TELEVISION NEWS

SECOND EDITION

A HANDBOOK FOR WRITING, REPORTING, SHOOTING AND EDITING

D0160868

Teresa Keller
EMORY & HENRY COLLEGE

Steve Hawkins
WCYB-TV

Holcomb Hathaway, Publishers

Scottsdale, Arizona

Library of Congress Cataloging-in-Publication Data

Keller, Teresa.
    Television news : a handbook for writing, reporting, shooting, and editing /
    Teresa Keller, Stephen A. Hawkins.—2nd ed.
       p. cm.
    Includes bibliographical references and index.
    ISBN 1-890871-57-5
    1. Television broadcasting of news--Handbooks, manuals, etc. I. Hawkins,
    Stephen A. II. Title.

    PN4784.T4K39 2005
    070.4'3—dc22

                                      2004012038

Copyright © 2005 by Holcomb Hathaway, Publishers, Inc.

Holcomb Hathaway, Publishers, Inc.
6207 North Cattletrack Road
Scottsdale, Arizona 85250
(480) 991-7881
www.hh-pub.com

Video/photos by Walt Reedy, A. D. Productions, Kingsport, Tenn.

10 9 8 7 6 5 4 3

ISBN 13 978-1-890871-57-4
ISBN 10 1-890871-57-5

Printed in the United States of America

CONTENTS

Preface   *xiii*
Acknowledgments   *xv*

CHAPTER 1   **All About News**   1

WHAT IS NEWS?   1

WHY IS NEWS IMPORTANT?   2

MAINSTREAM MEDIA   3

    Do the Mainstream Media Have a Bias?   4

    Mainstream Imitators with a Point of View   6

NONMAINSTREAM MEDIA   6

    Tabloid and Sensational Media   7

HOW DO REPORTERS ACHIEVE OBJECTIVITY, FAIRNESS AND ACCURACY?   7

    Objectivity and Fairness   7

    Accuracy   9

    Accuracy in Sound Bites   10

CHARACTERISTICS OF NEWS   11

    Conflict   11

    Uniqueness   12

    Prominence   14

    Impact   14

    Relevance   15

    Location   16

    Human Interest and Emotional Impact   17

CHARACTERISTICS OF GOOD REPORTERS   18

    Ethics   18

    Other Characteristics   20

CONCLUSION   *24*

KEY CONCEPTS   *25*

ACTIVITIES   *25*

CHAPTER 2   **The Television Newsroom**   27

KEY PLAYERS IN THE NEWSROOM   27

THE NEWSROOM ROUTINE   31

CONTEMPORARY NEWSROOM ISSUES   34

    Economics   34

Media Ownership   34

Media Convergence   36

News As Entertainment   36

Government by Fear and Name Calling   39

Politics in Sound Bites   39

Friendships and Conflict of Interest   40

Diversity and "isms" in the Newsroom   40

CONCLUSION   41

KEY CONCEPTS   42

ACTIVITIES   42

CHAPTER 3   **News Sources**   45

WHERE WE FIND NEWS   46

Observation   46

Listening   47

Printed Materials   47

The Press Conference   48

The News Release   49

PEOPLE AS SOURCES   49

Friends As Sources   50

Getting People to Talk   52

PREPARING FOR THE INTERVIEW   55

Do the Background Work   55

Talk to the Right Person   56

Plan What to Ask   57

Set the Ground Rules   58

GETTING THE MOST OUT OF THE INTERVIEW   63

Don't "Interview"   63

Be Skeptical   64

Begin the Interview   64

Guarantee Accuracy   65

Listen Carefully   66

Use Interview Strategies   67

Conclude the Interview   74

CONCLUSION   74

KEY CONCEPTS   75

ACTIVITIES   75

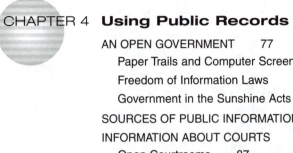

CHAPTER 4   Using Public Records   77

AN OPEN GOVERNMENT   77
   Paper Trails and Computer Screens   78
   Freedom of Information Laws   81
   Government in the Sunshine Acts   83
SOURCES OF PUBLIC INFORMATION   84
INFORMATION ABOUT COURTS   86
   Open Courtrooms   87
   Exceptions to Open Courtrooms   87
   Federal and State Courts   89
   Criminal and Civil Cases   93
   Cameras in Courtrooms   97
COURT RECORDS   100
   Information About Jurors   100
   Dockets   100
   Court Records   101
COMPUTER-ASSISTED REPORTING   102
CONCLUSION   107
KEY CONCEPTS   107
ACTIVITIES   107

CHAPTER 5   Storytelling and Writing for Broadcast   109

TELLING A STORY   109
PREPARING TO WRITE   110
   Review the "Five W's"   111
   Identify the Characters   111
   Personalize the Story   112
   Determine an Angle   115
   Keep It Simple   116
WRITING THE STORY   117
   The Lead   117
   Organizing the Story   121
   Choosing the Format   123
   Including the Sound Bite   125
   Ending the Story   131
   Writing for Radio and the Web   134

CONCLUSION   *144*

KEY CONCEPTS   *144*

ACTIVITIES   *145*

CHAPTER 6   Writing in Broadcast Style   149

USING VERBS CORRECTLY   150

    Avoid the "Verb-Free Zone"   150

    Avoid Distortion of Verb Tense   151

    Choose the Correct Verb Tense   153

    Use Active Voice   157

PUTTING THE WORDS TOGETHER   159

    Choose Words Accurately   159

    Attribute When Necessary   159

    Include Necessary Names   160

    Avoid Unnecessary Names   160

    Place Titles Before Names   161

    Delay the Name   162

    Do Not Use Age   163

    Use Pronunciation Guides   163

    Write for Breathing   164

SPECIAL STYLE REQUIREMENTS   166

    Numbers   166

    Ordinals   167

    Symbols   167

    Scores, Times, Dates   167

    Abbreviations and Acronyms   168

COMMON MISTAKES   169

ADDITIONAL TIPS   171

CONCLUSION   *173*

KEY CONCEPTS   *173*

ACTIVITIES   *174*

CHAPTER 7   Shooting Video I   177

DEFINING PHOTOJOURNALISM   178

THE LANGUAGE OF VIDEO   179

FRAMING SKILLS   182

    Fill the Screen   182

Think in Thirds   183

The 10-Second Rule   185

Hold the Camera Still   187

Use a Tripod   187

When a Tripod Can't Be Used   187

SHOOTING VIDEO IN THE FIELD   188

Get Plenty of Shots   188

Shoot Wide, Medium and Tight   188

Angled Shots   189

Pans and Zooms   190

SHOOTING INTERVIEWS   193

Leave Head Room   193

Leave Lead Room   195

Include Action in the Interview   198

CONCEIVING AND SHOOTING THE STAND-UP   200

LIGHTING   203

Camera Settings   203

Lighting Scenarios   204

CAPTURING GOOD AUDIO   214

CONCLUSION   217

KEY CONCEPTS   218

ACTIVITIES   219

CHAPTER 8   **Shooting Video II**   221

CUTAWAYS AND JUMP CUTS   221

Interview Cutaways   221

Sequence Jump Cuts   224

Transition Shots   226

THE SHOOTING AXIS   228

Neutralizing Shots   229

SHOOTING SEQUENCES   231

Wide, Medium and Tight Sequences   231

Match the Action   233

A Series of Related Shots   233

Completion   234

Action/Reaction   234

Reversed Point of View   236

Action Sequences   237

SHOOTING VIDEO USING ARTISTIC PRINCIPLES   242
   Leading Lines   242
   Movement   246
   Color   247
   Light and Dark   247
   Balance and Symmetry   248
   Foreground   250
   Background   251
SHOOTING TIPS FOR NATURAL SOUND PACKAGES   251
GENERAL TIPS   252
   Practice Assertiveness   252
   Understand the Story   253
   Broaden Your Skills   254
   Avoid Complacency   254
   Communicate   254
CONCLUSION   *255*
KEY CONCEPTS   *255*
ACTIVITIES   *255*

CHAPTER 9   **Editing**   257

THE EDITING PROCESS   257
ELEMENTS OF EDITING   258
   Pacing   258
   Repetition   260
   Timing and Punctuation   261
   Surprise   261
   Characters   262
LINEAR EDITING   262
   The Countdown   263
   Laying Black   263
NONLINEAR EDITING   264
LAYING THE VIDEO TRACK   265
   Establishing Shots   267
   Illustrating the Narration   268
   Stories Within the Story   269
   Using Cutaways   270
   Editing Sequences   272
LAYING THE AUDIO TRACK   277

Natural Sound   280

Nat Sound Breaks   281

OVERLAPPING AUDIO AND VIDEO   282

USING GRAPHICS   284

THE EDITOR'S RESPONSIBILITIES   285

Ensuring Truth and Accuracy   286

Adhering to Legalities   287

Exercising Creative Control   287

Avoiding Sensationalism   288

Providing Graphics   289

Creating Animations   289

CONCLUSION   289

KEY CONCEPTS   290

ACTIVITIES   290

CHAPTER 10   **Presentation and Voice**   293

VOICE QUALITY   293

Breathing   293

Warming Up   296

DELIVERY   296

Enunciation   297

Phrasing   297

Emphasis   299

Pitch   300

Pacing   303

Overall Tone   305

Additional Considerations   306

Techniques for Improving Delivery   308

THE QUALITIES OF A SUCCESSFUL COMMUNICATOR   310

Appearance   311

Courtesy   312

Nervousness   313

PRESENTING STAND-UPS   314

Use of Clear, Simple Language   314

To Memorize or Not to Memorize?   315

Stationary Stand-Ups   316

Action Stand-Ups   316

LIVE SHOTS   317

The Wraparound   319

The Live Shot Interview   321

Extended Live Coverage   322

CONCLUSION   *324*

KEY CONCEPTS   *324*

ACTIVITIES   *324*

CHAPTER 11   Legal Considerations   327

THE CONSEQUENCES OF CARELESSNESS   327

LEGAL VS. ETHICAL   328

LIBEL   329

Libel and Public Figures   332

Libel and Private People   333

Defenses Against Libel Lawsuits   334

PRIVACY   339

Intrusion   339

False Light   342

Private Information   342

Appropriation   343

Defenses Against Invasion-of-Privacy Lawsuits   343

COPYRIGHT   344

Licensing Fees and Permission   345

Fair Use   345

MEDIA ACCESS ISSUES   347

Courtrooms   347

Public Meetings   347

Prisons   347

Schools   348

Crime Scenes   348

COURT ORDERS   348

Confidentiality and Contempt   348

Shield Laws   350

Subpoenas   350

Newsroom Searches   351

CONCLUSION   *351*

KEY CONCEPTS   *352*

ACTIVITIES   *352*

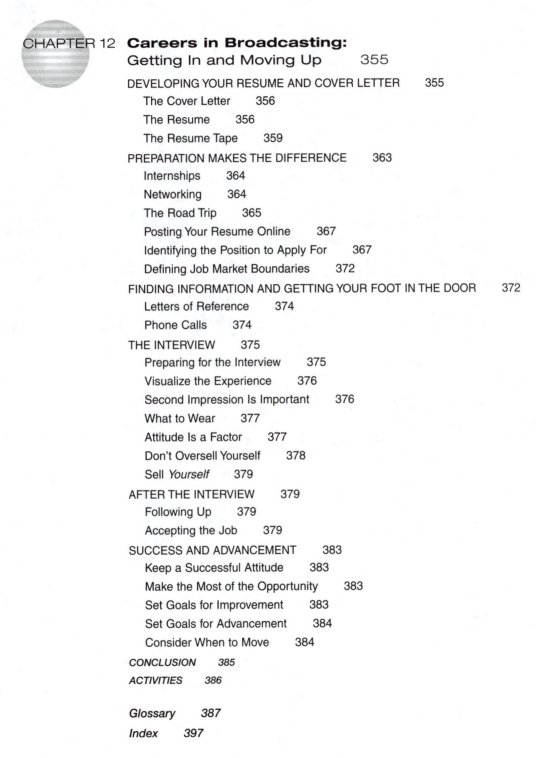

CHAPTER 12   **Careers in Broadcasting:**
Getting In and Moving Up   355

DEVELOPING YOUR RESUME AND COVER LETTER   355

The Cover Letter   356

The Resume   356

The Resume Tape   359

PREPARATION MAKES THE DIFFERENCE   363

Internships   364

Networking   364

The Road Trip   365

Posting Your Resume Online   367

Identifying the Position to Apply For   367

Defining Job Market Boundaries   372

FINDING INFORMATION AND GETTING YOUR FOOT IN THE DOOR   372

Letters of Reference   374

Phone Calls   374

THE INTERVIEW   375

Preparing for the Interview   375

Visualize the Experience   376

Second Impression Is Important   376

What to Wear   377

Attitude Is a Factor   377

Don't Oversell Yourself   378

Sell *Yourself*   379

AFTER THE INTERVIEW   379

Following Up   379

Accepting the Job   379

SUCCESS AND ADVANCEMENT   383

Keep a Successful Attitude   383

Make the Most of the Opportunity   383

Set Goals for Improvement   383

Set Goals for Advancement   384

Consider When to Move   384

CONCLUSION   *385*

ACTIVITIES   *386*

Glossary   *387*

Index   *397*

PREFACE

Television News: A Handbook for Writing, Reporting, Shooting and Editing, Second Edition, examines television news reporting in its practical, applied sense, as the application of a set of vital skills within the context of a career. More important, it recognizes news reporting as a foundation of our free society. Truthful information presented ethically, objectively and accurately is a requirement of news reporting in our democratic society, and our goal here is to provide a foundation for skilled reporting that meets those objectives. This book examines the legalities and the ethics of television reporting. In fact, a discussion of ethics is woven throughout the text, because ethical considerations are too important to be relegated to a single section or chapter.

The initial chapters of *Television News: A Handbook for Writing, Reporting, Shooting and Editing* examine the structure of a television newsroom, the personnel and their responsibilities, and the challenges that exist as broadcast professionals attempt to apply reporting ideals to real-world scenarios.

Chapters 3 and 4 provide detailed instruction regarding interviewing, news sources and public records, with special emphasis on covering court stories. Gathering and gaining access to information, however, is merely the foundation work. Chapters 5 and 6 demonstrate how to use information to greatest effect by writing clear, concise, accurate and informative stories.

Chapters 7, 8 and 9 could stand alone as a textbook for TV news photographers and editors. We cover the type of real-world shooting and editing that occurs on site and in newsrooms every day, and we provide ample visual examples. (Many of the photographic illustrations are taken directly from the videotape available to instructors who teach the course so that they may share it with their students.) Unlike many books, we also cover on-camera presentation, including voice, appearance and credibility. Chapter 10 also includes an important section on doing standups and live shots.

Chapter 11 covers the important topic of legal issues, providing simple guidelines for remaining alert to and avoiding legal risk. Finally, the book concludes with advice on how to get into broadcast news and succeed in this important and challenging field.

Television News can be used in sequence and in its entirety, but it also works well to extract chapters for specific purposes. For example, the chapters on news sources and writing can work for introductory courses in television or radio newswriting. The chapters on video shooting and editing can be used for concentrated video production courses. The book is an excellent companion for advanced television reporting courses.

In preparing the second edition, we sought to ensure that it reflects current trends and practices in the field. Highlighted changes to this new edition include:

- Inclusion of material on writing radio scripts and writing for the Web
- Additional instruction and examples on the role of the news producer
- Improved organization of video chapters
- New, applied exercises throughout the text
- Additional script examples in various formats: readers, VO-SOTs and packages
- More specific discussion of newsroom software
- More photographs and exhibits
- Updated information on media ownership
- Revised approach to conceiving and shooting standups

In today's busy, up to the minute and budget-conscious world, television news reporters are often called upon to perform several different tasks for each story. This book's inclusion of all aspects of reporting, including shooting and editing video, makes it ideal for the real-world applications in which one individual is called upon to do it all.

Television news is so vital to all of our lives and our system of government that we need the best and brightest people doing their best work in this field. This book offers specific practical and ethical guidelines for those preparing to enter the field and for those interning and working in the field. *Television News* is intended as a handbook that can be used for basic instruction for beginning reporters and as a reference or instruction for those who continue to learn the craft both in advanced classrooms and in newsrooms.

ACKNOWLEDGMENTS

The authors would like to acknowledge the generous support of the following programs and individuals: The Radio Television News Directors Foundation (RTNDA), for keeping broadcast educators up-to-date on contemporary newsroom practices through its Excellence in Journalism Education Program; Walt Reedy of A.D. Productions, for his steadfast commitment to perfection; Emory & Henry College; WCYB-TV; KCNC-TV News Director Angie Kucharski and the entire newsroom staff; Jim Shaver, WDBJ-TV; Dave Cupp, WVIR-TV, Charlottesville, Va.; and Eric Scott, WJZ-TV, Baltimore.

We would also like to thank the many excellent journalists who volunteered for long conversations, informed the book in many ways and who are quoted throughout the text. First, special thanks to Dale Solly, formerly of WJLA-TV, Washington, D.C., who passed away before this new edition of *Television News* could be published. We decided to include his worthy and informative quotations. Thanks also to contributors: Paige Beck, WCJB-TV, Gainesville, Fla.; Lisa Mitchell, WCYB-TV, Bristol, Va.; Jay Webb, WHSV-TV, Harrisonburg, Va.; Shelly Harper, WNBC-TV, New York; Lee Ann Necessary, Conus Communications, Washington, D.C.; Jeff Gurney, KCNC-TV, Denver; Angie Kucharski, News Director, KCNC-TV, Denver; Brian Maass, KCNC-TV, Denver; Mike Schuh, WJZ-TV, Baltimore; Karen Harris, WNBC-TV, New York; Ann Curry, The Today Show, NBC News, New York; Richard Frohlich, WFTV-TV, Orlando, Fla.; Melissa Charbonneau, CBN News, Washington, D.C.; John Antonio, WABC-TV, New York; Ellen McDonald, NPR, Washington, D.C.; Deborah Potter, NewsLab, Washington, D.C.; Stephanie Riggs, KCNC-TV, Denver; Dave Wertheimer, KSTP/KSTC-TV, Minneapolis/Saint Paul; Les Rose, CBS News Bureau, Los Angeles; Jeff Gurney, KCNC-TV, Denver; Kathy Soltero, KCNC-TV, Denver; Steve Youngerman, KCNC-TV, Denver; Mike Porras, KCNC-TV, Denver; Bob Burke, Chief Photographer, KCNC-TV, Denver; Don Stevenson, KCNC-TV, Denver; Pat Barry, KCNC-TV, Denver; Everett McEwan, KCNC-TV, Denver; Doug Hoffacker, KCNC-TV; and Taylor Cleveland, KCNC-TV, Denver. We would like to thank Washington County Circuit Court Clerk Kathy Crane; Bristol Officials Tony Massey and John Gaines; and Abingdon Virginian Editor Martha Weisfield.

Our sincere thanks go to those individuals who reviewed this text and offered their suggestions for its improvement. We would like to thank the following people for their expertise and guidance. *For the second edition:* Penny M. Byrne, Utah State University; Willaim R. Davie, University of Louisiana; Roger Hadley,

Oklahoma Baptist University; Pat Hahn, Palomar College; Bambi Landholm, Kansas State University; Steven Miller, Rutgers University; Paula I. Otto, Virginia Commonwealth University; Donald Pollock, University of La Verne; Gary Potter, Northeast State Technical College; Lillian Williams, Columbia College Chicago; and Stacey W. Woelfel, KOMU-TV, University of Missouri-Columbia. *For the first edition:* Steve Beverly, Union University; Dom Caristi, Ball State University; Lance Clark, Huntington College; Sandy Ellis, University of Wisconsin-River Falls; Joseph Glover, University of Florida; Marilou M. Johnson, James Madison University; Kenneth R. Keller, Southern Illinois University at Carbondale; Karen Slattery, Marquette University; Paul Smeyak, Oklahoma State University; and Edward Welch, Jackson State University.

Finally, we would like to thank our editor, Colette Kelly, and production director, Gay Pauley, of Holcomb Hathaway. Their professionalism and good ideas have helped us produce a first-rate textbook.

TELEVISION NEWS

SECOND EDITION

A HANDBOOK FOR WRITING, REPORTING, SHOOTING AND EDITING

If I give someone my word, it's just that simple.

**PAIGE BECK, WCJB-TV,
GAINESVILLE, FL**

ALL ABOUT NEWS

WHAT IS NEWS?

Many have tried, but no one has really succeeded in defining **news.** Definitions range from simple, general ones such as "anything people don't know" and "anything that's new," to "timely information" and "what people want to know." According to the commonly used "water cooler" definition, news is whatever the office staff is discussing around the water cooler. However, the definition of news can and should be much more complex. Additionally, journalists must consider that while there may be no limit to what people *want* to know, what they *need* to know is another matter entirely.

News is more than just facts and information; it is information that affects us. News affects how we live our lives, how we perform our jobs, how we function as students, and how we make decisions. We decide whether or not to carry an umbrella or cancel a picnic based on weather reports. We look to the media for sports scores, stock market reports and details about entertainment events. Information we have learned from news broadcasts may affect our choice of a college or a major field of study. We learn about candidates for public office, election results and the winner's effectiveness through media reports. Announcements about new industry and new jobs or, conversely, about plant closings and layoffs come to us through the media.

This book examines news as a product of credible news organizations attempting to present an accurate, fair and objective look at stories and issues that have importance and relevance in the lives of listeners and viewers. This approach to news plays an important role in the successful functioning of our society. We will return to a discussion of how to define news, but first, we must emphasize the importance of news in our society.

WHY IS NEWS IMPORTANT?

The First Amendment guarantees freedom of speech and freedom of the press. Nearly every American can recite these respected freedoms, but few understand their full implications. The authors of the Bill of Rights of the United States Constitution wanted citizens to be able to speak freely about the government. Our forebears believed that if citizens were free to criticize the government for its failures, voters would be well-informed. The press would fulfill a role as "watchdog of the government."

The media today fulfill the role of **watchdog** of the government and maintain surveillance over business, the social value system and all aspects of life in our society. In this respect, our system of government is no better than the quality of news the public gets. An effective system of government requires that the public get quality news, but there's another part of the equation: the public must pay attention and become involved. For example, if local government repeatedly cuts the budget for schools, reporters may examine the effect of the budget cuts on education. If the school system tightens its operation and makes better use of less money, we expect to get that information from the media. If the budget cuts mean that the condition of the school buildings deteriorates and students are attempting to learn in classrooms with poor heat or crumbling ceilings, the news media hold the responsibility for finding this information and presenting it to the public. When the media play this "watchdog" role effectively, voters have the information they need to exert influence and control for improving the situation either during public meetings or in the voting booth.

Media critics today point out that too much political reporting concentrates on who is winning and who is losing in the polls, rather than detailing the policies of potential leaders. When our information about candidates focuses on who is winning the contest, we might as well be watching a professional wrestling match. The entertainment value of a fight is fine, but we gain little important information. Although elected representatives in state legislatures, in Congress or in the White House have immense power, the voters have ultimate power and ultimate control over the operation of government. To exercise this power responsibly, the public needs good information. Accurate information leads to good decisions.

I'm worried that young journalists don't hunger for history and context. They've got to want to do the hard work, the heavy lifting. TV is not a toy and it's not just writing cute teases. It's a responsibility. You've got to get the facts right. The mission is to give people an understanding of their community and their world. That's why people need to get into the business.

Bob Burke
KCNC-TV, DENVER

Just as the public holds control in the voting booth and can guide the direction of government, citizens also establish guidelines for acceptable business practices through the democratic process. If prescription drug prices rise much faster than the overall trends for prices, the public may demand that the government regulate the pharmaceutical industry. Empowered voters express their will based on the accurate information they get from media reports on pharmaceutical companies or other business operations. The watchdog role of the media extends to our national system of social values. If individual levels of anger and frustration reveal themselves in increasing incidents of road rage, people may begin to look for solutions to the problem. Campaigns and public service announcements may appear advising people to show courtesy on the roads we share or to give way to angry drivers. Just as watchdogs alert owners to unusual activity, the media alert citizens to important information. This important role for the media gives citizens the information they need to govern the nation and to manage their own lives.

> Reporters must also know the difference between right and wrong. . . . Once you cross the line, you're no better than the crooks you're reporting on.
>
> *Brian Maass*
> **KCNC-TV, DENVER**

People watch news and read newspapers in search of factual information and at times to correct misinformation about a story. Without the credibility of offering accurate information, news makers have nothing. If a news organization loses its reputation for accuracy, it has nothing else to offer.

MAINSTREAM MEDIA

Network news and local TV news departments; major news magazines, such as Newsweek, Time and U. S. News & World Report; and local, weekly and daily newspapers are examples of **mainstream media** outlets that we expect to present information without a particular viewpoint. The "News Hour" on PBS, the Public Broadcasting System, and the news programming on National Public Radio are credible news sources. The New York Times, The Washington Post and USA Today are nationally distributed newspapers that many people trust. News media have had an enormous impact on the course of our nation's history from the very beginning. Printed publications rallied support for the revolution against the British. In more recent times, media reports of the status of the Vietnam War caused the administration to lose public support for the war and eventually resulted in the U. S. withdrawal from Southeast Asia. Media coverage of the early stages of the women's movement began a fundamental shift in relations between men and women and the role of women in our society.

We rely on mainstream media to present contrasting viewpoints on issues so we can formulate our own opinions. For example, a story about a confrontation between loggers and the protesters who are attempting to stop the logging by placing themselves in front of the logging equipment has at least two sides. On one side of the issue, reputable news organizations would probably find hard-working loggers who need to support their families, employed by owners trying to operate a successful business. On the other hand, the protesters are probably caring individuals who truly believe that their actions can help protect the environment.

Mainstream media will attempt to show both—or many—sides of an issue or conflict. Each individual, however, including those who gather information, holds certain biases. Good reporters must always make a conscious effort to present news objectively, but the task is not simple. Reporters in mainstream media outlets can sometimes succumb to deep prejudices that affect their presentation of the news. In good news operations, editors and others should forestall the broadcast of stories that fail to present a fair picture of opposing viewpoints.

Prominent news operations that we are describing as "mainstream" strive to present news stories objectively and fairly, but even the best news outlets sometimes fall short. No single news operation is perfect, but some basic characteristics should be apparent. Respected news operations should present stories because they are important in some way and not merely for their entertainment value. Mainstream media will not pay for their information, and the sources will be closely connected with the story. If the public is moved to action because of a story, the motivation should come from the factual information—not from influence by the reporter's point of view. To write objective stories, news reporters gather and present the most important facts and viewpoints.

Do the Mainstream Media Have a Bias?

Despite our identifying network news and major daily papers as the type of mainstream media that attempt to be objective, many argue that mainstream media outlets do have a bias. Bias, however, is often in the eye of the beholder. Conservatives in our nation accuse mainstream media of liberal bias, while liberals say that media are typically owned by large corporations, managed by wealthy people, and show a conservative bias.

The question whether media hold a bias must be answered for each individual media outlet. Some claim that The New York Times and The Washington Post have a liberal bias—and others see a conservative bias in the pages of the Washington Times and The Wall Street Journal. The major network newscasts have been accused of liberal bias—and some say they have a conservative bias. People often think they see a bias in their daily papers. In mainstream media, however, there is a fairly clear line defining where such points of view are found. Ethical mainstream news media exhibit a clear difference between *editorials and commentaries* and *news items*. While a local paper's editorials may tend to be conservative, the news articles should, and most probably will, show fairness, balance and an effort to be objective. More and more often, however, the line is becoming blurred between news and opinion—especially in the world of cable programming and talk radio (see Exhibit 1.1).

Examine the top stories of these news sites. Is there evidence of liberal or conservative bias?   **EXHIBIT 1.1**

Here are the headlines that appeared on these sites on January 28, 2004.

CNN NEWS	www.cnn.com
Top story:	Democrats dash to next contest states (Kerry follows win in Iowa with win in New Hampshire)

ABC NEWS	www.abcnews.go.com
Top story:	Kerry wins in New Hampshire
Other stories:	Girl survives after days in car with dead mom
	Will Michael Jackson hype force impersonators out of work?
	Fed leaves interest rates unchanged
	At least 50 dead in killer snow storm

FOX NEWS	www.foxnews.com/topstories/index.html
Top story:	Car bomber targets hotel in Baghdad
Other stories:	Digging out after nasty weather
	U.S. plans major offensive against Al Qaeda
	Worldwide shark attacks on decline
	NASA releases photos of Martian rocks

MSNBC NEWS	www.msnbc.msn.com/id/3032092
Top story:	Kerry is frontrunner of Dem election
Other stories:	Kay denies politics behind Iraq charge
	British probe clears Blair
	Four killed in Baghdad car bombing
	Drought threatens millions in Africa
	Two blasts hit Afghan capital
	Storm strikes light blow in northeast

CBS NEWS	www.cbsnews.com/sections/home/main100.shtml
Top story:	We were almost all wrong (David Kay)
Other stories:	Kerry talks with Rather
	Bizarre illness terrifies Sudanese
	A little slice of Elvis

Mainstream Imitators with a Point of View

Within the ever-expanding number of media outlets, a new type of programming increasingly imitates mainstream media, but, in fact, presents a distinct and sometimes unstated point of view. Some radio talk shows and some cable news talk shows are hosted by intelligent, articulate broadcasters who pretend to air a variety of viewpoints but who engage in behavior that mainstream news media would find to be both unethical and unacceptable. Some of the programs deal in anger and insult but may be highly rated and feature award-winning, popular hosts.

One obvious characteristic of these programs is name-calling. The hosts will use emotionally charged words to describe those with whom they disagree: *socialists, communists, fascists, femi-nazis, tree huggers, greens, morons, idiots, sodomites, reactionaries, fanatics* and *murderers.* They may claim that these people whom they label in insulting ways want to destroy the country and don't care about families or life.

Such programs have developed in recent years, partly because of the 1987 elimination of the Fairness Doctrine. The Fairness Doctrine required broadcasters to present differing viewpoints if they addressed controversial public issues. The courts found the regulation to be in violation of the First Amendment because it consisted of the government dictating programming content to broadcasters.

All broadcasters certainly have full First Amendment protection for their opinions, but some make no effort to achieve fairness or objectivity. In a number of cases, the hosts have been found to misrepresent statistics and factual information to support their own viewpoints. The danger is that citizens will respond to the emotion and fail to find facts. As it is often said, great freedom requires great responsibility, and the media explosion puts more and more responsibility on the shoulders of the citizen, especially when media programmers don't take responsibility for fairness, accuracy and objectivity.

NONMAINSTREAM MEDIA

In some cases, **nonmainstream media** outlets take a more positive approach to promoting a specific, clear and open point of view. These media do not intend to be mainstream and are geared toward a particular, supportive audience base with a specific perspective. They do not intend to inform the general public. The accuracy of information in these media can vary from intentional misrepresentations to complete accuracy.

For example, a religious broadcast station or network may present news from a perspective that opposes abortion and encourages prayer in schools, either omitting the merits of different viewpoints or presenting them as weak. In contrast, a newsletter from the ACLU might talk about the prayer in schools issue from the perspective of a Muslim student who does not want to participate in Christian prayer. In the example of a protest against logging, nonmainstream media may operate with a specific agenda in mind. Information provided by loggers might present the protesters as "tree huggers" who are trying to destroy jobs. The environmental viewpoint might describe a fight against "greedy profiteers" who don't care about nature. An environmental organization's media might present information about the danger of corporate pollution without showing the difficulties the company would face in reducing or eliminating the pollution. Various organizations design broadcast programs or edit newsletters to promote a specific point of view.

Always be armed with both sides of the story.

Shelly Harper
WNBC-TV, NEW YORK

Tabloid and Sensational Media

Some newspapers and television programs strive to excite and entertain readers by exaggerating, overstating and stretching the facts—or by presenting sensational and outlandish stories. In some cases, the stories are total fiction. In all these cases, the driving force is profit. We refer to these media as the **tabloids** and describe their reporting as **sensational.** The primary difference between tabloids and mainstream media is that tabloids are willing to pay people to talk or appear in their stories. The National Enquirer and Star are examples in print. Some television tabloids do the same. These publications/programs make an art of stretching the truth while avoiding libel and privacy charges. For example, a headline in a tabloid might exclaim, "Psychologists Say Congressman Is Suicidal." You can be sure the story is true in that the tabloid will have interviewed more than one psychologist who says the congressman shows signs of endangering himself. The story will not point out that the psychologists have never met the congressman and are basing their opinions on very little information.

The tabloids also tend to use unreliable sources, or people who have little or no connection to the heart of the story. Interviews with people who knew a celebrity 20 years ago become the basis for dramatic headlines. In some programs the facts may be correct, but the information is insignificant, such as details of the lives of celebrities provided for an audience as entertainment.

HOW DO REPORTERS ACHIEVE OBJECTIVITY, FAIRNESS AND ACCURACY?

In this text, we are assuming the goal of presenting credible news as part of mainstream media. With this in mind, we will discuss how a reporter achieves these goals in her writing.

Objectivity and Fairness

Being **objective** means examining facts or events without allowing feelings or opinions to interfere. In fact, objectivity may be impossible, but responsible reporters must do their best to avoid letting personal beliefs and biases creep into news stories. Good reporters will battle the urge to slant or misrepresent information and will strive to present all sides of an issue. A balanced presentation allows the public to evaluate the situation for themselves.

Although total objectivity may be impossible, reporters must strive to present factual stories that are free of opinion. We all have opinions and will inevitably be forming opinions as we come in contact with news stories. In fact, the decision to cover a story was based on someone's opinion. Being objective does not even mean that opinion is excluded from mainstream news. However, when the opinions of reporters and editors are included, such as in the opinion and editorial pages of newspapers, they are clearly labeled as such. Broadcast professionals, likewise, should clearly identify those stories that include editorial opinion. News stories are different. They will certainly include other people's opinions but should not include the reporter's opinion.

> Never get emotionally involved in any story you are covering. The more sure you are that you are right about something, the more likely you are to be wrong.
>
> *Dave Cupp*
> **WVIR-TV, CHARLOTTESVILLE, VA.**

Objective does not mean positive. Objective does not mean negative. Being objective requires finding the facts and presenting different viewpoints fairly. **Fairness** means presenting both sides—or many sides—of a story. Suppose a reporter is told to look into accusations by a group of parents that a particular high school principal is so ineffective that students are not getting a proper education. The reporter may first find out who is making the accusations and determine the basis of the claims. Following some initial finding that the accusations appear to have some credibility, the reporter will begin investigating the story. Who else would know about the principal's performance? Students and teachers; school workers, such as the secretaries, janitors and cafeteria workers; guidance counselors; parents and PTA officers; and others could become sources of information. The reporter should contact the principal's supervisors at the school board. Are there any written records about the principal's job performance? Has the issue been discussed at any public meeting from which minutes are available? The principal is certainly the central figure in the story. What does the principal say? The reporter should give the principal a chance to respond to the charges and remain open to that side of the story. While gathering all the facts, the reporter may see many reports of the principal's incompetence. By this time, although the reporter may have developed an opinion about the principal's effectiveness, he will strive to maintain as much objectivity as possible. When the story reveals a large body of negative information, it does not mean the reporter was biased. The reporter may well have gathered the facts fairly and objectively.

When a reporter presents only one side of the story, the information can be factual but unfair. For example, it may be factual that a citizen is accusing a public official of misusing public funds; however, anyone can make an accusation. Where's the evidence? Where's the proof? A good reporter, even if suspicious of the accused, should not be satisfied with presenting one side of the story. A good reporter will verify the charges and make certain the official gets a chance to respond to them.

Reporters must also be very careful to ask the right questions in the right way. The reporter can phrase questions so they lead people to answer in a certain way, but her goal should be to find out what people really think. In the example of the school principal, suppose that a student had reported finding the principal watching television in the office during the school day. When the reporter interviews a parent, the question could be phrased as follows: *Students have reported that the principal watches television during the school day. What do you think of such behavior?* Obviously, a parent would find such behavior unacceptable and might provide dramatic language about how disgusted he is. The question leads the parent to make negative comments about the principal, even though the parent may not have known of such an incident. Since the reporter is trying to find out about the principal's job performance, a better question would leave the parent to respond either positively or negatively: *What do you think of the principal's effectiveness?*

Reporters must constantly remind themselves to look at news with fairness and objectivity. Even though pure objectivity may be impossible, reporters can always be fair. There is always more than one side to a story, and the reporter must find it in order to present a true picture. In addition to presenting various perspectives on a story, the reporter must be sure that every single word is precisely *accurate*.

> Sometimes you'll have sources on both sides of a story and you may believe one more than the other. You've got to constantly ask yourself if you're presenting a fair picture.
>
> *Lee Ann Necessary*
> **REPORTER, ROANOKE, VA.**

Accuracy

Accuracy is the degree to which information is precise, exact and free from mistakes, and it is the only thing news departments have to offer. Unfortunately, too many reporters make too many mistakes, which harms the credibility of the news media in general. In a Washington Post story, one reporter committed a violation of accuracy standards in a story about Senator Robert Byrd from West Virginia. The article addressed the senator's efforts to get funding for renovating a train depot in his home state. The article noted that Senator Byrd "glides past on Amtrak's Cardinal Limited from time to time, heading to and from his home in Sophia, a few miles south." In fact, Senator Byrd *did not regularly ride* the train past the depot in question and had not ridden that particular train within the past 10 years. Moreover, he had *never* ridden the train to

> The Golden Rule applies to reporting. Treat the subject of your story the way you would want to be treated if the story were about you.
>
> *Paige Beck*
> **WCJB-TV, GAINESVILLE, FLA.**

> Never hesitate to "bother" someone by calling back to double-check facts. You will be respected for your commitment to getting the facts right. If you have the smallest nagging doubt about the information, do something to double-check your interpretation of the information.
>
> *Jay Webb*
> **WHSV-TV, HARRISONBURG, VA.**

Sophia because it *did not go there* (Brill, 1998). What would possess a reporter to write down information without knowing whether or not it was true? Was it pride in clever writing? An *assumption* that the senator regularly rode that train? A desire to portray the senator in a particular way? If the details are wrong, how can the public believe the rest of the story?

A good reporter *must* be confident that each and every word of the story is correct. *Can you prove the information?* The news writer should pay attention to every minor, nagging question about a story. Read your story to someone else and see if he has questions you have not thought of or have not answered. If there is any question, any doubt or any uneasiness about what you're writing, check it out before the story is printed or broadcast. People are often hesitant to bother someone after they have taken that person's time for an interview, but news sources will have much more respect for the reporter who interrupts dinner to clarify a point than for the reporter who gets the information wrong. Be sure that everything in your story is *exactly* right.

Accuracy in Sound Bites

In broadcast news, the reporter usually prepares a news package that includes narration plus taped comments from one or more people she interviewed for the story. A source's taped comments that are edited into the story are called **sound bites.** Good reporters make sure that the part of the interview selected for the news story presents an accurate picture of the person's comments. Obviously, a story will sparkle when it includes a dramatic, emotional comment, but good intentions should not lead the reporter astray.

Suppose a city council member has spent most of an interview talking about the benefits of a planned shopping center, such as jobs, tax revenue, improved merchandise selections for buyers and a shiny new look for a declining business area. The official also explains that property values will go up for those who live nearby. When asked about traffic flow, the official explains that roads will be upgraded adequately to handle increased traffic and then comments in an offhanded way, "During road construction, everything will be a mess for the neighbors. I'm glad I don't live there." This sentence would make a lively addition to the story, but does it really reflect the attitude of the council member? If the reporter uses this sentence, can it be put in the proper perspective, as an offhand comment within a long conversation about the benefits of the construction? Reporters can easily misrepresent or slant stories by the choice of sound bites, but they must avoid doing so.

CHARACTERISTICS OF NEWS

General definitions that identify "news" are not always helpful in determining whether a specific story has news value. Considering the following characteristics might help you decide whether a story should be broadcast.

Conflict

Most news stories contain a central conflict or disagreement that contributes to the news value. The stress point may be found among people or in opposing social forces. The tension can be the old way vs. the new way. Good vs. evil. Right vs. wrong.

Some people call the tension between humans and nature a conflict. One example of a human vs. nature conflict is memorable from the 1980s. When scientists said the volcano at Mount St. Helens, Wash., was ready to erupt, people within several miles were evacuated. But a man named Harry Truman refused to leave. The suspenseful story was news around the world because no one knew exactly when the deadly eruption would occur, and the man refused to leave. To this day, people remember the story of Harry Truman, who shared his name with a former president, and who died as molten lava and debris swept down the mountainside and over his tiny cabin.

Stories about conflict between the old and the new are always interesting and can have important news value. A new generation of young people chooses body piercing, tattoos and going out for the evening at 11 p.m. An older generation resists, having grown up in a time when the end-of-the-evening curfew was 11 p.m. and having long hair was a rebellious statement. The struggle of immigrant families in modern America can present a picture of colliding cultures. How does a family adjust to a new country with different customs and values? How do middle-class suburbanites who have always been surrounded by people like themselves adjust when the new neighbors don't speak English? These tensions between generations, cultures or neighbors provide the basis for news stories that go beyond simple conflict to represent some of the major social shifts of our times.

Conflict makes stories easy for the viewer to grasp because we can all relate to struggle. But reporters should understand that social conflict isn't necessarily the complete picture. The story of Harry Truman, killed by the volcano, also had a timeless, universal theme. It involved an individual against the system, and life vs. death. The old man sacrificed his life believing his right to stay was greater than someone else's right to force him to leave.

Presenting conflict should be one of the tools reporters use to illustrate the points of a story. If the conflict is important, it must be put in perspective. Although conflict almost always guarantees interest, seldom does the conflict alone reveal the full scope of the situation. For example, broad social issues often involve the struggle between political parties, one seen as conservative and the other liberal. The conflict is not as simple as conservative vs. liberal, and reporters should be careful to avoid seeing political fights as an issue of good vs. evil. Each side is convinced that its ideas and policies will work for the good of the community. The seemingly simple conflict represents complex ideas and reasoning.

In the case of two opposing political candidates and two viewpoints about school vouchers, the story should go much deeper than the conflict. Good reporters will find the reasons each side believes as it does. WHY does one person think vouchers will destroy public schools? WHY does someone else think vouchers will improve public schools? Does either side have any evidence for its beliefs? When the reasoning and the evidence behind the conflict are presented, the public can make an informed decision about which side has the best argument. Informed voting follows—and perhaps improved education. The story is not just who is for and who is against. How will the whole community be affected by the outcome?

Uniqueness

The more unusual the story, the more newsworthy and interesting it is. In fact, stories about crime are considered newsworthy because they are unusual. In today's society, people may have a hard time believing that crime is unusual. Watching the news and reading the newspaper can make it seem that crime is quite common—almost normal. However, remember that most people go through each day in a fairly routine manner: to work, to the grocery store, maybe to a movie or out to dinner. When someone hurts someone else in a violent way, it is indeed unusual, so crime becomes news.

Even though crime is statistically unusual, reports about crime are included in virtually every newscast. The daily parade of crime stories can lead to anxiety and fear, and this public anxiety may eventually result in a change in the way news is presented. More often, viewers complain that watching the news is gruesome and depressing. Some critics accuse news media of focusing on the salacious and sensational topics of rape, murder and robbery rather than reporting other important news.

Some news organizations reserve coverage of robberies and shootings for stories where the suspect is still at large and the public may need to know, or when the crime represents some unresolved social problem that the media can examine through the specific crime. For example, two persons drink heavily on a Saturday night, they get angry, and a fight escalates until one shoots or stabs the other. In many television markets, the story is not newsworthy, but a reporter might compile statistics on the number of people killed in domestic settings that

> In some markets, it's no holds barred. If you get it, it goes on the air. Here, we're more community oriented and it's better.
>
> *Jeff Gurney*
> **KCNC-TV, DENVER**

involve drinking and present an important, informative story. When the police arrest a drunk driver or answer a call to a home where the wife is afraid her husband is going to kill her, these stories do not normally make the newscast. Individual conflicts, however, may combine to provide an important insight into our society. Crime reporting is based on the understanding that crime is not a normal part of the day. Whether individual crimes are over-reported is open to discussion.

Reporters may not have the authority to determine whether a news department places too much emphasis on reporting crime, but even young reporters can evaluate the importance and relevance of the crimes they cover. Can the crime be put into some context? If the story is about a murder, how many similar murders happen each year? What do authorities say about the significance of the particular crime? Does it illustrate a trend or is it extremely unusual? What does the particular crime indicate about general public safety? Is there an important reason to inform the public about the crime?

Crime is reported because it is unusual, and many other varieties of stories also become newsworthy because they are unusual or unique. The chance of a woman giving birth to seven babies at once is one in many million. Obviously, the birth of septuplets is unusual, and because most people are acquainted with the difficulty of caring for one infant, they want to know all the details of how it's possible to care for seven babies at the same time. People are attracted to the uniqueness of the story.

A man working at a construction site bumps into a nail gun and winds up with a three-inch nail thrust into his brain—an accident that could easily result in death. However, the man remains conscious and walks and talks until surgeons remove the nail. To the astonishment of the medical community, the construction worker reports only one consequence—he can no longer do math. The unique nature of the story makes it newsworthy.

A community of Amish people in Pennsylvania has long fascinated neighbors and tourists because of its simple lifestyle. Wearing mostly black clothing with no buttons or zippers, the Amish operate successful farms and eat from bountiful gardens, but they don't use municipal electricity and they travel by horse and buggy instead of cars. They don't own televisions and don't go to movies. The children are home-schooled and generally isolated from the modern world. When an Amish teenager was arrested for selling cocaine, the story stunned the nation. How has such a modern-day problem penetrated the Amish community? The unusual nature of the story makes it newsworthy.

Reporters learn to recognize that most news stories are unique or unusual in some way. Even though crime is routine in a general sense, it is unusual for most people to come in contact with criminal activity, making crime newsworthy. Unusual stories often have important hard news value, such as the significance of a teenager firing a gun at classmates or a city council member stepping down to attend to a sick child. Sometimes the unique story is important simply in providing perspective on the varied and colorful world in which we live, such as the story of the doctor who composes symphonies or the 10-year-old chess champion. The unique and the unusual provide important news and important information about our world.

Prominence

Most of us can stub a toe or catch a cold and our misery carries no great significance because we do not live lives of prominence. On the other hand, points about prominent individuals can easily become a headline in the news. If the President of the United States catches a cold, the condition could easily become national news, especially if symptoms of the cold are evident in a major appearance. In such a circumstance, news reporters would be finding out when the Chief Executive contracted the cold, what treatment is being administered and how long the effects of the virus are expected to last.

Hundreds of people get traffic tickets each week with no media attention, but if police give the mayor a traffic ticket, the violation may become a local news story. In local communities, elected officials, community volunteers and persons who are active in community issues are usually considered newsworthy because of their high profiles. Events in the lives of these people become important news because routine patterns and procedures often change in their absence. Clearly, prominent people are those who are known by name and need no other title or identifier: The general public easily recognizes the names of actors Tom Cruise and Nicole Kidman. Even those who don't keep up with sports recognize the name Tiger Woods, and every American citizen should know George Bush and Dick Cheney. In some cases, a single name may give enough identification: Cher, Madonna, J. Lo.

The prominence can be a place or thing rather than a person. Vandals spray paint buildings every day, but vandalism at the Vietnam Memorial would be news. The Mona Lisa is such a well-known painting that moving it from one museum to another might become news. Electrical problems that shut down the elevators at the Empire State Building for several days might get news attention.

Reporters should easily recognize prominent people, places and things and will understand that prominence is news. Our culture is partly defined by the people and places that are known to everyone. When these icons change in some way, the result is interesting to us all.

Impact

People are naturally interested in information that affects them in a personal way. For this reason, occurrences that have an impact on a large number of people become important news. When taxes go up or developers propose a new shopping mall in a community, the story is newsworthy to that community. If a company announces a layoff of employees, the information is vital to those employees and their families, but also to people whose businesses are supported by those paychecks. A large layoff or a factory shutdown could have a far-reaching impact: The tax base could be reduced, and that reduction could affect plans for improving a city park. Enrollment could decrease in the school system if a lot of people leave the area, and teachers could lose their jobs. A shutdown could mean that the elderly couple who have operated the convenience store across the street from the factory for 30 years lose their business.

Anything that affects daily routines, health or finances is important and interesting to an audience. Examples of information important to our daily routines include new public services, crime, changes in education and employment issues. Individual finances are affected by changes in interest rates, price hikes in food and gas and changes in expenses related to travel. Disasters that affect insurance rates or food prices are important; a drought in Florida affects the grocery bill of a family in Tennessee. An individual's health determines quality of life, so health news can be extremely important. New drugs for allergy control and breakthroughs in cancer treatment or eye surgery can change lives. Problems with Health Maintenance Organizations (HMOs) become important business, social and political issues. The latest information about the effects of caffeine, sugar, fat and tobacco affects everyone. Food safety is an important health issue. Sometimes, food safety problems appear in foods imported from countries with less stringent processing standards than in the United States. Microorganisms in imported fruit can cause serious illness and even death, so changes in food import regulations are interesting and important to everyone.

News about issues that affect daily routines, finances and health has a major impact on people's lives; thus, stories on these issues can become important news stories. Reporters must learn to recognize those events that have an impact on large numbers of people as news.

Relevance

Information that is relevant or that connects to people in some way is newsworthy. Some stories may be interesting and give insight into the lives of other people but may be irrelevant to the lives of viewers. For example, if OPEC raises oil prices, the information is relevant to anyone who buys gasoline. The fact that Robert Downey Jr. has been arrested again or checked into a detox center may be interesting but is actually irrelevant to most lives. The more information connects to the lives of the audience, the stronger its news value.

Tabloid or "infotainment" stories are designed more to entertain the audience than to give information that is relevant to their lives. Even in mainstream TV news, decision makers often are tempted to use stories that include dramatic pictures simply because the video is so mesmerizing. TV news departments may use visually powerful stories for competitive reasons, with the idea that viewers will stop surfing the channels to look at dramatic pictures. Despite today's competitive pressures, news judgment should be based on impact and relevance rather than drama. For example, if a train hits a truck three states away and a videographer captures the resulting fire on tape, the drama of the footage does not mean that the story is important to viewers hundreds of miles away. If a news photographer captures video of a man shooting a woman, the drama of the video does not mean the story has any importance to viewers in another state. Often, such footage is made available to local stations all over the country, but quality news departments avoid using dramatic pictures that have no local connection and are purely intended to shock.

Decisions on news value and relevance are always debatable. Therefore, reporters must understand that relevance is an important characteristic of news and evaluate whether a story connects to the lives of viewers in a meaningful way. In the short term, an audience may find entertainment value in a story that is not pertinent to their lives, but in the long term the audience will seek news sources that consistently provide relevant information.

Location

The location of a story can determine whether it has news value or not. A widespread 24-hour power failure in a town 100 miles away would not be very important or interesting unless the cause was unique or unless it affected people in an unusual way. The story meets the criteria of being unusual (the power doesn't usually go off for long periods of time) and affecting a lot of people, but the impact is minimal. On the other hand, a local power failure would be newsworthy if it lasted more than a few hours. People would want to know what caused it, when they will have their own power restored and whether it will happen again.

When a large manufacturing company issues Christmas bonuses, the story might be very important in the surrounding towns even though the information might be met with yawns an hour's drive away. When an employer of 15,000 people gives bonuses that average 20 percent of their annual salary, the economic impact will be immediate and impressive. Nearby furniture stores, computer stores and car dealers may run promotions and special sales to try to capture a share of the nonbudgeted money people will be eager to spend. Location can determine the impact and the news value of a story.

Localizing a Story

Because close proximity contributes to news value, reporters can often find an important local story by looking for connections to major stories outside the immediate area. Finding the local angle to a regional or national story is called **localizing** a story. Journalists learn to examine national issues from a local perspective and to determine who is affected by the story.

National employment figures may not sound important locally until you consider the many ways the news may affect your viewers. One story could compare the national statistics to the local data. Is the local rate of people looking for jobs lower or higher than the national figures? Why? Another story might show how national economic events influence a local company. If national defense cuts are announced, the trickle-down from the cuts will affect most localities. Reporters can look for local companies or businesses that have ties with defense contractors. Similarly, a drop in national automobile sales may affect car dealers in the community, but local banks will also feel the effects, along with nearby companies that make auto parts or the materials that go into auto parts. The national story can lead to interesting local news.

Consider a network news story about a group of people getting sick from tainted fruit at a national convention banquet. Local reporters might investigate the fruit that is available in local grocery stores. Where does it come from? Who decides where to buy it? What safety procedures are in place to prevent a local situation similar to the national story?

National statistics may indicate that tourism is down. The national story may provide some explanations about why fewer people are traveling, but the story may or may not hold true locally. If the national picture applies locally, a reporter might discover that a local tourist attraction is losing money for the first time in several years. Perhaps fewer college students are finding jobs at hotels and restaurants. If the trend continues, the city or county may lose hotel and restaurant tax revenue, which could cause budgeting problems. Localizing a national story can provide important information for the audience.

Because information that connects to the lives of the audience and has an impact in some way is high in news value, stories that occur nearby rather than far away tend to be the most important. Reporters can learn to examine national stories or regional stories and look for the local connection as a way to develop important news reports.

Human Interest and Emotional Impact

Much of the reality of our daily lives exists in our thoughts and feelings. Many of us carry out similar actions and routines each day, but our individual reactions to people and events can be very similar to—or very different from—those of others. As we go through life, we discover and define ourselves in part by this comparison to others. Stories about other people are interesting and important to us. For this reason, stories that stir emotions become news, but in a different way from the stories that lead the newscast. Stories that focus on emotional elements and do not generally affect people's lives in other ways are known as **human interest** stories.

A reporter did a story years ago about a dog that died. The story is memorable today to listeners because it invoked strong human interest. It was a chronicle of a daily routine that ended with death but began with a man's long-time working routine and the faithful companionship of a canine. For years, this dog was cared for by its owner, who left each day on a morning train and returned home each afternoon. The dog accompanied the man to the train station, left, and returned each evening to meet the train from which the owner emerged. One day, the pet owner died from a heart attack and did not get off the train at the regular time. From that day on, the dog returned to the train station each afternoon at the same time and waited until the regular train arrived. After all the passengers were unloaded and the train departed, the dog sadly went away. The process continued for years. People in the town had taken over the care and feeding of the dog, but the animal's life became a constant vigil for the return of a master who no longer lived. The end of the dog's life and the end of the routine became the basis for a news item. The story evokes powerful emotions: sorrow for the dog who did not understand why it was no longer cared for by its master, concern for creatures that depend on us for their care, fear of abandoning someone who needs us or fear of being abandoned. Psychologists could probably write books on why the story is so memorable, but the basic reason is the emotion the story evokes.

Interestingly enough, many human interest stories relate to animals: the dog that miraculously finds its way home, the poodle mothering a baby squirrel, a pony that rides in a boat. We are also fascinated by the struggles and conquests of other human beings: the teenager's survival of a suicide jump from a high bridge, the 90-year-old woman who walked across the continent to promote campaign-finance reform, the maintenance worker who saved his meager earnings and gave away a million dollars.

> Being a reporter never entitles you to take free things. . . . Use your brain and your heart, too. Is that too much to ask?
>
> *Dale Solly*

Reporters learn to recognize and develop stories that appeal to the audience and have news value because of an emotional element. Finding these stories presents a special challenge because they often occur in people's private lives. The owner of the poodle that is mothering the squirrel may be so shocked that she will think to call a reporter, but in many cases reporters have to put forth special effort to find human interest stories. While covering more conventional news, reporters may ask people to tell them about the most phenomenal person they know or to think about the most unusual event they've seen. A reminder to news sources to call if they hear of something interesting may lead to these occasional, but very special stories that tug at the heartstrings.

CHARACTERISTICS OF GOOD REPORTERS

Ethics

The most important characteristic of a reporter is *ethical behavior*. When a reporter fails to operate according to a strong ethical and moral code of behavior, that one individual's failing can damage the overall credibility of the news media in long-term, serious ways.

Recently, a New York Times reporter was discovered to have acted unethically as a reporter in several ways. Jayson Blair quoted people he had never met and described locations he had never seen. He used bylines from several different states when, in fact, he had never left New York City. He made up facts, invented dramatic scenes, stole words from others and turned in false expense reports. He not only violated the trust that journalists hold, he boasted that he had "fooled some of the best minds in journalism" ("Top Editors," 2003). The Times fired Blair, and two top editors resigned as a result of the fiasco.

As another example, in 1980, Janet Cooke, a reporter for The Washington Post, won a Pulitzer Prize for writing a powerful story about an 8-year-old child who was addicted to heroin. The story was fiction—a lie. The powerful words were made up by a woman who claimed to be a journalist and were presented to readers as truth. More than 20 years later, the damage from Cooke's deception had just begun to fade when the Blair scandal came to light.

Even honest reporters seem to be making too many mistakes. As a result of major episodes of dishonesty combined with too many factual errors, readers and viewers of news are having a harder time believing what they read and see in news reports—even in the places they should be able to trust. Polls show that almost half of the American public believes that the news is "often" wrong. Only a small percent even believe all or most of what they read in their newspapers. It's no wonder. NBC's "Dateline" news program faked an explosion on a truck, and a number of other high-profile news outlets have recently had to confess to their staff members' lies, plagiarism and invented quotes (Brasch, 2003).

If character is what we are when no one is looking, we hope that reporters operate as if they are the subject of a constant hidden-camera investigation. Temptations are great—to help a friend or to write the story without being absolutely certain of the facts. In addition, reporters also have opportunities to use their power for personal financial gain. Many individuals and businesses could benefit from stories in the news, and they are sometimes willing to offer bribes to get their viewpoint expressed. Individuals and businesses may also offer to pay for a reporter's travel or may entertain reporters and editors with the same goal: getting the story they want in the news. If a reporter is grateful for an expensive meal and wants to return the favor with a news story, the story may not be objective—and the story will surely not *look* objective.

Our economy as well as our democracy depends on people dealing honestly with each other. We expect our citizenry to operate with some sort of moral foundation, and journalists especially need an ethical code. But what is ethics?

Ethics is a system of deciding what is right and wrong. As a student, you may have had to develop your own code of ethics to help you make decisions about cheating or plagiarism. As a reporter, you will surely be called on to make ethical choices, and you should give some thought to developing a personal process for making moral decisions. The Radio-Television News Directors Association (RTNDA), the National Press Photographers Association and other groups offer ethical guidelines that can help reporters. (See the box on the following pages.)

The right ethical decision is not always clear, and even those with strong moral systems and the best of intentions can make mistakes. At the very least, journalists must examine their personal ethical codes and realize that behaving honestly in the pursuit of truth is the most important characteristic of a reporter. Honesty and credibility are the only product mainstream media have for sale.

Other Characteristics

Another important characteristic for a reporter is *curiosity* or *inquisitiveness*. Although some people may declare a lack of interest in certain subjects, the reporter may not. The reporter should be curious about everything, including science, psychology, literature, history, politics, differing cultures, children's games, animal behavior and economics. The reporter wants to understand all subject areas, because they eventually relate to or intertwine with news stories.

> Reporters must be naturally curious. You can't teach someone curiosity.
>
> *Ellen McDonald*
> **NPR**

A good reporter also has a *desire to get the story right*. Lunch conversations and water cooler chats are usually full of rumor, alleged conspiracies and sloppily drawn conclusions. There's great satisfaction in hearing others discuss an issue and to be the one who knows the real story—or the one who's willing to find the full story.

A *healthy skepticism* leads reporters to important information that others might miss and can be a vital characteristic for those who want to bring news to light. Skepticism takes the form of constant questioning or continual doubt. When the city treasurer resigns and says it's because he wants a job with less stress and wants to spend more time with family, the reporter wonders about the *real* reason for the resignation. When a local company issues a news release announcing layoffs because of the need to "streamline operations," the reporter will be skeptical. Why the need to "streamline"? Could there be other reasons for the downsizing?

Please notice that the characteristic should be a *healthy skepticism,* not cynicism. Cynicism—a pervasive distrust of people's motives—is not a good characteristic for

Characteristics of a Good Reporter

- A strong sense of ethics
- Curiosity
- Desire to get the story right
- Healthy skepticism
- Enjoying being with people
- Persistence
- Organization
- Ability to be a team player
- Willingness to accept criticism
- Flexibility

RTNDA Code of Ethics

The RTNDA Code of Ethics and Professional Conduct is a statement of guiding principles for the practice of electronic journalism. It cannot anticipate every situation electronic journalists might face. Common sense and careful judgment should be applied in all cases.

CODE OF ETHICS AND PROFESSIONAL CONDUCT OF THE RADIO-TELEVISION NEWS DIRECTORS ASSOCIATION

The Radio-Television News Directors Association, wishing to foster the highest professional standards of electronic journalism, promote public understanding of and confidence in electronic journalism, and strengthen principles of journalistic freedom to gather and disseminate information, establishes this Code of Ethics and Professional Conduct.

PREAMBLE Professional electronic journalists should operate as trustees of the public, seek the truth, report it fairly and with integrity and independence, and stand accountable for their actions.

PUBLIC TRUST: Professional electronic journalists should recognize that their first obligation is to the public.

Professional electronic journalists should:

Understand that any commitment other than service to the public undermines trust and credibility.

Recognize that service in the public interest creates an obligation to reflect the diversity of the community and guard against oversimplification of issues or events.

Provide a full range of information to enable the public to make enlightened decisions.

Fight to ensure that the public's business is conducted in public.

TRUTH: Professional electronic journalists should pursue truth aggressively and present the news accurately, in context, and as completely as possible.

Professional electronic journalists should:

Continuously seek the truth.

Resist distortions that obscure the importance of events.

Clearly disclose the origin of information and label all material provided by outsiders.

Professional electronic journalists should not:

Report anything known to be false.

Manipulate images or sounds in any way that is misleading.

Plagiarize.

Present images or sounds that are reenacted without informing the public.

FAIRNESS: Professional electronic journalists should present the news fairly and impartially, placing primary value on significance and relevance.

Professional electronic journalists should:

Treat all subjects of news coverage with respect and dignity, showing particular compassion to victims of crime or tragedy.

Exercise special care when children are involved in a story and give children greater privacy protection than adults.

Seek to understand the diversity of their community and inform the public without bias or stereotype.

Present a diversity of expressions, opinions, and ideas in context.

Present analytical reporting based on professional perspective, not personal bias.

Respect the right to a fair trial.

INTEGRITY: Professional electronic journalists should present the news with integrity and decency, avoiding real or perceived conflicts of interest, and should respect the dignity and intelligence of the audience as well as the subjects of news.

Professional electronic journalists should:

Identify sources whenever possible. Confidential sources should be used only when it is clearly in the public inter-

(continued)

RTNDA Code of Ethics, *continued*

est to gather or convey important information or when a person providing information might be harmed.

Journalists should keep all commitments to protect a confidential source.

Clearly label opinion and commentary.

Guard against extended coverage of events or individuals that fails to significantly advance a story, place the event in context, or add to the public knowledge.

Refrain from contacting participants in violent situations while the situation is in progress.

Use technological tools with skill and thoughtfulness, avoiding techniques that skew facts, distort reality, or sensationalize events.

Use surreptitious newsgathering techniques, including hidden cameras or microphones, only if there is no other way to obtain stories of significant public importance and only if the technique is explained to the audience.

Use the private transmissions of others only with permission.

Professional electronic journalists should not:

Pay news sources who have a vested interest in a story.

Accept gifts, favors, or compensation from those who might seek to influence coverage.

Engage in activities that may compromise their integrity or independence.

INDEPENDENCE: Professional electronic journalists should defend the independence of all journalists from those seeking influence or control over news content.

Professional electronic journalists should:

Gather and report news without fear or favor, and vigorously resist undue influence from any outside forces, including advertisers, sources, story subjects, powerful individuals, and special interest groups.

Resist those who would seek to buy or politically influence news content or who would seek to intimidate those who gather and disseminate the news.

Determine news content solely through editorial judgment and not as the result of outside influence.

Resist any self-interest or peer pressure that might erode journalistic duty and service to the public.

Recognize that sponsorship of the news will not be used in any way to determine, restrict, or manipulate content.

Refuse to allow the interests of ownership or management to influence news judgment and content inappropriately.

Defend the rights of the free press for all journalists, recognizing that any professional or government licensing of journalists is a violation of that freedom.

ACCOUNTABILITY: Professional electronic journalists should recognize that they are accountable for their actions to the public, the profession and themselves.

Professional electronic journalists should:

Actively encourage adherence to these standards by all journalists and their employers.

Respond to public concerns. Investigate complaints and correct errors promptly and as with as much prominence as the original report.

Explain journalistic processes to the public, especially when practices spark questions or controversy.

Recognize that professional electronic journalists are duty-bound to conduct themselves ethically.

Refrain from ordering or encouraging courses of action which would force employees to commit an unethical act.

Carefully listen to employees who raise ethical objections and create environments in which such objections and discussions are encouraged.

Seek support for and provide opportunities to train employees in ethical decision making.

In meeting its responsibility to the profession of electronic journalism, RTNDA has created this code to identify important issues, to serve as a guide for its members, to facilitate self-scrutiny, and to shape future debate.

reporters. Reporters generally devote energy to bringing information to the public in the belief that an informed citizenry is able to make wise decisions. Furthermore, even though human beings can have tendencies toward selfishness, disregard for others and dishonesty, the media offer an important balance of power that helps keep people honest and helps weed out those who misuse their power. Doomsayers don't make good reporters, but those with a healthy skepticism help keep the system strong.

Persistence is a helpful characteristic for a reporter. When someone says "no comment," some people may become discouraged, but a good reporter finds challenge in such a refusal and becomes more determined to get the story. The reporter goes on to ask, How can I get the person to agree to comment? Or how can I get the information another way?

Another important characteristic for a reporter is to *enjoy interacting with people.* It's hard to imagine anyone getting any pleasure out of a reporting job if she doesn't enjoy talking to people. The job often involves approaching strangers and asking questions that many people would consider too personal to ask even their closest friends. Although you may not think of yourself as an extrovert, you may find that with a little practice and experience, talking with people can become enjoyable.

> The reality of the business is that if you're not knocking on the door of the parents of the dead children, the competition is.
>
> *Richard Frohlich*
> **WFTV-TV, ORLANDO**

Regardless of whether an individual is an extrovert who enjoys working with people, anyone interested in working in a newsroom should be willing to be a *team player.* The process of putting a newscast together happens in a group of people. The reporters and anchors are most visible to the audience, but the producers, writers and assignment editors hold vital responsibilities as well. Just like most jobs, no one does it alone, and enjoying the group effort and recognizing the contributions of others will make the work much more pleasant.

Most successful professionals share the characteristic of being *organized,* and reporters need this skill as well. Working on deadlines and dealing with lots of different people on many different subjects requires self-imposed structure. Reporters must manage their time effectively and give attention to managing many details and lots of information. The simple ability to keep names, addresses, phone numbers, fax numbers and e-mail addresses in an accessible format becomes an important job skill. Finding the name of a contact and a phone number quickly could mean the difference between getting or losing a story.

> I'm a fan of failure. It teaches the best lessons.
>
> *Mike Schuh*
> **WJZ-TV, BALTIMORE**

Broadcast reporters must also be *willing to accept criticism.* Everyone makes mistakes, and in the broadcast business the mistakes are usually seen by many thousands of people. News directors and producers should tell the reporter how to be more effective. Audience members may write or call to criticize the story content or more personal aspects of a presentation such as the reporter's delivery or appearance. Stations may bring in consultants to work with on-air personnel in making changes. Because of the nature of some stories, there will be people who will not like you. In short, the broadcast reporter will work more successfully by learning to accept criticism.

Some consider reporting to be an *important calling* in preserving democracy and facilitating social justice. Citizens need a free flow of information about their government. Sometimes the fear of public exposure helps prevent bad deeds. As Joseph Pulitzer said, "The press may be licentious, but it is the most magnificently repressive moral agent in the world today. More crime, immorality, and rascality is prevented by the fear of exposure in the newspapers than by all the laws, moral and statute ever devised" (Swanberg, 1967). Television was not a factor when Pulitzer wrote these words, but in a more modern context he surely would have commented on fear of exposure on television as well.

Reporters must also show *flexibility*. Those who want the routine of a 9 to 5 desk job should avoid the world of television news. Few reporters, editors and producers work Monday through Friday during normal business hours, and as your career advances, you'll probably work a variety of schedules that may include weekends.

Newsroom personnel must be able to change plans in an instant and make the change with a positive attitude. You may be on your way to cover a council meeting and be diverted to the scene of an accident. You may have dressed for a live shot in front of a theatre and find yourself trudging through mud during a driving rain. Reporters and photographers work with a variety of people and will meet and interview all types of people. Although some days in the newsroom are routine, most days are not, requiring people to be flexible.

> Perceptions matter. It seems like no big deal to take a free t-shirt, but what do people think when they see a reporter wearing a specific t-shirt? And if the t-shirt is no big deal, what about when a company wants to fly you somewhere and put you up in a hotel? Would those perks affect your coverage of the company? What would be the public's perception?
>
> *Lisa Mitchell*
> **WCYB-TV, BRISTOL, VA.**

CONCLUSION

News is important to us as individuals and as a society. Mainstream news operations perform a vital function in preserving our democracy. In today's high-tech world, however, it can be very difficult to identify credible sources of news. We generally trust broadcast network news, local television newscasts, major national newspapers and magazines, public broadcasting, local daily and weekly papers and cable news. However, some news outlets imitate mainstream media in production quality and talent, but are not faithful to the standards of good journalism. Some nonmainstream print and broadcast outlets promote a specific point of view to a specific audience and may or may not be faithful to facts. Tabloid and sensational media outlets have a more general audience and exist strictly for profit without even a pretense of accuracy, fairness and objectivity. Generally, legitimate news items will have the characteristics of conflict, uniqueness, prominence, impact, relevance, location and human interest or emotional impact. Good reporters will be called on regularly to make ethical decisions and should examine their own procedure for making moral choices. Above all, they must be honest in the pursuit of truth. Other characteristics of good reporters include curiosity, skepticism, persistence, flexibility, organization and the ability to work well with others and to accept criticism.

Journalists hold the nation's trust for providing accurate, fair and objective information, and quality news organizations safeguard our democratic system.

KEY CONCEPTS

news	tabloids	accuracy
mainstream media	sensational	sound bite
mainstream imitators	objectivity	ethics
nonmainstream media	fairness	

Activities

1. Find examples in current news that demonstrate each of the following characteristics of news:

    Uniqueness

    Prominence

    Impact

    Relevance

    A localized national story

    Human interest/emotional impact

2. Find an example of nonmainstream media. Explain how it lacks objectivity.

3. Read a story in a tabloid such as the National Enquirer. List the sources in the story and their qualifications.

4. Listen to several of the following news sources and compare coverage of a topic: a major network evening newscast, the "News Hour" on PBS, a CNN and a Fox News prime time program, and an afternoon or evening radio talk program. What are your observations about the ways the topic is covered?

5. Buy a National Enquirer or other tabloid newspaper. Compare the content with the stories in the daily newspaper in your city. Compare the importance of the stories as they relate to your life.

6. Determine when the next election is in your locality. What do you know about the candidates or issues? Listen to a newscast and determine which stories provide information important and informative to voters.

7. Listen to a newscast and evaluate whether there is more than one viewpoint presented in each story. In your opinion, have certain viewpoints been overlooked or omitted?

8. Listen to a newscast to determine which news characteristic makes each story newsworthy. Is there conflict, uniqueness, prominence, relevance, wide impact, emotional impact? What does the location have to do with the importance of the story?

9. Assume that you are working for a broadcast news outlet and you are told to make sure a local company looks good when you write your story. What would you do?

10. Define and explain the code you use in making moral and ethical decisions. Is your process consistent, and does it apply to others in the same way it applies to you?

WORKS CITED

Brasch, Walt. "The Hollowed Holes of Ethics." *Liberal Opinion Week,* June 2, 2003, p. 24.

Brill, Steven. "Quality Control." *Brill's Content,* Aug. 1998, p. 19.

Swanberg, W. A. *Pulitzer* (New York: Charles Scribner's Sons, 1967), p. 51.

"Top Editors Step Down From N.Y. Times." comcast.net/smedia/domestic. Accessed 6/5/03.

Get a grip—this is not glamour. You get called out of bed. You plan to go to a concert and you wind up going to a rock slide. You don't have defined hours. You think it's neat to be on television and then you realize you don't have Christmas with your family. You need thick skin.

**TAYLOR CLEVELAND,
KCNC-TV, DENVER**

THE TELEVISION NEWSROOM

TELEVISION NEWSROOMS vary in size, technology and budget, but the basic process and the key players in putting together television newscasts are similar everywhere.

KEY PLAYERS IN THE NEWSROOM

The **news director** governs the structure of the newsroom. Responsibilities include hiring and firing, managing the budget, dealing with personnel problems and working with the station manager, engineers and other department heads concerning equipment, purchases, promotion and station image. The news director is responsible for the overall effectiveness of the newscast and may work with consultants and advisors about how to improve the look of the set or the effectiveness of the reporters and anchors. The news director's amount of involvement in the daily decisions about which stories to cover and how to schedule reporters and photographers varies from station to station. Even when news directors try to work closely with daily details, they are often called away for meetings with other managers, conferences or involvement in community affairs.

Producers have control and authority in the newsroom because they supervise and coordinate the overall editorial content and production of a newscast. Working with assignment editors and reporters, producers set up the day's schedule and determine which stories will be covered and how much time each one will get in the newscast. During the day, producers stay in touch with reporters to ensure that the stories develop as planned and to make decisions on schedule changes. They may decide that a reporter will develop a story in a dif-

The producer has control and authority in the newsroom.

ferent format than assigned—or will abandon a story altogether.

As the day progresses, the producer develops a *rundown* for the newscast—a list of stories in a logical order that will appeal to the target audience. (See Exhibit 2.1.) Producers think in terms of *news blocks*—the news content between commercial breaks. The *A-Block,* the first part of the newscast, includes the most important news of the day and must end in a way that entices viewers to stay tuned through the commercials for news in the second part of the newscast, the *B-Block.* News blocks are typically followed by the weather block, more news, and sports. The producer writes *teases*— short introductions to upcoming stories that make viewers want to stay tuned. For example, at the end of the A-Block, the anchor might say, *Put steak back on your shopping list. We'll tell you why when we come back.* The B-Block story might explain a new scientific study showing health benefits of eating meat.

As the reporters' stories begin to shape up, the producer plans graphics and other production elements of the show and stays in contact with the editors, anchors and newscast director as the newscast comes together. The producer writes headlines and promotions for stories and reviews scripts for accuracy and good writing before the reporter records the audio track. During the newscast, the producer communicates with the director in the control room and with the anchor on the set, keeping the show on time. Stories may have to be added or cancelled as the broadcast progresses.

Producer Responsibilities

Supervise newscast content and production

Determine timing and format of stories

Interact with reporters as stories develop

Make decisions about schedule changes

Develop a rundown sheet for the newscast

Write headlines, promos and teases

Review stories for accuracy and good writing

Supervise newscast in contact with anchors and directors

Consider legalities and balance of presentation

Producers hold high-stress jobs and make split-second decisions on a routine basis. If an important news story is being reported live, the producer is sitting in the control room deciding what gets on the air for how much time. The producer must also consider the legalities and the balance of the presentation. The primary skill for a producer, in addition to the ability to work carefully and pleasantly under pressure, is the ability to write well.

Assignment editors handle the daily scheduling of the newsroom, deciding which

Producer's rundown sheet.   **EXHIBIT 2.1**

PRODUCER   6PM WEEKDAY   **1/29/2005**

Page	Story Slug	Segment	OTS	Anchor	Est Duration	Actual	Back
A1	DAVE'S WX OPEN	LIVE				0:00	5:59:55 PM
A2	PREOPEN	no open			0:10	0:00	5:59:55
A3	SMYTH HEADSTART	PKG		STEVE	2:15	2:17	6:00:05 PM
A4	METHADONE BILL	VOB		STEVE	0:45	0:47	6:02:20 PM
A5	FATALITY	VO		STEVE	0:20	0:20	6:03:05
A6	SUSPENSION PENALTY	VO	TOUGHER	STEVE	0:40	0:38	6:03:25 PM
A7	DOG POISONING	VOB	WHO DONE IT?	STEVE	0:45	0:43	6:04:05 PM
A8	WILDFIRES	VOB		STEVE	0:40	0:42	6:04:50
A9	COMMUNITY COLLEGES	VOB		STEVE	0:45	0:57	6:05:30 PM
A10	UMWA BENEFITS	VO	EXTENDED BENEFITS	STEVE	0:30	0:28	6:06:15 PM
A11	BRISTOL HOUSING	VOB	HOUSING HELP	STEVE	0:40	0:39	6:06:45 PM
A12	AIRPORT COMMISSION	VOB		STEVE	1:05	1:04	6:07:25 PM
A13	WX TEASE	VO		STEVE	0:20	0:23	6:08:30
B0	BREAK ONE				1:40	0:00	6:08:50
B1	WX SUMMARY	LIVE			3:00	0:27	6:10:30
B2	STATS & BIRTHDAYS	FONT			0:15	0:00	6:13:30 PM
C0	BREAK TWO				1:40	0:00	6:13:45
C1	FORECAST	FONT			1:10	0:00	6:15:25
C2	INDEPTH SCHOOLS AND SODA	PKG		STEVE MELISSA MELISSA	5:25	5:24	6:16:35 PM
C3	SPORTS TEASE	LIVE		STEVE PJ	0:20	0:07	6:22:00 PM
D0	BREAK THREE				1:45	0:00	6:22:20
D1	SPORTS				3:30	0:00	6:24:05
D2	PJ LIVE	LIVE		PJ		0:17	6:27:35
D3	SUPER BOWL PRAC	VO		PJ		0:42	6:27:35 PM
D4	NUCKLES	VO		PJ		0:34	6:27:35
D5	NUCKLES BITE	SOT				0:16	6:27:35 PM
D6	AGASSI	VO		PJ		0:33	6:27:35
D9	STOCKS	FONT		STEVE	0:15	0:14	6:27:35
E0	BREAK FOUR				1:30	0:00	6:27:50
E1	LOOKAHEAD	LIVE		GARICK	0:20	0:15	6:29:20
E2	NIGHTLY NEWS TEASE	LIVE		STEVE	0:10	0:07	6:29:40 PM
E3	CLOSE				0:10	0:00	6:29:50

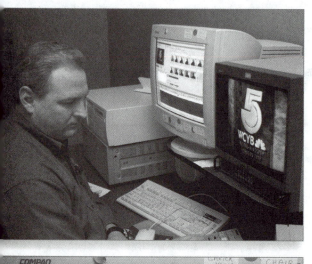

The video editor combines the various video and audio portions of a story to make a cohesive whole.

reporters and photographers work together, where they go and when. They maintain contact with crews in the field by radio, cell phones and pagers, and work with the producers as schedules change in the reporter's day. The assignment desk also maintains a file of upcoming stories. For example, city council sends a date, time and agenda of an upcoming meeting, and the assignment editor keeps track of the information and makes sure that producers know about the meeting and what may be important about it. The assignment desk keeps track of important court cases as they progress through the judicial system and makes sure that other important issues get appropriate follow-up coverage. Like producers, assignment editors work under pressure every day to make sure that everyone gets the information, time and assistance necessary to complete their individual tasks.

Photographers shoot appropriate video that clarifies and enhances the news story. Television photographers often prefer the term *photojournalist,* which reflects the fact that they gather information in addition to shooting video. Photojournalists often work alone in covering an event, carrying the responsibility for finding the facts, conducting interviews and shooting the video. They are sometimes called upon to write stories. Photographers understand how to compose a good shot and must be able to determine what shots are appropriate. In addition, they must work well with reporters and be able to edit video.

Video editors combine reporter narration, portions of interviews, video and natural sound as required for packaged news reports or for pictures and sound that accompany the news anchor's presentation of a story. Video editors usually spend part of their time in the field shooting news stories, although some work full time as editors in the newsroom.

Anchors present news and introduce reports live from a news set. In addition to speaking in a clear and captivating manner, news anchors must have an overall personal appeal to viewers. News anchors must understand news values and be able to write well. News anchoring is not an entry-level job, and the best anchors work for long periods of time as reporters before they become news anchors. Those who don't are often seen merely as attractive people without experience and can be resented by others in the newsroom. However, anchoring a newscast while maintaining the loyalty of viewers is a very difficult responsibility, even though those who do it well make it look easy. News anchors hold enormous responsibility for the image of the television station. At the most basic level, everyone in the newsroom, including anchors, is a reporter.

Reporters gather information and write and present it in the required format for viewers of the newscast. They may record narration for editing into a packaged news story, or they may write the story that the news anchor reads. Reporters sometimes do live broadcasts from the field, or they may introduce a story live from the newsroom or from the set. Television news reporters must interact well with people to gather information, recognize important news and be able to use public records and the Internet efficiently. Television reporters should be familiar with basic legal issues related to gathering and reporting the news. Often, they are required to shoot and edit video in addition to gathering the information, interviewing sources and writing the story. Being a television news reporter does not require glamour, but does require a neat, pleasant appearance and a pleasing vocal delivery. An understanding of basic English grammar and the ability to write simply and clearly are fundamental requirements for reporters. Television reporting requires a great variety of skills and hard work.

The remainder of this book is devoted to providing instruction for all areas of television reporting. First, we'll look at the basic operation of a newsroom, including current issues in covering the news.

In a typical newsroom, producers, reporters, anchors and others carry out a variety of responsibilities with the goal of presenting important information to an audience.

To work the assignment desk, you have to like the chaos.

Doug Hoffacker
KCNC-TV, DENVER

THE NEWSROOM ROUTINE

Television newsrooms are busy and exciting places, often staffed 24 hours a day, seven days a week with bright, ambitious professionals. Staff members are arriving and leaving at all hours, and someone is always under extreme pressure, wrapping up the last-minute details for the next news presentation. Irregular hours and deadline stress are part of the business for everyone.

Most stations have morning newscasts with anchors arriving in the early hours to review the news and prepare for the next broadcast. Everyone knows NBC's Matt Lauer and Katie Couric and may envy their jobs, but their routines include going to bed very early and getting up when most people are in the deepest sleep of the night. Producers of the morning show generally arrive for work at 11 p.m. to review the last newscast of the day and begin preparing the rundown, writing stories and making decisions about the presentation of their programs. Their workday concludes around 7 a.m. Morning anchors often present both morning and noon newscasts.

The assignment editor arrives early in the morning to begin reviewing possible news stories and think about organizing the day. Later, the assignment editor will participate in a meeting where final decisions are made about which stories will be covered and who will cover them.

Producers, reporters and news directors begin gathering about 8 or 9 a.m. for participation in the morning meeting. Assignment editors participate in this decision-making event, and photographers sometimes attend to offer their input as well. Everyone offers story ideas, and the group discusses them. Those who have a strong belief in the importance of a story often have to defend the idea vigorously against those who disagree. The news director holds ultimate authority for decision making, but often yields the role to the producers.

When story assignments are made, reporters begin making phone calls and setting up appointments. Throughout the day, producers work on rundowns at their computers in the newsroom, communicating with reporters through the assignment desk while reporters work in the field talking with people and uncovering information. The number of stories a reporter completes in a day varies from newsroom to newsroom. In the best scenario, a reporter works on one story a day and may be given a day off from working in the field to develop a story. More commonly a reporter will do two stories a day, and occasionally more. The more stories a reporter is required to produce in a day, the less time he has to work carefully and accurately.

In the afternoon, after the noon newscast, an assignment editor and another set of anchors, reporters, photographers and producers begin arriving to plan for the late evening news. Another editorial meeting will be held to decide what stories to cover and how to schedule the staff. While this is happening, the reporters who arrived in the morning will be returning to the station to write their reports, record their

> The hard part is working your way up in towns where you don't know anyone and you're lonely. Working nights and weekends and holidays is hard . . . and getting laid off for nothing you did wrong, but because they've got to cut somewhere. Local news is fraught with egotistical news directors that are sometimes just plain mean and there are others who just want lunch. The same newsrooms have people you'd walk through fire for. In any newsroom, you can find the best and the worst the profession has to offer. It's all up to you.
>
> *Les Rose*
> **CBS NEWS BUREAU, LOS ANGELES**

narration and turn their stories over to the editors. After the primary afternoon and early evening newscasts conclude, the newsroom becomes a bit quieter with evening producers at work while reporters and photographers are in the field. They, of course, return in time to write and edit their stories, which air on the late evening newscast. After the late news, the overnight producers work to prepare the early morning newscasts and the cycle repeats.

As stated earlier, most days the newsroom seldom settles into a routine. A breaking story such as a major fire or weather disaster may require news staff to work overtime or change their hours. If the city suffers an earthquake, a reporter most certainly won't go home at the normal time. In some markets, plane crashes, floods or riots have kept hardcore news people at their jobs for days, catching a little bit of sleep when possible. When a reporter or anchor is reporting live from a major breaking news story, she will most likely want to stay to follow up on leads and to track down the details so the audience gets accurate information fast. Some people thrive on this kind of excitement and mark their career achievements by the adrenaline rushes that come with these major stories. Reporters and photographers may cover extended news events such as forest fires that can't be controlled or may travel to cover more pleasant stories like the Olympics. In these situations, normal hours are unheard of for reporters and photographers. Producers may work around the clock as well, making decisions about live coverage, ensuring that satellite or microwave signals are ready when called for, and guiding those who are presenting the information on the air so that they know how much time they have and what they need to introduce next.

Working in a newsroom is a rare opportunity. Like any job, it has its ups and downs—days when the job seems perfect and days when any other job on the planet sounds preferable. As in any work environment, there will be people who are impossible to work with as well as those who become life-long best friends. Some managers will be good and some will seem to delight in torturing employees. Some

Computer Skills in the Newsroom

The better your computer skills, the more efficient and valuable you will be in a newsroom. Newsroom personnel do not usually hold the responsibility for hardware problems with computers, but any computer skill is helpful. If you can troubleshoot computer problems and manage the interaction between hardware and software, you will find yourself holding more and more responsibility—and becoming more and more valuable in the newsroom.

Prospective reporters do not need to worry about learning specific newsroom software in advance. Those who are comfortable with a variety of computer programs will be able to learn appropriate software in a particular newsroom with little difficulty.

Sometimes you can't worry about the big decisions in the newsroom. That's management's job. I have to be sure I do my job well so I can look myself in the mirror and be happy with what I see. It's like sports. If everyone does their job, we'll win the game.

Pat Barry,
KCNC-TV, DENVER

stations will be well-financed and well-run while others will operate on a shoestring, squeezing impossible amounts of work out of people and giving minimal compensation. However, as we emphasized earlier, news is an important calling and a vital requirement for our society. Those with special skills combined with a positive attitude and other demanding personal characteristics can thrive in and enjoy the newsroom.

Despite the many individual differences in newsrooms, they share the major challenges and controversies that come with the effort to bring information to television audiences. These issues relate to economics, politics and ethics.

CONTEMPORARY NEWSROOM ISSUES

Economics

These early days of the 21st century find media critics, journalism scholars and often the general public expressing serious concern over the hypercompetitive environment that now encompasses news. The effect of economic pressure on news content is one of the major topics of contemporary concern about television news.

Television stations are in the business of making money, and running a successful business can be an honorable endeavor. In early television days, however, serious broadcast news was not expected to make money because news was viewed as a station's public-service responsibility. The expenses for reporters, investigations and travel were considered part of the cost of doing business. Later, station managers learned that news attracts large audiences and news programs can make lots of money. In recent years, most stations have added more local newscasts, sometimes presenting as many as five or more hours of local news per day. The fact that programs are often added for the purpose of making money rather than for the purpose of informing the public has been a significant shift. In addition, as news becomes more profitable, television stations have become more desirable acquisitions for large corporations. Hence control of the media has become an important issue.

Media Ownership

Media ownership has become a hot topic in newsrooms, and it has attracted increasing interest among the general public as fewer and fewer companies own more and more media, both in the United States and worldwide. Media serve the public best when they offer many, varied voices and opinions. If a town has one newspaper, the owner could refuse to cover an important event or might give more coverage to a particular political ideology. The current debate pits those who want to allow more U.S. media ownership consolidation against those who oppose it.

Is there an adequate number of voices in the media marketplace? Some say yes: In addition to broadcast network news and local newscasts, there are more cable networks than ever before. There's the Internet. There are myriad national and local newspapers.

Others say no: Today, giant corporations own the major broadcast networks that influence news coverage at the local level, and they also control numerous other media. For example, the Walt Disney Corporation owns ABC and 10 television stations, mostly in large market areas. ABC has affiliate stations in 200 market areas that cover the entire country. The situation is similar with all the major networks.

In addition to owning a network, major media conglomerates like Disney, Viacom, General Electric and Fox typically own dozens of radio stations and several cable networks, as well as magazines and newspapers. Some own a major movie studio, a book-publishing company, and other media-related businesses.

Historically, the Federal Communications Commission had limited the number of broadcast stations an individual or a company could own. The FCC philosophy had been that smaller, local operations would serve communities better than large corporations that might be located far away from the public they are supposed to serve. Today, there is no limit to the number of stations a company can own, as long as the station coverage does not exceed 35 percent of the national audience, and even that limit is being challenged.

Government regulations also used to prevent ownership of both a television station and a newspaper in the same market area—called **cross ownership.** Ownership of more than one broadcast station of the same kind in one market was also prohibited. These regulations have also been relaxed.

Large broadcast companies argue that economic times are tough, partly because of declining audiences, and that owning more stations helps them survive. Some small broadcast companies object to increased media concentration because they fear being bought out and losing control to a large owner.

For television reporters, media ownership issues show up in salaries, in news assignments and in programming decisions. When a media company buys a television station, the new owner may downsize in an attempt to increase profits, and newsroom expenditures, positions and salary levels may get cut.

The most dangerous potential of huge media conglomerates is in controlling news and information. An incident several years ago at ABC demonstrates the problem. ABC News pulled a story charging that Disney World in Orlando had employed pedophiles and had not been fully cooperative in investigating sex crimes at the theme park. Some believed the network did not want to offend the parent company (McClellan, 1998). On the other side of the issue, supporters of fewer limits on media ownership say such incidents are few and that there is very little overall evidence that the number of media a company owns affects the content or quality of news coverage.

Media Convergence

Media ownership is related to another growing trend in television newsrooms. As large corporations come to own more media outlets, they are combining their newsgathering efforts—a move known as **convergence.**

In one model of convergence, a single company owns the major daily newspaper, a television station and an online news operation in Tampa, Fl. All three operations work from the same building with news managers orchestrating news coverage together. In other examples, broadcast newsrooms and cable news operations are joining together.

For television news reporters, convergence might mean preparing a version of the story for both broadcast and the Internet—and maybe even for newspaper publication. Newspaper reporters may find themselves speaking into a camera to explain the information they've gathered. Everyone may be involved in reworking the news product for the Internet. Convergence will require broader skills from news professionals: those who can use computers most easily and who can write well in a variety of styles will be the most sought-after employees.

Some defend convergence as a way to keep news operations financially strong. Others fear that converged media will limit the number of voices and viewpoints in a market area. If the same people run the newspaper, the television station and even a few radio stations, and the same people report, write, edit and shoot video for all the media in a market, citizens may need to look further to find varied voices and opinions.

News As Entertainment

Operating a business and making a profit are respectable goals, but the drive for profit can put pressure on news operations to be entertaining. Entertainment generally attracts more viewers than news does, so entertaining news might attract more viewers than a more serious presentation. However, presenting entertainment and calling it news can mean that the audience is not getting the real news. For example, few people would choose to hear a story about details of the federal budget rather than a story about a runner who overcame cancer to win the Boston Marathon. In fact, the budget story may be more important because of its potential impact on a large number of people's everyday lives. But broadcast managers quickly learn that stories like those about the runner lead to bigger audiences, and the station begins to present more of them.

The pressure to entertain and attract large audiences can lead to questionable ethical decisions. For example, a news anchor in Las Vegas showed up on a witness stand in court during ratings month telling jurors about her jailhouse interview with the defendant—a violation of the journalistic principle that reporters should protect their sources and that prosecutors should make their legal cases without the help of journalists. Moreover, the evening newscast featured excerpts from the courtroom testimony along with comments from the anchor about her exclusive interview (Cooper, 2001).

News departments often attempt to present more exciting programming during ratings periods to attract viewers. It is not uncommon to see "special" undercover reports on prostitution, homosexual activity in public areas or other dramatic topics during sweeps periods.

News producers may succumb to economic pressures in choosing the lead story in the evening news. If a celebrity has been arrested again on drug charges, how important is the story? Which would be more important—the celebrity arrest or a story about a bombing in the Middle East? Which would attract more viewers?

The economic pressure is intensified when the newscast is in competition with sensational tabloid programs. The evening news may be scheduled against programs that focus on sensation-seeking individuals. Serious news is not likely to win the competition for ratings. But what happens to those audience members who really do want serious, important news and tune out because the news is mostly fluff? These viewers may permanently lose interest in mainstream broadcast news.

> Reporters need to remember that there's a distinction between journalism and television.
>
> *John Antonio*
> **WABC-TV, NEW YORK**

The challenge for the news media today is to maintain a perspective on the importance of real news and information and to present them in a way that appeals to viewers. Is this possible? Perhaps not. Perhaps a small percentage of news junkies will get their information from C-SPAN and the few remaining public affairs programs, plus mainstream newspapers, magazines and broadcast news reports. The votes of this small number of informed people will be dwarfed by those who make their voting decision the day before the election based on campaign commercials that are guaranteed to be misleading, no matter which party produces them. This prospect is a frightening one for the future.

Broadcast news is journalism, not entertainment. Despite the enormous pressure to excite the audience, the audience is the government. The audience votes. The audience holds the future of our democracy in its hands. Reporters must constantly assess whether they are giving voters the information they need to make wise decisions on Election Day.

Lowest Common Denominator

As competition for television viewers has intensified, the desire to attract large numbers of viewers has resulted in programming that appeals to the lowest common denominator of viewers. The **lowest common denominator** is a common term in the broadcasting world and deserves clarification. In math, the lowest common denominator is used to add and subtract fractions. For example, to add 1/3 and 1/2, one must convert them to fractions with the same bottom number—

a common denominator. (Six is the smallest, or lowest, number that can be divided evenly by both three and two, so it is the lowest common denominator.) In broadcasting, appealing to the lowest common denominator means providing programming that can be understood by the largest number of people. The intellectual level of the programming must be low enough that everyone can understand it.

Simply put, most people are not educated enough, interested enough or sophisticated enough to understand or care about complicated subjects. Everybody in broadcasting knows this, but it is rarely stated. The goal becomes finding subjects that everyone understands. In sitcoms, sex appeal and sexual conquest play a role in almost every plot because everyone understands sexual attraction. In news, everyone can understand simple conflict, but not everyone grasps the subtleties of conflicting opinions. It's easy to understand one politician accusing the other of stupidity. It's more difficult to sort out why one politician supports a trade agreement and another opposes it.

In crime and disaster news, everyone understands flaming buildings and crews hauling murder victims away in body bags. Fewer people show interest in the details of fire codes or sociological questions about the causes and cures for high crime rates. More and more often, network news avoids complexity, apparently for fear that audiences won't understand and enjoy the program. For example, network news coverage of Medicare prescription drug reform often featured stories on polls and the likelihood of the bill's passage, with much less information on the content of the proposal. Stories about funding for war often showcase the political battle over spending, but do not often explain how the money will be spent. If citizens don't get the necessary information about issues of importance in the network news, they will need to seek out other sources of information.

Sensationalism

Simple presentations that appeal to the lowest common denominator of viewers often focus on the sensational aspects of the story. The term "sensationalism" also bears a word of explanation. In a mainstream newscast, a murder might be reported as follows:

> A high-school drama teacher is dead—shot as she left school today.

A sensational version would emphasize senses and emotion rather than facts:

> As a popular drama teacher walked to her car this afternoon, a bullet pierced her skull. She lay dying as blood drained from her body and a group of shocked students watched in horror.

The sensational version appeals to our emotions in much the same way we would be titillated and excited by reading a novel. Unlike feature stories presented solely because of the emotional appeal, news stories should be presented because of the value of the information and facts. Although we may feel sorrow that a teacher was killed, the purpose of the news story is not to make us feel bad, but to inform us about a serious, violent incident at a school.

There may be a place for sensationalism in our society, but mainstream newscasts are not that place. Appealing to the audience's baser instincts may deny people important information they need.

Government by Fear and Name Calling

"We have nothing to fear but fear itself," a famous statement President Franklin Roosevelt made during World War II, seems applicable to this discussion of contemporary news. When politicians frame issues to frighten the public into supporting them, the battle escalates into which side can scare the public more about the policies of the other side. "My opponent will destroy Social Security while I will work to protect the family." Politicians have found success and support when they paint their opponents as liars, cowards and extremists. Rarely is any conflict such a clear choice between good and evil. Rarely are issues black and white; instead, the issues of our day reflect differing ideas of good in complex situations—many shades of gray. When the public bases decisions on fear, the decisions are probably not good ones. Yet, the public is often attracted to stories of fear and sensationalism that charge the emotions.

When the speaker of the house calls the president a "tax and spend liberal" or a "right-wing extremist," the fight can be entertaining, but the serious issue of whether a specific policy is good or bad is lost. What are the goals of the policy? What is the cost? What are the chances the policy will work? What evidence exists about the potential success of the project? Have similar policies succeeded or failed? The news media and individual reporters hold the power to avoid insignificant political struggles and to present important policy news in an interesting way.

Politics in Sound Bites

Sound bites have become an issue of concern in modern-day news coverage. A **sound bite** is a short segment of an interview or a short excerpt taken from someone's comments that the reporter chooses to edit into a story. Skilled politicians know how to speak in short, colorful comments that are likely to be included in a story. In this way, a public person can exert some control over news stories. Ideally, viewers would be able to hear politicians defend their proposals at some length with reasoning based on evidence. If the president is accused of proposing policies and ignoring the costs, viewers should hear the exact cost, the relationship of the expenditure to the cost of other plans and the rationale for the policy. Broadcast news stories, however, generally allot fewer than 10 seconds for the sound bite in a story that lasts about a minute. The narration usually provides the facts, and the sound bite is used to add emotion and color. In earlier decades, sound bites ran closer to 30 or 40 seconds. Neither amount of time is adequate for any kind of detailed explanation, so responsible citizens will always want more information for good decision making.

Friendships and Conflict of Interest

A **conflict of interest** arises when two desires are difficult or impossible to satisfy at the same time. For example, the conflict between the need to report a story and the desire to protect a friend can pose serious problems for a journalist. If you're dating a politician, you may be reluctant to follow up on a story that criticizes your partner, or you may ask easy questions and save tough questions for the opponent. If your neighbor's teenager is charged with vandalizing the local school, you may feel protective of the kid who has grown up next door. When reporters feel uncomfortable or recognize conflicts of interest, the situation should be acknowledged to an editor or news director. The best course of action may be to withdraw from the story and let someone else cover it.

Sometimes, a conflict of interest may not really exist, but appears to. For example, when a reporter is married to an elected official, observers might expect the reporter to protect the politician and the political party. Viewers could believe the reporter would not cover political news fairly. Even though this reporter might be willing to examine both political parties with the same intensity, some might never believe that the reports are objective. In this case, the appearance of a conflict of interest is as damaging as a real one. Reporters must always pay attention to nagging doubts about whether they can cover stories fairly and whether they are keeping the necessary distance between the personal and the professional. In addition to avoiding real conflicts of interest, reporters must avoid the *appearance* of conflict of interest.

Diversity and "isms" in the Newsroom

As broadcasters write for general audiences, they must take care not to offend specific groups of people. Stop for a second and imagine this: A manager of a business is giving instructions for a project to a secretary. What picture do you see in your mind? Do you see a male manager and a female secretary? Are they both white? Our cultural expectation that managers are white men and secretaries are women is based on old stereotypes. Although it may still be true that many top managers are white males, women and minorities also occupy important leadership positions and are gaining more power and authority. When women are not promoted, partly because people so commonly think of them as wives and mothers rather than competent professionals, this unfair treatment is an example of sexism. Even today, reporters can be found talking about "businessmen" in news stories where the video plainly shows women as part of the group.

Stereotypical thinking related to race is also the product of a long history, and old discriminatory assumptions often go overlooked in media writing. For example, even though there are many more white women on welfare than black women, the term "welfare mother" probably conjures up an image of a black woman in an inner-city ghetto. This picture is the one we see often because it's easy to find pictures of poverty concentrated in inner cities and because newscasts have often combined the images of black women with stories about welfare. Reporters don't generally search rural areas to find scattered nests of poverty when they need pictures for the evening news. Viewers are left with the image of inner-city minorities as the picture of poverty. Reporters have the opportunity to break harmful assumptions by avoiding unfair stereotyping. When looking for sources, remember that leaders of black, Asian and other minority groups may offer valuable insights on matters unrelated to race and gender. All segments of a community contribute to its vitality or to its failure and must be fairly included in news coverage.

Do your best and take pride in your work.

John Antonio
WABC-TV, NEW YORK

In addition to avoiding stereotyping in news writing, broadcasters should not stereotype fellow employees. Newsroom staffs have all kinds of people. You may be working with someone from Japan, Mexico or Nigeria; a gay man or a lesbian; or someone from a small rural community or a large city. You will work with Christians, Jews and atheists. It sounds cliché, but it would truly be a dull world if we were all alike. It is also true that it is easier to get along with and understand those who are most like us. An extra effort in breaking down barriers will bring great rewards. Broadcast reporters have an unusual opportunity to combat discrimination and exclusion simply by recognizing the full potential of individuals in all groups. To do so will improve both broadcast writing and the broadcast work environment.

Enjoy that first job in the small market. Most people are young, just out of college and everybody's learning. It's all new and fun.

Pat Barry
KCNC-TV, DENVER

CONCLUSION

Television newsrooms employ a variety of professionals, including the familiar faces in front of the camera. Everyone in a newsroom affects news content to some degree, and those who determine the information that the public gets determine the strength of our democracy. This responsibility takes place in a stressful, fast-paced environment. Moreover, pressures from corporate ownership for high ratings and profits may come to bear at all levels, from the station manager to the reporter on the street. News professionals must focus clearly on the details in front of them, but they also need to understand how they fit into a larger purpose. They must understand the pitfalls of programming to the lowest common denominator and avoid sensationalism, conflicts of interest and stereotyping. For those with the intelligence and the energy, the television newsroom can be exciting and rewarding.

The first step in reporting news is to have information to report. Chapter 3 examines effective ways for reporters to get information from people.

KEY CONCEPTS

news director	anchor	lowest common denominator
producer	reporter	sensationalism
assignment editor	photojournalist	sound bite
photographer	cross ownership	conflict of interest
video editor	convergence	

Activities

1. Pay special attention to the watchdog role of the media in a newscast. Which stories are important to voters? Why?

2. Evaluate a political story. Is the issue presented clearly? Has the reporter avoided making the story a simple conflict between opposing politicians?

3. Evaluate the overall balance of important news vs. entertainment in a newscast.

4. Go to the Web page of the *Columbia Journalism Review* (www.cjr.org) and find the section titled "Who Owns What in the Media." Bring in a report on three of the giant media corporations and compare your information with information your classmates find.

5. Find out who owns the newspaper, television stations and top radio stations in your market area.

6. Make a list of current events that impact you. Ask how the political process affects these events. For example, if some people in your community don't have enough money, are there laws that might be affecting their salary? If tuition at your university is increasing, are state budget cuts affecting the cost? Make a list of potential follow-up stories related to the events.

Regarding Ethics . . .

7. Pretend that you are the news director and you are in a fight for first place in the ratings in your market. If you can improve your numbers in the next rating book, you will get a raise and your news team can promote its first-place status. You know that stories involving sexual preference can bring in viewers. Consider the option of doing an undercover story about homosexual activity at the nearby rest area on the interstate. Offer reasons for and against doing the story.

8. Pretend that a member of your family is suing a local business. The assignment editor brings up the lawsuit in a news meeting and asks you to cover it. What would you do?

WORKS CITED

Cooper, Gloria. "Dubious Decisions; Details at Six." *Columbia Journalism Review,* May/June 2001. http://archives.cjr.org/year/01/4/darts.asp.

Jefferson, Thomas. "Letter to Colonel Charles Yancey." *The Writings of Thomas Jefferson* (Washington, D.C.: The Thomas Jefferson Memorial Association, From 1903), *14,* p. 384.

McClellan, Steve. *Broadcasting & Cable,* Oct. 19, 1998, pp. 50–51.

Swanberg, W. A. *Pulitzer* (New York: Charles Scribner's Sons, 1967), p. 51.

"Who Owns What." www.cjr.org/tools/owners/. Accessed 10/4/03.

Interacting with people is the most important skill of all. When you're

genuinely interested in people and when you genuinely respect

people, they respond by talking to you. If you're a

reporter, that's the beginning of quality

news reporting.

**NIKKI WOLFE, WBTV,
CHARLOTTE, N.C.**

NEWS SOURCES

THE PREVIOUS CHAPTERS emphasized the importance of news and of the reporter's curiosity and perseverance in finding information. But how and where do broadcast reporters find the facts? The answer is *everywhere*. Although the average citizen may hear about an accident at the corner of Elm and Main, the reporter may realize that there seem to be a lot of accidents at that location and begin questioning the overall safety of the intersection. When the paint is peeling and the plumbing leaks at City Hall, the reporter may look for explanations. A store clerk's complaint about shoplifting could prompt a reporter to launch an investigation into security at the mall. Friends and associates may all seem to be complaining about allergies or the stifling summer heat. For most people, these topics fall under the category of general conversation. For the reporter, the complaints may spark an informative, important news story.

When a reporter decides that something is newsworthy and begins to investigate, most topics will yield a wealth of information, though there is no guarantee that the facts will be easy to obtain. The first step in finding a subject for a report is usually to pay attention to what you see and what you hear from others. From there, the reporter searches for supporting written documentation.

A reporter's investigation usually incorporates three basic sources of information: what he sees, what he hears and what he reads. These simple categories represent complex areas of reporting skill. Can you be sure that your observations are correct? How do you know whether to believe what someone tells you, and how do you get the person to talk to you in the first place? Where can you find documentation and supporting evidence for your story? This chapter and the next examine the sources of news and offer guidelines for gaining credible information from observation, from people and from public records.

WHERE WE FIND NEWS

Observation

The old saying that "seeing is believing" may or may not be true. Reporters can be most confident in what they see with their own eyes. The reporter who covers the story of a fatal car accident reports on personal observation at the scene. The eye-witness account becomes the basis of the story, with the reporter serving as the representative of the listeners or viewers, describing the scene of the accident for the person who was not there. The reporter knows, without doubt, that the victim was pulled from the blue Ford and taken away in an ambulance because he saw the event happen. The reporter may know that police gave a ticket to the driver of the truck that was involved in the accident, because he saw it. But things are not always as they seem, and reporters must learn to double-check even what they see with their own eyes. For example, police may drive someone away from the scene of a crime in the police car, but this does not necessarily mean the individual is being held or even questioned in relation to the crime. The fact that the police officer handed the truck driver a piece of paper does not mean that it was a ticket. Reporters learn to question everything for accuracy, even their own observations.

To verify what they think they saw, reporters will talk to other eye witnesses. At an accident or crime scene, authorities on the scene can give the official version of what happened. If the information is noncontroversial, the reporter may use it as background to reconstruct the events. If the information could be damaging to someone, however, the reporter will attribute the facts, as in, *Police say Mr. Smith walked out onto the porch and fired three shots.* If the interview is videotaped, the reporter may choose a comment from the source that will be edited into the video package. In the accident example, officials can verify whether the truck driver was actually cited and what the charges were or can comment on the version of events given by the eyewitnesses.

Things that most people see and pay little attention to may capture the curiosity of the reporter. Seeing the city manager walking around the outside of City Hall with someone carrying a clipboard and making notes as they look at the structure might be worth checking out. Perhaps the clipboard-carrying professional is an architect who is examining serious structural problems with the building. While commuting to work, the reporter may notice the large number of 18-wheel trucks that seem to be speeding and wonder if they're safe. The observation could lead to a report on truck inspection records or the frequency of truck accidents and fatalities on a certain roadway. The reporter may notice children in a school bus without seat belts and report on the laws governing transportation of school children. A sign advertising Saturday-night bingo could initiate a report on state gambling regulations and practices. Noticing the color of leaves on a tree could lead to a story about disease or environmental threats to plants. Reporters learn to see things carefully and curiously, and as they question their observations, important news stories may develop.

Listening

Reporters may find news just by really listening to what people say and the conversations they overhear. When the waitress at the diner comments that she's afraid she may be losing her job, the reporter may discover that new highway construction is planned that may require the restaurant to be torn down—or that the Health Department has issued another bad report. When the baby-sitter says another mother will be late because she's going to court with her son, the reporter may discover that a teacher is being charged with assault. When the neighbor says he's going to a meeting of the Little League-steering committee, the reporter may discover that a new sportsmanship contract is being drawn up for parents to sign before their children can join a team. When a friend of the family mentions that Mr. Smith is worried about his business, the reporter may come away with a story about the influence of a new international trade agreement on the local textile manufacturer. Reporters hear people talking just like everyone else, but the reporter is listening on a different level as well, for important news.

Printed Materials

Reporters learn to observe and listen with exceptional intensity, but they may also find news in readable form. Reporters can be more comfortable and confident when they know their story is backed up in writing. After covering an accident and talking to eyewitnesses and officials at the scene, the reporter will pick up a copy of the formal accident report at police headquarters. The official document will provide more information concerning the circumstances and any charges that have been filed. In the case of the story on security at the mall, a spokesperson from the mall may give information about how many arrests were made in the last month for shoplifting and assault, but police records can confirm the numbers. Remember that it might be in the interest of the mall to keep information about crime quiet, so the reporter may be misled. Because we can't always believe what people tell us, the job of reporters is to be skeptical and find proof for everything they present to their audience. In the case of the waitress who fears losing her job, plans from the Department of Transportation can verify new highway plans, or if the problem is health-code violations, the inspection records of the restaurant will be available. Because public records are such an important source of information, we will discuss their use in more detail in the next chapter.

As they develop story ideas, broadcast reporters also rely on what they read in newspapers. As previously discussed, print and broadcast reporters often see themselves in competition, when, in fact, both media serve different and important purposes. Broadcasters certainly don't want to repeat a story already in print, but newspaper stories may spark additional investigation or related stories. A report on a fire in an abandoned warehouse that contains dangerous chemicals may lead a broadcast reporter to a story on environmental requirements for disposal of chemicals. A report on new standards being implemented in the schools may lead to a story on high school graduates who can't read. A story about Russian visitors to a local civic club may lead to a story about children learning Russian in a public school. Just as good reporters listen and observe with unusual intensity, they read with the same radar for news ideas.

Reporters are often working under short deadlines and must be careful about interpreting what they read. They may read a news release about a unique development in the government of a church that will affect millions of people. Or they may return to the newsroom after covering an event and find information that has been faxed to the station offering a perspective on the story. The reporter may read a story from a wire service about an event before going to cover it. In the pressure of the moment, reporters often fail to read carefully and interpret correctly. Those who present facts to the public must be very careful not to misinterpret and not to jump to conclusions about what they read.

Reporters can quickly learn to be careful about what they think they see and can develop sophisticated listening abilities. They can develop the skill of reading between the lines and thinking "outside the story" for additional news ideas. Learning to find and develop sources and get information from people is much more difficult.

The Press Conference

When an organization or individual wishes to present information, in person, to reporters from many news outlets, she may organize a press (or news) conference. The event begins with a planned announcement by the individual or organization, and an opportunity for additional questions and answers usually follows. A public official may call a press conference to announce plans to retire or approval of federal funds for a new recreation center. A company may announce an expansion, or a celebrity may unveil plans to establish a new charity.

By holding a press conference, the organization or individual portrays the information to be presented as newsworthy. Reporters must evaluate whether the information is in fact newsworthy. Sometimes, individuals and organizations simply want their names before the public as much as possible. A well-known company name may translate into more product sales and more profit. The attention a celebrity gets may mean more contracts and a longer career. The fact that someone presents information in a formal, professional way does not mean it meets the criterion of being important to a significant number of people.

Journalists should always look for background to information presented at news conferences. The reporter should look at the information as a starting point and should not pass it along to viewers at face value.

The News Release

The news release is similar to the news conference but is much more common. The news release is a written notice about information that may be of interest or importance to the public. Again, a news release is an attempt to portray information as newsworthy, and this claim is often not true. Most organizations have a public relations staff that spends a lot of time issuing news releases and hoping for media coverage. Banks announce their promotions; colleges announce their upcoming lecture series; businesses announce their quarterly profits; politicians announce government projects that bring money to a locality. All are hoping for a positive mention that will enhance their reputation. Sometimes these announcements are newsworthy, but rarely should they be more than a beginning point for a story.

PEOPLE AS SOURCES

Without doubt, people make the best news sources. Despite the reporter's best use of observation, listening and careful attention to printed material, it is human beings who can spot the unusual, recognize injustice and draw conclusions. Individuals have areas of expertise and know what is important in their own areas where reporters cannot be expected to have sophisticated understanding.

Anyone can be a source, from the judge to the janitor. Taking notice and showing an interest in everyone can lead to relationships that yield news. Reporters learn that a secretary is more than a tool for scheduling appointments and leaving messages. Those who take time to get to know the secretary may wind up with an inside scoop about an impending bankruptcy or corporate takeover. Reporters have taken doughnuts to secretaries in the courthouse and in the police department, knowing that these staff members can provide guidance in public records and tips to other important information.

One long-time reporter revealed that some of her best information over the years had come from two confidential sources: one within the courthouse and the other an employee at the morgue. These people never appeared on camera and were never quoted as the source of information, but dur-

It can take a long, long time to develop good news sources, but if you establish trust, the payoff is enormous. I enjoy the challenge of developing a good contact. Remember, though, that over time, people view you not just as a news person, but as a friend. You need to keep this in mind.

Brian Maass
KCNC-TV, DENVER

ing private and confidential conversations and phone calls, they provided background that allowed the reporter to ask the right questions of others and find stories that otherwise may never have been revealed. Establishing relationships with people who trust you does not happen overnight—especially when the private information they share could cause someone to lose a job and income. These kinds of sources usually develop after they have observed the reporter's work to be accurate and when they feel comfortable on a personal level with the reporter.

> You don't get stories inside the newsroom. Go to church in a new community. Play on a ball team and shop in the same places so you get to know people.
>
> *Paige Beck*
> **WCJB-TV, GAINESVILLE, FLA.**

One of the best ways to develop news sources is simply by being seen. Just showing your face is part of the equation—and letting people know that you're interested in news is another. If you're only a voice on the phone, it's more difficult for people to relate to you than if you can ask questions face to face. Sincerity and real interest in people are more apparent in person, especially when you can take a few minutes to get to know someone personally. Developing sources takes time. Spending a few extra minutes at City Hall before or after a story gives you the opportunity to get to know the janitor and hear about his son's career success, or to talk sports for a few minutes with the city treasurer. This extra time can be an important investment in finding news. Always remind people to let you know if they hear of anything interesting. The goal is to have people think of you when they think of news.

Sometimes, sources emerge after they see a reporter's work in high-profile stories. When you become associated with careful reporting and gain respect from your audience, people will more likely think of you when they want to reveal important information. Sometimes, important sources may remain totally anonymous even though they know you and your work. One reporter found a piece of paper under her windshield one morning—an ambulance report about a judge's drunk-driving accident the night before. The reporter never discovered the source of the information.

> Go there. Show your face.
>
> Be known.
>
> *Richard Frohlich*
> **WFTV-TV, ORLANDO, FLA.**

Friends As Sources

Friends may often serve as a source of news. Because your friends like and respect you, they may bring you story ideas from their own observations or from what they hear from others. However, friendships can present reporters with a conflict of interest—the tension between concern for a friend and the desire to report the truth. When friends come to you willingly with information, there is usually no problem. In other cases, difficult questions may arise. For example, is it fair to use information you overhear from your friends as the basis of a news story? Do you have to notify them that you intend to use the information you got from them?

What if the information is about illegal activity that your friends are involved in? Is the reporter ever off duty? Can the friends of a reporter ever let down their guard, or must they always evaluate everything they say as a potential news story?

If a friend is talking at a party about rumors of layoffs at the nearby factory, the conversation may be a tipoff to an important news story and there is no problem for the friend. However, if the friend discusses violations of environmental law at his workplace, the use of the information could be traced to the friend and could even cause him to be fired. What if the friend does not want to be a news source and refuses to provide additional information to the reporter? What if the friend asks the reporter not to follow up on the information? Perhaps the friend is the mayor who is talking about a recent personal vacation disguised as a business trip. Balancing job responsibilities with personal and social life is a constant struggle for a reporter.

If they're friends, they'll understand when you have to do the unfavorable story. It can't be personal.

Karen Harris
WNBC-TV, NEW YORK

Reporters handle the overlap between friendship and job responsibilities in a variety of ways. Some reporters assume they can use any information they hear and expect their friends to understand the assumption. Everything is considered "on the record" when the reporter is present. Some reporters believe that their true friends will understand that any newsworthy information must be investigated. Other reporters choose not to use any information they hear in a social situation without special permission and assure their friends that they don't need to be on guard about what they say socially.

When a friend becomes involved in a news situation, the reporter must decide whether or not to cover the story and how to approach the friend. One investigative reporter suggests a matter-of-fact and nonjudgmental approach. The goal is not to judge the person but to question the action. Suppose a friend is accused of defrauding the bank where she works. The reporter's approach can make it clear that the friend is in trouble and the reporter has a job to do while at the same time letting her know that the friendship is not threatened: *I see you've gotten yourself into a jam here. You know I have to ask you about it.* The implication is that the relationship remains the same, but the reporter must confront the situation. Other reporters may not believe they can report objectively on a friend. They recognize the difficulty of evaluating evidence impartially when the natural tendency would be to believe and offer help to a friend. If a reporter thinks it will be difficult to be impartial, he may request that the editor assign someone else to the story. One reporter withdrew from a malpractice story because the doctor was his neighbor. Even if the reporter believed he could report on the lawsuit objectively, his reporting could cause stress in the relationships between his family members and the doctor and her family.

Occasionally, the reverse happens and someone who is a reporter's source becomes a friend as well. In this case, expectations about the news-source relationship and about the friendship should be clarified. Sometimes, a reporter will develop a romantic interest in a news source, or the source may express an attraction to the reporter. If the reporter is not interested in a relationship, the challenge will be to overcome the source's rejected feelings and continue the professional relationship. However, when a mutual sexual attraction develops, the attending feelings make it very difficult to report on the person objectively. In addition, those who know about the relationship may have difficulty believing that the reporter could be objective even when he is. If there is a question about the ability to be objective—or about the appearance of neutrality—a reporter should see that someone else covers the story.

Reporters can find news sources just about anywhere when they take the time to get to know people and to let people know that they're interested in hearing their news tips. Sometimes reporters are looking only for background or for news tips, but other times they want more than background information. In those cases, a reporter must convince the source to talk publicly, as we discuss next.

Getting People to Talk

How did one reporter get Michael Jackson to agree to be followed with cameras for weeks when others couldn't even get a short interview? What would make a man who beats his wife admit to and talk about his actions in a taped interview? Why would a busy executive take time from daily responsibilities to make a comment to a reporter about newly released unemployment figures?

In some cases, interviews are as straightforward as asking a witness to describe what happened. At other times questions can be as delicate as asking an elected official, face to face, about allegations of criminal conduct or asking someone about a marriage or divorce. Reporters seek interviews with people who have facts and information the reporter doesn't, and the skill of the reporter in asking questions often determines the quality of the information obtained.

> Friendly or hostile, deep down people want to talk.
>
> *Melissa Charbonneau*
> **CBN NEWS, WASHINGTON, D.C.**

Reporters benefit from knowing that people expect to be asked questions and expect to give information when they're talking to a media representative.

Request an interview only after you're clear about whom you need to talk to and what you need to know. Sometimes the request will be made by telephone, but in sensitive situations, it's almost always better to make a request in person. First and foremost, when arranging an interview, as in any other aspect of broadcasting, reporters must exercise the most fundamental interpersonal skills—good manners. Good manners form the basis of professionalism.

Be Professional

General rules of etiquette apply to reporters. Be pleasant and considerate. You are asking for time and information from someone, and your initial approach sets the tone of your conversation. Show general respect for people and the positions they occupy, even when their actions may diminish your positive feelings. People are likely to feel comfortable with you when you engage them in conversation and show an interest in them, their activities and their interests. Make an effort to make things pleasant. Be on time. Be neat, clean, tucked and pressed, and dress professionally—with a personal style if possible. Return phone calls promptly—return *all* phone calls. Say please and thank you. Answer your mail and e-mail. Write thank-you notes. Be yourself; don't pretend to be someone you're not. Don't try too hard to impress. Listen at least as much as you talk. Listen for hints and look for body language. If someone is moving toward the door or talking about things they need to do, you may be taking too much time. Don't be too pushy, but don't be intimidated. Be a person of your word, and do what you say you'll do.

> You could lie and get the information, but if you're good, you'll say who you are and still get it. That's the good journalist.
>
> *Shelly Harper*
> **WNBC-TV, NEW YORK**

With a professional approach, you will likely find that people are pleasant and cooperative. From that point, your goal is to get the information you need. Some general guidelines for good interviews appear later in this chapter.

Offer Motivation

People resist talking to reporters for a variety of reasons. However, individuals have a variety of motivations that may help reporters convince them to give information. For the sake of this discussion, we will discount the recent surge in "reality TV" and the all-too-common talk-show guest who reveals personal information for the sake of an expense-paid trip to a city and a moment of celebrity. Nor are we talking about the tabloid television shows that pay people for sordid or sexy stories. We restrict our discussion to journalists' efforts to persuade those who have information with legitimate news value—that is, stories that have some meaning for and impact on a significant group of people—to discuss it publicly, on the record.

There are as many motivations for people to talk as there are people, and as journalists mature and learn more about people and life in general, finding ways to work with people will get easier. Knowing *why* someone wants to talk can be very important information. Being aware of the following motivations can help reporters convince news sources to agree to talk.

For justice. Despite the impression we may get from news reports, most people understand that society's rules preserve order and improve the quality of our lives. Those who break the rules diminish the possibilities for everyone. Therefore, when good people know that others are cheating on their taxes, defrauding insurance companies or misusing public funds, they want the bad behavior exposed and stopped. They want justice.

For status. Feeling respected and important may be one of the strongest motivations on the planet. If someone is seeking your analysis on a public matter, it verifies your status. For this reason, a busy CEO may enjoy offering comment on changing social forces. With increased visibility, the executive may gain positive comments from friends and acquaintances or new business opportunities. Similarly, the average person whose opinion is rarely sought out may feel important being the guest on a television show. Even when the revelations are embarrassing, the person may feel special, simply because of the appearance. People will talk to gain status and respect.

To tell their side of the story. When people are accused of misdeeds or poor judgment, they may agree to talk to a reporter as a way of presenting their personal view. If a citizen complains that the county government is running water lines to a commissioner's property at taxpayer expense, the commissioner would surely want to defend against the charges and offer alternative explanations for the water-line path. An accused murderer may want to explain why he believes he pulled the trigger in self-defense. Strikers on the picket line surely want the public to understand why they believe their demands are justified. People want their views to be known.

To set the record straight. News reporters are not the only ones who value the truth. When false information harms someone's self-interest, that person may be willing to supply factual information to the news media. If a teacher's group is complaining that the county's new health insurance plan offers poor coverage, the county treasurer may want to point out the ways the new plan saves money and exactly how the coverage changes. The treasurer wants to set the record straight.

To get revenge. Revenge may not be the most noble of motivations for talking to reporters, but bad intentions can sometimes bring good results. In a fairly common scenario, an employee who gets fired will reveal negative information about the company or the boss—perhaps misuse of funds or violations related to labor law or environmental regulations. Obviously, the dismissed worker is angry and wants revenge. Reporters must be skeptical and careful to verify information when it is presented in anger, but sometimes that information is important. Anger can drive people to talk.

To help others. Despite the many human acts of cruelty and lack of consideration we see and hear about, people generally enjoy helping each other and working toward a better world. People will often reveal private, painful information in the hope of comforting others in similar situations. An alcoholic mother will perhaps describe how she deceived herself about her problem, hoping that others may recognize the pattern in themselves, seek help and stop hurting their families. One reporter managed to get an interview with the parents of a man just arrested after a five-state murder spree. The reporter confessed to the couple that her boss was pushing her to get the story and that she was desperate. Even while struggling with their own personal tragedy, the pair found sympathy for the struggling young reporter. As media competition increases, especially in high-profile stories, personal requests for help from reporters may become overused and ineffective. Nevertheless, people like helping others and will often talk to reporters for that reason.

> Take care of people and they'll take care of you. Be responsible and respectful. . . . Ask the questions correctly rather than going fishing. You've got to know what you're looking for.
>
> *Ann Curry*
> **"THE TODAY SHOW," NBC NEWS, NEW YORK**

Getting people to talk is sometimes very easy and the individual welcomes the attention. At other times, convincing someone to talk can be a challenge. In any case, once the arrangements are made for a conversation between a reporter and a source, the reporter must make the most of the conversation. Reporters must devote the necessary time to prepare for the interview.

PREPARING FOR THE INTERVIEW

Good reporters don't just schedule an appointment, walk in and start asking questions. Much of the reporter's work in an interview is done in advance. The reporter must develop background for the story, schedule a time to talk, develop appropriate agreements with sources about how the information will be used and attributed, and prepare to ask the right questions during the conversation. The first steps involve understanding the scope of the story and knowing what to ask.

Do the Background Work

News sources lose respect for reporters who come to the interview without a basic understanding of the subject and the source's background. For example, a basketball coach was asked for an interview just before the first round of the end-of-season tournament. A sports reporter began the interview by asking what the team's win and loss record was. The coach was insulted that the reporter hadn't taken time to find out the season record before asking for comments about the playoffs. No doubt, the sports reporter was covering many teams and was on a tight schedule. Nonetheless, people like to feel important and respected. When the coach realized that the reporter had not really been interested in the team or in his coaching, he put little effort into his answers.

Another news source noticed that the reporter didn't have any prepared questions and seemed to be relying on her to determine the direction the interview would take. Also offended, she decided that it wasn't her job to make the interview a success, so she began offering extremely short, simple answers to the few nondirected questions the reporter asked. Because the reporter was ill-prepared and the source declined to elaborate or reveal unsolicited information, the interview was a failure. The young reporter may never have even realized why the conversation went nowhere.

Preparation can be time consuming. If a company announces a new product, the reporter should not attempt an interview until he is acquainted with the plant's current operations. Check the company's Web site. Law requires publicly held companies to provide annual reports, and private businesses or agencies may be willing to make them available. Be careful not to overlook the obvious. Information may be available in newsroom files and in newspaper databases. Effective use of such sources of information ensures that the reporter approaches the subject with sophistication, enhancing the credibility of the individual, the broadcast station and the news media in general.

If you don't do your homework, your interview may suffer. Many, if not most, people enjoy talking about their vocational and personal interests and want to be helpful to reporters, as long as they feel the reporter is genuinely interested and respectful. Knowledgeable professionals pride themselves on hard work and achievement and resent those who confuse the facts, don't do their homework and look for the easy route. In that event, as one city official put it, "It's easy to clam up."

Talk to the Right Person

A source is less likely to clam up if she is the right person to talk to. If you're not sure what you need to know and why—and whether you're asking the right person—don't schedule the interview. The person to give the best information may not be the first one you think of.

A reporter's initial instinct may be to find an official to talk to, and the official viewpoint on a story is certainly mandatory. Moreover, public officials and public figures are easy to interview. They're well-known and easy to find. People in the public eye often enjoy media attention and are experienced at dealing with media representatives. Sometimes, however, the best approach may be to take notes from the official and save the on-camera interview for someone else. The best story may come from the person who doesn't come immediately to mind, and may even be difficult to locate. For example, the mayor will have the latest information about plans for a new bypass in town, but talking with the elderly couple whose home will be jacked up and trucked to another location to make way for the road would make a much more fascinating story.

The caution about depending too much on public officials also applies to high-profile individuals in the private

> I have failed if my piece includes a public official. That means I couldn't find a real person to carry the story.
>
> *Mike Schuh*
> **WJZ-TV, BALTIMORE**

sector. The official spokesperson at the factory that's closing down will have a polished presentation about company plans to help retrain those who lose their jobs, but an interview with the 56-year-old employee who has no experience with computers and is afraid of failing at a new endeavor makes a richer, more meaningful story. A personalized story will always be more memorable than one that does not show the impact on people. Some reporters believe they have failed if they even include an interview with an official in a broadcast news story.

Plan What to Ask

Early in their careers, reporters may get a sense of accomplishment from merely coming up with enough good questions to conduct an interview. The next stage in development comes when the reporter can generally plan the questions, *the answers* and the follow-up questions. This ability is directly related to the necessity for doing background research and being prepared. Without knowing a particular political affiliation or agenda of a news source, the reporter might miss the source's attempts to slant or misrepresent. If the groundwork has been thorough, the reporter will be able to formulate questions and have a good idea what the answers might be. One reporter may not have realized how embarrassed he should have been by this unprofessional question to a former astronaut and airline president: *What do you think is a good question for me to ask you?* The most minimal thought and preparation for the interview would have yielded a stronger question. For more in-depth preparation for an interview, imagine your source's possible answers and prepare follow-up questions for each of them.

Many professionals maintain the habit of writing down planned questions throughout their careers. Everyone has surely seen Barbara Walters holding her question cards as she talks with the famous person-of-the-hour. Those cards guarantee that the best questions will get asked, and they also serve as a sign that the interview is serious and carefully planned. A surprise turn in the conversation could cause a reporter with less experience than Barbara Walters to forget the major points that need to be addressed. When the questions are written down, the reporter can listen more carefully to the answers without worrying about formulating the next question.

Not everyone agrees, however, that writing the questions down is a good idea. Some reporters believe that trying to follow a list of questions written in advance interferes with the natural flow of an interview and distracts the interviewer from concentrating on the answers. Each conversation takes on a life of its own, and the reporter must be able to ask the logical follow-up questions at the appropriate moment. In fact, a middle ground might be the best. Writing some questions in advance surely cannot hurt and may help the reporter form an idea about the direction of an interview, but if the news source unexpectedly comments about something important, the reporter will need to abandon the outline and ask for an explanation. You can always return to the list of prepared questions to continue the interview or to check that you've covered all the topics you intended to.

When formulating questions, remember to avoid yes-or-no questions. Instead of asking, *Do you think the new water plant is necessary?* ask *What is your opinion about the necessity of a new water plant?*

Once the reporter identifies the proper source and completes the background work, he will often need to establish the conditions of the interview in advance.

Set the Ground Rules

After you've persuaded someone to talk to you, the source may try to insist on knowing the questions in advance. In addition, news sources may demand certain conditions before they are willing to talk.

Typically, reporters refuse to say what specific questions they will ask, for several reasons. Subjects may prepare and rehearse their answers and wind up sounding canned and insincere. Additionally, people sometimes reveal themselves in the most candid way when a question takes them off guard.

One famous example of an excellent unplanned response took place during Ted Kennedy's primary campaign for the 1980 presidential election. When CBS reporter Roger Mudd asked Kennedy why he was running for the country's top office, the candidate seemed stumped. He had great difficulty formulating an answer to the question. Some scholars believe this interview marked a downturn in voter support for Kennedy, perhaps because voters expect presidential candidates to have strong reasons for wanting to lead the country. Kennedy was defeated, and political candidates have been prepared for the question ever since (CBS Reports, 1979). Clearly, if Kennedy had been able to look at a list of questions in advance, he would have planned something that he thought voters would like to hear. Usually, indicating the general subject area of the conversation is sufficient to allow an interviewee to prepare, and reporters should resist pressure to provide specific questions in advance.

Celebrities and public officials will sometimes insist that certain subjects be off limits in an interview and may demand restrictions in exchange for their appearance. The reporter must decide whether the interview is worthwhile if editorial control is given to the subject. Some professionals believe in proceeding with an interview despite the requirement to put certain subjects off-limits. These interviewers hope that once the person begins talking, she will say more than intended, bring up valuable new information or even agree to answer questions on the taboo subject.

The question of whether to break such a promise obviously has ethical aspects. Is it right for the reporter to agree to conditions for the interview and then disregard them? Does the importance of the information gained for the public justify a broken promise to an individual? Broadcasters must behave ethically and should be careful about agreeing to limits they have no intention of observing.

Source Agreements

Sometimes news sources for television do not appear on camera but give sensitive information in off-camera conversations with the reporter. Reporters often make very specific agreements with these sources about the conditions under which they are willing to talk. Unfortunately, there are no clear, standard definitions for source agreements. People use the expression *off the record* as if they know what it means. In fact, you will probably get a different definition of **off the record** from every reporter you ask. In general, the expression refers to an agreement between a reporter and a source that provides some level of protection for the source's identity. However, there is no standard agreement on the specific meaning. Does it mean that you can't say where you got the information, or that you can't use the information at all? Can you use the information to ask other people questions?

Sometimes reporters accept information from sources **on background.** Background information can mean a variety of things. Sometimes the source means there must be absolutely no identification of where the information came from or even acknowledgment that there is a source. Sometimes the source intends that the reporter should not use the information even as background for questioning others.

The agreement to use information on background sometimes simply means that it cannot be attributed to an individual. Press aides to government officials will sometimes conduct a news conference with cameras rolling and then proclaim that the news conference is over. From that point, with cameras off, the spokesperson will continue answering questions on background. In this case, reporters can't say who gave the information other than a general "source on Capitol Hill," "source within the Pentagon" or other broad identifiers. For all the viewer knows, the source could be either a powerful official or the janitor. The term **deep background** is sometimes used to specify that a source's information is not to be used by the reporter at all. Such an agreement is suspect because it asks the reporter to know something but pretend not to know it.

To many journalists and many news sources, *off the record* means the same as *deep background*—that is, it cannot be used at all. Again, once the reporter knows something, he can't *not* know it. At other times, sources and reporters say *off the record* when they really mean the information won't be attributed to an individual—the same as *on background*—and they both expect the reporter to use the information in pursuing the story.

Not for attribution is another term used between sources and reporters. With an agreement that the reporter won't say where the information came from, it can be included in a story. It will appear as general knowledge or as an understanding by the reporter. An astute viewer will, of course, wonder where the reporter got the information and how credible the source.

According to one long-time journalist, the competitive reporting atmosphere in Washington, D.C., has resulted in an "ad hoc system of agreement in which each reporter and source negotiate how the information will be used. The source may begin the conversation, not with 'Now this is off the record,' but with 'Now here are the conditions on which I'm willing to talk'" (Kovach, 1998).

Because there are no widely available, clear definitions of the terms that apply to source agreements, the best policy is to clarify with the source exactly what you mean when you promise protection in some way. Ask sources to explain precisely what they expect when they ask that the story not be attributed to them, that it be used for background only or that it remain off the record.

Getting the Information on the Record

Revealing secrets of grand injustice and impropriety is not a daily event for reporters. A news source coming forward to provide news of major importance on the condition of anonymity is not a regular occurrence either. When sources do provide important information and their identities remain secret, viewers may question the credibility of the story.

Many times, people demand confidentiality because they fear losing a job or making enemies. Suppose the mayor's secretary knows that the mayor is giving city business to a personal friend who owns a contracting firm, and the building contractors who offer lower bids are routinely turned away and their paperwork destroyed. Each time the city awards a building contract to the friend, a check arrives for the mayor. The secretary wants people to know about the mayor's possible abuse of power but knows that he will be fired if he goes on record with the accusation. The secretary offers to give you the story and provide written evidence if you promise to keep his identity secret. (Maybe the low-bid proposals weren't really destroyed, and maybe there are photocopies of checks that have an amazing correlation in time and percentage to contract agreements.) This scenario presents a dilemma for the reporter. When information is not attributed to someone, as in, *Sources say the mayor is handing too many city contracts to personal friends,* the audience may question the truth of the information. If the reporter can say, *The mayor's secretary claims . . . ,* viewers have a much better idea how to judge the truth of the story. But, if the reporter requires the secretary to go on the record, there may not be a story at all. Reporters, along with their editors and producers, must often decide whether a story is important enough to report without attribution. And if the story results in a libel suit, the reporter may have to decide whether to reveal a confidential source or go to jail.

Whistle-blower is the name for a source inside an organization who reveals improprieties to the outside world. Those who "blow the whistle" to alert the community to serious problems serve an important role in society. Whistle-blowers have alerted the public to safety hazards in airplanes and automobiles, to knowledge by tobacco company executives that their product is addictive despite public testimony to the contrary, to racist practices in major corporations and to abuses of power by government officials. These individuals commonly ask to have their identities protected.

Some evidence indicates that reporters often do not try hard enough to get sources to go on the record. If someone offers confidential information, the first step should be to try to convince the source that if the story is important, it is worth going public. After all, public attention can provide some protection. If the secretary mentioned previously goes public with information about the mayor's illegal activity, the mayor may find it difficult to fire him without trying to disprove the accusations. When the story is made public, with supporting evidence, the heat should be on the mayor—not on the secretary. Other partial remedies may be in order since the secretary may not trust that public attention will provide adequate protection. Since the consequences to the mayor and to the reporter may be very serious, the reporter may reach an agreement with the secretary that his identity will be protected to a point. The secretary may be willing to agree that if the case goes to court and if the reporter faces jail for refusing to name the source, he will admit to giving the information to the reporter. By that time, other ways to verify the charges may have come to light.

Another partial remedy comes in offering the most information possible about the source or sources of the story. The reporter might reveal that the source is an employee in the mayor's office. If the mayor's staff is small, the secretary will surely veto this possibility, but he might agree to citing a source in city hall. What can the reporter say that will assure the audience that the story is true? *A source in city hall with information confirmed by printed documents?* Reporters must be able to prove their stories and need to give the audience reasons to trust the information. Some reporters challenge the source about the importance of the information: *Why should I stick out my neck to report this information if it's not important enough for you to talk about it? Why should I throw mud at your boss if you won't?*

All journalists prefer clearly identified, credible sources for their stories. In fact, experienced reporters will sometimes stop a source from giving information if they insist that it's off the record. Believing that the source really wants to talk, the reporter will push instead for full use of the information. The attempt to persuade may take a variety of forms: *Wait. Don't tell me unless you're going to let me use it. . . . Sorry, but I don't want to know if it's off the record because I may be able to find out from someone else. . . . I prefer not to know if it's off the record, but I believe you really think this is important enough to tell me on the record.*

For broadcasters, the task often requires getting the source to go on camera rather than merely on the record. Some reporters say they are not satisfied unless a source of an important revelation goes on camera. If that fails, the source's appearance can be disguised and only the voice can be used. Only under exceptional circumstances should the reporter disguise both the identity and voice.

The agreement to talk can be viewed as a test of the source's credibility. Sources who are convinced of the importance of a story should agree to talk. If they retreat, the reporter should become more skeptical about their information. (Please note that a reporter should never put serious accusations on the air based on information from only one source. Regardless of the source agreement, the reporter should insist on supporting documentation, physical evidence and verification from other sources as well.) Whatever agreement the reporter makes with a source, experienced reporters recommend getting the agreement on tape—and of course the agreement must be kept. News sources have won lawsuits because their agreements about confidentiality were broken. The courts have viewed the agreement not to reveal a source as a contract and have held the media accountable for contract violation. Breaking a promise in this case becomes more than an ethical issue—it becomes a legal one.

Going to Jail to Protect a Source

Reporters go to jail in this country almost every year for refusing to reveal their confidential sources in court. There is no federal law protecting a reporter's right to keep a source confidential. Some states have **shield laws** to protect reporters from testifying about where they got information, but these laws often provide limited protection. For example, Tennessee's shield law offers some protection to reporters from disclosing information in both civil and criminal court and covers anyone connected with the news media or the press. The law does not protect the reporter if the information relates to a violation of the law, however, or if the court finds there is a public interest in the information that overrides the need of the reporter to protect the source. In Florida, the shield law offers some protection to professional journalists who refuse to reveal the sources for information they get in the newsgathering process, but the protection does not hold when information is material to an unresolved issue raised in a legal proceeding, can't be gotten any other way and is overridden by some other compelling interest ("The Reporter's Privilege," 2003). The Florida law applies only to "professional journalists" and excludes book authors. California's law is included in the state's constitution and seems to offer broader protection than many other states', although state courts have narrowed the protection. When you begin a reporting

Shield Laws

The following states have a shield law according to the Reporters Committee for Freedom of the Press Web site **www.rcfp.org** (as of 7/2003): Alabama, Alaska, Arizona, Arkansas, California, Colorado, Delaware, Florida, Georgia, Illinois, Indiana, Kentucky, Louisiana, Maryland, Michigan, Minnesota, Montana, Nebraska, Nevada, New Jersey, New Mexico, New York, North Dakota, Ohio, Oklahoma, Oregon, Pennsylvania, Rhode Island, South Carolina and Tennessee.

job or move to a job in another state, be sure to find out whether there is a shield law and how strong its protections are ("The Reporter's Privilege," 2003). For more information about shield laws, see Chapter 11.

News organizations may have policies that limit the confidentiality that reporters are able to offer. These limits exist, in part, to help reporters resist the temptation to make a story sound better than it really is, and they are being taken very seriously in the wake of Jayson Blair's dishonesty as a reporter for The New York Times, discussed in Chapter 1. Despite a number of high-profile ethical breaches, we could hope that a discussion of honesty among reporters would not be necessary. Over and over, we emphasize that news reporters seek the truth, but there's another side to the coin: Reporters must also be truthful. As citizens, we must be able to trust our reporters.

Understanding available legal protections and preparing for the interview can be as important as the interview itself. The reporter must identify the proper source, set the ground rules for the conversation and prepare to make the most of the opportunity. The next step is to take full advantage of the time with the news source.

GETTING THE MOST OUT OF THE INTERVIEW

Don't "Interview"

The ability to interview is one of the reporter's most important skills. However, "interviewing" doesn't really work, so the first rule is *Don't interview.* Your goal is to have conversations where you simply talk to people and they talk to you. Being "interviewed" sounds like being cornered—up against the wall. When situations are too formal and uncomfortable, an individual may be more concerned about ending the interview than about giving helpful information. When people are comfortable and enjoy talking with someone, they are more likely to relax and reveal what they know along with their personal thoughts and feelings. Those who give sources the feeling of being the reporter's new best friend are likely to get the most information. The reporter learns to establish an immediate sense of friendship and trust so that people feel comfortable giving information. With the understanding that we really want to "talk," we will continue to use the term "interview" and will proceed with some guidelines that may help you make the most effective use of opportunities to talk with news sources.

Broadcasters should also remember that some people are nervous and intimidated by interviews, especially in front of a camera. When you put inexperienced people before a microphone or TV camera, reassure them and try to make them comfortable. Knowing that stumbles and false starts can be edited out of a taped

> Don't do "interviews." Your goal is to have a conversation. The only way to get close to people is if they don't know they're being interviewed.
>
> *Mike Schuh*
> **WJZ-TV, BALTIMORE**

interview—or that an answer can be repeated—will help some people relax. Something as simple as using a small clip-on microphone rather than holding a stick microphone in front of someone's face can help the subject relax. Encouraging people simply to look at the reporter and ignore the cameras sometimes helps them concentrate. Videotape allows flexibility and a comfort level that is not possible in live broadcasting.

Be Skeptical

Reporters must play a dual role. Although they should establish a sense of trust and close friendship, they also must remain skeptical of everything they're told. Because the fundamental role of the media is to serve as a watchdog over government, reporters often take an underlying adversarial approach to every source. Good reporters always wonder if the source is telling the truth. Even if they believe what they're being told, they will want verification. Reporters must always be skeptical about why the source is talking and be concerned about the spin they may be getting on the facts. Especially in the world of journalism, skepticism is a virtue. For example, if a city official announces a cutback in highway workers as a "streamlining" measure, the reporter will examine whether the move was truly for streamlining or whether there might be other explanations.

With healthy **skepticism,** reporters will always wonder if the information they're getting is true and why the source is willing to give the information. Sometimes information is true, but slanted. The reporter should know if a source has a specific agenda so that the source's comments can be put in perspective. For example, you can count on the fact that new statistics about crime will be interpreted in widely different ways by Republicans and Democrats.

Although skepticism is a virtue, **cynicism** can be a destructive force. Cynics deny positive motivations and tend to be distrustful, expecting deceit and dishonesty everywhere. While a skeptic may demand evidence that someone is telling the truth or acting with good motivations, the cynic may refuse to accept true sincerity. Reporters are well served by skepticism, but they should avoid giving in to cynicism.

In maintaining a healthy skepticism, reporters should never be satisfied with one source of information in any questionable issue. An old rule of journalism demanded three independent sources for a story, and the reporter had to be sure that the three sources didn't get the information from the same place. Contemporary standards are often less stringent, but today's journalists will demand enough evidence and verification to be sure the story is true.

Begin the Interview

Be sure to begin the interview. This advice may sound obvious, but it wasn't to a reporter who once scheduled an interview, sat down and began to chitchat. This went on for 10 to 15 minutes, and the news topic never came up. Finally, the inter-view*ee* had to suggest that perhaps it was time to discuss the arranged subject.

When any two people get together for business, informal conversation can go a long way in establishing rapport and making the interaction more comfortable. Talking about the weather, last weekend's golf game or a recent vacation can help people uncover common interests and feel comfortable with each other. Casual conversation serves an important purpose, but it should not take precedence over effective use of time. A simple comment can move things along: *Well, I could spend all day talking about beach vacations, but let's take a minute for you to explain a few things about the new industrial park before we do the camera interview.* People are usually busy with lots of responsibilities, so the reporter must make sure the interview proceeds efficiently.

When beginning a taped interview, it's a good habit to ask the interviewee to say and spell her name and to specify the proper title. This process ensures that you will know the proper pronunciation as well as the correct spelling. Remember that Jane "Smith" could be "Smyth" or "Smythe."

Guarantee Accuracy

Broadcast reporters are guaranteed accuracy when the interview is preserved on tape, as television interviews generally are. On the other hand, there's usually much more to the story than the information you get when the camera is rolling, so reporters also use note taking and audiocassette recording to help guarantee the accuracy of their information.

When you call to set up an interview and describe the subject you want to discuss, the source may make important comments. Often during the preinterview (the conversation before you turn on the camera), you will be gathering information in preparation for asking the best possible questions while the camera is rolling. For the sake of accuracy, you will want to take notes. Note taking can serve several purposes. Our memories are fallible and we always think we can remember more than we do. By the time you've left the interview, talked with other people and perhaps had lunch, the precise words and meaning of a conversation may fade. Taking notes provides insurance for accuracy and makes it easy to double-check the facts. Like the Barbara Walters question cards, note taking also inspires confidence in the person you're interviewing that you're going to get the story right. A professor being interviewed about her research noticed that the reporter was not taking notes and doubted that the reporter understood the subject. The professor suddenly had very little to say.

Print reporters almost always use handheld audiotape recorders to guarantee accuracy, but broadcast reporters also use audiotape recorders as a secondary recording, in addition to the primary camera recording. The secondary audiotape recorder can be used in the preinterview before the camera is rolling, and it's a good idea to record the on-camera interview as well. With a handheld audio recorder, you can listen to the tape while riding in the car or sitting at your desk without having to cue up a videotape. This allows the reporter to choose the sound bite for the story from the secondary audio before returning to the newsroom or to easily double-check the meaning of a comment.

Thus, while the camera operator is shooting the primary recording, the reporter may simultaneously be operating a handheld audio recorder and taking notes. Each medium has an important purpose. As digital video becomes more common, it will be possible for a reporter to check the audio and video at a computer terminal without having to use full production facilities to watch the tape. With this technology, the secondary audio of the camera interview may not be as vital, although the handheld tape recorder can still be used more easily while traveling and when time limitations are important.

Listen Carefully

The importance of the ability to listen carefully cannot be overstated. The reporter must personally, thoroughly and totally understand the information in order to prepare the story. The temptation is great to ignore the fine details and focus on the simple basics, but the more the reporter understands, the more information he can pack into the precious little time allowed for the story. Even though the process may be difficult, time consuming and even embarrassing, keep asking for explanations or material that can clarify until you *understand*. If you don't get it, your lack of understanding will show.

One broadcast interviewer learned the hard way about listening carefully, stunning his interviewee into silence and embarrassing himself. The guest on the live morning talk show was encouraging citizens to consider organ donation. The guest explained that there are just three options for a victim of kidney failure: ongoing dialysis, a transplant or death. The host made a mental note that there were three options and asked questions about the first two options. The guest discussed medical scenarios that would make it possible for some people to incorporate dialysis into a normal lifestyle, while others would succeed in finding transplantable kidneys. The semialert interviewer then delivered this follow-up question: *Now, please tell us about the third option. Who would find it appropriate?* There is no time out allowed on careful listening for reporters.

Not paying careful attention can cause the reporter to miss follow-up questions about unplanned revelations. A reporter was interviewing a woman who had recently been appointed to a dean's position at a widely respected college. In answering a general question about whether other

> Reporters like to talk, but be sure to listen. . . . Get your agreements on tape. . . . Little mistakes are the worst. We should hope that someone points them out to us. Otherwise, we might get complacent.
>
> *Lisa Mitchell*
> **WCYB-TV, BRISTOL, VA.**

women had held such a high position, the new dean responded that no women had held the position before. She said she was pleased to have gotten the job because she had, herself, experienced sexism in her former position at the college. Because the reporter was concentrating on the simple perspective of this individual's new position and because she wasn't really listening carefully, she missed the opportunity to follow up on the kinds of sexism the new dean had most recently experienced.

When reporters think they know the situation or jump to quick conclusions, they may not hear what the source is really saying. A good test of whether you're hearing what the source is saying is to repeat what you just heard: *Let me make sure I've got this right. Am I understanding you to say that the budget cuts will not hurt the schools because of the administrative reorganization?*

Use Interview Strategies

Ordinarily, the best policy for the reporter is to be straightforward and honest. But dealing with experienced news sources who have something they're trying to hide may require other strategies. Following are some interview techniques that may help you elicit information from difficult sources.

Play Dumb

Sometimes you may know more than you show. Or you may be fairly confident that you understand, but need some assurance. Playing dumb can sometimes help you get a clearer answer to a question, or even encourage sources to reveal their dishonesty. Never use this technique as a substitute for background work.

Suppose you are assigned a story about your county's filing of a lawsuit against the state. The county claims that it is not getting enough of the state's money for education because it is a small locality. Most of the money goes to larger counties and cities. As a reporter, you will need to understand that there are both local and state funds for schools. Locally, the money probably comes from property taxes and other local taxes. At the state level, income tax, sales tax and other taxes provide the pool of money. The state then returns a portion of the money to local school systems, usually based on the number of students. Because your county is a small county with few students, it gets very little money. Your county attorneys say that big cities and counties have too many advantages. They collect more local tax because they have more people and more business and industry. Then, they collect a larger portion of state money because they have more students. As a result, children in your county do not have the money needed for buildings, computers and special

> Some reporters want to show they know everything. If you don't know, people will try to help.
>
> *Mike Schuh*
> **WJZ-TV, BALTIMORE**

programs. You are interviewing the school board superintendent, and the comments sound complex. By playing dumb, you may get a sharper, clearer answer: *This issue seems pretty complex. Can you explain to me in simple terms why the funding system is unfair?*

Occasionally, despite having done your background work, you may remain confused about complex issues. In this case, you're not playing dumb—instead, you're revealing your lack of understanding, and the advice in this case is *don't be afraid of looking dumb.* Ask for explanations as many times as it takes. Ask the source to explain again, more simply. Remember, if you don't understand, there are others who won't either, and until you understand thoroughly, you certainly can't write the story clearly. For example, legal rulings can be especially challenging to understand and clarify for general audiences. If a plea of *nolo contendere* is documented in court records, a TV news story announcing that the defendant entered a *nolo contendere* plea will not be clear to most viewers. When you ask for an explanation, the court clerk may tell you that it means "no contest." This sounds more like the English language, but a good reporter can make it clearer by asking a few more questions: *I think I know what "no contest" means, but will you make sure that I understand by explaining it again in simple terms?*

Playing dumb may make it easier for sources to reveal important information—or to show themselves being dishonest. Suppose the mayor has fired the city's marketing director. The marketing director has informed you that she was fired for complaining repeatedly to the mayor about a misuse of funds from a government grant—and has given you documentation to prove it. Instead of asking the mayor directly about the marketing director's complaints, the reporter casually asks about the dismissal of the marketing director. The reporter may even appear to accept, without asking for details, the mayor's explanation that there had been numerous complaints about the marketing director's performance. To prevent the mayor from becoming defensive, the reporter may present the first question about the spending of the grant money as a casual question later in the interview. Without showing how much information he knows, the reporter can ask more and more penetrating questions and eventually ask directly about charges of misusing money. If the mayor repeatedly lies and attempts to mislead the reporter, these efforts will be revealed.

Understanding scientific matters can also be difficult. If you're covering a hazardous material spill on the interstate highway, you may need to report the name and characteristics of the chemical. Be sure you learn all you can about the chemical and its uses so that you can explain it to the listener: *I'm not a scientist . . . just a reporter. Help me understand this.* Reporters are not encouraged to lie and misrepresent themselves, but sometimes withholding what you know or playing the role of someone who does not understand can help you get the information the public needs.

Be Tough

Occasionally, a reporter can gain information by being tough and making people angry. When news sources become upset, they may let their guard down and talk. Sometimes being off guard leads people to reveal important information.

One reporter tells the story of a mayor who drove away from City Hall just as she and her TV crew arrived for a scheduled interview about missing city funds. After waiting far longer than the mayor believed she would, she saw him drive back toward City Hall, see the TV truck and drive away again. Undaunted and unwilling to give up, the reporter found the mayor's home address and went there, where the car was, indeed, in the driveway. But no one answered the doorbell. Finally, the reporter began taping in front of the house, explaining into the camera that the mayor had canceled an appointment and was refusing to comment. At this point, as you've probably already guessed, the mayor appeared on the porch and agreed to make a statement. Playing tough can sometimes yield results.

> Have thick skin. Sometimes people don't like what you represent. They'll hang up on you, slam doors and be rude. You can't take it personally.
>
> *Mike Schuh*
> **WJZ-TV, BALTIMORE**

Another common tough tactic is to remind the subject that you have the story from other sources and the story is scheduled to run—either with her comment or without. A statement within a story that a public official is refusing to comment can create the appearance that the person is hiding something. In the above example, if the mayor is accused of knowing about missing funds and refuses to comment, the mayor looks bad. Since mayors are usually elected, looking bad can translate into losing votes or losing political support for favorite projects. This threat can provide the proper encouragement for talking to a reporter.

Being tough does *not* mean being rude. The reporter can ask the toughest questions diplomatically. The purpose is to gain information, not for the reporter to use the power of the press to bully someone. On the other hand, reporters may occasionally push someone to the point of anger as a way of taking the person off guard and getting him to talk. The tactic may work, but you need to be aware that the reporter will surely lose any future opportunity to get information from the angered source.

The Ambush Interview

Reporters face a serious ethical question about whether it is ever acceptable to force someone to talk. In an **ambush interview** the reporter surprises a person who won't agree to an interview, catches her off guard and forces her to answer questions. Some journalists insist that ambush interviews are always wrong. Instead, the reporter should have enough background information to persuade the source: *I've got this information, and I need you to talk.* Others believe that good arguments don't always prevail and that ambush interviews can sometimes produce a benefit greater than the damage done by using the questionable technique.

If a reporter has learned that the owner of a business is locking up immigrant women and forcing them to work 12-hour days with less than minimum-wage pay, the owner is not likely to agree to a pleasant, sit-down interview. If the reporter has sufficient evidence that the abuse is taking place and has tried repeatedly and unsuccessfully to schedule an interview, he may wait somewhere for the owner to appear and try to get him to explain why workers never enter or leave the business. Without absolute confidence of the facts, the reporter could wind up looking foolish, but if the charges are true, the owner will be forced to try to answer the reporter's questions.

> I don't ambush people. I say, "I've got this and I need you." I have a history of fair dealing and making good arguments.
>
> *Dale Solly*

Because an ambush automatically implies guilt, responsible media outlets use them only as a last resort. Reporters should consider an ambush only after every other attempt to get a subject to talk has failed—this means diligent and persistent attempts, not just a couple of phone calls.

In addition, the reporter must be confident the ambush is necessary to the story. The reporter should explain within the story why the ambush was necessary and should avoid using the ambush to lead the story, as this suggests it was done for the sake of the drama rather than the information. Some media critics argue that ambushes at someone's home are never appropriate. Only when getting the story is more important than the method of getting it should the reporter and producers agree that surprising someone with tough questions is acceptable. However, ambushing a source is very different from asking tough questions.

Ask the Tough Questions

Asking tough or sensitive questions is not easy, and the reporter must approach them carefully. When a reporter properly prepares for an interview and can accurately guess what the answers to questions will be, she can establish an order or strategy to lead up to the most difficult questions. If you're talking to the city manager about an illegal city sewage discharge into the lake, you may begin with a review of the facts and ask about consequences of the discharge and plans for cleanup. If you're going to confront the official with allegations that he knew about plans for the illegal discharge, you would surely not begin the interview with that question. Save the tough questions for the end, or the first question may be the last one you get to ask.

By doing it properly, a good reporter can ask almost anything without offending. Asking a tough question does not have to mean being confrontational or accusing. Remember that when people know you're a reporter, they know it's your job to ask questions. People expect you to ask questions, but they don't want to feel insulted. In the case of the city manager, you may begin by establishing that city officials are aware of the sewage discharge problem and are working on a cleanup. When it's time to ask the city manager about allegations of knowing in advance and perhaps approving the illegal activity, you don't have to ask the question in anger or in judgment. You just need the facts.

Remain calm and do your job professionally. Your approach might be something like this: *The city manager's office oversees the Waste Department, and you supervise the department closely. A former worker is claiming that the sewage was dumped with your approval. What is your response to this allegation?* The question includes a reference to the city manager's authority (respect and status) and an assumption that he does the job well by knowing the details of the operation he supervises. The request for comment does not contain a judgment of guilt, and the request is phrased in a positive manner, thereby preserving the manager's dignity.

The manager may resent the question, either because of guilt or innocence, and may refuse to answer: *I have no comment.* Or, *I resent the implication that I have done anything illegal and I am not responding to these fabricated charges.* Or, *That's a lie and I am ending the interview now.* Here's where the reporter's skills are challenged. Being confrontational will not help. The reporter should remain calm and nonjudgmental: *I understand this question is upsetting, but I'm sure you can see why people need to hear your response to the allegations. Please tell us how such a discharge could have taken place without your knowledge?* There is never an excuse for being rude, even when asking tough questions. Moreover, the reporter should not appear judgmental.

Avoid Judgment

Given a choice, people will always prefer to talk to the person who can understand them—not the person who will sit in judgment. Our closest friends are usually similar in age, with similar life experiences and attitudes, which makes us comfortable. News sources also appreciate talking to someone who understands them. If the mayor is charged with accepting bribes in exchange for city construction contracts, you have to ask questions—but you don't have to be condescending and judgmental. A matter-of-fact approach will probably make it easier for the mayor to talk about the charges. *Well, Mayor, I understand the D.A. has pressed charges against you. I know this is difficult for you, but I have to talk to you about it.* This is not to say you won't ask the personal questions, but you will begin by talking about the charges. *Let's begin by having you explain the charges and the court procedures you are expecting.* As the interview proceeds, you will ask more sensitive questions, but attempt to frame them in a way that helps the mayor preserve some dignity. *I'm sure you knew the law related to bribery. Can you explain how you allowed yourself to do something you knew could get you into such big trouble?* Even though you may privately conclude that the reasons are absurd, you will try not to show your personal feelings in the interview. Appearing nonjudgmental encourages people to be more open with you.

Ask for Proof

If a defense contract worker calls a reporter to reveal that the company is manufacturing defective bolts for airplanes, you cannot broadcast the story based on one person's claim. The whistle-blower may want to give the tip and no additional information, leaving it to the reporter to ferret out the truth and investigate the story. Acting like you're not particularly interested in the story unless the source can offer proof that the story is true may encourage the worker to give more information or even go public with the claim. *What evidence to you have? Why should I believe you? I don't believe this story can be proven. Do others know about this? If this is true, why can't you get me any documentation? Why can't you give me the name of someone else who can verify your claim?*

Reminding sources of the importance of your reputation for accuracy can help. *Remember that my reputation is on the line with this story. If you want your message to get out, prove it to me and I'll work with you. But remember—nothing is more important to me than the facts.*

Repeat the Question

Sources can be pretty stubborn about refusing to answer questions. The reporter may have to be persistent. Sometimes asking the same question in different ways circumvents the source's defensiveness and yields an answer. For example, reporters are often in the position of trying to find out whether incumbent senators are running again and whether newcomers will challenge their seats. From the senator's viewpoint, it may be advantageous to keep plans secret for as long as possible to protect power or to conceal campaign plans. Asking the senator about plans to run for re-election can be a challenging exercise, and politicians usually have experience dodging questions. A typical response might be, *I've been so busy working that I haven't had time to consider whether I'll run again.* Nonsense. Of course, the senator has a very good idea whether he will run or not. Reporter: *I'm sure you have been busy. Maybe you could tell us what kinds of considerations will affect your decision.* The senator may continue to dodge, and the interview may proceed to other topics. Later the reporter might return to the topic: *Senator, our viewers will remain interested in whether you will continue as their representative in Washington. What could possibly make you decide to leave office voluntarily?* If the senator has been thinking about retiring, rephrasing the question and asking it later in the interview may yield an honest answer.

Ask Why

Why? is the best question on earth. When sources refuse to talk, they can sound very firm and immovable. *I cannot answer that question. Sorry, I'm unable to respond to that question.* The stonewalling can be very frustrating. Occasionally, asking why they can't answer can provide some insight.

Other Interviewing Techniques

1. *Avoid yes-or-no questions.* If you ask the mayor, *Were you aware of the illegal payments?*, you'll get a one-word answer and no explanation. Questions that begin with "how," "what" or "why" will yield more useful information. *How is it possible that the mayor would not be aware of large sums of money being paid out of the city treasury? What could have explained these large payments other than some kind of fraud? Why were you not suspicious about these large sums of money being deducted from the treasury?*

2. *Keep the questions brief.* When the question becomes convoluted and complex, the source won't be able to answer clearly.

3. *Ask one question at a time.*

4. *Try not to interrupt.* Even though tape is rolling and the photographer may be getting tired, let people make their points. The interview can be cut and edited later.

5. *Interrupt politely.* Sometimes people get excited about the interview or about the opportunity to talk about a subject that interests them and don't know when to quit. If time requires or if your patience is totally gone, find a polite way to interrupt: *Excuse me. This is very interesting, but we have another appointment and have to go. Could you please sum up your point in another sentence or two?* Or, *I'm sorry, but our time is running short and I have one more question I must ask you before we go.*

6. *Know when to keep your mouth shut.* In television and radio interviews, be careful about vocalizing your encouragement. As people are talking in normal conversation, we encourage them by saying things like "uh-huh" and "OK." However, these utterances can overlap the words of the interviewee and make editing very difficult. Remain silent for a second or two after the subject quits talking before you comment or ask another question.

7. *Silence is golden.* In addition to preventing editing problems, there are other reasons to wait before you speak. People have a natural tendency to want to fill up silence. For this reason, reporters often jump in with another question when the subject quits talking. But if you wait until the silence is uncomfortable, you will be amazed to see the *subject* fill up the silence, and perhaps reveal important information. Regarding the effort to get important information from sources, one reporter has the philosophy that *he who talks next loses.*

Conclude the Interview

Make it clear when the interview is over. Like the advice to begin the interview, this may also sound painfully obvious, but conversation can easily drag on and gradually drift away from the subject at hand. The reporter needs to keep the interview on track. As the interview concludes, review important points, either by asking the source to summarize or to verify your summary of what was said. Ask if there's anything the subject would like to add. Sometimes the source may have important ideas that the reporter didn't think to ask about.

Before you leave, exchange business cards. Having names, titles and phone numbers handy can be helpful when you need to find information in a hurry. When you leave your card, remind people that you're always interested in news tips—you may wind up with the scoop on a future story. Before leaving, it is also a good idea to ask permission to call later in case you need clarification on anything as you're writing your story. This agreement will make you more comfortable with calling if you do need a better understanding of something as you are writing. The request also shows your source that you are serious about avoiding mistakes in your story.

Strive to maintain a good relationship with your source, even after a tough interview. People generally understand that a reporter's responsibility may involve asking difficult questions. One tactic is to deal with the strained situation directly: *I'm sorry about having to ask that question about your bankruptcy, but I guess you understand that I had to. I hope you realize it's nothing personal and I'm just doing my job. Perhaps we can talk again soon.* Finally, don't forget your manners as things wind up. Be sure to say "thank you."

CONCLUSION

Gathering information is fundamental to broadcast reporting, and the broadcast professional must learn to pay careful attention to observations and casual conversations. Gathering written information and supporting documentation for stories is also important. However, it is human beings who analyze and provide leads to important news. Getting information from people can be either simple or difficult. The police officer at the scene of an accident is generally happy to provide details of what happened. However, when reporters are digging for important information, especially about the misuse of power by government officials or official actions that involve public money, sources may have a wide variety of reasons to keep the information secret. Private individuals may also hold important information but may be reluctant to reveal it to reporters. In these cases, getting information from people can be extremely difficult.

For reporters to work with people successfully, they must keep several things in mind: First, the reporter should view most everyone as a possible news source, treat them courteously and professionally and let them know that the reporter is interested in hearing news tips. Often, the reporter needs to provide some motivation for a source to talk and must make clear agreements about conditions under which the information will be used. The reporter must do appropriate background work for a complete understanding of the story, its context and the agendas of the people involved in the story. If the reporter doesn't understand, the story won't be clear.

The reporter must conduct the interview carefully so that it proceeds in a comfortable, conversational manner, but she may also need to employ techniques that press the source to reveal crucial information. Reporters must approach all sources with a healthy skepticism about the information they receive and the individual's motivation for giving it. Working with people is always a complex endeavor, especially in the role of a reporter. Getting information from people is a skill that can be learned and for which experience alone will provide advanced training.

In addition to learning how to get information from people, reporters should also master the skill of finding written information for developing and supporting stories. Sometimes written records provide insights that initiate important stories. Fortunately, we live in a society that provides enormous access to information, much from public records. To benefit from these sources, reporters must learn what information is available and how and where to get it. This is the subject of the next chapter.

KEY CONCEPTS

off the record	not for attribution	skepticism
on background	whistle blower	cynicism
deep background	shield law	ambush interview

Activities

1. Work on developing news sources. When you do your banking, take an extra minute to make conversation with the clerk. Take your utility bill in person rather than mailing it and talk with people. Don't hide the fact that you are a reporter and, when appropriate, remind people that you are always interested in hearing about anything newsworthy.

2. Practice getting people to open up to you in your general conversations. Show an interest in those you come in contact with. Ask people about their families, their frustrations, their worries.

3. In the next 24 hours, pay close attention to the things you see during your normal routines. Is there anything out of the ordinary? What do you wonder

about? Write five questions that you could pursue to find out more about things you see.

4. Make a list of five story ideas you believe should be covered in your market area. List key documents and key people you would need to pursue the story.

5. Write down the guidelines you would follow if a source asks you to keep her identity secret.

6. List three potential ways to resolve the conflict of interest if one of your friends became the subject of a controversial news story or was charged with an illegal activity. Also consider how you would approach your friend if you felt you must cover the story. What motivations would you use to get the friend to talk to you?

7. Watch a newscast or news magazine program like "60 Minutes" and examine the motivations of those who are giving information. Are they talking to set the record straight, to give their side of the story, to help others or for other reasons? List the three most interesting reasons you see.

Regarding Ethics . . .

8. Imagine that you are discussing your reporting responsibilities with a relative, and she comments that she can't understand why a journalist should not tell a judge what he or she learns about a crime from a news source, even if the reporter had promised not to reveal the source. List the major arguments your family member might make along with reasons you could offer for reporter confidentiality. Which argument is stronger?

9. Assume that charges have just been made against the mayor for misusing public money. You would like to get an interview for the evening news, but the secretary says the mayor left a message that there will be no comment on the charges and has left town for the day. On a hunch, you drive to the mayor's house and realize that she is there, working in the back yard. List several reasons for and against surprising the mayor and getting an ambush interview on camera.

10. Suppose you have promised a source about drug use never to say where you got the information. Your story runs and makes quite an impact on the community. Later, you are called into court and told either to reveal the source or go to jail. What would you do?

WORKS CITED

CBS Reports: Teddy. Transcript provided by CBS. Sunday, Nov. 4, 1979.

Kovach, Bill. Personal e-mail communication, Dec. 3, 1998.

"The Reporter's Privilege," at www.rcfp.org/privilege/ (July 22, 2003).

There are so many stories buried in public records. Reporters who know where and how to look can use them to develop fascinating and important reports.

TARAH TAYLOR,
WCYB, BRISTOL, VA.

USING PUBLIC RECORDS

AN OPEN GOVERNMENT

In this country, we have the right to get information that might be considered confidential or secret in other societies. This unequaled access has developed because our government is run by the people. If citizens are to decide important questions about how the government should run or evaluate how the system is working, they must have the facts upon which to base their judgments.

The amount of information that is public record in this country is truly astounding, and some are uncomfortable with this vast freedom. Great freedom requires great responsibility, and it cannot be denied that some people use their freedom in irresponsible ways. In the face of abuse of our freedom, public officials and citizens alike often tend to react by trying to eliminate the freedom. For example, after complaints that chiropractors were using access to public accident reports to solicit business, one police department closed the records to everyone. Such a simple action could have unintended consequences. It might prevent reporters from compiling a story about the danger of accidents at a particular intersection or about teenagers involved in drunk-driving collisions. Regaining access to those reports will require time, energy and legal action by people who recognize the seriousness of such restrictions.

Access to public information is becoming easier through computer technology. Government records are now posted on Web sites, and anyone can access information from their home computers. As records of trials, property sales and arrests; building permits and other records are becoming available by a simple mouse click, some people are becoming increasingly uneasy about access

Knowing how to use public records is a constant building block for what we do, and staying within the law is critical.

Brian Maass
KCNC-TV, DENVER

to information. Even though this information has always been available, in the past it required a trip to the courthouse and significant research effort.

Now, the information is readily available, and more people know about it. The explanation for this access is both simple and profoundly difficult to grasp. In essence, individuals are safer when government actions are open to public inspection. Even though one family selling a piece of property to another sounds like a private transaction, the government exacts a tax on the transfer. Citizens must be able to see how taxes are levied to make sure that everyone is treated equally. If the government is paying a private business to build a highway, people must be able to know the cost and who the contractor is. When judges distribute property and assign custody of children in divorces, citizens must stand watch to make sure the judges apply the law justly. More obviously, the public must know who is being arrested, what the charges are and what punishment is applied.

Although some people become frightened and willing to eliminate freedoms that make them uncomfortable, some others are not even aware of the full scope of our freedom of information. Reporters cannot even assume that public officials know the extent of information they must provide to any citizen upon request. A small-town sheriff recently argued that he did not have to provide arrest records to a reporter. He was wrong. Do we want to live in a society where the local sheriff can arrest people and not have to reveal whom he arrested and why? The fact that someone is elected to a local government position, to state legislature or to Congress does not mean he understands the principles and practices of constitutional law. Reporters should remember that access to public information is a hard-won right and remains a battleground.

Paper Trails and Computer Screens

Information available through public records is wide-ranging. As one newspaper editor put it, "You can get information about anything you're interested in." The problem for young reporters is developing topics of interest and knowing what to ask for. In addition, beginning reporters often lack the time to research important information. News departments often focus on stories that can be done in a day and fail to allocate staffing and resources for more in-depth news.

Bright, energetic reporters should not be satisfied until they can sink their teeth into serious, important stories behind the news. Many of these important news stories require following paper trails and staring at computer screens rather than putting microphones in front of public figures. For example, a Nashville television station examined public records to discover that the governor had given millions of dollars in state contracts to his friends. Using public information, WKRC-TV found illegal use of taxpayers' money in charter schools ("Investigative Reporting Contest," 2003). This reporting involved extensive evaluation of financial records—certainly not an exercise in fun—but it resulted in stories that help protect the integrity of our government.

Journalism operates at its best in careful examination of our society, and the potential for stories is unlimited. Reporters can find ideas and assistance with in-depth investigations and use of computer records through the National Institute for Computer-Assisted Reporting (nicar.org) and its parent organization, Investigative Reporters and Editors, Inc. (ire.org). For a quick introduction to the kinds of public information available, go to the phone book and look up the listings for the town or county where you live. You will find listings for the fire department, police department, city or county court system, health department and more. In short, you are entitled to know the business taking place in any of those offices. You may ask for a list of employees and their salaries. You may ask for a list of monthly expenditures or an annual budget. You may ask for statistics and reports, and you may attend scheduled meetings where decisions are made regarding these departments. Imagine the possibilities for stories:

- How many people have AIDS?
- How many people died of tobacco-related illnesses last year?
- How much are the street sweepers paid?
- How much money is spent on local basketball courts? Is it the same in all parts of town?
- What condition is the local school building in, and how much money is allocated for maintenance per year?
- Who owns the sole vacant lot in the middle of downtown, and why does it remain vacant?
- What crimes are most common in the city?
- How many people are on welfare, and how long, on average, do they receive public assistance?
- How many babies were born out of wedlock in the last year?
- What restaurants did not pass the last inspection?
- Where is the next subdivision being built, and who sold the lots?
- What were the topics at the last city council meeting?
- What is the assessed value of the house at 155 Main Street?
- How many people are in the county jail, and how much does it cost to keep them?
- Which city officials are overdue on their local tax bill?

- How much tax money was used to send town employees to the tourism convention?
- Where did the money go when Mrs. Smith died?

The fascinating stories that you can find in public records are limited only by your curiosity and patience for research.

The fact that the previously mentioned information is public does not mean that you can always obtain it easily. You may need to persist and insist on getting access to public information, but remember first that you have a right to the information and, second, that rules of etiquette and good manners always apply. Make it clear that you know the information is available to the public, but be courteous. Remember that most everyone feels stressed and busy, and your request will add to the workload. Introduce yourself, in person if possible, and try to be specific about what you want. If you want a divorce file and you don't know the exact date of the divorce, at least be very clear about the name, including proper spellings and initials.

Secretaries and receptionists may be the least likely to understand the law about revealing public information. Unless they have been carefully instructed, they are likely to resist requests for information, or, at the very least, they may not be helpful. As the saying goes, knowledge is power, so when you know you have a right to the information, you will be more successful in getting what you want. The deputy at the sheriff's office may tell you that you are not entitled to see the mug shot from a recent arrest file, or the secretary may tell you that the inspection records of a restaurant are not available. When you know you have a right to those records, you can insist and ask to speak with supervisors or managers with confidence until you find someone who will see that your rights are respected.

If possible, deal with the person in charge. Say please and thank you. Sometimes, the best first step is to put your request in writing on your company's letterhead. Official requests are not always necessary, and public employees are certainly free to give the information based on a simple, oral request. If you feel you're being put off, continue to call and ask for what you need. Be pleasant each time, but if the story is important, don't give up. Finally, a public office or agency can charge fees that cover photocopying and other processing fees. Occasionally, they may attempt to charge exorbitant fees as a way of discouraging requests.

Again, the right of access to public information is a precious freedom that is always under assault. Media professionals are helping to protect everyone's freedom when they challenge efforts to withhold public information. Congress recognized the tendency of government to withhold information and the danger of government secrecy when it passed the Freedom of Information Act. Much of the public's right to information comes from this law, and reporters should be familiar with it.

Freedom of Information Laws

The Federal Freedom of Information Act

Much public information will be made available to you because of federal requirements deriving from the **Freedom of Information Act,** frequently referred to as FoI or FoIA. The FoI began as the 1966 Federal Public Records Law and was intended to restrict needless government secrecy. The underlying principle of democracy is that government serves the people, and the people need information to be well served. This access that we take for granted has not always come easily. After a long tradition of the executive branch of government illegitimately withholding information from reporters and the public, Congress passed a law mandating that federal agencies in the executive branch provide information to the public.

The business of federal agencies is the business of the public; therefore, virtually all documents and records must be provided to those who ask, with some specific exceptions. Federal agencies in the executive branch include the departments of Agriculture, Commerce, Defense, Education,

> FoIA is your friend. Use it.
>
> *Dale Solly*

Energy, Health and Human Services, Homeland Security, Housing and Urban Development, Interior, Justice, Labor, State, Transportation, Treasury and Veterans Affairs. All these agencies are covered by the federal Freedom of Information Act. (Information from Congress and federal courts is not covered by the Freedom of Information Act, although much information from these branches of government is also available to the public and will be discussed shortly.)

The full content of the federal Freedom of Information Act (5 USC Sec. 552) is too long to include in this text, but reporters can easily find the full text on the Internet (http://foia.state.gov). In general, the act says that each government agency in the executive branch must make all its records available to the public in any existing form or format. If the records exist in computer files, they must be made available in that format. Agencies must provide indexes of the information that they have on file. There are exceptions.

Nine exceptions to information that has to be provided through the Freedom of Information Act are precisely specified. The government does not have to release information to the public that deals with national security, internal personnel issues, trade secrets, certain internal memos and letters, personnel and medical files, information about law enforcement investigations and geological data. Sometimes government officials will stretch the meaning of the exceptions to withhold information. For this reason, reporters should have a basic understanding of the categories of information that the government can legitimately withhold.

Agencies may require that requests for information through the Freedom of Information Act be made in writing, although officials often give reporters information based on an oral request. Formal requests may take longer than

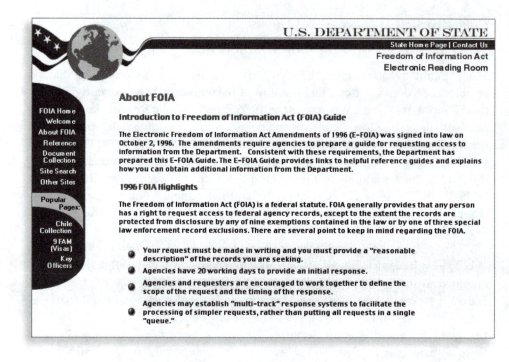

informal ones, but the agency must respond to the request within 20 days, either by providing the requested information or by explaining its delay or refusal to provide it. The agency can charge fees for copying and for employee time in searching for information.

If reporters believe information is being unjustifiably withheld, they can challenge the decision in federal court. Furthermore, disciplinary action, including contempt of court charges, can be brought against the person responsible for the withholding. The law is clear for all citizens that the inner workings of our government are open to public inspection.

Help for Reporters

These Web sites can help guide reporters to public information:

Society of Professional Journalists, spj.org

Reporters Committee for Freedom of the Press, rcfp.org

Radio-Television News Directors Association, rtnda.org

The Poynter Institute, poynter.org

State FOI Laws

The Freedom of Information Act applies to federal agencies only. However, each state has adopted some version of the Freedom of Information Act for state government. Specific state laws are readily available on the Internet, for example, through the Web page for the Reporters Committee for Freedom of the Press (rcfp.org). Some regulations specify that all agency records are considered official

Exceptions to the Freedom of Information Act

The following are exceptions to the information available through the Freedom of Information Act:

1. Information related to national security.

2. Internal personnel rules and practices.

3. Matters protected by specific statute, such as tax records and patent applications.

4. Trade secrets and privileged financial information.

5. Some internal memos and letters, such as working papers used in agency decision making.

6. Personnel and medical records.

7. Certain law enforcement information, such as ongoing legal investigations.

8. Private information related to regulation of financial institutions.

9. Geological data.

government business, including books, papers, letters, notes, presentations, reports, forms, documents, meeting minutes, telephone logs, contracts, position descriptions, job classifications, payment records, maps, charts, diagrams and graphs. Documents related to security, internal personnel matters and some other types of information are exempt. Reporters should become acquainted with the state Freedom of Information Act where they work.

Government in the Sunshine Acts

The federal government and state governments require that their agencies conduct business in public. In other words, government employees cannot go behind closed doors to make decisions. The federal open meetings law is found in 5 USC Sec. 552. In general, agencies must provide advance notice of all meetings, with an agenda of matters to be discussed. Citizens and reporters alike may attend meetings to see how decisions are made involving public policy and taxpayers' money. Citizens may challenge an agency for violating the open meeting requirements any time two or more agency members use their authority to conduct government business in private and without advance notice to the public. Reporters can challenge the closure of meetings by protesting to the governmental body when they close the meeting. If the reasons for closure do not seem legitimate, reporters can challenge the closure in court, and actions taken in the closed meeting can be overturned. As usual, certain exemptions apply, by which government bodies can go into closed sessions to deal with personnel matters, legal matters and other issues similar to those exempted in the Freedom of Information Act. Good reporters should acquaint themselves with the laws of their state.

SOURCES OF PUBLIC INFORMATION

Viewers appreciate interesting and important information on many topics. Health information, for example, is vital information about a community and is available from the local health department. Developing health-related stories does not have to begin with a massive search of statistics. Ask a nurse at the health department what the staff is most concerned about. Important stories are often revealed by the topics of conversation at coffee-break time. Searching the public files may come later when you attempt to verify the validity of staff complaints. Following is a list of other sources for noncrime information that could lead to important news.

Birth and Death Records

Birth and death certificates are public record. If they cannot be found locally, they are kept in the government's Bureau of Vital Statistics. These records are critical to reporting. Checking someone's date and place of birth can verify a public official's claims about upbringing, education or other listings on a resume. Death records list a time and cause of death that can confirm—or raise questions about—how someone died, or they could provide the basis for investigating conduct by coroners or medical examiners.

Zoning and Planning Documents

City and county planners can provide a wealth of information. Zoning and planning offices are unlike courthouses, where procedures exist for allowing the public to search information themselves. To find information about proposals for zoning or plans for a new subdivision, reporters may need to ask for what they want, perhaps using the interviewing techniques suggested in the previous chapter to find out what's going on. Although generally low-profile workers, employees in these offices can explain long-range plans for roads, subdivisions, malls, sewers, major business developments and more.

The proposals from planning and zoning offices often come before a governing body for action. If a plan to include business in a residential area is being proposed, the city council will need to approve the plan. Perhaps the city is trying to annex land as space for a giant conference center. As the issue becomes part of a public decision-making process, the city council will list the agenda item in public notices, and the proposal may appear as a public notice in the newspaper. Zoning and planning issues can be important and interesting to the public. For example, citizens could appear at a planning meeting to object to designs for a new shopping complex.

Building Permits

If you see a new construction and wonder what it is going to be, you can find out from the building permit. Law usually requires posting the building permit at the construction site. If it is not posted, the reporter can use the address to get information from the office that issues building permits. Information on the permit can lead to further detail in the public records about the history of the property or about who the building permit is issued to.

Tax Records

The local treasurer's office, commissioner of revenue or clerk's office contains a great deal of information about people's taxes. A reporter, or anyone for that matter, can find out the total amount of real estate value a certain person pays tax on or the total assessed value of a specific property. The amount of taxes that public officials pay can become important information. Many localities are making plans for electronic imaging of maps that will allow reporters and others to look at tax maps on home or office computers.

Although tax records of corporations are not public information, nonprofit, tax-exempt organizations must file their records for public inspection. GuideStar, the national database of nonprofit organizations, makes this information available on the Internet at guidestar.com.

Disclosure Forms for Elected Officials

Elected officials put their lives in the limelight. You can find out almost anything about their activities and interests from disclosure forms.

Financial disclosure. All elected officials and candidates for public office report their personal business so that voters can determine whether they have any conflicts of interest in their jobs. For example, a congressional representative who is paid $100,000 a year to sit on the board of directors of a tobacco company might not be very objective when voting on tobacco issues. Voters need to know this. Citizens would certainly want to know if a city council member showed part ownership in a company that the city routinely hires to do work.

Financial disclosures include the following types of information: offices and directorships; debts owed; stock interests; payments for talks, meetings and publications; gifts received; salary and wages; and business and real estate interests. You can usually obtain the information by calling the office of the public official, but it is also available through city or county offices.

Campaign disclosure. A candidate's campaign spending is public information. Campaign disclosure forms are filed before, during and after an election with the voter registrar's office and are usually on file for quite some time after the election. The reports include the following types of information: the names of people who contribute more than $100, a list of expenditures and a list of debts. Comparing where money comes from for each candidate, how much money there is and where it is spent can be an interesting and informative news story in a campaign.

News Files

News files kept by organizations and local newspapers can provide valuable background information on people or issues.

Phone Book

The phone book should not be overlooked as a valuable informational tool, and telephone information is readily available on the Internet.

City Directory

A city directory can tell you who lives at a certain address. Private companies compile and sell city directories, which contain amazing amounts of information. They include alphabetical listings of residents and businesses, which may list the marital status, occupation and address of each adult in the locality. The city directory includes the names and addresses of businesses, with information about the nature of the business. One section lists street addresses in numerical order along with the residential occupant or business concern *and* phone number. So, if you hear on the police scanner that there is a fire at 213 Glendale Ave., a city directory will tell you the names of people who live there, their occupations and the phone number. Obviously, some of the information will be out of date, but a current directory provides a lot of accurate information. City directories also include a numerical telephone listing. If you have a number scribbled on a piece of paper and can't remember who it's for, the directory can tell you. Newsrooms should have city directories available for reporters' use, and the Internet site anywho.com allows reverse lookup (using a phone number to find the associated name and address).

Business and Organizational Reports

Most businesses and organizations prepare annual reports. Publicly held businesses are required by law to provide annual reports. Often, private businesses will make reports available upon request or via their Web pages.

INFORMATION ABOUT COURTS

Freedom of Information acts and **Government in the Sunshine** acts generally apply to the executive branch of the government, but the public has a right to a lot of information from the judicial branch of the government as well. The nation's courtrooms are generally presumed to be open to public inspection for the protection of the person on trial. The defendant is likely to be treated fairly when the public can easily observe or find out what happened in a courtroom.

Open Courtrooms

Authorities cannot take a defendant behind closed doors for a trial and emerge with a verdict and a prison sentence. In England in the 16th century, officials did conduct secret trials in a court called the Star Chamber. Behind closed doors, they would torture confessions out of people and sentence them to prison or death, and no one was allowed to watch the proceedings or know what the evidence was. Founders of our system of government were determined to prevent Star Chamber–type activity and insisted that a defendant have a right to a public trial. When a trial is open to the public, the media are included. (When we talk about trials, we also automatically include various pretrial proceedings, from the first appearance when charges are placed through the trial and final sentencing.)

Reporters may generally assume that courtrooms are open—a right guaranteed by court interpretations of the First and Sixth Amendments. Occasionally, however, a judge will attempt to close a courtroom in the belief that a public and media presence will interfere with a fair trial. Media attorneys have fought many battles to maintain access to courtrooms, arguing that there are better ways to ensure a fair trial than shutting out the public. Judges have several options other than closing courtrooms, such as delaying the trial, sequestering the jury or changing the location of the trial.

Like many other freedoms, the media right to access to courtrooms has been a hard-fought battle. Decades ago, the Supreme Court upheld a judge's decision to shut the media and the public out of a courtroom. Within weeks, dozens of courtrooms around the country were closed, and hundreds more were closed within the year. Soon thereafter, the Supreme Court established stricter guidelines, making it more difficult for judges to keep the public and the press out. Reporters should take the issue very seriously if a judge attempts to close a courtroom. First, they should contact the news director or someone who can contact station attorneys. Then they should make a formal protest by identifying themselves to the judge. They may say that they believe the closure to be a violation of the First Amendment and that they do not plan to make a case themselves but that attorneys can point out issues for the court to consider. They can request the opportunity to be heard through counsel. Reporters need to be aware of the potential for closed courtrooms and must be prepared to object.

Exceptions to Open Courtrooms

Courtrooms can be closed to the public and press when the government has a reason that overrides the need of the public to witness the court action. For example, juvenile proceedings are sometimes closed, and grand jury proceedings are always held behind closed doors.

Juvenile Proceedings

In some states and localities, juvenile proceedings, and sometimes the court records, are closed to the public. The rationale for protecting information about juveniles is the belief that young people may have poor judgment and commit crimes in the process of growing up that they would not consider as adults. The closed system, in essence, lets young people make mistakes without having the information follow them into maturity, when they are making better decisions. Even though 18 is the legal age for adulthood, a state may decide to open the court when a child is at least 14 and involved in a felony. Adult cases may be closed when the cases involve children. For example, when an adult is charged with abusing a child or when the case involves child custody or child support, the courtroom may be closed. The general national trend, however, is toward opening juvenile courts and records.

Even when information about juveniles is available from public record or open court, the media often voluntarily withhold it. For example, when an adult is convicted of sexually abusing a child, the name of the child is usually not revealed, even though it is readily available from public record. If the adult charged with sex abuse is a parent of the victim, the name of the adult is often withheld, because revealing it would clearly indicate the identity of the child. People are generally surprised at the many situations in which media voluntarily withhold information in respect for privacy considerations. For example, broadcasters have widely and routinely withheld the identities of juveniles unless a court has ruled that the child would be tried as an adult, although the trend has been to more openness in these situations. Recently, especially in cases of school violence, the media have revealed identities of underage suspects without waiting for court rulings on trial status. For example, a 13-year-old suspect was shown on network news broadcasts being taken into custody on charges of shooting a teacher at his school. Society is now beginning to abandon privacy considerations for juveniles, especially in the face of increasingly dangerous and violent actions by young people. More often, young people are tried as adults with courtrooms open and records related to the case readily available.

State laws vary widely regarding when courtrooms are open in cases involving juveniles. Journalists should check the laws where they work. The information is easily accessible on the Internet sites listed in this chapter.

Grand Jury Proceedings

A **grand jury** is a group of citizens called together to examine claims against a defendant. When they determine that there is enough evidence for placing charges, they issue a formal notice, or **indictment.** Grand jury hearings are always held behind closed courtroom doors. The only information available from grand jury proceedings is the record of an indictment. Testimony is secret, and no transcripts of the proceedings are available. This secrecy protects individuals who may be wrongly accused of a crime and are never formally charged. It makes sense that if there is not enough evidence to charge someone with a crime, the deliberations would not be open to the public. In fact, law prohibits members of a grand jury from discussing a case. (A major historical exception was made in 1998 when transcripts of grand jury testimony in the investigation of President Bill Clinton were provided to Congress and released to the public.) It is also noteworthy that even though members of the grand jury are legally bound to maintain secrecy about proceedings, grand jury witnesses are not.

Federal and State Courts

Reporters must understand the difference between state and federal courts. (We also assume that all reporters know the three branches of the government: executive, legislative and judicial. If a reporter has any question, a quick review of a basic government text is strongly advised.) An overview of the major differences in state and federal courts follows.

Federal Courts

Federal court cases focus on issues related to federal law, which is law that applies in all states. Federal courts preside on three levels, the titles of which are preceded by U. S.: U. S. District Court, U. S. Circuit Courts of Appeal and the U. S. Supreme Court. U. S. District Court is the first level of the federal court system, where most cases originate (see Exhibit 4.1). U. S. Circuit Courts are the middle level of the federal court system; they hear appeals from U. S. District Courts. Each of the 13 circuits includes several states. The U. S. Supreme Court is the final authority in federal law, with decisions rendered by nine justices. A U. S. Supreme Court justice serves a lifetime appointment after being nominated by the president and confirmed by the U. S. Senate.

Because U. S. presidents are affiliated with a political party, a Supreme Court justice could conceivably issue rulings affiliated with political party philosophy in gratitude to the president for the appointment. Because the justices hold lifetime appointments, however, they generally sit on the high court much longer than the president who appointed them is in office. It is assumed that these powerful justices will lose any feeling of debt to political parties they might have and will become faithful to their consciences and to the law. In fact, a number of justices have been appointed by either conservative or liberal presidents and have proceeded to find an independent voice on the court, sometimes adhering to the opposite political viewpoint from the president who appointed them. Some, however, remain partisan throughout their tenure.

EXHIBIT 4.1 The U. S. federal court system.

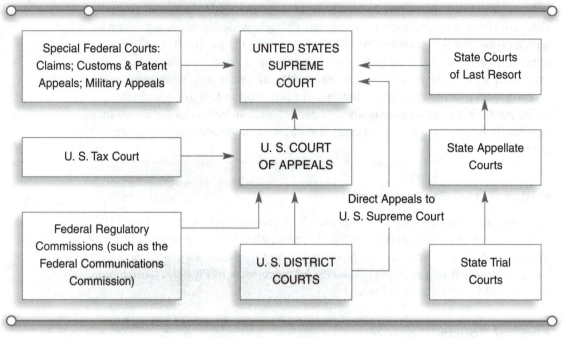

Besides making judgments related to laws that affect the entire nation, federal courts also solve disputes between residents of different states and between U. S. citizens and people from other countries. Federal violations are not always restricted to serious matters. A minor law violation could be heard in federal court if it takes place on federal property. For example, making too much noise in a U. S. Parks Department campground would be a federal issue and would be adjudicated in federal court.

Much federal law comes from statutes passed by Congress. Other federal cases arise from requirements in the U. S. Constitution. For example, the Fourth Amendment protects citizens against "unreasonable searches and seizures." So, if city police break down a woman's door, search her house for drugs and confiscate any cash they find, they may be violating constitutional law. If the woman challenges the action, she may take the matter to federal court rather than state court.

In addition to statutes passed by Congress and constitutional law, federal law is derived from the judiciary. For example, the Supreme Court has ruled that citizens have a right to march, protest and speak in the public streets. This ruling came decades ago as a "new" interpretation of the First Amendment. Prior to that ruling, city officials often prohibited individuals or groups from assembling and speaking in public areas. The new Supreme Court ruling became law that now applies in all states.

U. S. Circuit Courts

1st Circuit: Maine, Massachusetts, New Hampshire, Rhode Island and Puerto Rico

2nd Circuit: Connecticut, New York and Vermont

3rd Circuit: Delaware, New Jersey, Pennsylvania and the Virgin Islands

4th Circuit: Maryland, North Carolina, South Carolina, Virginia and West Virginia

5th Circuit: Texas, Mississippi and Louisiana

6th Circuit: Kentucky, Michigan, Ohio and Tennessee

7th Circuit: Illinois, Indiana and Wisconsin

8th Circuit: Arkansas, Iowa, Minnesota, Missouri, Nebraska, North Dakota and South Dakota

9th Circuit: Alaska, Arizona, California, Hawaii, Idaho, Montana, Nevada, Oregon and Washington

10th Circuit: Colorado, Kansas, New Mexico, Utah, Oklahoma and Wyoming

11th Circuit: Alabama, Florida, Georgia and the Canal Zone

DC Circuit

Federal Circuit

State Courts

State courts deal with matters of state law—statutes passed by state legislatures or local governments—and with issues related to the state constitution. There are many levels of state courts. Some state courts may hear only juvenile cases, traffic charges or other narrowly focused matters, such as small-claims court. Others handle more serious matters. (Like federal courts, state courts may also be called district or circuit courts, but they should not be confused with U. S. District and U. S. Circuit Courts.) See Exhibit 4.2 for an example state court system.

Lower state court matters can be appealed in state appeals courts and eventually to the state supreme court. Rulings related to state laws cannot be appealed further than the state's highest court, unless the state law potentially conflicts with a U. S. constitutional requirement. For example, a state law requiring protesters to post a $10 million bond before getting a parade permit would likely be challenged in state courts, state appeals courts and the state supreme court. The protesters would argue that the bond is so high that they could not realistically be expected to pay it. Thus, they would say their free speech has been abridged. This case could continue on appeal to the U. S. Supreme Court because it involves a constitutional issue, a possible abridgment of the First Amendment. In fact, such a state law would likely be ruled an unconstitutional infringement on freedom of speech by the U. S. Supreme Court, if the case got that far. On the other hand, if a state passes and enforces a 45-mph speed limit on every highway in the state, federal courts would have no basis for becoming involved in the matter. The U. S. Constitution does not specify how fast a state should allow its people to drive.

EXHIBIT 4.2   Example of a state court system.

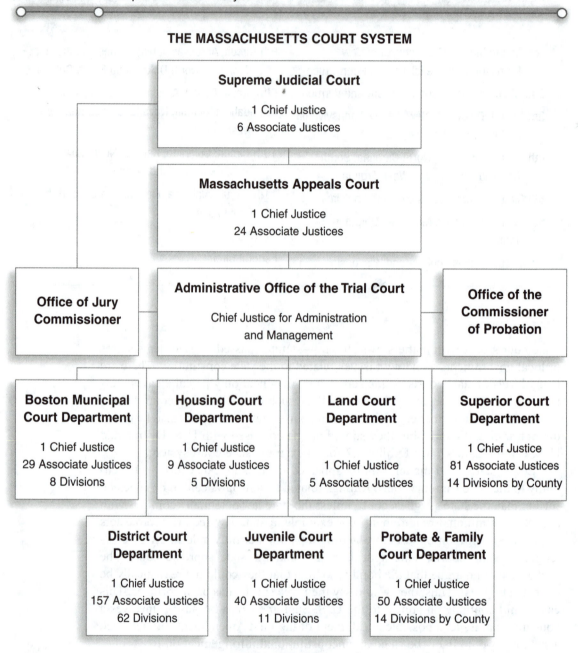

THE MASSACHUSETTS COURT SYSTEM

Supreme Judicial Court

1 Chief Justice
6 Associate Justices

Massachusetts Appeals Court

1 Chief Justice
24 Associate Justices

Office of Jury Commissioner

Administrative Office of the Trial Court

Chief Justice for Administration
and Management

Office of the Commissioner of Probation

Boston Municipal Court Department

1 Chief Justice
29 Associate Justices
8 Divisions

Housing Court Department

1 Chief Justice
9 Associate Justices
5 Divisions

Land Court Department

1 Chief Justice
5 Associate Justices

Superior Court Department

1 Chief Justice
81 Associate Justices
14 Divisions by County

District Court Department

1 Chief Justice
157 Associate Justices
62 Divisions

Juvenile Court Department

1 Chief Justice
40 Associate Justices
11 Divisions

Probate & Family Court Department

1 Chief Justice
50 Associate Justices
14 Divisions by County

The number of justices for all courts is the maximum authorized by statute; the actual number of judges varies depending on vacancies.

Criminal and Civil Cases

There are two kinds of legal cases: criminal and civil. Both federal and state courts hear both kinds of cases. Criminal trials take place when a governmental body charges an individual with breaking a written (statutory) law. The crimes range from breaking the speeding law to more serious violations such as robbery, rape and murder. The penalty for breaking criminal, statutory law may be a fine, serving time in jail or both.

The **defendant** is the person facing a criminal charge brought by the government; for example, O. J. Simpson was the defendant in *California v. Simpson.* In *U. S. v. McVeigh,* the trial related to the bombing of a federal building in Oklahoma, the federal government brought charges against Timothy McVeigh. **Prosecutors** are the government attorneys who argue the cases against defendants.

Criminal charges come about from *arrests* or *indictments.* In an **arrest,** law enforcement officers confront and detain someone against whom they have evidence of violating a law, and they indicate the reason in a sworn statement that becomes part of the arrest report. If the crime is serious, the suspect is taken to jail. A court official of some sort must approve holding someone in jail—an individual cannot be arrested and held in jail by police officers unless a judge agrees that there is probable cause that the individual is guilty of a crime. These court officers who grant the right to hold someone in jail until a more formal court appearance are not necessarily trained attorneys in every state, and they don't necessarily operate out of a courtroom. These officers of the court who act as judges with the specific responsibility of consenting to an individual's incarceration before a formal placing of charges are sometimes called **magistrates.**

After an arrest, at the first available opportunity the suspect will be taken to a formal court hearing for a reading of the charges by a judge. If it is a nighttime arrest, the suspect will most likely have a hearing the next day. If the arrest is made on a weekend night, the court appearance will be on Monday morning. If the judge does not believe there is sufficient evidence that the suspect was likely to have committed the crime, no charges will be filed and the suspect will be released.

In many cases, an individual is charged with a crime but never taken to jail. When the person is not considered a threat to the community and is expected to respond, a subpoena may be issued instead of an arrest warrant. A **subpoena** is simply a written order, in this case, to appear in court. (The subpoena can also be an order to provide written material or other evidence for the court.) Others involved in the case as it proceeds through court may be called by subpoena, including witnesses. Subpoenas are issued in both criminal and civil trials.

The procedures for charging people with crimes, accepting their pleas, ensuring their right to an attorney and setting trial dates vary somewhat from state to state. Generally, the **arraignment** is the open court hearing where the accused appears before a judge to hear a formal reading of criminal charges and has the opportunity to claim innocence or admit guilt. The **preliminary hearing** is a court hearing where a judge determines whether the state has enough evidence that a crime has been committed by the accused and that therefore the person should be held for trial. A trial date will be set at the preliminary hearing. At one of these initial appearances, the defendant enters a **plea,** or formal claim of guilt or innocence.

During the early court appearance, the judge can set a bond. A **bond** is an amount of money the defendant gives to the court as a guarantee that he will show up for trial. If the person charged does not show up at the scheduled trial date, the state keeps the money. If the suspect cannot afford the bond, he must stay in jail. Sometimes a suspect is released on **recognizance,** which means he is trusted to show up for court dates without posting a bond. In very serious cases, suspects are **held without bond,** meaning the court suspects that a defendant might flee or harm someone and does not allow the individual to use money as a guarantee to appear in court. The person is required to stay in jail until trial. For wealthy defendants facing serious charges, the bond may be millions of dollars, whereas a drunk who is accused of assault may be released on a very small bond. Official reports will indicate whether a suspect has been released on recognizance or a bond has been posted.

The public is allowed to know the details of the state action after any of these steps. If someone is arrested in the middle of the night and is being held in jail, officials are free to release this information. Some police departments routinely allow reporters to review daily arrest records. Others use red tape as a way of delaying the release of the information and may require reporters to get information from court documents. After the initial arrest, everything happens in an open courtroom, and reporters can attend and print or broadcast what they learn. They can get access to court records after the session is over. In localities where reporters have good relations with court officials, they often get information by phone immediately. In less desirable situations, court officials make reporters wait for official paperwork.

After a judge has formally filed the charges, a plea has been entered, attorneys retained and arrangements made through bond or recognizance ensuring that the defendant will show up, a trial date is scheduled. (If release arrangements are not made, the suspect remains in jail—because she either could not post bond or is being held without bond.)

Prior to the trial, the defendant may bring issues to the court in a **pretrial hearing,** where a judge listens to requests from attorneys and decides matters about how the trial will be conducted. For example, the defense attorney may attempt to have a confession suppressed, claiming that it was induced without the suspect being advised about the right to an attorney. A judge may decide whether evidence is admissible in the trial based on whether it was legally obtained. Throughout all these activities, the case file will be growing. It may include witness statements, police reports and other official documents before the trial begins. Reporters are wise to take the time to read the case file before covering a trial.

During felony trials, court reporters keep official records. Sometimes they produce complete transcripts that become available upon request. At the very least, an official record of the **disposition,** or final ruling of a court case, will be made. A **sentencing hearing** usually follows a trial where a suspect is found guilty, and the judge decides how much time the defendant will spend in jail or on probation, or may issue other consequences. A formal record of the sentence will be made and filed. Official records of court appearances will be filed in the appropriate court clerk's office and are open for public inspection.

Related Police Information

Arrest warrants and mug shots are commonly made available to the media immediately after an arrest. An arrest warrant may follow a police search granted by a **search warrant.** The search warrant will specify what police are looking for when they search someone's property and why they believe the items reveal information about a crime. A search warrant is accompanied by an **affidavit,** a sworn statement revealing information about the suspected crime that supports the need for the search warrant. The affidavit should be available to reporters after the execution of the search warrant.

> Don't just take the information from your sources. Get a copy of warrants and affidavits. Don't just sit in the courtroom. Read the court records.
>
> *Lisa Mitchell*
> **WCYB-TV, BRISTOL, VA.**

For the same reason that court records are available to the public, these police reports are also public information—as a protection for the person who is arrested. Normally, people think that making information about someone's arrest available to the public and the press is a violation of privacy and harmful to the person arrested. In fact, the information makes the police answerable to the public for arrests they make. The public information requirement prevents police from arresting people in secret and forces law enforcement officials to make public reports showing why they take people into custody.

You may know of instances in which information from police files caused the system to change. For example, a study of police arrests on cocaine charges in Los Angeles showed that blacks were likely to face stiffer charges in federal court while whites faced lesser charges in state court. This information could force the LAPD to examine how it treats people of different races on similar charges.

> Pull the file before you go to trial. You may be the only reporter to know about a confession that has been thrown out.
>
> *Dave Cupp*
> **WVIR-TV, CHARLOTTESVILLE, VA.**

A problem sometimes arises when police officials aren't used to dealing with the media and do not realize that their records are public information. Exerting pressure on police departments and law enforcement agents can be a challenge for a reporter, but reasonable efforts must be attempted to obtain the necessary information. If a polite explanation does not work, editors and media owners may be able to help by making phone calls or exerting legal pressure. Otherwise, people who supervise the department and media attorneys can help. If you keep talking, you will find someone who understands the nature of public information and will see that you get the information you ask for. (*Special note:* Remember that your dispute is not with the individual who is failing to provide the information you need, but with the institution. Do not make it personal, and always be polite. Maintaining your professionalism will benefit you and reporters who follow in your footsteps in the long run.)

Grand Jury Indictments and Civil Actions

Charges can also be placed against individuals by a grand jury indictment. State or federal grand juries can be called together, or **convened.** A state grand jury may examine evidence regarding the sale of illegal drugs. For example, police investigators may spend several months trying to track down drug dealers in a community. They will present their evidence to a grand jury, who will determine whether or not to place charges against certain individuals. If the grand jury indicts, the charges are formalized, and officers will proceed to make arrests. If the grand jury finds that there is insufficient evidence to place charges, the case is over. As mentioned previously, grand jury records are closed unless charges are filed.

Courtroom activity involves much more than criminal trials. Some of the most important issues in society take their legal form in civil actions. Civil matters usually involve money. In **civil court,** one party takes another party to court to settle a grievance. The judgment that is issued by the court may require one party to pay the other party or to do something specific, like make the workplace more hospitable to women and minorities. Civil actions can be based in statutory law or in constitutional law. For example, a plaintiff might file a civil lawsuit against an employer for wrongful dismissal from a job or for failing to pay for a service provided. When a citizen claims that a local television station has committed libel against him, he will file a civil lawsuit in state court (because libel laws are state laws). If the television station loses the case, it pays money to the citizen who has proved that false information damaged his reputation. The person filing the civil lawsuit is called the **plaintiff.** The person (or organization) against whom the civil lawsuit is filed is called the **defendant.**

Federal civil issues include society's most perplexing debates on topics like sexual harassment, affirmative action and police brutality. A plaintiff might bring a federal civil action against an employer for alleged sexual discrimination. The governing law derives from the 14th Amendment, which guarantees equal protection under the law. If a person is fired and the reason is that the boss doesn't like women employees, the woman can ask for money to compensate for the loss of wages and for pain and suffering. The argument is that the woman did not receive equal protection, because a man would not have been fired under the circumstances.

In summary, generally both state and federal courtrooms are open to the public and the press in both criminal and civil actions, with a few exceptions. Information about arrests should be available at the police department immediately after the arrest. Subsequently, formal charges, dates of upcoming trials and records of all court decisions are available as they happen or immediately thereafter, usually from a clerk of the court. All this information is public information and should be available upon request. Sometimes, full transcripts of court proceedings are available. In short, the public, which includes media representatives, has a right to know what happens in courtrooms.

Cameras in Courtrooms

Even though courtrooms and trials are generally open, you cannot assume that television reporters can take their cameras into courtrooms. More and more state courts are open to news cameras, but federal courtrooms are not, and reporters must be aware of the policies governing both.

Most states allow cameras in at least some of their courtrooms, but state rules governing cameras vary widely. Usually, only news cameras are allowed, and the judge must grant permission for the cameras to be present. Be sure to find out what your state law allows and secure permission in advance before showing up at a courtroom with a news camera. The Radio-Television News Directors Association Web site (www.rtnda.org/foi/scc.html) provides a summary of state camera coverage rules (see the following pages).

In some states, you may photograph the jurors and not in others. Some states readily admit cameras to criminal court but not to civil court; in others, rules permit cameras in civil court and not in criminal court. Some courts require a dress code for news personnel, perhaps prohibiting jeans or sneakers. Some states require ties for men and business dresses for women. It is the judge's duty to enforce the regulations, and he may strictly enforce them or perhaps ignore them. Coverage of certain court actions is frequently prohibited, such as coverage of juvenile proceedings, divorce cases and cases involving sexual offenses. Courts generally prohibit photographing police informants, minors, undercover agents, jurors and victims of sexual abuse—even when they allow coverage of other aspects of the trial from within the courtroom.

Judges hold nearly total control in their own courtrooms and can exclude anyone who might interfere with a fair trial. Some judges try to use this power to exclude all cameras from all proceedings, asserting that the mere presence of cameras interferes with a fair trial. In cases where state law permits camera coverage of courtrooms, however, the media can object to being shut out and can appeal the decision to another court. Because of the potential for distraction by television equipment, state law may limit the number of cameras covering a trial and may restrict movement of camera crews to official breaks in proceedings. In high-profile cases where the number of cameras is restricted, the media usually cooperate in *pool coverage,* where one station shoots the video and shares it with others. For example, in the O. J. Simpson trial, one camera captured the courtroom activity, and the footage was widely distributed to networks and individual stations.

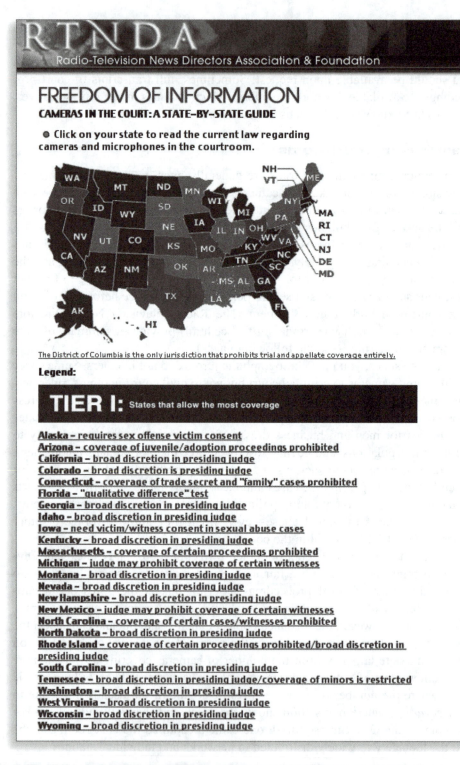

RTNDA
Radio-Television News Directors Association & Foundation

FREEDOM OF INFORMATION
CAMERAS IN THE COURT: A STATE–BY–STATE GUIDE

● Click on your state to read the current law regarding cameras and microphones in the courtroom.

The District of Columbia is the only jurisdiction that prohibits trial and appellate coverage entirely.

Legend:

TIER I: States that allow the most coverage

Alaska – requires sex offense victim consent
Arizona – coverage of juvenile/adoption proceedings prohibited
California – broad discretion in presiding judge
Colorado – broad discretion is presiding judge
Connecticut – coverage of trade secret and "family" cases prohibited
Florida – "qualitative difference" test
Georgia – broad discretion in presiding judge
Idaho – broad discretion in presiding judge
Iowa – need victim/witness consent in sexual abuse cases
Kentucky – broad discretion in presiding judge
Massachusetts – coverage of certain proceedings prohibited
Michigan – judge may prohibit coverage of certain witnesses
Montana – broad discretion in presiding judge
Nevada – broad discretion in presiding judge
New Hampshire – broad discretion in presiding judge
New Mexico – judge may prohibit coverage of certain witnesses
North Carolina – coverage of certain cases/witnesses prohibited
North Dakota – broad discretion in presiding judge
Rhode Island – coverage of certain proceedings prohibited/broad discretion in presiding judge
South Carolina – broad discretion in presiding judge
Tennessee – broad discretion in presiding judge/coverage of minors is restricted
Washington – broad discretion in presiding judge
West Virginia – broad discretion in presiding judge
Wisconsin – broad discretion in presiding judge
Wyoming – broad discretion in presiding judge

TIER II: States with restrictions prohibiting coverage of important types of cases, or prohibiting coverage of all or large categories of witnesses who object to coverage of their testimony.

Hawaii - coverage of certain cases and witnesses prohibited
Kansas - many types of witnesses may object
Missouri - many types of witnesses may object
New Jersey - coverage of sexual penetration cases prohibited
Ohio - victim/witness has right to object to coverage
Oregon - witnesses discretion to object to coverage of certain cases
Texas - no rules for criminal trial coverage, but such coverage allowed increasingly on a case by case basis
Virginia - coverage of sex offense cases prohibited

TIER III: States that allow appellate coverage only, or that have such restricting trial coverage rules essentially preventing coverage.

Alabama – consent of all parties/attorneys required
Arkansas – coverage ceases with objection by party/attorney
Delaware – appellate coverage only
Illinois – appellate coverage only
Indiana – appellate coverage only
Louisiana – appellate coverage only
Maine – appellate coverage/civil trial/arraignments, sentencings and other non-testimonial proceedings in criminal matters
Maryland – appellate coverage/civil trial only
Minnesota – appellate coverage/trial – consent of all parties required
Mississippi – appellate coverage only via the Internet
Nebraska – appellate coverage/audio trial coverage only
New York – appellate coverage only
Oklahoma – consent of criminal defendant required
Pennsylvania – any witness who objects won't be covered, civil trials only without a jury
South Dakota – Supreme Court coverage only
Utah – appellate coverage/trial coverage – still photography only
Vermont – broad discretion in presiding judge

From the Radio-Television News Directors Association Website. Reprinted with permission of RTNDA.

Allowing cameras in courtrooms is very controversial. Critics argue vigorously that the presence of cameras interferes with a fair trial and causes attorneys and witnesses to play to the camera rather than focus on the pursuit of justice. The O. J. Simpson trial in 1995 is often cited as an example of the out-of-control circus atmosphere that cameras can cause. First, it is important to remember that O. J. Simpson has been, to date, the most famous murder defendant in history. Second, most of the circus was outside the courtroom, where some of the media did, indeed, act irresponsibly in many ways. Inside, however, one camera, mounted to the wall, showed the world what was going on in the courtroom. Many problems and concerns about the Simpson trial can be attributed to the judge's inexperience with celebrity trials and with cameras in his courtroom. The hot emotional issues of racism and sexism also complicated this trial and turned it into a forum on society's major problems. However, very few mistakes were made in the thousands of reports presented about the trial.

Other celebrity trials earlier in the century also drew thousands of reporters and media abuses in a circus-like atmosphere. In the 1935 trial of the man accused of killing the baby of American aviator Charles Lindbergh, thousands of reporters descended on the trial and became extremely intrusive. Many states subsequently passed laws inhibiting media coverage of trials. Sometimes trial coverage can be sensational, but this is not typically the case: nationwide, news departments routinely capture and broadcast video of all or parts of noteworthy trials. The cable network CourtTV often shows gavel-to-gavel coverage of trials. Even though coverage remains restricted in many courts, the public is accustomed to seeing more and more televised courtroom action, a trend that is likely to continue. Again, eliminating the freedom of access may seem like the easiest way to eliminate abuses, but giving up freedom rather than finding other solutions is more dangerous in the long run.

COURT RECORDS

Court records include much more than just information about what happens in courtrooms. Courts process and make formal records of divorces, wills, marriage licenses, property transfers and more. Reporters can certainly use court dockets and visits to the courtroom to follow important criminal and civil cases, but court records can lead reporters to other important stories as well.

Information About Jurors

The names of jurors may or may not be public record, depending on state law. If you are in the courtroom during the jury selection process, you will certainly hear the names, but it may also be possible to obtain the names from the clerk's office. If addresses and phone numbers are not available there, many other avenues exist to locate jurors.

(*Special note:* The fact that you *can* contact jurors doesn't mean you *should.* Reporters must always act responsibly, and trying to contact jurors during a trial is illegal—with serious consequences. When a trial is over and reporters want information about the deliberation process, jurors may be willing to comment. Remember to respect a person's wishes and privacy. "No" usually means no and is not an invitation to repeated phone calls or harassment.)

Dockets

The starting point for covering courtroom action is the *docket*. A **docket** is a schedule of cases to be presented in the courtroom. Since a docket can change quickly, it may not always be posted. The reporter may need to call and ask about the schedule for a day or about the schedule for a specific case.

(*Special note:* Court personnel are usually willing to help when they are treated with respect. Remember that everyone is busy, and the more specific information you can provide when asking for assistance, the more successful you will be. Do not be afraid to talk to judges. Although judicial codes prevent judges from discussing particular cases, they may be willing to talk to you about applicable law and even to explain a lot of detail as long as it is off-the-record or background information. One reporter says the judge in cases has often served as her off-the-record source for information: "If a case goes into the night and all the court offices are closed, I've been known to call the judge at home." Prosecutors will enjoy talking to reporters because they have an interest in making their cases look strong. Remember the biases of those you talk with, and try not to become too dependent on any one source. Again, clerks may resist giving information, but the law requires that the public have access to court dockets.)

Divorce Records

Unless a judge issues an order to seal the file, all the information about a divorce and divorce settlement is available to the public. If you know the name and the approximate date of the divorce, you can get access to the case file and to all the details of the marital dissolution. In some cases, details of a divorce can provide important background information about a news subject or could reveal important information for the public. For example, a divorce file might reveal that a strong antiabortion legislator had paid for his wife to have an abortion. A divorce file could reveal that a public official was not at a conference for which taxpayers reimbursed expenditures, or an investigation of a judge's divorce decrees might show a bias against men in child custody issues.

Deeds

If you know the name of the buyer *or* the seller of a house or other property, you can find the boundaries of the property and trace all previous owners. You can use the deed as a path to a tax map and can likely discover the amount that was paid for the property, even if the price is not listed in the deed. Just by knowing the exact location of a building or tract of land, you might be able to trace the name of the person or company that owns it. You may also be able to find a tax map and information about owners by determining the owner of *adjacent* property. Tax maps may be cross-referenced to deed books, which may reveal current and previous owners and even the sales price.

Deeds can give a reporter someone's address and an idea of the person's net worth. Sometimes these real estate records can help a reporter locate someone from whom they need information. The process may not be easy and may take detective work, but it can be done, and discoveries about who owns or has sold property sometimes have important news value. Property ownership can also sometimes be traced through wills.

Wills

The court records include an index of wills. If you know the name of the person who died and at least an approximate date of death, you can find almost everything about the disposition of the estate. For high-profile people or financial investigations, wills can give important background information.

Marriage Licenses

Your local court records have an index of marriage licenses that may date back to previous centuries. If you know a name, you can find a copy of the person's marriage license. If you don't know an approximate date of the marriage, the process may take lots of time and even more patience. Information in a marriage license can sometimes help locate people who don't want to be found. Also, a marriage license often includes a wife's unmarried name—helpful because those trying to hide their business interests will sometimes put property and contracts in the spouse's name. Checking someone's marriage license can lead to other important information.

COMPUTER-ASSISTED REPORTING

Information is getting easier to find on the Internet. You can type in someone's name and search the entire country for the individual. Directories on Web sites of businesses list employees and e-mail addresses. You can find information about topics ranging from race, politics and culture to pet care and cleaning. In addition, information designed specifically to help journalists with computer-assisted reporting is available by the click of a mouse. Today's journalists must master the ability to search out information on the Internet. Several organizations for journalists provide guidance on finding and using databases, and Web sites offer reporting guidelines, tips on sources and additional training. They can also put you in touch with other journalists who are working with Internet sources for investigative stories. The Web site for the nonprofit National Institute for Computer-Assisted Reporting (NICAR) makes databases in the following areas available to journalists:

Online Reporting

Web sites provide assistance and information for advanced online reporting:

Investigative Reporters and Editors, Inc.
www.ire.org

National Institute for Computer-Assisted Reporting www.nicar.org

The Poynter Institute www.poynter.org

The Reporters Committee for Freedom of the Press www.rcfp.org

Society of Professional Journalists www.spj.org

transportation, election campaigns, health, public safety, business, federal spending and others. Exhibit 4.3 lists the databases available under the topic "transportation." Exhibit 4.4 shows the NICAR home page, www.nicar.org. Clicking on a link to any of the databases will lead to a description of the database. The Web site of Investigative Reporters and Editors Inc. provides numerous educational services to journalists. At both these Web sites, reporters can see examples of important stories that were developed using computer resources. For example, reporters have used public records about education to find disparities in resources, teacher expe-

Online Directory

To find a person's address and phone number or to look up the person associated with a phone number, visit anywho.com.

NICAR's databases for transportation.   **EXHIBIT 4.3**

AIR

FAA	Enforcements
FAA	Service Difficulty Reports
FAA	Accidents and Incidents
FAA	Aircraft Registry
FAA	Airmen Directory
NASA	Aviation Safety Reporting System
NTSB	Investigations of Aircraft Accidents

ROADS

DOT	Fatal Accidents
NHTSA	Vehicle Recalls and Complaints
DOT	Truck Accidents
Truck Census	
Truck Inspections	

WATERWAYS

Boating Accidents
Boat Registration

GENERAL

Hazardous Materials

EXHIBIT 4.4 NICAR home page.

National Institute for Computer-Assisted Reporting

www.ire.org

Search IRE:

[Search!]

♀ Member sign-in

History
How we started, Bylaws, The Arizona Project, Endowment

Membership
Benefits, How to Join, Find an Investigative Journalist, Listservs, Update Your Address

Training
Conferences, Seminars, Fellowships, Training Materials

Resource Center
19,000-plus investigative stories, 2,000 Tipsheets, Reporting Guides, Beat Sources

Broadcast Center
Videostreamed clips, IRE feeds, IRE videos

Database Library
Government database collection, Data analysis

Campaign Finance Information Center
Campaign Finance Database, Stories

FOI Center
Columns, Awards, FOIA Database, Tipsheets

The IRE Store
Books, Audio tapes, Databases, Periodicals, IRE Logo Goods

Job Center
Hot jobs in journalism, latest fellowships and grants

IRE Awards
Latest contest, Past winners, How to enter

Educators
IRE Journalism Educators' Center

IRE Board
Elected members, Committees

NICAR is a program of Investigative Reporters and Editors, Inc. and the Missouri School of Journalism. Founded in 1989, NICAR has trained thousands of journalists in the practical skills of finding, prying loose and analyzing electronic information.

THE LATEST:

• **IRE Annual Conference:** Don't miss Investigative Editors and Reporter's premier event, June 17-20 in Atlanta. The preliminary panel schedule, expected speakers, highlights and more are available now.

• **Data update:** The IRE and NICAR Database Library has just updated its OSHA inspection workplace database, consisting of all federal inspections at companies in the U.S. and its territories between January 1972 into February 2004. Journalists can help protect public safety by identifying patterns of workplace dangers and abuses, by type of industry, geographic location or specific employer. A journalist could use the data to pursue stories anywhere in the U.S.

• **Federal contracts data update:** The IRE and NICAR Database Library has just updated its federal contracts database to include fiscal year 2003. For about 70 federal agencies — including the Department of Homeland Security and the Department of Defense — the database includes a record of every contract transaction of more than $25,000. The database includes the specific agency, the company, a basic description of the product or service, the location of where the work is performed, and the amount. Archived data going back to 1979 is also available.

• **CAR Conference:** More than 300 journalists attended panels, hands-on classes, demonstrations and networking opportunities at the 2004 Computer-Assisted Reporting Conference in Cincinnati.

• **CAR Tool:** During the March 2004 Cincinnati CAR conference, Tom Torok, database editor at *The New York Times* shared some CDs with CAR SQL Server tools -- including ways to handle non-standard names, use ASP techniques and automate tasks. If you missed the conference, you can click here to download a copy.

• **New data:** The Database Library now offers a database of Securities and Exchange Commission administrative proceedings. It includes cases before the SEC administrative judges, as opposed to criminal cases or civil cases filed in federal courts. Journalists can use the database to look up a company or broker's history with the SEC, using the data as a tipsheet for additional exploration of a company or person.

• **Extra! Extra!** Get inspired by IRE's online guide to investigative and computer-assisted reporting stories. Extra! Extra! is updated regularly with the latest work from newspapers, broadcast outlets, magazines and online newsrooms.

• **Inside the March/April** *Uplink*: The latest issue features articles showing how to examine emergency response times using computer-assisted reporting. Included: How the *Arizona Daily Star* used mapping to find areas of Tucson with poor response times and a guide to working with computer-aided dispatch data. Subscribe now.

• **Serving journalists:** NICAR, created in 1989, has provided data and services to more than 365 news organizations just since Jan. 1, 2000. NICAR has helped journalism organizations ranging from the *Wall Street Journal* and NBC News to the *Billings Gazette* in Montana and WQAD-Moline, Ill.

• **Data and the news:** See how IRE and NICAR can help you cover the latest news using data, tipsheets and archived stories.

• **Math test for journalists:** Test your skills with this interactive test developed by Steve Doig, Arizona State University, and inspired by Phil Meyer, UNC-Chapel Hill.

• **Math help for journalists:** The fourth volume in the IRE Beat Book Series is titled "Numbers in the Newsroom: Using Math and Statistics in News." The guide, written by *Washington Post* database editor and former IRE training director Sarah Cohen, focuses on putting numbers into perspective for stories. It's also a great deadline guide! Others in the series: Understanding Crime Statistics, Covering Aviation Safety, Home Mortgage Lending: Detecting Disparities and Unstacking the Deck: A Reporter's Guide To Campaign Finance.

• **The Election Machine:** If you're looking for a better way to cover the next election, check out this suggestion from Neil Reisner, of the *Miami Daily Business Review*, for using Access, Excel and ArcView to run the numbers.

• **Census Help:** The NICAR Database Library is available to help out with questions regarding Census data. Send your questions to censushelp@nicar.org.

From IRE.org. Reprinted with permission.

rience and student achievement in elementary schools in Columbus, Ohio, based on race and income. Reporters have used FBI statistics available by computer to identify local rates of police shootings. Public files and computer databases showed reporters that children were being abused and neglected in Colorado's foster-care system. The Poynter Institute, The Reporters Committee for Freedom of the Press and the Society for Professional Journalists all provide training and assistance to journalists as well as national and international links to public records, other organizations and industry news. See Exhibit 4.5 for the Poynter home page.

Reporters don't necessarily have to search extensive, specialized databases to find stories or verify facts. Simply using a basic search process on the Internet can lead reporters to enormous amounts of information. For example, if the topic is lactose intolerance among school children or the dangers of ozone to the environment, you can type the topic into the subject line of any number of search engines and get more information than you can process. To find search engines, type the topic *Internet Search Engines* and several listings will appear. Google tops the list of most popular search tools and has become so commonly known that it's changing the language. People talk about *googling,* as in, "I *googled* by own name and came up with three listings." Yahoo!, Ask Jeeves, AllTheWeb, aolsearch, HotBot, Teoma, AltaVista, Gigablast, LookSmart, Lycos and MSNSearch are other examples.

These search engines provide links to news articles and databases and also to images, maps, product information, chat rooms, links to finding people and businesses and more. Using the search engines becomes easier and easier as each one competes to attract more users and simplifies the search process. For example, Google and others provide a help page with instructions on effective searching and advanced search tips.

A reporter who can use a computer, read and follow directions can use the Internet to help provide depth and detail in news stories. The challenge and sophistication comes in evaluating the quality of the information. Anyone can post a Web page and there's no guarantee that the content is accurate. With a little practice and experimentation, however, reporters can learn to do advanced searches and discern quality sources of information on the Web.

EXHIBIT 4.5   Poynter home page.

CONCLUSION

The ability to get information from people will be the most valuable skill for a reporter. Human beings can analyze information and indicate how situations affect others. People can also direct the reporter to printed material that can reveal important information or provide proof for the claims that they or other people make. Much of the information will be documented in public records that are available for review by any citizen. Both federal and state Freedom of Information laws guarantee public access to government records. Courtrooms and court records, police documents and records of public meetings are readily available. Moreover, the public has a right to attend public meetings, from city council to the floor of Congress. Besides information that is public because it relates to the functioning of our government, an enormous amount of information is available through private sources and over the Internet. In short, if you want to know, chances are good you can find out.

KEY CONCEPTS

Freedom of Information Act	subpoena	sentencing hearing
Government in the	arraignment	search warrant
Sunshine Act	preliminary hearing	affidavit
grand jury	plea	convened
indictment	bond	civil court
defendant (criminal court)	recognizance	plaintiff
prosecutor	held without bond	defendant (civil court)
arrest	pretrial hearing	docket
magistrate	disposition	

Activities

1. Look in the phone book under the name of your city or county and count the number of public offices. List three offices along with a question you could ask about an activity of public interest related to the department. If you have difficulty, call the office, explain what you're trying to do and ask for assistance.

2. Search on the Internet for information about the three offices you chose in Activity 1. You may need to begin by searching for the name of the town or

county and finding links to the offices. List the public information that you find available on the Internet.

3. Using the Web sites listed in the chapter that assist reporters, find the state laws that govern cameras in courtrooms. Select another state and find these laws. How do the two compare?

4. Using the Internet, find the laws that govern juvenile courts and juvenile records in your locality. List the circumstances under which a reporter might be able to observe the proceedings.

5. Make a list of the local courts in your area. What are the names of the various courts, and what kind of cases do they hear?

6. List three examples of criminal cases that would be tried in state court and three that would be heard in federal court.

7. List three examples of civil cases that would be tried in federal court.

8. Find and read the Freedom of Information laws and the open meetings laws for your state.

9. Watch a local newscast or read a local paper to find out about a high-profile arrest or trial. Go to the courthouse and ask to see the defendant's file.

10. Go to the local health department and ask to see last year's inspection records for your favorite restaurant. Be prepared to defend your right to see the information. Try to get the information based on your oral request only, but be prepared to make a formal request if necessary, as specified in your state FoI laws.

WORKS CITED

"Investigative Reporting Contest" at www.ire.org/contest. (July 24, 2003).

The heart of what we do is writing. We have pictures, but they don't matter unless you have a cohesive narration to go with it. Anybody can string a few facts together, but not everyone can tell a story.

JOHN ANTONIO,
WABC-TV, NEW YORK

STORYTELLING AND WRITING FOR BROADCAST

TELLING A STORY

Modern-day broadcast reporting, no matter how sophisticated or complex the issue, boils down to telling a story. The impact of storytelling does not change over time. Thousands of years ago, storytellers passed along important information, preserved history and promoted cultural traditions by telling stories around a campfire. This early reporting was always face-to-face, person-to-person. Today, technology makes it possible for sound and pictures to travel around the globe on a path through phone lines and over the air, with a side trip into space included—all in a matter of seconds. But the underlying process has changed little in thousands of years. Even though modern broadcasting technology distributes the story to a mass audience, the reporter prepares the message as if one individual hears it. No matter how technology changes or improves, good storytelling is and will always be one-to-one, one person telling a story to another—even if the audience numbers in the millions.

In preparing to write an effective story, the broadcast reporter makes careful analysis of the news situation and information. The background work must be in place, and the importance of the story must be clear. Now, as storytellers have done for millennia, the writer must prepare the story for his audience. The reporter should identify the central characters and determine an appropriate storytelling style. As the words begin to come together, the information must be conveyed to the listener in short, simple sentences that are easy to understand. Techniques for beginning, devel-

There's a difference in storytelling and reporting. Broadcasters have to do both.

Mike Schuh
WJZ-TV, BALTIMORE

oping and concluding the story must be evaluated. And finally, the broadcast reporter must apply some rules that pertain specifically to broadcasting. Before we discuss presentation style, however, reporters need to remember the background work and careful evaluation that take place before the first word hits the computer screen.

PREPARING TO WRITE

Writing begins and ends with thinking. Before the writer can tell the story, she must have complete command of the information. Remember that you cannot tell someone a story effectively if you do not understand it yourself. You can repeatedly read the printed information you gathered and you can play back the taped interview over and over, but if you don't understand it, you can't explain it.

Once you know that you thoroughly understand the story, put yourself in the listener's seat. You must explain the information in a way the listener will understand. You may have spent a lot of time learning terms and concepts to understand an issue, but now your goal is to make the story clear and simple so that the person who hears it once will also understand.

The first step in relating a story effectively is to review why the story is important. A large audience will hear your news story. But will they listen—and why should they? Why is it important? An effective news story will have a clear purpose and mission. As you begin writing your story, be sure that you can answer the most basic questions. What is this story about? Why is it newsworthy?

If the story is about the International Monetary Fund, viewers may immediately quit listening because they don't see how the story affects them in any personal way. The fund is out of money. So what? The writer may need to explain how economic failure in Asia hurts the U. S. economy. An even stronger approach would connect the Asian money crisis to local businesses:

> Telling a good story should be like a good movie: a clear beginning, middle and an end . . . with characters you care about . . . a clear line of thought and surprises with proper leads up to them. It's a bonus if the audience actually feels something. . . . If you don't care about your story or subjects, it's going to show FAST. And if you don't like people, go fix copy machines or find another occupation.
>
> *Les Rose*
> CBS NEWS BUREAU, LOS ANGELES

A local factory is worried about future business as Congress debates the International Monetary Fund crisis.

News broadcasts abound, and people are bombarded with lots of information every day. Your story must strike a chord if you want people to stop and listen. The story must have an answer to the important question, "So what?" The answer to this question is always found in the way the story affects people, so the storyteller should explain the impact of the news on human lives.

Review the "Five W's"

Every story should include minimum factual information, which can generally be summed up as the "Five W's." Every communication student learns to recite them: Who, What, When, Where and Why. Forgetting one of the Five W's invariably leaves a gap. Who did What? When and Where? Why? This formula covers the fundamentals of any story. "How" is often added as an important aspect of a news story.

"Where" is usually one of the most important elements of a broadcast news story. In fact, location is listed as a fundamental characteristic of news in Chapter 1. For example, filling in a pothole on a road through campus might become news on the college radio station because of where it is happening. If the hazard had been obvious for a long time and students had become accustomed to driving around the hole to avoid damage to their cars, they will welcome the information about the road repair. Obviously, road work is not usually noteworthy, and a pothole somewhere across town, away from the campus, would not make the campus newscast. Likewise, a boating accident in Florida does not usually find its way onto a newscast in Albuquerque—unless there's a local connection. If so, the Albuquerque news story will begin with the local connection so the audience can immediately recognize the significance of the story:

> An Albuquerque couple are presumed dead after their chartered fishing boat sank in stormy Florida waters over the weekend.
>
> Who: Albuquerque couple
>
> What: presumed dead
>
> When: over the weekend
>
> Where: Florida
>
> Why: possibly because of the storm (although the story may offer other reasons)

The Five W's can help reporters ensure that the basic information for a news story is in place. These basic facts should appear somewhere close to the beginning of the story, if not in the very first sentence.

Identify the Characters

Any story—even a news story—has central characters, a plot and a resolution. The central character of a story about a woman with quintuplets is obviously the woman and perhaps her husband. Who are they? Where do they live? How are they coping with five babies? How will they afford the expenses? The reporter should determine how to introduce them to the audience in a way that makes the

Think emotion—don't think linearly. Tell what touched your soul. . . . Remember that the television audience can see the pictures, but they can't touch or smell. Make the sensations real when you write your story.

Stephanie Riggs
KCNC-TV, DENVER

audience care about what is happening. The plot is fairly simple: a couple has five babies, sorts out the way they will handle the situation and braces for the future.

Looking for the expert—not necessarily the professional—can lead to more compelling stories. If the story is about increasing depression among middle-school children, the expert is the depressed 11-year-old. In terms of plot, the child is depressed, cannot enjoy life and needs a solution to the problem. The expert on why kids join gangs is the young gang member who needed a sense of belonging and found it in the gang. Rising interest rates may be of concern to the audience, but the young couple who have to postpone the construction of their new home bring reality to the new interest-rate numbers. The Department of Transportation spokesperson can certainly explain why the department has closed a bridge to traffic, but the woman who has to drive 40 extra miles each day may cause people to care about the story. Professionals can certainly provide valuable context and broad understanding, but the real stories lie with those whose lives are affected.

We can cover the city council meeting where a tax increase is approved, get the mayor's opinion and some comments from council members, and give our viewers the facts. Or, we can introduce them to an individual who is involved in the news event. They will still get the facts, but they are more likely to care if the story shows someone specific. Bringing an individual to the attention of the audience can bring emotional life to an otherwise dry story. Perhaps the audience meets Gladys Wilson, who has simply come to observe the council meeting. Throughout the story, we can use her facial expressions and reactions to parts of the meeting to keep the audience interested. Even if they indicate pure boredom, they will still enliven the story. Gladys becomes a story within the story. A very short comment from Gladys at the end of the meeting brings a character to life in conjunction with information about tax rates or other important city business. Remember that we relate to people and are interested in how different people behave. Few of us identify with the police chief or the mayor, but most of us can empathize with the person who is facing that tax increase and shows concern about its effect on the family's vacation plans. People are fascinated by other people, and writers who can use individuals to tell news stories will add an emotional element to the information and maintain the interest of the audience.

Personalize the Story

Often, the character in the story serves a larger purpose than providing a focus or an interesting, emotional element. To **personalize** a story means to use a single person to explain a large issue or event. Typically, in order to personalize a story, the reporter will have to search for the right person to represent a larger story.

A story about new, tough state requirements for evaluating teachers and schools does not have an obvious central character who represents the issue, but the information will have a stronger impact on the audience if the reporter finds one. Perhaps the central character is a teacher who can demonstrate the seriousness of the new dictate. Imagine a teacher talking about how intimidating the new requirements are. The teacher is worried about how her 25 students of different capabilities can prove, through standardized tests, that they understand the concepts behind the American Revolution in addition to demonstrating the math and language skills designated for their grade level. The teacher could lose her career if students cannot demonstrate clear historical concepts and are weak in math. Low scores throughout the school could threaten school accreditation or funding. Through this presentation, the information has new meaning. The teacher we are now acquainted with faces a tough challenge and is frightened and skeptical about the appropriateness of the new standards. The teacher's skepticism provides the opportunity for the reporter to explain the reasoning behind the new requirements. The story ends with a reminder to the audience that testing begins before Christmas break.

Often, stories are simply about people themselves. When U. S. Senator Bill Frist, also a physician, rushed from his office to resuscitate a gunman who opened fire in the Capitol building and killed two security officers in 1998, networks ran stories that focused exclusively on Frist's activities during the mayhem. Those stories were simply about Frist, the person. However, if a reporter received an assignment to find out about members of Congress who hold professional credentials outside politics, he might personalize the story through Frist and follow it with information on the number of law, accounting, architectural and medical licenses held by the nation's lawmakers.

Again, people are interested in other people. Statistics, government policy and economics become important and interesting only because of the way they affect individuals. Although a story about the Dow Jones Industrial average may sound dry and uninteresting, a story about a college student who gained or lost several hundred dollars in a single day on the stock market can be captivating. A story about the challenges of changing insurance coverage is important, but the situation is more understandable when presented through the eyes of a cancer patient who has to give up the doctor who has treated him for the past 12 years because the doctor is not on the patient's PPO's approved list of physicians. The cancer patient gives a human face to a social issue and offers viewers a clearer understanding of the statistics.

> Real stories are about real people and how they are affected.
>
> *John Antonio*
> **WABC-TV, NEW YORK**

Instead of beginning a story on locally decreasing unemployment rates with the numbers, tell the story of John and Jane Smith and how their lives have changed because of Jane's new job. After introducing the issue through the eyes of individuals, you can bring in broader information about unemployment trends with more meaning. To explain the implications of decreased car sales, introduce a local car dealer who complains about paying interest on the unsold cars on the lot. If you report a story about tainted fruit that made people sick at a national conference, build it around an individual who attended the conference. After giving an introduction to the person, progress to the facts about other people who were affected and the reasons for the sickness. If your story is about a luxury cruise liner that caught on fire, try to find a local person who was aboard it. (How do you find these individuals? A travel agency may be a good place to inquire, or tips may come from people who call to ask for more information about stories.) By focusing on the experiences of people, you can clarify and enliven a story about a complicated issue. TV news reporting is most effective when it talks to people about other people.

The Diamond Effect

To structure a personalized story, think of a diamond. In the **diamond effect,** the story begins with a single viewpoint, then expands to discuss a broader issue, and ends by returning to the perspective that began the piece. The reporter introduces the viewer to a single person or a small group of people and how the story relates to them. Then she broadens the scope to tell a more general story. In the end, the story returns to the person(s) we met in the beginning (see Exhibit 5.1).

If a bridge in the community is closed for replacement, the story might focus on one of the children who used to walk across the bridge every day to catch the school bus. The child may talk about how fast it was to get to the bus stop and how the walk will now take 30 extra minutes. Then the story can outline the reasons why the bridge is closed, detail some effects it will have on other people who live nearby and give the expected date of completion. At the end, the report can return to the child and end with his feelings about the situation and how he is coping.

The person around whom the diamond-effect story is built does not have to represent the larger picture in a literal sense. In a story about welfare reform, a

EXHIBIT 5.1   The diamond effect.

One child and
the long drive to school
because of the closed bridge.

The more general story, i.e., numbers affected,
reasons for closure, effects on others.

Same child as beginning, on the
drive home from school—
looking to future.

woman who is still on welfare may become the focus of the story, even though she doesn't represent the fact that most people are now working. The audience may meet Jane Wilson, who continues to pick up her welfare check each month. Then they learn that Wilson is unlike most of last year's welfare clients, who are now going to work each day.

We emphasize again that people relate to other people. Whether the central character of your story represents a larger group or serves to introduce a larger issue (as in the diamond-effect welfare story), or simply shows one person's involvement in a news event, the audience will be more interested and care more about a story when you focus on how it affects real people.

Determine an Angle

Part of our task in telling a story is to determine the **angle,** or the approach we'll take in explaining it to viewers. What is the most interesting aspect of the story? How can you help viewers understand it? After you gain a full understanding of a news situation, choose a particular focus—or angle—from which you will introduce and tell the story. For example, you might present information about a drug bust in a straightforward manner, telling who was arrested, when and how. When a serious story is brand-new, it is considered hard news and requires more urgency in presenting the facts:

> Thirty suspected cocaine dealers are sitting in jail this morning, as police wrap up a three-county drug sting.

Another approach, or angle, might tell the story from the police officers' point of view:

> Washington County police officers are congratulating themselves for a job well done after last night's drug sting.

After the basic facts of the story become known, the reporter might find additional, softer angles to the story. The drug sting could be told from the point of view of police families who were worried about the officers' safety during the operation:

> The husbands and wives of police officers involved in last night's drug sting are recovering from a night of worry and lost sleep.

The examination of family concern during the drug sting would be more of a feature story—an approach that focuses on human emotion. To find the angle for the story, part of the reporter's work includes deciding how urgent the information is. Do the facts need to be presented quickly, or will a softer approach work?

Reporters decide on the angle of every story. A story on welfare reform could be told from the perspective of someone on welfare, or from the point of view of an employer who regularly hires people as they leave the welfare rolls. In covering a group of concerned citizens presenting a petition at a city council meeting, the reporter may choose an individual protester—or an individual council member—as the focus of the story. If the petition relates to a traffic problem, the reporter may focus on a recent traffic accident as a way of introducing and developing the story. A story about a speech may develop around the speaker, the significance of the occasion or the audience reaction. A story about a murder can be approached from the viewpoint of the person who discovered the body, from the angle of the investigation process or from conversations with the surviving family members. If a hospital is planning an expansion, the reporter may develop the story by looking at the hospital's financial status, by talking to an emergency room doctor or by focusing on a patient.

You may find a fresh angle by approaching a story from what you do *not* see. Sometimes a sports team is closely identified with the voice that broadcasts the football games. Although the audience may recognize the name and voice, few may know anything about the man behind the Saturday afternoon play-by-play. A feature story related to the team's most recent victory may show what fans could not see—an interesting story about the announcer and his extensive home gardens. A Fourth-of-July fireworks show could provide an interesting story based on what patriotic Americans do not see. Did you ever wonder how the music and fireworks are synchronized? What goes into that 15-minute burst of color? A behind-the-scenes feature on the preparation for the fireworks show could portray the trained specialists who spend hours meticulously lining up dozens of varieties of rockets and calculating the length of fuses. In reports about floods, hurricanes and other disasters, viewers are accustomed to seeing reports on damage to lives and property, but what about a different angle? Where does the trash go in the cleanup process, and what challenges arise for sanitation crews?

By considering different approaches to the story, we vary our ways of presenting information. This variety helps ensure that viewers do not get bored. Further, the angle the reporter chooses may determine the presentation style of the story.

Keep It Simple

Like early storytellers, broadcasters prepare information for the ear. Viewers cannot reread or relisten to what we say in the way they can study a paragraph in a newspaper if the writing is unclear. In most instances, TV reporters get one opportunity to get listeners' attention and interest. We have one chance to help them understand. In short, broadcast writers must keep it simple. Keeping it simple means writing in short, declarative sentences.

Even though we must keep broadcast writing simple, reporters must never confuse simple writing with simple ideas. Complex ideas can be made clear and simple, and simplifying does not mean dumbing down. One successful executive attributed his long resume of achievement in the business world to making complex ideas simple. He contended that every promotion came because he had been able to simplify concepts for people. Broadcasters can and must do the same thing.

The long-running, successful news program "60 Minutes" provides an example. "60 Minutes" has set the standard for hard-hitting broadcast journalism that tackles difficult topics in a limited time. No matter how complex the topic, the veteran broadcasters boil it down to a simple, understandable level. You can do this in your own stories, and ensure that the major point of the story is clear, by reducing the story to its simplest form, usually three words: subject, verb and object. Who did what to whom? Or, what did what to what?

Suppose a local hospital has been found in violation of the Hill-Burton Act. A reporter's investigation may reveal that the hospital is turning poor pregnant women away from its emergency room. Reduced to the essential words, the core of the story is "Hospital turns away women." Before the first word hits the screen, the writer needs to boil the story down to three or four words, to make the point absolutely clear.

It is a great mistake to believe that complex issues must be left to newspaper and magazine writers. In fact, broadcast reporters can present complex issues in a clear, understandable way by writing deeper, not longer. Shortening an explanation from 20 seconds to 15 seconds can be quite a challenge, but good writers develop the ability to both simplify and clarify.

As we have emphasized, the most interesting stories involve people. Newscasts, however, don't always offer time to present every bit of information in story form with real people at the center of the issue. Sometimes, the news story presents basic facts and leaves the audience to evaluate how the information will affect individuals. The goal remains to present the information as an interesting story, told simply and clearly. Although some people may think broadcast-style writing stifles creativity, complex prose works better in places other than radio and television. Broadcast writing can, of course, be creative, with exciting leads and clever turns of phrase, but the primary goal is to be simple and clear.

> Find the story in its simplest terms. State in one sentence what you want the viewer to get from it. It's a commitment statement and you'll discuss everything from the opening shot to the sound bite to moments of transitions in relation to that simple sentence. It could be, "Farmer Fred is upset about decreasing prices and he's doing something about it." Keep it short and simple.
>
> *Dave Wertheimer*
> **KSTP/KSTC-TV,**
> **MINNEAPOLIS/ST. PAUL, MINN.**

WRITING THE STORY

The Lead

When small children hear the words "Once upon a time," they pay attention, tune in and anticipate an interesting story. Broadcast reporters strive to get the same reaction from the audience. Even though the first line won't be the dramatic "Once upon a time," the first sentence must get the viewer's attention and evoke the same type of anticipation. For this reason, reporters—our modern-day high-tech storytellers—must pay special attention to the first sentence of the story, or the **lead.** In a newspaper story, the first paragraph is considered to be the lead, but since broadcast stories are much shorter, the lead is only the first sentence. The lead is the most important sentence because it draws the viewer's attention, sets the tone for the story that follows and often includes many of the basic facts of the story. If you do not succeed in getting the viewer's attention in the lead, your writing will never be heard.

Put your best stuff first.

Dale Solly

There are infinite ways to begin a story, but you should be aware of some commonly used leads. These include the *hard, soft, throwaway, umbrella, question* and *suspense leads*. This list of lead types provides a place to start. Seasoned journalists don't generally think about the category their leads fit in. However, at times when it's difficult to begin the story, one of the following concepts might help.

The Hard Lead

The **hard lead** is a straightforward first sentence that begins giving information immediately. There is no delay because this is new information and it is important. The hard lead is the most common way to begin stories and the type reporters generally like best, because it means they are conveying crucial information. The lead includes the basic facts—the who, what, when and where—and the audience can make an educated guess as to how and why. There is no question about the subject and where the story is going. If terrorists have bombed an embassy, or a city building is burning, could there possibly be a reason to delay the point of the story? When the information is serious, the writer doesn't worry about building in surprises or suspense. Breaking news begins with a hard lead, and the audience learns who, what, when and where very quickly.

> Thirty county residents are locked in jail tonight after a countywide drug bust.
>
> City employees are evacuating Town Hall at this time because of a dangerous gas leak.
>
> U. S. forces are striking military targets in Iraq this morning.

The Soft Lead

Whereas the hard lead gets right to the point in telling the story, the **soft lead** gives listeners only a general idea of what the story is about. The writer introduces the subject and attempts to evoke interest without giving basic facts in the opening sentence. The Five W's follow the lead. The soft lead is never the best choice for a hard news story; you commonly find it in feature stories or in the section of the newscast that follows the hard news story or stories. When used to add perspective, the soft lead can provide an interesting angle and make the story stand out in the newscast.

Police officers are preparing for even more guests at the county jail. They have already put 30 suspected drug dealers behind bars.

Town Hall employees are hoping to return to their desks in the morning.

A story about military strikes as they are underway would always require a hard lead, and many of the follow-up stories will follow in a breaking news fashion with hard leads. However, a **sidebar story**—a story that gives related information about a more significant news story—might employ a soft lead. In the following example, the reporter is talking to people at a local coffee shop.

Americans are drinking coffee this morning and forming opinions about last night's air strikes against Iraq.

The Throwaway Lead

With a **throwaway lead,** a popular way to introduce a subject, the writer entices the viewer to listen further without giving any real information about the story itself. Unlike the soft lead, the throwaway does not even reveal the subject. There may be a general suggestion about the who, what, when and where, but nothing is clear . . . certainly not the how or why. The throwaway lead teases the viewer into spending more time learning the details. Most of the time, the throwaway lead could be totally eliminated—thrown away—without affecting the viewer's ability to understand the story.

Several area businesses shut down last night, but no one is complaining.

Town workers may have wished for a day away from the office, but they didn't plan it this way.

Conflicts are not usually between good and bad . . . but between different ideas of good. This is surely the case in the Middle East.

The Umbrella Lead

The **umbrella lead** introduces more than one subject—or different parts of the same story. This type of lead includes a lot of information, but if the umbrella is well-written, the viewer will be interested enough to see how the two parts or two subjects fit together. In the umbrella lead, the who, what, when, where and why may be there, but more questions arise in the mind of the viewers, and they continue listening to find the answers.

Numerous drug dealers are on their way to jail, while families of police officers wait to hear whether their loved ones are safe.

The Board of Supervisors is proceeding with one multimillion-dollar project, but has rejected a plan for improving county schools.

U. N. leaders are deciding the next course of action in Monrovia, while refugees are flooding out of the war-torn city.

The Question Lead

Reporters are generally in the business of answering questions rather than asking them. However, a **question lead** asks viewers a question at the beginning of the story that helps involve them as they listen to the details. The real subject of the story may not be clearly introduced until later. Some experts advise against ever using a question lead, and these leads should certainly be used sparingly. However, if used appropriately and written well, the question will make the viewer want to hear the rest of the story.

Using some kinds of questions in the lead may irritate some audience members. You must structure the question lead so the viewer cares about the answer—and be certain to answer the question. Asking yes-or-no questions can be dangerous: *Should county citizens bother to vote in the upcoming election?* The viewers might be answering aloud as they reach for the remote. Asking sarcastic questions (*Are our citizens illiterate when it comes to signs that say "No Parking"?*) can lead to sarcastic answers from your *ex*-viewers as they look for more intelligent writing.

Question leads are most effective when you use them in stories about debatable subjects and when the answer to the question is an important one, as in the following examples:

> Are the streets in our town safer for our children and for our police officers tonight?

> Will Israel's new prime minister become a nightmare for Palestinians?

Again, reporters should take care not to overuse this type of lead. Generally, it is too easy to begin with a question. More thought and more work usually produce a declarative statement that will make a stronger lead.

The Suspense Lead

The **suspense lead** creates anticipation and expectation for a resolution. With a suspense lead, the story becomes a mystery waiting to be solved. The facts are often told in chronological order, and the payoff may not come until the end of the story. The reporter should not overuse the suspense lead and should make the payoff worth the wait, so viewers won't feel they have wasted their time. Although suspense can be a very effective way to create interest in your story, the drama must be effectively built to keep the story from falling apart before the ending.

> A telephone call began and ended a dangerous evening for area police.

> Israel's new leader might signify trouble for a group meeting this week in Washington.

There are many ways to begin a story, and the common types listed above may serve as helpful guidelines. Each story is different, however, and creativity has no limits. You may find other effective ways to gain viewer attention.

Remember that the objective is to help the viewer understand the story—not to demonstrate your cleverness as a writer. Always keep the audience in mind.

Organizing the Story

By this time, you have done the legwork in gathering the information and support for the story. You have interviewed all of the key figures and examined all supporting documents. You have verified all the information and created a captivating lead. Now it's time to arrange the information, write the script and decide how to use interviews and stand-ups.

Developing the story is basically an exercise in organization. Which information is vital? Which information is interesting but not necessary for the viewer's understanding? The reporter must constantly be thinking from the perspective of the viewer who knows nothing about the story. In what order would the viewer ask questions? What proof would the viewer need that the story is true?

Individuals can be endlessly creative in finding story angles and appropriate writing styles to suit the information they present. Sometimes, however, a formula can help you put a story together. Typical story patterns include the following:

Chronological Order

Some stories are told best in **chronological order,** the order in which they actually happened. Recounting events exactly as they unfolded can be effective and even dramatic. For example, a feature on a day in the life of a NASCAR driver could begin at sunrise as the driver walks into the garage to talk with the crew, and proceed through practice laps and the meal before the race. Of course, the race competition and results will play a prominent part in the story, which might end after a late-evening celebration as the driver heads back to the trailer or hotel for sleep.

A missing-person story will surely include a chronological report of the person's last-known activities. A feature on astronaut Sally Ride's historic space mission would likely follow a chronology of her major life events. Interpersonal storytelling—the story at bedtime or around the campfire—is almost always in a real-time sequence.

Time is always limited in broadcast news, however, and does not allow for telling everything chronologically. Using chronological order can tempt the writer to include unimportant details and could mean that the writer hasn't sorted out the information or found a way to tell a story. Broadcast stories must communicate the message quickly and therefore often begin with the most important point.

The Main Point

Writing from the **main point** of the story is often more effective than a chronological approach. Instead of recounting the football game from kickoff to the end of the game, begin telling the story with the main point or the turning point, and then recount the major events.

> With a 40-yard touchdown pass in the fourth quarter, the Hornets began a three-touchdown comeback to defeat the Tigers.

Even though the long struggle for a peace agreement is an interesting story, the most important point is that the agreement has been reached.

> The Mideast peace agreement has been signed despite three days of tense negotiation and two threatened walkouts.

A feature on an athlete's life accomplishments would not have to follow chronological order. A kidney transplant at age 20 might be the best place to begin, followed by information about a major childhood illness. After details of the health battles, the story might proceed to information about marriage and children. A chronological telling might not be as effective in this story. News stories often succeed by beginning with the most important information.

What is happening right now can also form a captivating lead. When a story begins in the present, it will often follow the pattern of present, past and future.

Present, Past, Future

Many stories work well by looking at the present, reviewing the past and then looking to the future: present, past, future. Some say it is really present, past, *controversy,* future. Here's where we are, how we got here, the sticking point or problem that caused this to become a story, and what is expected to happen next. This approach works well for breaking stories. Consider a major fire at an industrial plant:

> *Present:* Twenty firefighting units continue their battle with the flames at Gose Industries this morning.
>
> *Past:* The fire broke out last night in a chemical storage room.
>
> *Controversy:* The fire chief says the company had been warned to remove old chemicals during the last fire safety inspection.
>
> *Future:* Officials say they hope to have the blaze under control by early this afternoon.

A version of this style will also work for a lighter story or feature. If no controversy is involved, use the part of the story that made it interesting for you in place of the controversy. Here's the story, here's how it became a story, here's why we're interested, here's what is expected to happen.

> *Present:* A new parents' group is fighting to keep Greendale Elementary School open. The group is called "Save Greendale."

Past:	City Council voted last month to close the school because of the small enrollment and high operating costs. Consultants had recommended the change last year.
Controversy:	Area parents say that school enrollment will increase in the next few years. They claim the consultants' report did not include the future impact of the county's new industrial park. They also insist that the school is too important to the community to be closed.
Future:	The group is raising money for a new study of business and population trends in the area. They plan to present the findings to City Council in July.

The writer should always double-check that all the important facts—who, what, when, where, why and how—are included, but beginning the story in the present, reviewing past events and looking to the future is a formula that can also help ensure that the story is complete.

Choosing the Format

As part of the writing process, the reporter will need to find out how the broadcast story will be presented. Producers may want a news package, a voice-over or a combination of voice-overs with a sound bite. The **news package** is a report produced and edited prior to broadcast time, typically consisting of a reporter's recorded voice telling the story, pictures with accompanying natural sound to cover the narrations, sound bites and (usually) a stand-up.

Sometimes, a reporter gathers information and writes a story that the news anchor reads as the audience watches video. This type of presentation—the anchor's voice covered by video—is referred to as a **voice-over** or **V-O.** The editor gets the anchor to read and time the script to determine how much video is needed. Then, the editor prepares the pictures and sound that the viewer will see and hear while the anchor reads the story.

At other times, the anchor reads a story under video that leads into a sound bite and then resume reading when the sound bite is over, as video continues. This presentation is called a **VO-SOT,** for Voice-over/Sound on Tape; a **VO-B,** for Voice-over/Bite—short for sound bite; or a **VSV,** for Voice, Sound, Voice. To produce a VO-SOT, the editor finds out from the anchor how long it will take to read the lead-in to the sound bite, lays that amount of video, adds the sound bite and then adds the amount of video required to cover the anchor's words after the sound bite.

The reporter may also write a **reader**—a short six- to eight-line story that the anchor reads, looking directly into the camera with no accompanying video.

For any broadcast story format, the writer will provide a **slug**—a one- or two-word description of the story. Different stations will have different story formats, but the page heading almost always includes the slug, the reporter's name and the date of the newscast (see Exhibits 5.2 to 5.5).

EXHIBIT 5.2 Format for a news package.

	Commission	(slug)
	Spalding/Chang	(names of reporter and photographer)
	7/14/05	(date of the newscast)

ANCR ON CAM — The County Commission insists that property tax rates will stay the same, and the decision may mean an end to football and art for students this fall. Larry Spalding reports.

ROLL PKG — (Nat sound of meeting)

Time: 1:15 — Despite protest by a roomful of teachers, Commissioners refused to raise property taxes at Tuesday night's meeting. Several of the elected leaders argued that the budget short-falls are because of state budget problems and that local citizens should not have to pick up the bill.

Super:*
Commissioner
Rita Wilson — *Our citizens are already taxed to death with higher property taxes than any other county in the state. If the state officials want to destroy the education of our children, let people remember them at election time.*

But teachers say they already have to conserve chalk and reduce copying in the face of losing football and art altogether this fall. They want a higher property tax if that's what it takes.

Marcus Jones
President
SCEA — *We've got to do what it takes to educate our children, even if we have to pay more. I don't want higher taxes any more than anyone else, but we're talking about our future, and, as I see it, we don't have a choice.*

The local government has lost almost 60 million dollars in tax revenue that previously came from the state. County School Board officials had said that if property tax rates were not increased, they would definitely ax the football and art programs for fall.

(Stand-up) School officials don't expect improvement in the state budget any time soon. They say that closing schools will be the next step. Larry Spalding for WEHC News.

###################

* Super—short for superimpose. The words are superimposed over the picture.

Format for a voice-over.   **EXHIBIT 5.3**

Commission
Spalding/Chang
7/15/05 – 7 a.m. newscast

ANCR ON CAM   Some citizens may be glad that property taxes will not be going up, but one result is that football players won't be suiting up for play or practice this fall.

ROLL TAPE   Commissioners refused to raise property taxes at Tuesday night's meeting. Some of them say that the budget shortfalls are because of state budget problems and that local citizens should not have to pick up the bill. One commissioner says she hopes that voters will show their objections when state legislators come up for re-election. County teachers say local citizens should pay more taxes if it's for the sake of children and education. But the vote is final, and school officials have already decided to eliminate football and art this fall.

ANCR ON CAM   If the budget doesn't improve, school officials say they will look at closing schools as another way to save money.

#################

Including the Sound Bite

The **sound bite** is a short segment of a taped interview that is edited into the news package. The sound bite serves several important purposes: it adds credibility, emotion, opinion and variety to the story. *Credibility* means that the source of the information is believable. The audience can understand why the person you interview would have knowledge about the issue or event. If a story names a suspect in the bombing of an abortion clinic, including a comment from an FBI agent about why the agency believes a specific individual may be involved adds weight to the report. The sound bite should therefore come from a credible source. If the maple trees in the city park are all dying of a disease, the sound bite should come from someone knowledgeable about the problem. A jogger in the park might make a dramatic comment about the tragedy of the dying trees but would not be a credible source about the disease.

EXHIBIT 5.4 Television format for a VO-SOT.

	Commission Spalding/Chang 7/15/05 – Noon News
ANCR ON CAM	Football and art programs will be cut from county schools this fall as a result of a vote at last night's Commission meeting.
ROLL TAPE	Commissioners blamed local budget woes on decisions by state lawmakers and decided that local citizens should not pick up the bill with higher taxes. The property tax increase was defeated. School officials had already decided to eliminate football and art without an increased budget. Teachers say the move is short sighted.
Marcus Jones President SCEA	*We've got to do what it takes to educate our children, even if we have to pay more. I don't want higher taxes any more than anyone else, but we're talking about our future, and, as I see it, we don't have a choice.*
	The local government has lost almost 60 million dollars in tax revenue that previously came from the state. School officials say that closing schools may be the next step.
TAPE OUT	##################
ANCR ON CAM	In other county news . . .

Because reporters strive for an objective presentation of facts, the sound bite can add emotion or opinion to the story that the reporter cannot. The reporter can say that 100 people marched in protest of a car tax, but the protester can make an angry comment, call the tax "stupid" or give glowing praise for the lone official who voted against the tax. Sound bites also add variety to the story. Instead of just hearing the reporter's voice, the audience can see and hear different people with their different emotions, opinions and attitudes, from a variety of locations. There may be one sound bite or several. You can intersperse them throughout the story, or they can come early or late.

The reporter should not use the sound bite alone to relay the basic facts of the story. If the mayor describes the schedule for completing a new bridge in town, there

Commission
Spalding/Chang
7/15/05 – 10 a.m. newsbreak

ANCR ON CAM

Property taxes stay the same next year in Sullivan County, but some teachers and some former football players are upset with the decision. The Commission voted last night against raising property taxes, which means the end of football and art in county schools this fall. Teachers say citizens should pay the cost of a good education. Commissioners say the budget shortfall comes from the state legislature and local citizens shouldn't have to pay more. Meanwhile the School Board says the next step may require closing some schools if a solution to the budget woes is not found.

################

will likely be stumbles and "uhs" while he simultaneously speaks and gathers his thoughts. The reporter should be able to present the facts more clearly and concisely.

Sound bites are never very long, usually about 10 seconds. In fact, media critics often worry that the sound bite prevents the listener from gaining important insight into individuals. How much can you tell about a political candidate in 10 seconds? Even though 20 seconds is also very short, perhaps the candidate can give a little more explanation of viewpoints that would be helpful to voters. However, because a major purpose of sound bites is to add emotion or credibility to the story, a short one can often suffice. Additionally, reporters include the information from important segments of an interview in the narration. For example, consider the following comments from the mayor:

Mayor: The bridge repairs were scheduled for completion at the first of June. Now it appears that it won't be ready until December. That means school buses will have an extra 30-minute drive to get kids to school on time. The bridge schedule is totally unacceptable. There's no excuse for our citizens to have to wait six months on that project. The City Council is fed up with this construction company and I'll guarantee you they won't be getting another city contract. They're a hundred thousand dollars over budget, too. Ridiculous. Just ridiculous.

The comment has some important information that the reporter can shorten and simplify:

Narration: School children may have an extra-long bus ride this fall because repairs to the Center Street bridge are behind schedule. The June completion has been moved to December, and the mayor says the project is already a hundred thousand dollars over budget.

Mayor's sound bite: The bridge schedule is totally unacceptable. There's no excuse for our citizens to have to wait six months on that project.

Narration: The mayor insists that the Wilford Construction company won't be contracted for any other city jobs.

The reporter gives the facts, but cannot add opinion and human emotion. The sound bite enhances the story with color and feeling. It also adds variety and breaks up the reporter's narration. The sound bite usually comes after the basic facts of the story (the Five W's). By this time, the viewer understands the basics and is ready to consider additional emotional elements. The *why* and *how* may follow. After you tell the audience that the president made a major policy statement on the Mideast summit in Maryland today, the sound bite will bring the story to life.

I have told the leaders that I am willing to stay in these negotiations for two weeks without sleep, if necessary, but the United States will not continue to provide military assistance to countries that are not working toward peace.

Rules are seldom absolute. At times, the sound bite may be more factual than emotional, and sometimes the interviewee may say things so simply and clearly that the reporter does not need to rewrite the information. Additionally, the sound bite does not have to be a single profound comment. The reporter may include several short comments from one person or from several people throughout the story. Sometimes, the sound bites may be short segments of the natural sound of the event—an exclamation or a round of applause.

The "How Do You Feel?" Question

The need to add life and emotion through the sound bite has led to one of the most often heard complaints about the news media: Why do they stick the microphone in front of people's faces and ask *How do you feel?* You probably have heard reporters ask homeowners how they feel as they wade through water in their home after the flood. After a mine collapse, reporters ask the families of victims what they think and how they feel. After the Olympic gold medalist steps down from the victory platform, the question is, *Can you tell us how you feel right now?* The audience objects, in part, because of the drumbeat predictability of the question and because, in a way, they already know the answer. The public also identifies with the pain victims feel and considers the question an invasion of privacy. Some media scholars strenuously object to any suggestion that reporters should ask the "How do you feel?" question.

But there is another viewpoint. Even though the responses are somewhat predictable, each expression of suffering or success is unique. In fact, the story does need the emotion of the people involved. The audience remembers the story better when they relate to the individuals in the situation. Victims of tragedies often appreciate the fact that someone will listen to their frustrations. In fact, surviving family members often want people to know something about their lost loved one.

> My husband was one of the finest men on earth. We'd been married for 30 years and he worked faithfully in that mine every day to provide for our children. I don't think I'll be able to go on living without him. . . .

Even though the emotion may seem predictable, it serves as an important reminder to the audience that the victims were individuals, important in the lives of others—just like the viewers themselves. The fact that 228 people died in a plane crash is very different from the fact that William Molina lost his pregnant wife as she returned from a business trip, and that he is willing to talk about how excited they were at the prospect of having their first child. The sound bite offers an aspect of the story that brings it to life.

Hearing "How do you feel?" inspires immediate resentment in many people, so reporters must exercise care in this area and work for more creative questions. Because the question itself seems to be the irritating factor, you might ask it of the person you are interviewing but leave it out of the edited package. You may not even have to ask the question. A comment to the owner of the damaged home such as "This looks devastating" may lead the person to talk about the devastation and reveal her emotions. Saying to the parents of a murder victim, "I can't imagine what such a loss would be like" would probably bring descriptions of the deep impact of the tragedy. There's a fine line between being assertive in a way that encourages people to talk and being rude and inconsiderate. People's feelings are truly individual and usually private. Reporters must be respectful, creative and careful when probing for expressions of emotion, but the impact on individuals remains an indispensable part of any story.

Writing to the Sound Bite

As you decide how to put a news package together, the sound bite should be your first consideration. Some reporters say that choosing the sound bite is the first step in writing the story. Finding the short comment from a long

Reveal. It's much better than announcing.

Deborah Potter
RTNDF

interview that represents the overall emotion of the subject or that clarifies an aspect of the story is not always easy. Some public people are experts at speaking in sound bites as a way of exercising some control over the news coverage, but most subjects don't tailor their comments so precisely.

The right sound bite may be hard to find, but once you do, the rest of the story may fall into place around it. The first part of the story will clarify the important facts, and the *lead-in* will set up the sound bite. A **tag,** the information after the sound bite, provides a transition and may refer to the sound bite to strengthen the cohesiveness of the story. For example, the sentence following the president's sound bite about peace negotiations could connect directly to his words:

> *Sound bite:* I have told the leaders that I am willing to stay in these negotiations for two weeks without sleep, if necessary, but the United States will not continue to provide military assistance to countries that are not working toward peace.

> *Subsequent narration:* The president may be losing sleep alone. Israel's prime minister says he's going home tomorrow—agreement or not.

The reporter will need to write out the content of sound bites. Transcribing the sound bite is usually required because of closed captioning, but there are other benefits to typing it out. Looking at the words, rather than just hearing them, makes it easier to see ways to write into and out of the bite to strengthen the story. Connecting different parts of the story makes it better. Here are some suggestions for including sound bites effectively in your stories.

Lead in to sound bites. The narrator's introduction to a sound bite is referred to as the **lead-in.** Because every word counts in a broadcast story, the lead-in serves two purposes: it introduces the person who will be speaking, and it gives additional information to the viewer. The lead-in should help establish the qualifications of the interviewee. In radio news, the lead-in must identify the speaker, although television news provides the opportunity to superimpose the person's name and title over the picture instead. Even in television, the identification is often part of the script.

> *Lead-in:* Emory Police Chief Wallace Ballou says students are much safer in the commercial crossing area because officers are using radar and giving more tickets.

Avoid echo lead-ins to sound bites. An **echo lead-in** repeats what the interviewee says in the sound bite. Echo lead-ins are weak and should be avoided.

> *Echo lead-in:* The police chief believes the radar is slowing traffic and making students safer.

Sound bite: We think the increased use of radar has slowed traffic, and we believe students are now much safer in the commercial area.

The sound bite should give additional information or provide emotion or opinion that would not be appropriate for the reporter to offer. Good lead-ins provide context for the information, opinion or emotion expressed in the sound bite.

Better lead-in: The police chief believes the radar is slowing traffic and making students safer.

Sound bite: I know a lot of citizens complain about so many tickets, but I think everyone can see we're doing what we have to do. We care about our citizens.

Echo lead-in: The fire chief says the fire started in the chemical storeroom.

Sound bite: The fire started in the chemical storeroom.

Better lead-in: The fire chief says the cause of the fire has been identified.

Inform with lead-ins to sound bites. Because every word counts, the lead-in should be used to add important information to the story rather than simply notifying the audience that a sound bite is coming. The lead-in to the sound bite should be an informative, complete sentence. Weak writers may waste words by stating the obvious as a lead-in:

Weak lead-ins: The fire chief says . . .
                   The fire chief explains . . .
                   According to the fire chief . . .

Sound bite: The fire started in the chemical storeroom. It appeared to be a poorly maintained area and I think the wrong two chemicals came into contact with each other and caused this disaster.

The audience clearly understands that the fire chief is speaking and that the purpose is to explain or give information. Here the writer wastes time by stating the obvious fact that the reporter was asking questions of the fire chief:

Weak lead-in: We asked the fire chief how the fire started.

Better: The fire chief says that better housekeeping could have prevented the fire.

Sound bite: The fire started in the chemical storeroom. It appeared to be a poorly maintained area and I think the wrong two chemicals came into contact with each other and caused this disaster.

Ending the Story

If the most important sentence in the story is the first one, the second most important sentence in any news story is the last one. The audience is most likely to remember the last thing they hear. The ending completes the story and, in a newscast, helps to make the transition to the story that follows.

Often, the way you begin a story will help determine the ending. If you introduce a story about food allergies in children through 5-year-old Susie, who has to take her own lunch to kindergarten and will wind up in the emergency room if she eats peanut butter, you will want to return to Susie at the end of the story. However, reporters must resist the temptation to write grand, dramatic conclusions to news stories: *And so, while other kindergartners go through the cafeteria line, Susie will always be sitting somewhere else with her safe, packed lunch.* This long view into the future may end the story with punch, but the grand conclusion may be inaccurate. We really don't know that Susie will never get her lunches like the other kids. Perhaps medical treatment will allow Susie to eat like everyone else, or maybe the childhood problem will disappear in a few years. Give the information and stop.

Grab them at the top of the story.

Hook 'em at the bottom.

Shelly Harper
WNBC-TV, NEW YORK

Reporters should resist the temptation to add finality by giving advice: *Be sure to attend tonight's council meeting. It promises to be controversial.* The reporter's role is to pass along factual information for the listener to evaluate; the job description does not include taking sides or giving opinions. News anchors may sometimes make editorial-type comments in chatter time before commercials, and editorial writers are paid to give opinions—but reporters report facts. Even without opinion, suggestion and grand drama, there are many ways to bring your story to a close, such as the following:

What happens next. The final line in the story looks to the future and the results expected from the information related in the body of the story. It leaves the viewer looking ahead.

> As many as 20 additional arrests are expected in the next 24 hours.
>
> The bill goes to the president on Monday to be signed into law.
>
> County residents can appeal their property assessment by calling the Treasurer's Office.

A summary. The final sentence recounts the important information included in the story and what it means to the viewer. Generally speaking, you've been successful if you can place an imaginary "So . . ." at the beginning of the last sentence. We leave the viewer with a capsule of the facts.

> *So . . .* Police believe almost half the city's drug dealers have been put out of business in the last few hours.
>
> Protesters insist they met their goals by disrupting afternoon traffic and forcing people to see their antiwar demonstration.

The FCC granted the radio license to the Goldberg group because of its small size and the plan of the owners to manage the station.

The other side. This type of conclusion tells us who else is affected and how. If the story is about a labor strike, the last line might describe the efforts of law enforcement to contain violence. It leaves the viewer with information about someone other than the subject.

Those charged could face up to 25 years in prison if convicted. For tonight, jailers are trying to accommodate the first full house in city history.

The Emerson group claims the FCC misjudged its application and made the wrong decision.

Tax assessors insist the property taxes remain lower here than in all surrounding counties.

Tired workers just wanted to be out of the traffic jam—and home for dinner.

A bit of information. The story can end with an extra bit of information that is not critical to an understanding of the story. The information, though not vital, is interesting—and viewers will likely talk about it in discussions related to the story.

Police have seized four cars and will sell them to finance future drug stings.

The Goldberg company president says she'll celebrate the FCC decision by shopping for a new transmitter.

Ending the suspense. A suspense ending goes with the suspense lead and delivers the anticipated punch to close.

Lead: A telephone call began and ended a dangerous evening for area police.

End: The night ended with officers calling home to assure family members they were OK.

Lead: An antiwar protest today disrupted traffic—but it also led to peace.

End: But neighbors Kevork Staeva and Dale Smith talked while they watched the protest—for the first time in 20 years. For them, the protest did lead to peace.

The ending to the story may come in the form of a reporter stand-up that includes a standard outcue, or the ending and outcue may be recorded narration to be used under video that leaves the viewer with a strong impression of the story. Using a sound bite is almost never an effective way to end a story, because the reporter should be in control of the story from beginning to end. The reporter always must carefully consider the most effective way to conclude the story.

Writing for Radio and the Web

More and more, television reporters are preparing their stories in different formats—sometimes even for newspaper publication. More commonly, broadcast news operations put their stories on a Web site. In some situations, television reporters may also do radio news broadcasts. For those who have the skills outlined in this book for gathering information and writing in broadcast style, the adaptations for radio or Web writing are not difficult.

Radio Scripts

Preparing a script for radio news is very similar to writing a script for television broadcast. Writing for a reader is the same, with slight variations in the format. Packages are similar for radio and television: important information appears up front, followed by a lead-in to the sound bite, then a *tag* with information at the end of the story and a *SOC* (standard outcue) with the name of the reporter and the station. The primary difference is that a radio package is much shorter—approximately 30 seconds rather than 1 minute 15 seconds to 1 minute 30 seconds for television news. Notice that in Exhibits 5.6 and 5.7, the time allotted for the reader is 20 seconds, and the package time totals 30 seconds. For more information about preparing radio scripts, visit the Newswriting for Radio Web site at www.newscript.com.

EXHIBIT 5.6   Format for a radio reader.

```
FORMAT FOR A RADIO READER
REAGAN—NOON
ALVANAS
JUNE 8, 2004                    :20

THOUSANDS OF MOURNERS CONTINUE TO FILE PAST THE COFFIN OF FORMER
PRESIDENT RONALD REAGAN IN SIMI VALLEY, CALIFORNIA TODAY. THE LINE
PASSED BY THE CASKET ALL THROUGH THE NIGHT AS PEOPLE PAID THEIR
RESPECTS. AFTER 6:00 THIS EVENING, THE FAMILY WILL ACCOMPANY THE
BODY TO WASHINGTON, D.C., FOR A FUNERAL PROCESSION IN A HORSE-
DRAWN CARRIAGE AND TWO FUNERAL SERVICES.  THE STATE FUNERAL IS
SCHEDULED FOR TOMORROW IN THE CAPITOL ROTUNDA, AND THE BODY
WILL LIE IN STATE FOR 24 HOURS. ON THURSDAY, A SECOND FUNERAL SER-
VICE TAKES PLACE AT THE NATIONAL CATHEDRAL. ON FRIDAY, PRESIDENT
REAGAN WILL BE BURIED AT HIS LIBRARY IN CALIFORNIA.


###
```

Format for a radio package. **EXHIBIT 5.7**

REAGAN—NOON PKG
ALVANAS
JUNE 8, 2004   :30

THE LINE OF MOURNERS FOR FORMER PRESIDENT RONALD REAGAN
CONTINUES AT THIS HOUR—AS IT DID ALL NIGHT LONG IN CALIFORNIA.
THE NATION WILL CONTINUE TO GRIEVE DURING A FUNERAL PROCESSION
AND TWO FUNERAL SERVICES IN WASHINGTON, D.C. DURING THE REST OF
THE WEEK.

WALTER WINGSTON AND HIS FAMILY TRAVELED FROM ARIZONA AND FILED
PAST THE BODY AT 2:30 THIS MORNING.

　　CART= N 3
　　"I will always remember him as the president who helped end the evils of
　　Communism and I wanted my children to pay respect to this great man."
　　(RUNS : 08)

THE STATE FUNERAL TAKES PLACE TOMORROW IN THE CAPITOL ROTUNDA.
THEN, THE BODY WILL LIE IN STATE FOR 24 HOURS BEFORE A SERVICE AT THE
NATIONAL CATHEDRAL. PRESIDENT REAGAN WILL BE BURIED IN CALIFORNIA.
SARALYN ALVANAS. WEHC NEWS.

###

Web Journalism

Web journalism is in its infancy, and it is unclear how it will evolve over time. It is clear, however, that those who are skilled in gathering information, evaluating it for accuracy and importance, organizing it and writing a simple, clear presentation will be involved—and broadcast journalists should easily adapt to the demands of the Web.

News outlets of all types are increasingly putting their information on Web sites. This coming together of media, where reporters present their information in more than one format, is known as **convergence.** As a result, broadcast and print reporters may be asked to prepare a version of their stories for Web presentation.

Media corporations are converging their media operations in innovative ways. For example, in Media General Corporation's TriCities, Tennessee market proper-

EXHIBIT 5.8 Web site that converges television and newspaper reports.

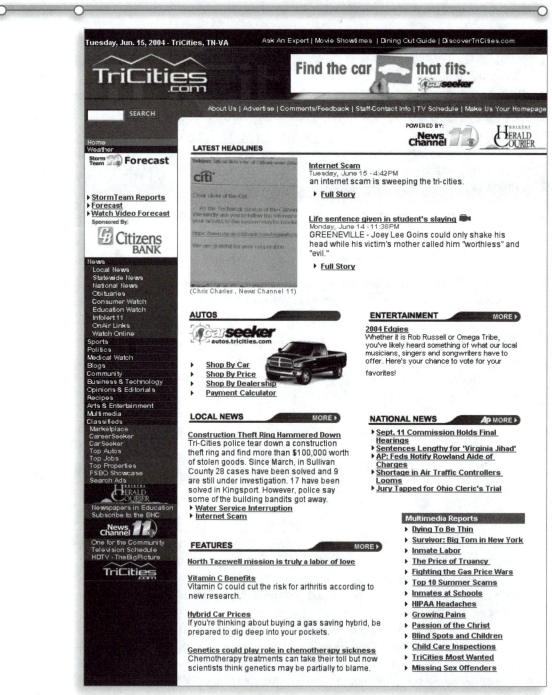

From Tricities.com. Reprinted with permission.

ties, WJHL-TV works alongside the daily newspaper, the *Bristol Herald Courier,* and both are represented on the Web site, tricities.com. On the Web site, you can find stories in both print and broadcast versions, with additional information developed specifically for the Web. Exhibits 5.8–5.11 illustrate the varied writing styles used when media converge. Exhibit 5.10 shows the full *print story* accessed by link from the multimedia reports menu. Exhibit 5.11 shows the full *broadcast script* for the related story. Modern reporters will increasingly be asked to present their information in more than one format.

For Web writing as for other media, the basic skills are the same: getting the story and writing it simply and clearly. Stories for the Web can be presented in a variety of ways, including text, video, graphics and other images. Sometimes the presentation style is more like newspaper, sometimes more like broadcast and sometimes unique to the Internet. Regardless of the style, the following basic elements almost always appear in Web presentations.

Headlines. Like newspaper stories, every Web story has a headline. These are short, usually with a subject and an action verb that causes the reader to want to know more. *(text continued on p. 143)*

A converged Web site.   **EXHIBIT 5.9**

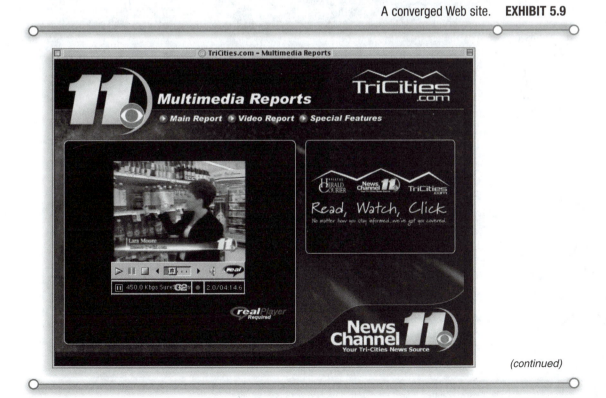

(continued)

EXHIBIT 5.9 Continued.

Print version of the story accessed by link from Tricities.com.   **EXHIBIT 5.10**

PRINT STORY— GASTRIC BYPASS

By Lara Moore

How many of us have tried diet after diet, but the weight keeps coming back? A number of people in the Tri-Cities are now taking big risks to make the weight stay off.

Gastric bypass surgery is being performed here every day, but it comes with a price. Here are the numbers:

In the past year alone, 283 gastric bypass surgeries have been performed at the Johnson City Medical Center. One person died following an operation. One person died after gastric bypass surgery at Holston Valley Medical Center, where 84 of the procedures were done in one year.

Six persons who opted for gastric bypass surgery died after operations at Bristol Regional Medical Center. Doctors have performed nearly 600 of the operations there since 1994. At Russell County Medical Center, 350 people have had the surgery; two have died as a result.

Startling numbers, but despite the risks, News Channel 11 found out there are still hundreds of Tri-City area residents taking the chance of dying, to be thin.

Our stomachs on average are about the size of this one liter bottle. After stomach bypass, they are about the size of an egg, leaving little room for food and forcing big lifestyle changes.

Patti Gold should know. In August 2003, gastric bypass was her last ditch effort to lose weight. "My dream was to wake up and be 100 pounds lighter," she says. She soon learned that wasn't reality, but she is 60 pounds lighter and breathing easier.

"I couldn't go up a flight of steps without huffing and puffing, but now my husband and I can hike at Buffalo Mountain," says Gold.

To make that hike, she's had to slow down on food. Gold tells me she can still eat out so I challenged her with a trip to a cafeteria. She rose to the challenge, putting in a special request for a grilled chicken breast, which she ate only half of along with a few green beans and a couple of bites of fruit. Gold has no regrets about the surgery.

(continued)

EXHIBIT 5.10 Continued.

But the same can't be said of Sharon Matney. Her health was in jeopardy and doctors said she'd die without the surgery. "My focus wasn't on, oh, gee, I want to look good in this bathing suit," she says. "I wanted to be able to go hiking with my daughter; I wanted to be around for my grandkids." In a year and a half, she's lost 125 pounds, but there's been no hiking.

Matney suffers from severe abdominal pain. "To lose weight is going to be the beginning of your new life. I didn't know it was going to be the beginning of my daily pain," says Matney.

She's now living with physical and emotional pain. So bad that she lost her job and her insurance. "Part of me is still right there. Mentally, I'm still that heavy person," says Matney as she looks at her old pictures.

Surprisingly, she would do it again, because despite the pain, she is healthier. "I can tie my shoes now. I can cross my legs." And she feels like her daughter is proud to call her "Mom."

Tony Payne spends his days in the water teaching at the YWCA, but it's not always been smooth sailing. "It took everything I had to walk from my car in here. Sometimes I even had to sit down twice to get in here," he says. "I was dying every day; I could tell it."

To Payne, the risk of surgery was less than the risk of living at 500 pounds. After about 18 months, he's down to 300 pounds and taking less medication, but he realizes his surgery is not a sure thing. "The challenges are there. I've gotta work hard every day at it. It's not something that's given to you. You've gotta work at it," says Payne.

This controversial surgery is not a magic pill, but hundreds in the Tri-Cities are taking their dose. Most are happy with the results. "I keep a smile now, since I'm not 500 pounds," says Payne. Gold takes a look at her before and after pictures and reacts. "I see someone happier and I just think I look a lot healthier and feel a lot healthier."

Doctors say it's not the surgery that's risky. It's the patients who are at risk when undergoing any type of surgery. Tri-Cities hospitals that offer the surgery also offer and encourage support groups before and after the procedure.

From Tricities.com. Reprinted with permission.

Script for video portion of the Web story. **EXHIBIT 5.11**

BROADCAST SCRIPT—GASTRIC BYPASS
By Lara Moore

[NEWSCAST=6]
[WRITER=lm]

[ANCR=Jim 2-shot] How many of us have tried diet after diet but the weight just keeps coming back? A number of people in the Tri-Cities are now taking big risks to try to keep the weight off.

[ANCR=Sara] That's right. Gastric bypass surgery is being performed here every day. . . but it may come with a price. Take a look at these numbers.

[GRAPHIC #tc41-FULL]
[ANCR=Sara reads Graphic:]

JCMC 283 surgeries—1 death

Holston Valley 83 surgeries—1 death

BRMC 600 surgeries—6 deaths

Russell County Medical 350 surgeries—2 deaths

Startling numbers, but despite the risks, News Channel 11's Lara Moore found out there are still hundreds taking the chance of dying to be thin.

[ROLL ENG PKG-TAPE #05-16]
[RUNS 1:48]

On average, our stomachs are about the size of this one liter bottle. After stomach bypass, they are about the size of an egg, leaving little room for food and forcing big lifestyle changes.

Patti Gold should know. This is what she looked like just a few years ago . . . and what she looks like now. Gastric bypass service made the difference. It was her last-ditch effort to lose weight.

[SOT]
[SUPER= O1-Patti Gold]
My dream was to wake up and be 100 pounds lighter.

[NATS - STAIRWAY]
She soon learned that wasn't reality, but she is 60 pounds lighter and breathing easier.

[SOT]
I couldn't go up a flight of steps without huffing and puffing, but now my husband and I can hike at Buffalo Mountain.

[NATS - MILK SHAKE MACHINE]

(continued)

EXHIBIT 5.11 Continued.

To make that hike, she's had to slow down on food. Gold tells me she can still eat out so I challenged her with a trip to a cafeteria.

[NATS: Would it be possible to get a plain chicken breast, grilled?]
She rose to the challenge, and has no regrets about the surgery.

But the same can't be said of Sharon Matney. Her health was in jeopardy and doctors said she'd die without the surgery.

[SOT]
[SUPER 02 - Sharon Matney]
My focus wasn't on, oh, gee, I want to look good in this bathing suit. I wanted to be able to go hiking with my daughter; I wanted to be around for my grandkids.

In a year and a half, she's lost 125 pounds, but there's been no hiking.

[SOT]
To lose weight is going to be the beginning of your new life. I didn't know it was going to be the beginning of my daily pain.

She's now living with physical and emotional pain. So bad that she lost her job and her insurance.

[SOT]
Part of me is still right there. Mentally, I'm still that heavy person.

Surprisingly, she would do it again, because despite the pain, she is healthier.

"I can tie my shoes now. I can cross my legs." And she feels like her daughter is proud to call her "Mom."

[NATS - SWIMMING POOL]
Tony Payne spends his days active in the water ....but it's not always been smooth sailing.

[SOT]
[SUPER -03 - Tony Payne]
It took everything I had to walk from my car in here. Sometimes I even had to sit down twice to get in here.

His life was in danger.
[SOT]
I was dying every day; I could tell it.

So the risk of surgery was less than the risk of living at 500 pounds.

Now, he's down to 300 and taking much less medication but realizes his surgery is not a quick fix.

[SOT]
The challenges are there. I've gotta work hard every day at it. It's not something that's given to you. You've gotta work at it.

This controversial surgery is not a magic pill, but hundreds in the Tri-Cities are taking their dose.

[NATS-CON ɹRSATION —Moore: Are you wearing a smile more now than you were before?
Payne: Oh, you better believe it. I keep a smile now since I'm not 500 pounds.]

[SOT]
(Gold takes a look at her before and after pictures and reacts.)
I see someone happier and I just think I look a lot healthier and feel a lot healthier.
[OUTQ= A LOT HEALTHIER]
[ENG OUT]

[ANCR= SARA]
That was Lara Moore reporting. Now, Tri-Cities hospitals that offer the surgery also offer and encourage support groups before and after the procedure. If you'd like to learn more about gastric bypass surgery, just log on to tricities.com. There, you'll find the top 10 reasons why gastric bypass surgery is not the easy way out.

From Tricities.com. Reprinted with permission.

Summary. Somewhat like the lead-in that an anchor reads to a news package, the summary of a Web story gives an idea of what the story is about without revealing the most important details. Sometimes the summary reaches deep into the story for interesting facts that will entice the reader to read the full story. A summary is usually two or three sentences long, and it should not echo the beginning of the story.

Links. Stories written for the Internet include links that lead readers to more information. Often the reader sees only the headline and summary at first; clicking on one of the links leads to the full story presented as a video file, a newspaper-style story, a broadcast script or a story written specifically for the Web. Occasionally, the link from the initial headline and summary leads to a second-level summary.

The full story. Writing that is prepared specifically for the Web usually resembles newspaper writing, with an inverted pyramid style—the most important information at the top and the least important information at the end. Web stories generally include direct quotes, and the story may include a link to a video clip of someone talking—the equivalent of a sound bite in a broadcast story.

Video packages. Sometimes, full video packages—or even full newscasts—are linked to headlines and summaries. *Nat sound* packages are sometimes posted on

Web sites; the viewer sees and hears the natural sounds of an event, without reporter narration or summary.

CONCLUSION

The best broadcast news writers tell stories with central characters, a plot and a resolution. Although broadcast news stories employ the creativity of fiction, they must also be truthful and accurate, including the basic Five W's: who, what, when, where and why. The fiction writer can concentrate on creativity, but the broadcast writer must make clarity and accuracy her primary goals. Before putting words on the computer screen, the writer can benefit by boiling the story down to its essence and examining its importance. What is the story in three words: subject, verb and object? So what? Who cares? The writer must certainly care, or the audience won't. Likewise, the writer must understand the information thoroughly or the listener won't. As broadcast writers become more sophisticated, they may become masters of style, including surprise, and of making strong writing connections to the available video. Broadcast-style writing is a difficult, complex process. The best broadcast news reporters are careful, precise writers and excellent storytellers.

Strong writers who are willing to be flexible will be called on to present information in a variety of styles as media increasingly converge. Web sites are bringing televisions and newspaper reporters together. Television reporters are being asked to write a print version of a story in addition to writing and narrating it for broadcast. They may be asked to present a Web version of the story—or to find new, additional information for the Web. Those who can adapt their writing styles will be increasingly in demand and are likely to be highly successful.

KEY CONCEPTS

personalize	umbrella lead	reader
diamond effect	question lead	slug
angle	suspense lead	convergence
lead	chronological order	sound bite
hard lead	main point	tag
soft lead	news package	lead-in
sidebar story	voice-over	echo lead-in
throwaway lead	VO-SOT/VO-B/VSV	

Activities

Watch a network newscast and answer the following questions.

1. Describe the different storytelling styles you see.

2. Identify a different angle a reporter could have used in a story.

3. Identify the type of lead in each story you see in the first block of the newscast.

4. Listen for the way stories are developed. Are they presented chronologically? Is the main point first? Does a story review past events?

5. Evaluate the sound bites. Do they give factual information or emotion?

6. What information is included in the lead-ins to the sound bites?

7. Make of list of the surprises you find in the stories in the newscast.

8. Make a list of places where the reporter has written copy that refers to the video.

9. What types of story conclusions do you hear? Summaries? Another viewpoint? A bit of information?

WRITING ASSIGNMENTS

The facts in chronological order:

1. *Tim Wilson, age 35, and his wife Nicole Wilson, 36, left their house on Elm Street, Meadowview, Connecticut, last night at 7:30 to go to the grocery store in Glade, Connecticut, which is 15 miles away. They were traveling north on Highway 11-W when a tractor–trailer crossed the center line and hit them head-on. They were driving a 1999 Honda. The truck was driven by Paul Roost and is owned by Gomez Trucking of Winston Salem, Maine. The Wilsons were taken to the hospital, but both died from their injuries before midnight. Nicole Wilson was the county treasurer, an office to which she was elected four years ago. She was scheduled to run for re-election in November. Roost was examined and released. The owner of the trucking company is on his way to Glade to pick up Roost. Police have investigated and say they will determine whether to place charges by 1 p.m. today.*

    a. Using the information from the chronological account above, write the Five W's of the story: who, what, when, where and why.

    b. Boil the Five W's down to the three most important elements. Who or what did what to whom or what? (subject–verb–direct object)

c. Write a six- to eight-line broadcast story for a 7 a.m. news break. Write a hard news lead, with the most important information first.

d. Interview a classmate or friend about the story of his or her life. Chronologically, the story will likely include the date of birth, graduation from high school, first job, enrolling in college, beginning or ending a relationship and so forth. Now, write a six- to eight-line broadcast story of your friend's life, beginning with the most important event and following with other important facts.

2. Use the information below for the exercises that follow.

NEWS STORY

EnCon
July 28, 20XX
Washington, D.C.

In a lawsuit against former EnCon Corp. executives, including chairman Joseph May, chief executive Bill Swilling and the company's directors, the Labor Department contends that company leaders misrepresented the company's value, even while they were selling their own stock, and caused 20,000 workers to lose their savings.

The lawsuit was announced this morning and is the first to be brought against the company's top two executives. A Labor Department official says the suit comes 18 months after the company filed bankruptcy and was delayed because of the necessity to review more than two million pages of company documents and interview nearly two hundred witnesses.

EnCon's stock fell from a high of $86 a share to less than 40 cents a share within a year, while company officials continued to claim that the stability of the company was sound and to tell investors to expect a 50 percent increase in stock value. Meanwhile, top officials were selling their stock while employees were prohibited from selling.

Julie Warren, a Labor Department spokesperson, says the lawsuit precedes expected criminal charges against EnCon executives.

ADDITIONAL WARREN COMMENTS

July 28, 20XX

We are pleased to announce this lawsuit against a corporate act of greed. Our staff has worked for many months preparing this case, and we are gratified to take this stand on behalf of corporate workers nationwide. The case represents a new legal precedent for holding corporate executives accountable for warning investors when they are at risk. We cannot allow executives to fill their own pockets while they lead their workers and investors to financial ruin with false claims. We believe the actions of these men represent the worst of fraud, conspiracy and money laundering, and we intend to follow up in court to make sure they are punished to the full extent of the law. In the future, corporate leaders who consider such horrible actions may remember what the consequences will be.

ENCON NEWS RELEASE

July 29, 20XX

Houston: EnCon Corp.

EnCon has announced the hiring of a restructuring specialist to help lead the company out of bankruptcy and to help guide corporate leaders through the legal entanglements the company now faces.

Bill Wilson joins EnCon as the company faces legal action by the U.S. Labor Department and says he believes the company's leaders will be vindicated against allegations of fraud and deception. Wilson brings experience in leading J.P. Logan Inc. through a major bankruptcy and civil action in 1999.

According to EnCon chairman Joseph May, "This is a difficult time for the company, but we are convinced that we acted ethically in the information we provided. We have believed and continue to believe that EnCon is a good company. We also have confidence that Mr. Wilson's expertise can guide us back to a position of strength."

EnCon was founded in 1983 and sells electricity and natural gas.

ENCON NEWS RELEASE

August 1, 20XX

Houston: EnCon Corp.

EnCon has announced the resignation of chairman Joseph May. Chief Executive Bill Swilling says the decision was reached by the Board of Directors in a meeting last night with the full concurrence of Mr. May.

According to Swilling, "We all realize that investigations into the corporation are continuing and we need to appoint a leader who will be able to devote 100 percent of the time to leading the company into the future."

Bill Wilson, EnCon's newly appointed restructuring expert, concurs in the decision. According to Wilson, "This change will help refocus company efforts on correcting problems and improving the company's image. We fully expect EnCon to recover from this difficult time and resume its position as a world leader in filling the energy needs of its customers."

COMMENTS FROM JOSEPH MAY

August 1, 20XX

Houston

I have enjoyed my past responsibilities with EnCon Corporation, but I am resigning my position so that the company can focus on the energy business rather than on my personal actions of the past year. The Labor Department's lawsuit is without merit, and the information I provided to employees and to workers was always a reflection of my belief that the company would rebound and continue its growth. I would never have misled the great EnCon employees who dedicated themselves to a company they believed in as much as I. Clearly, if I had done the things I am charged with, I would not have been able to sleep at night, and I remain confident that my name will be cleared. In the meantime, my wife and I will be selling our remaining possessions and moving to our cottage in Florida. We are finding support from our family and friends, and we cannot wait for this nightmare to be over.

a. Using the information in the July 28 story above, choose the Five W's of the story: who, what, when, where, why and how.

b. Boil the Five W's down to the three most important elements. Who or what did what to whom or what? (subject–verb–direct object)

c. Write a six- to eight-line broadcast story. Write a hard news lead, with the most important information first.

d. Find the two most important points and write an umbrella lead.

e. Using the information that was available through August 1, write a six- to eight-line broadcast story beginning with information from the *present,* followed by the important information from the *past,* and ending the story by looking to the *future.*

3. Write a news package, using the format given in this chapter. Use any information you need from July 28 forward, and follow these instructions:

a. Write a strong lead in active voice that gives the most important and up-to-date information.

b. Choose a sound bite from Joseph May.

c. For the lead-in to the sound bite, be sure to write a complete sentence that adds important information.

d. Review ways to conclude the story, and write the ending.

e. Think about the video and sound you would need for the package.

Some people have a malaise about writing. You don't have

a right to be sloppy because it's television.

JOHN ANTONIO, WABC-TV, NEW YORK

WRITING IN BROADCAST STYLE

TELEVISION REPORTERS are professional writers. As previous chapters indicate, the reporter must understand news value, know how to get information from people and from public records, and recognize the elements of a good story. Ultimately, all these skills come together when the reporter begins putting the words together.

The reporter must exercise skill in using language specifically for broadcasting. Writing in broadcast style means writing in a conversational manner and writing for the ears rather than for the eyes of the audience. As we emphasized earlier, the broadcast writer must keep the writing simple and clear. We want to write like we talk because the audience will understand better that way. Using simple, declarative sentences, we need to capture the audience's attention and make the story come alive.

Another goal of broadcast-style writing is to make the words easier to read, because the broadcaster will be trying to record narration or present it live. A good script makes reading the story with proper emphasis and without stumbling much easier. The writer must also consider some style requirements that are unique to broadcasting. We will offer specific guidelines for broadcast-style writing, but first we will examine two disturbing trends in broadcast writing that relate to verbs.

USING VERBS CORRECTLY

Sentences require a subject and a verb. An occasional use of a series of sentence fragments might be acceptable, but as a rule broadcast writers should write in complete sentences.

Avoid the "Verb-Free Zone"

Broadcast writing expert Deborah Potter points out the problem of missing sentence parts, particularly verbs. She says that some writers are eliminating all forms of the verb "to be," perhaps thinking they're avoiding passive voice. Rather than writing, "The body was found at noon," we hear, "The body . . . found at noon" (Potter, 2000). These writers may think they are saving time by leaving out words, but they are more likely to be distorting the meaning.

Broadcast writing is most effective when it sounds like normal conversation—the way the audience is accustomed to hearing information. Broadcasters seem to be developing a language that bears no resemblance whatsoever to the way people talk. More specifically, many broadcast stories today are "verb-free zones."

> Write in short, complete sentences. Have a beginning, a middle and an end. What's the plot? What's the logical conclusion? Every day I think of those things.
>
> *Dale Solly*

The "verb-free zone" results from the desire to be brief. Broadcasters are increasingly shortening the story by leaving out the verbs. The more time and trouble the reporter invests in the writing, however, the more likely the listener will find the story easy to understand. If the writer works harder, the story can be told well—and in keeping with the rules of grammar. When reporters fail to write or speak in complete sentences, they do a disservice to viewers.

Some knowledge of grammar makes it easier to understand how the "nonsentence" story is written: writers attempting to substitute participles for verbs. A participle is a verb form ending in *ing,* correctly used as an adjective that modifies a noun: the *returning* president. In a complete sentence, the verb would be *is returning*: The president *is returning*. The "is" functions as an auxiliary verb that makes the form complete. Reporters appear to be picking up the bad habit of dropping auxiliary verbs.

Verb-free: The president . . . <u>returning</u> home . . . <u>watching</u> protesters . . . gates <u>coming</u> down.

Better: The president <u>returned</u> home and <u>watched</u> the protesters break down the gates to the national park.

Verb-free: The secretary of state . . . <u>paying</u> special attention to signals from Israel . . . <u>hoping</u> for a peace agreement.

Better: The secretary of state <u>is paying</u> special attention to signals from Israel. She's <u>hoping</u> for a peace agreement.

Dropping auxiliary verbs may shorten copy, but the problem is that people don't talk that way. The least educated among us will construct complete sentences without thinking, even in casual conversation. Writing in complete sentences makes our stories stronger.

Writers also must accurately represent to the audience the timing of a news event. Increasingly, television reporters are distorting the verb tense—another disturbing trend.

Avoid Distortion of Verb Tense

Television news can give the audience information almost immediately, and reporters do well to emphasize the timeliness of the news. One way of doing this is to write the lead in present tense. However, when broadcast writers place too much emphasis on writing in present tense, they sometimes carry present tense throughout the story. The result is that they don't write accurately. In an effort to sound up-to-the-minute, writers misuse the tense of the verb and wind up with a distortion.

This language problem seems to have developed because instructors and consultants have emphasized over the years that reporters should write in present tense. This advice is meant for the lead of the story. Reporters should approach the story from the present—begin by telling viewers the most current information, or *what is happening now.* A present-tense lead makes the news sound more immediate and captures the audience's attention. The lead should be written in the present tense, however, *only if* the information truly represents what *is happening* at the very moment the reporter is speaking. Furthermore, the encouragement to find present tense for the lead is not intended to apply to the entire story. Unfortunately, it seems that the advice about writing the lead from the perspective of the present has spread around the country as a general rule to write everything in the present tense. The result is a **distorted present tense**—the use of present tense for events that have clearly happened in the past. For example, people die now and will continue to die in car crashes. To say that *people die* uses present tense to describe a continuing action. The following lead on a news story is *not* correct:

Incorrect: Three die in a car crash last night.

People will continue to die in car crashes, but not the three we're talking about here. We see this kind of headline in newspapers and hear it in broadcasts all the time, but the best reporters will write their stories with more accuracy and precision. In fact, *three people are dead,* or *three people died.* But, if the deaths happened last night and we are working on a news story for today, we need to update the story for the viewers. What is happening today?

Police are considering involuntary manslaughter charges against a driver in last night's deadly crash.

Suppose that three U. S. representatives are in Mexico on a trade mission. The actual events are distorted in this lead:

Distorted: Three <u>go</u> to Mexico on a trade mission.

In fact, the three are *now—at this moment—*<u>in</u> Mexico. To say they *go* suggests that they go on a regular basis and will continue to go in the future to Mexico. A more accurate description of what is going on at the current time is needed.

Better: Three U. S. representatives <u>are seeking</u> a new trade agreement in Mexico.

Distorted: Workers <u>repair</u> the damage to the East Bridge after last night's truck accident.

Better: Workers <u>are finishing</u> repairs to the East Bridge after last night's truck accident.

Distorted: The School Board <u>looks</u> into options for complying with the court decision.

Better: The School Board <u>is looking</u> for options in complying with the court order.

Distorted: The Senate <u>puts</u> together an education bill.

Accurate: The Senate <u>is putting</u> together an education bill.

Distorted: The city <u>finalizes</u> its budget.

Better: The city <u>has</u> a new budget.

This distorted use of the present tense imitates headlines in a newspaper and is somewhat more acceptable when it is used in the lead-in to a newscast. For example, the news anchor begins the newscast with a rundown of upcoming stories, the preproduced opening of the show runs, and then the newscast begins. Before the opening, the anchor might use a lead-in such as the following:

A rescue team <u>goes</u> to Iran . . . Republicans <u>prevail</u> in last night's vote on gun control . . . and transportation officials <u>propose</u> more funding for railroads.

But, as the newscast begins, each story should present a precise and accurate description of what is happening in the present for the lead. The rest of the story can include past tense accurately, because much of what we report has already happened. At this moment, the team does not *go,* the Republicans don't *prevail* and the officials don't *propose.* At this moment—*now*—the team is working in Iran. The Republicans *are celebrating* their victory in last night's vote. The transportation officials *are proposing* the plan for railroad funding.

This unfortunate tendency to distort the present tense results in some very bizarre juxtapositions of tenses. For example, in describing an out-of-control fire, one network reporter's script said, *Blazes destroy 100 homes . . . the flames reach within a few hundred yards of John Blevins' house.* Then the Blevins sound bite came up: *Yeah, we were scared to death. The flames were right there and we thought we would have to run for our lives.* Notice how awkward that sounds. The reporter was talking as if the blazes *are here* and *are close.* Then the subject described how they *were.*

In another example, a reporter's copy says that *School board members introduce next year's budget.* Of course, the meeting is over and the budget *has already been introduced.* In fact, the board *is struggling* to balance the budget and will revisit the issue. In a network news package, the reporter script says, *The president speaks tonight,* after which we see the president's taped comment, clearly *said* earlier. Unlike the use of present tense to describe a position the president *holds,* this lead-in artificially connects the present and the past. Of course viewers understand the process of reporting and can sort out present from past, but why should they have to? With more careful attention to writing, reporters can use present and past tenses correctly to report a coherent story with facts that are accurate as to when and where they took (or are taking) place.

Choose the Correct Verb Tense

Verb tense indicates to viewers when an action took place in relation to when they are hearing the story. If the information is not new, there's no purpose in having a newscast. Therefore, broadcast writers look for a way to write the lead sentence in *present tense.*

Present Tense

With a good command of verbs, the writer can make stories sound current, compelling and exciting so that the audience pays attention. In fact, reporters look for a way to make stories sound up-to-the-minute even if the information has not changed since the last newscast. They often write the lead in present tense even if most of the story recounts events of the past. For example, one newscast may report that police *are charging* the mayor with assault related to an altercation with a council member last night. The next newscast may report that the mayor *is sitting* in jail, and the rest of the story may talk about the past events that *led* to his arrest: He *lost* his temper after the council meeting, *argued* with a council member, *threatened* him and then *threw* a chair at him. A third newscast of the day may report that the mayor *is facing* an afternoon appearance in court on assault charges and then resume use of past tense to explain the lead.

In a precise use of **present tense,** the writer tells the audience that the action is happening now. This accurate description of what is happening now builds strong, compelling leads. When the reporter sits down to write a story, the lead should tell the audience the most up-to-date information—what is going on *at this minute*. In the following example, the present tense makes a more compelling lead.

Past: Rescue teams left camp this morning for the disaster site.

Present: Rescue teams are hiking toward the disaster site.

Although stories of rescue teams and disasters don't generally bore anyone, the second sentence sounds stronger than the first one because we can picture people doing something at the moment we hear about it. We see an action in our heads. The rest of the story may use past-tense verbs to talk about how the plane *crashed,* how another pilot *spotted* the wreckage and how the rescue effort *was planned,* but the strong present-tense lead will catch the listener's attention. The following examples illustrate how using current information makes a stronger lead than writing in the past tense.

Past: Two people <u>died</u> in a car crash last night.

What's happening now: Police <u>are sorting</u> out the cause of a car crash that killed two people last night.

Past: The School Board <u>examined</u> the legal ruling last night.

What's happening now: The School Board <u>is studying</u> options for meeting a judge's order.

The broadcast writer should use the present tense accurately. However, present tense does not always refer to events that are happening at the present time. Present tense can refer to an ongoing action.

Continuing present. Present tense is used to describe actions that are happening now, but present tense also describes actions that continue to happen or that happen repeatedly.

People <u>die</u> in car crashes.

I <u>eat</u> dinner at six.

The mayor <u>fires</u> city employees.

Appeals courts <u>stay</u> executions.

Police officers <u>enforce</u> the law.

Reporters must be careful not to use present tense for continuing actions when the action does not continue. This incorrect usage distorts the present tense.

Present progressive. The **present progressive tense** describes an action that is happening in the present but may or may not continue. Use the present progressive when you want to describe *what is happening now* without indicating that the action is certain to continue into the future.

The City Council <u>is asking</u> Treasurer Joe Smith for his resignation.

Police officers <u>are enforcing</u> the smoking law at area high schools.

Poor AIDS patients <u>are dying</u> because they can't afford medication.

The present progressive tense works well for broadcast leads when it is an accurate portrayal of what is happening now. Reporters should not, however, force a lead into present or present progressive tense when the verb does not represent what is going on right now.

Other uses of present tense. In addition to actions that are going on at this minute or actions that happen continually, present tense can also be used for universal, historical and literary truth; for summaries and quotes; and even for the future.

Present tense for a universal truth is similar to the continuing present in the sense that what is true now continues to be true in the future. *A stitch in time saves nine. What goes around comes around. A hint to the wise is sufficient.*

Historical events can be described in present tense. *Twain writes from his experience working as a river pilot on the Mississippi. Congress passes the Public Broadcasting Act in 1967.* The distorted present tense we often hear resembles the historical present, but a daily newscast is designed to tell the audience about current events, not to document history.

Likewise, in writing about literature, we often use the present tense. In a work of fiction, the action is always happening. For example, in Steinbeck's *The Grapes of Wrath,* drought *forces* the Joad family out of Oklahoma into a westward migration and search for work.

We sometimes even use present tense to talk about the future. *The new mall opens next week. The team goes to the playoffs in June.*

Present tense is used regularly for quoting, paraphrasing and summarizing. For example, we often use present tense when reporting what someone *said* in the past. The rationale is that when someone makes a comment, it probably reflects his ongoing thinking about the topic. In other words, the individual *believes* what he *said.*

The president says the budget decision will hurt middle-class families.

Even though the president may have *said* the statement yesterday, we suspect he has the same belief and would make the same statement today. The statement stands, so we use present tense.

Broadcasters are writers, and words are the tools of the trade. Using words precisely and carefully is part of what earns the paycheck. In an effort to make the news sound current and late-breaking, however, reporters sometimes clobber

Another key to being a good writer is being a reader. Those who read a lot have a better grasp of the English language, and they know more.

Stephanie Riggs
KCNC-TV, DENVER

the accuracy of the present tense. Be careful not to distort the present tense and to write in complete sentences.

Past Tense

The precise and accurate use of action verbs in present tense makes broadcast writing more effective. However, the audience also appreciates variety, so every story should not begin in exactly the same way. Sometimes we even choose to write a lead in past tense to describe an event that has ended. Using the past tense is perfectly acceptable for broadcast news.

> Unemployment rates <u>fell</u> by a full percent last month.

Listeners understand that if they are hearing about an event, it has already occurred.

> Witnesses <u>described</u> the two men who stabbed the victim.

> The attorney <u>convinced</u> his clients to resume negotiations.

Broadcasters may choose to use past tense for the lead with the addition of an adverb that lets the audience know that the past action happened recently.

> <u>Today,</u> the man charged with killing three women <u>confessed</u> to the murders.

> <u>This morning,</u> police <u>discovered</u> a new piece of evidence in the Oklahoma City bombing.

Past tense can often be the most effective and most accurate description for our news stories. Some say that the most powerful sentence in Christianity is *Jesus wept.* Not *Jesus . . . weeping . . .* Rather, simply, *Jesus wept.*

Present Perfect

While past tense is acceptable for broadcasting, especially for the sake of variety and accuracy, there is no question that the most interesting news presents new, up-to-the-minute information. One way to talk about something that has occurred in the past but to make it sound more current is to use the **present perfect** tense to describe an action that has recently ended. This tense implies that the action happened sometime before now, perhaps just prior to the immediate moment. It also suggests there has been a result from previous events. The present perfect uses a form of *to have* along with the past participle of a verb.

> *Past:*   The House <u>approved</u> a measure yesterday that will help working parents pay for day-care expenses.

> *Present perfect:* The House <u>has approved</u> a measure that will help working parents pay for day-care expenses.

Past:	A third victim in the bridge accident <u>died</u> last night.
Present perfect:	A third victim in the bridge accident <u>has died.</u>
Past:	The 12-year-old <u>went</u> to a detention center.
Present perfect:	The 12-year-old <u>has gone</u> to a detention center.

Even though broadcast news is most effective in its immediacy, everything cannot be accurately reported in the present tense. Sometimes, using the present perfect tense can help the news sound more up-to-date. Broadcast writers need to be able to use the present perfect to maintain the sound of immediacy when other present tenses are not appropriate and to imply that there has been a result or progress made since previous events.

Use Active Voice

Generally, writing captures attention much more easily when the writer talks about someone or something *doing* something, rather than something *being done* to something or someone. For that reason, broadcast writers must strive to use active voice rather than passive voice whenever possible. In **active voice,** the subject of the sentence is the actor doing the action of the verb. *The judge sentenced the defendant to life in prison.* In **passive voice,** the subject of the sentence is the recipient of the action. *The defendant was sentenced to life in prison.* Using active voice allows the writer to use exciting verbs. Sentences with action verbs will be more concise and more conversational. Compare the following:

Passive voice:	Even though writing is not generally seen by the audience, it may be seen by people in the newsroom. Close attention should be paid to the difference between "it's" and "its."
Active voice:	The audience won't see your writing, but people in the newsroom will. Be sure to pay close attention to the difference between "it's" and "its."
Passive voice:	The ribbon was cut this afternoon by the mayor to open the new recreation center.
Active voice:	The mayor cut the ribbon and opened the new recreation center this afternoon.
Passive voice:	Smith was freed by rescuers.
Active voice:	Rescuers freed Smith.

Isn't the active voice much livelier and better than the passive voice? Compare some more examples:

Passive:	The watermelon was eaten quickly and enthusiastically by the children.

Active:	The children enthusiastically gobbled up the watermelon.
Passive:	The county health center has been getting more and more requests for AIDS testing.
Active:	More and more people are asking to be tested for AIDS at the county health center.
Passive:	Fish are being killed in the city park.
Active:	Something is killing the fish in the city park.

To be sure you use action verbs, write about who *does what* to whom. Or, what *does what.* Instead of *the defendant was sentenced,* write *the judge sentenced the defendant.* The listener can then form a clearer picture of the action. Instead of *the students were given their grades,* write *the teacher passed out the grades.* You wouldn't tell someone that *three pizzas were eaten by my friend.* You'd say, *"My friend ate three pizzas!"* We naturally use active voice and action verbs in conversation. Sports writers are masters of action verbs. *The Hornets blasted the Panthers. The Tigers bruised the Bulldogs. The Yanks shut out the Indians. The Tornado overpowered the Falcons. The Yellow Jackets raced past the Wolfpack. The Seminoles dropped Miami. San Diego held off Cleveland.* Perhaps the sports action makes it somewhat easier to find action verbs for sports, but good writers can find the action even where none is obvious.

> You can never have enough vocabulary. We always want to say something differently than we just wrote it. There may be another word that describes what happened more accurately.
>
> *Kathy Soltero*
> **KCNC-TV, DENVER**

As an example of using action verbs, let's assume we're covering a story about a new kiosk-style coffee shop opening inside City Hall. We could write, *A new kiosk-style coffee shop will open this week inside City Hall.* The information is straightforward and accurate, and even includes an action verb. However, the lead could be much more exciting. If we take some time to think and imagine the action that could result from the new enterprise, we might come up with a more exciting lead: *City Hall workers will soon be able to grab a Danish and sip a cappuccino without leaving the office building.* Police may be planning extra surveillance on roadways during a holiday weekend, and we could write a lead that says just that. But if we imagine the action, the lead could be more compelling. *Drunk drivers are more likely than usual to see blue lights in the rearview mirror this holiday weekend.* The goal is to help the audience see an action in their heads from the words we choose.

In our day-to-day conversations, we naturally use action verbs. Broadcast writers should also use action verbs whenever possible, even when we have to imagine the action.

PUTTING THE WORDS TOGETHER

Choose Words Accurately

The English language offers many different ways of saying the same thing—and each way expresses the idea a little differently. The power and subtlety of our language become clear when we realize how many ways we can describe something as simple as how someone says something. This great variety demands great attention to accuracy when we are writing. For example, one would not likely need to *insist* that the sun will come up tomorrow, because few people are likely to dispute the claim. Similarly, when one *argues,* the word indicates that there is a strong opposing view. An interviewee would not likely *explain* that the City Council is meeting tonight, whereas the council member might need to *explain* why the budget projections missed by several million dollars. To *hint* or *suggest* means that the source did not make the situation clear but dropped subtle indications. To *assert* or *declare* means that the source made a very clear and strong comment. If the source *reveals* or *discloses,* the information was not previously known to many people. To say someone makes a *claim* suggests that evidence for the opinion may not be obvious. To say someone *acknowledges* something suggests that the person may have resisted admitting the information. Reporters must be very careful to characterize a source's comment accurately.

Attribute When Necessary

Not only must reporters be careful to characterize sources' comments accurately, they must also attribute them accurately when necessary. **Attribution** means identifying the source of information in a story or giving the audience as much information as possible about who says it.

Unless we tell them otherwise, viewers believe everything we say to be our own words, thoughts or opinions. If this is not the case, you must tell them otherwise. Be certain the listener knows where you got the information. If your story says the city is planning a new swimming pool and recreation complex, the listener will want to know the source of the information. If the city manager is the source, the listener will evaluate the story quite differently than if the information comes from a lifeguard at the existing pool.

Anytime information is controversial or disputable, the source should be attributed. Likewise, opinions should be attributed. In other words, "Who says so?" The reporter should not say that the suspect shot the victim twice. The story should indicate the source of the accusation: *Police say the suspect shot the victim twice.*

Reporters sometimes want to place a grand summary at the end of the story and include inappropriate opinion. For example, *The Million Moms march on Washington was a great success.* It is inappropriate for the reporter to make such conclusions. If, indeed, the march did appear to achieve its goals, a more appropriate comment would attribute and expand on the opinion. *March organizers say they think the day was a huge success in drawing attention to gun violence.* (Of course, a reporter would not include such a statement unless march organizers had truly made such a comment.)

The audience deserves to understand the context of information. Therefore, reporters should always attribute opinion or information that is controversial or disputable. Attribution enhances the accuracy of the story and the credibility of the news organization.

Include Necessary Names

Another issue of accuracy is to be precise in identifying people. Particularly when writing unflattering stories, such as stories about people involved in a crime, the reporter must exercise special caution and make the person's identity very clear. A story about the arrest of John Smith from Hometown on charges of assaulting his wife could surely cause distress for other John Smiths in the same town—and there is, no doubt, more than one John Smith in any town. The distress could easily turn into a lawsuit. Because the only thing reporters have to offer is accuracy, the story should include the full name and other identifying factors such as the age, address and place of employment of the John Smith who is accused of assault. (See Chapter 11 for more about libel and private citizens.)

Avoid Unnecessary Names

Sometimes a name is critical to a story, but sometimes the name is not at all necessary to the meaning of the story and is better left out. When the person's name is not commonly known and the position is the important factor, a title can suffice. Unless everyone knows Computer Services Director Sherry Davis, her name is not important to the story. The title, however, is significant.

Unnecessary name:	Computer Services Director Sherry Davis says students can't log on because of a corrupted drive on the main server.
Title suffices:	The computer services director says students can't log on because of a corrupted drive on the main server.
Unnecessary name:	Lead Detective Wilma Smith says the department is shutting down the arson investigation.
Title suffices:	The lead detective says the arson investigation has been shut down and no charges will be filed.
Unnecessary name:	Health Center Director Phyllis Blevins says ten percent more students have asked for AIDS testing in the last two months.

Title suffices:	The Health Center director says ten percent more students have asked for AIDS testing in the last two months.
Unnecessary name:	Assistant City Planner Janet Williams says the road project is behind schedule.
Title suffices:	The city planning office says the road project is behind schedule.

Only names that are widely recognized should be included in the lead. When Michael Jordan signs a business contract, his name is so commonly known that the story can begin, *Michael Jordan signed a new business contract today.* Likewise, the name of a major public official such as the secretary of state or a major music star might catch the interest of a listener from the very beginning of a story. Most names, however, would draw little attention.

Place Titles Before Names

When you do use both a name and a title, you can keep sentences short and simple by placing the title before the name. This allows the broadcaster to read a sentence smoothly and without pauses. You can see the difference by reading the following two sentences aloud:

Difficult:	Joseph Wilson, chief executive officer of Eastfield Corporation, announced the expansion of the Springfield plant this morning.
Better:	Eastfield Corporation's Chief Executive Joseph Wilson announced the expansion of the Springfield plant this morning.

This order makes the story easier to read and also keeps the information simple. The first instruction we gave about writing for broadcasting is to write for the ear—conversationally, in short, simple sentences. When we name someone and then give the title, the reader needs to pause at the commas that surround the title. These pauses interrupt the flow of the narration.

When the title goes before the name, a comma is generally not necessary because the name is an essential part of the identification. If the name is established first, however, the title is considered additional, clarifying information, and commas are required around the title. Since commas usually require the reader to slow down, pause and breathe, broadcast writing is more effective without the commas. Therefore, put the title before the name, eliminate the commas, and make it easier to read.

Difficult:	Sherry Davis, the director of computer services, says students can't log on because a drive on the main server is corrupted.
Better:	Computer Services Director Sherry Davis says students can't log on because of a corrupted drive on the main server.

Difficult:	Rachel Williams, congressional representative from the Eighth District, is introducing a bill to require mandatory trigger locks on handguns.
Better:	Eighth District Congresswoman Rachel Williams is introducing a bill to require mandatory trigger locks on handguns.

For easier reading and clearer communication, remember to put titles before names.

Delay the Name

When you use both a name and a title or some other identifier, delaying the name can make a story flow more smoothly. This helps the audience focus on one piece of information at a time and can also help listeners prepare to hear a name that may be important to them. Take a routine traffic accident for example. Using the names in the lead might actually cause listeners to miss them. In contrast, delaying the names and leading with the location will alert people from that area or those who know someone there to pay attention to see if they recognize the names.

Weak:	Joe Smith and Mary Jones are both in serious condition following a head-on collision on Cummings Street today.
Better:	Two Bristol residents are in serious condition following a head-on collision on Cummings Street today. Police say Joe Smith and Mary Jones hit each other when Smith ran a red light.

Using a title and location in the following story alerts those who know Bridgewater council members to pay close attention to the name that follows.

A Bridgewater city council member is dead. Joe Wilson was killed in a single-car accident last night on Interstate 95.

In the case of controversial information, it must be attributed to someone, but the person's position may be more widely recognized than the name. Combining the name and title can be too much for the audience to take in at once. Delaying the name solves the problem.

Weak:	Assistant Clerk Sandra Wilson in the treasurer's office says the city won't be able to meet its payroll by July.
Better:	An employee of the treasurer's office says the city won't be able to meet its payroll by July. Assistant Clerk Sandra Wilson points out that new sewer lines and recent school renovations have cost much more than expected and have put the city in serious financial jeopardy.

In the following examples, the names are important, but giving the title of the position first and delaying the name makes the leads stronger.

Weak: The mayor has appointed business owner Mary Weisman as the new director of tourism.

Better: The mayor has appointed a new director of tourism. Business owner Mary Weisman will take charge of the tourism office on June 1.

Weak: The director of the Washington County Health Department, Mary Davis, says the number of AIDS cases is on the rise. She has been keeping records since 1987.

Better: Washington County's Health Department director says the number of AIDS cases is on the rise. Mary Davis has been keeping records since 1987.

Do Not Use Age

Another piece of information that is often unnecessary is a person's age. If you are writing about an 86-year-old grandmother, the age is not pertinent unless she is skydiving or doing something unusual for her age. A 30-year-old grandmother would be interesting, however. When identifying someone charged with a crime, all information that distinguishes the suspect from others is helpful, including the person's age. Generally, however, don't include a person's age in the story.

Use Pronunciation Guides

Broadcasters must remember that other people may be reading their writing and may not know how to pronounce words or names that are clear to the reporter who was on the scene. Conversely, you may be reading a story that includes words you don't know how to pronounce. One of the worst mistakes in pronunciation would be to assume or guess at the correct way to say something. From the audience's perspective, the newscaster who mispronounces words looks uninformed and loses credibility.

In common practice, reporters often simply talk to or advise anchors about the proper way to say someone's name or an uncommon word. However, if the story is likely to be rewritten at times when no one will be on hand to offer guidance, the writer should include a pronunciation guide within the story. For example, Joe Smyth may not pronounce his name like the word *with* but may instead say it with the *I*-sound in *ninth*. The Associated Press Broadcast News Handbook offers a pronunciation guide that can be helpful in making these distinctions:

VOWEL SOUNDS*

a—bat, apple	oh—go, oval
ah—father, arm	oo—food, two
aw—raw, long	ow—scout, crowd
ay—fate, ace	oy—boy, join
e, eh—bed	u—curl, foot
ee—feel, tea	uh—puff
i, ih—pin, middle	yoo—fume, few
y, eye—ice, time, guide	

CONSONANTS

g—got, beg	sh—shut, fashion
j—job, gem	zh—vision, mirage
k—keep, cap	th—thin, path
ch—chair, butcher	kh—guttural "k"

When you include pronunciation guides in a script, type them in parentheses immediately following the word they describe. Individuals are free to establish their own methods to ensure they pronounce words correctly, but whatever the system you choose, *use it.* Mispronouncing words damages a reporter's credibility.

Write for Breathing

Broadcast reporters have an additional consideration in putting together a story: They must keep in mind how much the reader can easily say in one breath. As we have emphasized before, to ensure a clear presentation of the story, the writer needs to construct simple, declarative sentences with one idea to a sentence. Sentences should be short—really short. Complex sentences with introductory phrases and clauses—or with descriptive phrases and clauses within the sentence, like this one—are both difficult to read and difficult for the listener to follow. Read the following sentence out loud:

> *Difficult:*   Because part of the consideration in broadcasting includes how much the reader can easily say in one breath, the writer needs to construct simple, declarative sentences with one idea to a sentence.

The sentence is long and difficult to read easily. For broadcast presentation, simple, declarative sentences work better:

Reprinted with permission of the Associated Press.

Better: Broadcast writers must consider how much the reader can say in one breath. The writer needs to construct simple, declarative sentences.

It takes a lot more time to "write short" than to "write long," but good writers will always look for ways to write shorter and sharper.

Okay: Today is the day that veterans pause to remember soldiers who remain missing in action.

Shorter: Veterans are pausing today to remember soldiers who remain missing in action.

Okay: The mayor is using the occasion to take a swipe at City Council for failing to fund the ambulance service.

Shorter: The mayor is taking a swipe at City Council for failing to fund the ambulance service.

Remember to write simple, declarative sentences. Eliminate internal phrases and clauses.

Difficult: Pornographic material, loaded onto computers in the Miller lab yesterday, has been removed by computer services, and campus police are investigating.

Better: Campus police are looking for the person who loaded pornographic material on computers in the Miller lab yesterday. Computer services has removed the material.

Difficult: The woman thought, since she was eight months pregnant, that she was in labor.

Better: The woman was eight months pregnant and thought she was in labor.

Difficult: Funding for the industry, authorized by Congress in 1999, will bring private and public energy research efforts together.

Better: Congress approved money in 1999 so that private and public researchers could combine their energy studies.

Readers and listeners also have difficulty with lists. Consider this long sentence written for a broadcast story. Try to read it out loud.

Difficult: Students use their computers daily to gather information for school assignments, to communicate with other students and faculty on and off the campus and, of course, to keep in contact with friends and family—all of which are vital to the overall performance of the student.

A listener would barely be able to keep up with the information, much less remember it later. The writer must refine and simplify the ideas.

> *Better:*   Students need computers to complete assignments and to make good grades. They also use them to communicate with each other . . . with professors . . . and with their friends and family off campus.

> *Difficult:*   Local bank officials, meeting this morning, said they are concerned that increasing interest rates on home mortgages could depress the local housing market, causing layoffs in construction, in home-improvement businesses and in the trucking industry.

> *Better:*   Local bank officials warned this morning that rising interest rates may mean fewer home sales and fewer jobs. They say higher costs for home mortgages will cause layoffs for construction workers, truckers and some store clerks.

Broadcast writers need to stay away from big words. The short, simple sentences that are your goal are no place for showing off expansive vocabularies. If you want your listeners to understand, why use a big word when a small word will do? Why *initiate* when you can *start?* Is *subsequent to* better than *after? Prior to* better than *before?* Using simple words as you use them in conversation will make your writing clearer and more understandable to the listener.

SPECIAL STYLE REQUIREMENTS

Networks and large stations may have their own style requirements, or they may use style guides supplied by national organizations such as the Associated Press. Reporters will need to discover the style requirements of their stations and learn them. The following suggestions may help make your copy more readable.

Numbers

The rules for using numbers for broadcast writing are very different from the rules for numbers in print. Numbers must be written so that broadcasters can read them easily and so that listeners can understand them.

To write numbers, follow these three rules:

- Write out numbers one through eleven.
- Use numerals for 12–999.
- Write out words after 999.

Ordinals

Write out the ordinals for one through eleven: *first, second, third, fourth, fifth, sixth, seventh, eighth, ninth, tenth* and *eleventh*. For larger numbers, use abbreviations in accordance with the rules for numbers, such as the *12th, 100th, 999th* or *one-thousandth* customer.

Symbols

Symbols can easily be misread. Broadcast-style writing includes writing out words instead of using symbols. Write *percent* rather than using the symbol *%*. Write *dollars* rather than using the symbol *$*.

NUMBER/SYMBOL	BROADCAST STYLE
100,000	100-thousand
1,013	One-thousand-and-13 *or* Slightly over one thousand *or* About one thousand
$14,502,311.39	14-point-five-million dollars
10,000	Ten-thousand
12%	12 percent
3%	Three percent
1,100	Eleven-hundred
1/3	One-third

Because the numbers are spoken quickly, the audience won't be able to re-read them and analyze them. If the story says that a contractor has charged the city *$12,345,700* for a project, the reporter will have a difficult time translating the numbers into words. In addition, the audience won't be able to process so many numbers quickly. Instead, the script could say that the contractor charged the city *more than 12 million dollars* for the project. Because precise numbers are difficult to remember, simplify them to something more easily digestible. Don't expect viewers to remember that the total budget for next year is *one-million-982-thousand-948 dollars*. However, they might remember *one-point-nine million* or *almost two-million dollars*.

Scores, Times, Dates

Scores, times and dates are exceptions to the rules about writing numbers for broadcast style. Numbers in these three instances appear in such a unique form that it is unlikely that the reporter will misread them. In a series of sports scores, the reader can easily recognize the numbers and read them properly even though they are not written as words.

> Bristol over Kingsport 5–3 (five to three)
>
> The Falcons defeat the Tigers 3–2

And now for basketball scores:

> Atlanta over Pittsburgh 58–56
>
> Cleveland defeats Cincinnati 61–49

Some sportscasters may prefer including the word *to* in the score, but others are so accustomed to reading scores that the hyphen is clear enough. When desired, scores can certainly be written as follows: 5 *to* 3.

Times are also written in a very distinctive form and are not likely to be confusing to the reader.

> The game begins at 8:00 Wednesday night.
>
> The jury deliberated until 11:30 p.m.

Dates are numbers, too, and appear in a unique format. Specific dates should be used only when they are required to clarify a point. *By the middle of the month* is usually as accurate as *June 15,* and viewers are more likely to remember it. If you are referring to the sinking of the Titanic, *the middle of April* is probably close enough. If you're talking about the income tax deadline, you'll need to say *April 15.* When a full date is required, it can be written in the normal fashion: *The bomb was dropped on Hiroshima on August 6, 1945.*

Abbreviations and Acronyms

In general, avoid abbreviations in broadcast news scripts. The broadcaster must be able to read copy clearly and quickly, but an abbreviation requires translation. For example, a story about *Scottsdale, AZ* requires the reader to translate the *AZ* to Arizona without hesitation. Mistakes are less likely when the words are written as they are to be spoken. Exceptions may be made for very common abbreviations such as *Dr.* for *Doctor,* but only when you are sure the person reading the story will have time to become familiar with the copy.

An **acronym** is a word formed from the first letter of a group of words. Some very common acronyms may be used in broadcast copy, but only if both the person reading the story and the audience are familiar with the acronym. For example, in a story about the space shuttle, we could write *NASA* and expect the reader and the listener to recognize the acronym as a word. In a story about an airline, we could refer to the *F–A–A,* using dashes to indicate that each letter is to be read separately. In short, try to avoid abbreviations and acronyms. Only very common short forms should be used, and then only when you are sure the reader and listener will easily recognize them.

COMMON MISTAKES

The reporter should also avoid common mistakes in word usage. Following are a few examples of commonly misused words.

It's and its. If *it is* correct, *it's* going to have *its* apostrophe. More and more writers, even intelligent ones, belie their education and cause readers to question their ability to attend to details by confusing the use of *it's* and *its*. Some grammarians would consider denying the right to vote to those who can't sort out the difference!

It is simple, or, *it's* simple. **It's** is a contraction of the two words *it* and *is*. The apostrophe indicates that a letter is missing.

Its is a possessive—it describes something belonging to something. You can't judge a book by *its* cover. *It's* a good book even though *its* cover is tattered.

The reason people confuse the two similar words is logical. The problem is that the English language does not always follow logical patterns. Normally, apostrophes go after the thing or things that own something, indicating possession.

The book's cover was tattered.
The computer's hard drive failed.
The students' efforts were admirable.

It's is not possessive. *It's* the exception. In *its* case, the apostrophe means a letter is missing. Unfortunately, our language has many exceptions to the general rules. Professional writers, including broadcast reporters, should be among those who pay attention to the rules—and the confusing exceptions.

Even though the audience does not generally see your writing, other people in the newsroom do. To maintain the respect of your colleagues and others who may see your writing, pay close attention to the difference between "it's" and "its" and other uses of apostrophes.

Hopeful/hopefully. What's wrong with this sentence? *Hopefully, we'll know the answer by Monday.* The sentence is grammatically incorrect because *hopefully* is an adverb that tells how. As used here, the meaning is that we will know—in a hopeful manner.

Incorrect: Hopefully, they'll know the answer by Monday.

Correct: Commissioners hope to know the answer by Monday.

Prayerfully is another adverb telling how. Replace the two words to understand the problem more clearly.

Incorrect: Prayerfully, we'll know the answer.

Correct: Prayerfully, we entered the cathedral.

Hopefully, we watched the final play of the game.

We will not know the answer hopefully. We *hope to* know the answer. The misusage is such a common error that it sounds correct. Serious writers and journalists will make the distinction.

Affect/effect. *Affect* is a verb meaning to influence or to stir emotion. *Effect* is most commonly used as a noun meaning the result of something. The pollution is *affecting* the health of the forest. The *effect* of the pollution in the forest is that trees are dying. The confusion in usage of these two words comes partially because *effect* can sometimes be a verb; however, *effect* is used correctly as a verb only when it means *to bring about*. The plan will be *effected* by monumental effort.

> Master the English language.
>
> *Jeff Gurney*
> **KCNC-TV, DENVER**

Dilemma. Consider this sentence: *The mayor and city council are facing a dilemma—to cut taxes or to give tax refunds to voters.* Because the definition of *dilemma* is having two options that are equally bad, the word is used improperly in this instance. The mayor and council may have a problem, but they are not facing a true dilemma. A true dilemma might be exemplified in a choice over whether to increase taxes or eliminate art and music classes from the city schools.

Number/amount. Just as you cannot have a *number* of mashed potatoes on your plate, you can't have an *amount* of baked potatoes on your plate. *If it's something you can count, don't use amount.* Therefore, protesters can show a small or large *amount* of frustration, but they don't leave a large *amount* of cans and bottles on the ground when they depart—they leave a large or small *number* of cans and bottles, but a small or large *amount* of trash.

Former/latter. The viewer cannot go back and reread the story to be certain about the order of things. *City council considered tearing down the old library, but another group of citizens offered to restore the building from private contributions. The vote supported the latter.* By the time the viewers hear the last sentence they probably won't remember which was the former and which was the latter.

Unique/Unusual. *Unique* means the only one, different from *all* others. If something is unique, it has no equal. Therefore, something cannot be *more unique* or *most unique*—it's either unique or it's not. When something is rare, uncommon or strange, the word *unusual* may apply.

Literally/figuratively. *Literal* means following the exact words. If two people's hearts *literally burned* with passion, we would need to call the fire department—or probably the morgue. Likewise, if the audience *literally exploded* with laughter, we'd need a cleanup crew. However, the city council could *lit-*

erally bury their history by putting minutes of former meetings underground in a time capsule. The opposite of a *literal* use is a *figurative* one. In a figurative sense, two hearts can *burn* with passion and an audience can *explode* with laughter. Work hard to use these words correctly, but please don't literally die trying.

These are just a few examples of common mistakes in word choice. Pay attention to word usage, and make certain the words you are using are carefully and accurately chosen.

ADDITIONAL TIPS

Be careful with pronouns. Unless located near its antecedent, a pronoun can confuse listeners. *The mayor says he will run again* is easily understood, but *the mayor and the police chief confirmed that he would run again* is not.

Don't be an alleged writer. Reporters sometimes think that using the word *alleged* can substitute for attribution. This mistake can lead the reporter into court as a defendant in a libel suit. Lawyers who help broadcasters defend against libel suits will tell you the words *alleged* and *allegedly* offer us no legal protection from libel suits. Those two words are often used carelessly when a reporter does not know for certain whether what she is writing is accurate, so she includes a hedge word: *John Doe allegedly killed three people during his cross-state crime spree.* If John Doe has been charged with three murders, say *police accuse him of killing three people* or *Doe is charged with three murders.* But, as far as the courts are concerned, the words *alleged, allegedly, purported* and *supposed* do not exist. It is as if you have said *John Doe killed three people during his cross-state crime spree.* If you cannot back that statement up, you'll have committed a mistake that may very well cost you your career. When it comes to accuracy, we cannot afford to be wrong.

Use intonation for direct quotes. If you want to include in your story a direct quote that is especially colorful or important, avoid using the awkward "quote/unquote" method. The anchor's vocal intonation and emphasis will help clarify which words are a precise quotation.

> The president's words—I did not have sexual relations with that woman—will mark his historical legacy.

Remember to paraphrase information that needs to be attributed. If someone's exact words are used, vocal intonation should indicate the direct quotes.

Avoid the negative—write positive. Don't write about what won't happen. Reword to avoid the negative. Instead of saying *the local college band will not be* *making the trip to perform in Japan,* say *the band has canceled its trip.* Instead of saying the president *will not sign* the budget bill, say the president *will veto* the budget bill.

Avoid clichés. Resorting to clichés is natural when we can't think of something better. A **cliché** is a trite or stale expression: *Only time will tell. Slow as Christmas. Happy as a clam. No stone left unturned. The cart before the horse* in *shark-invested waters* in *the eye of the beholder* as *the tension mounts* in *the sands of time* with everything *up for grabs like clockwork* before something *bites the dust.* The best writers coin their own phrases and don't have one team *drawing first blood, winning the battle but losing the war* and *meeting their Waterloo* all in the same game. The solution is to think more. Avoid clichés.

Don't hyphenate. Don't break a word at the end of a line. Remember, the goal is for anyone to be able to pick up the story and read it cold.

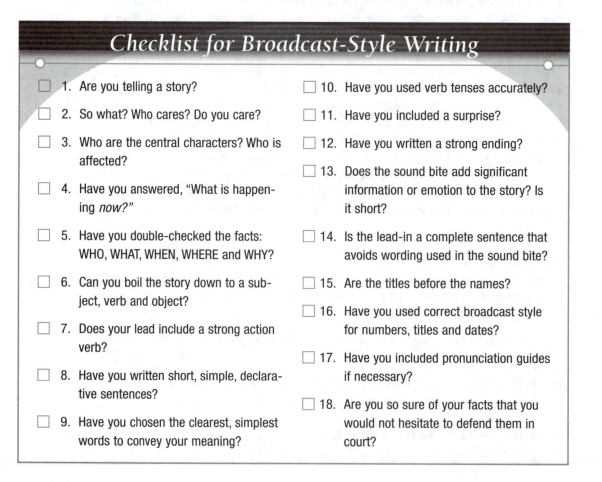

Checklist for Broadcast-Style Writing

☐ 1. Are you telling a story?

☐ 2. So what? Who cares? Do you care?

☐ 3. Who are the central characters? Who is affected?

☐ 4. Have you answered, "What is happening *now?*"

☐ 5. Have you double-checked the facts: WHO, WHAT, WHEN, WHERE and WHY?

☐ 6. Can you boil the story down to a subject, verb and object?

☐ 7. Does your lead include a strong action verb?

☐ 8. Have you written short, simple, declarative sentences?

☐ 9. Have you chosen the clearest, simplest words to convey your meaning?

☐ 10. Have you used verb tenses accurately?

☐ 11. Have you included a surprise?

☐ 12. Have you written a strong ending?

☐ 13. Does the sound bite add significant information or emotion to the story? Is it short?

☐ 14. Is the lead-in a complete sentence that avoids wording used in the sound bite?

☐ 15. Are the titles before the names?

☐ 16. Have you used correct broadcast style for numbers, titles and dates?

☐ 17. Have you included pronunciation guides if necessary?

☐ 18. Are you so sure of your facts that you would not hesitate to defend them in court?

Defend every word. Literally, be able to defend every word you use in a story in case you have to do so in a courtroom. Be sure that every word is accurate—every sentence is true. Speaking of clichés, the one that says *when in doubt, don't* is a good one to remember. If you are not absolutely, positively sure of the information in your story, do not include it. If you're unclear or confused about some of the information, do not try to make it sound good and include it. Find clarification and eliminate your confusion. If you don't get it right, the audience doesn't get it right, and you have failed at your job.

Do have someone else proofread. It is a good idea to read aloud to someone else in the newsroom so she can help you edit and finalize your story. Beginning reporters sometimes don't want anyone to hear or see their story until it goes on the air. In essence, they would rather make a mistake in front of an audience of tens of thousands than in front of one or two. Let someone else read your story. Seek out someone to read it. If reporters look out for one another, they will all become better writers. And you'll catch errors before you suffer the embarrassment of hearing your mistake on the air.

CONCLUSION

Writing for broadcast has different style requirements from other types of writing because the copy should be conversational and is intended to be read aloud. Because the purpose of news is to bring an audience up to date on important events, verb tense must be managed carefully. The writer wants to report what is happening in the present, but he must be careful not to distort the use of present tense by using it to describe events that clearly happened in the past. Similarly, broadcast writing sounds much more interesting in active voice rather than passive voice. Finally, broadcast writers must learn a few very specific rules that are designed to make their stories easier to read aloud. Television news reporters earn their salaries in large part by their command of the language, and they must constantly work to fine-tune these word skills.

KEY CONCEPTS

distorted present tense	present perfect	acronym
verb tense	active voice	it's/its
present tense	passive voice	cliché
present progressive tense	attribution	

Activities

1. Find a story in a newspaper and rewrite it in broadcast style using the broadcast-style checklist.

2. Make a list of the surprises you find in stories from a newscast.

3. Listen for verb tenses. Do the tenses you hear accurately represent when the action happened?

4. Listen for titles and names. Are the titles stated before the names? Is information attributed to someone whose title is given, but whose name is omitted?

5. Listen for numbers. Are they simplified?

6. Tape and transcribe three stories in a particular newscast. Analyze the writing. Is it conversational? Do the reporters tell interesting stories?

WRITING ASSIGNMENTS

1. For each of the following stories, find the most important information and write seven different broadcast leads, as described below the stories.

STORY 1:

A public hearing was held yesterday in Franklin County about proposals to change regulations on surface mining of coal. Current regulations allow miners to use dynamite to clear away mountain tops to remove coal and deposit the refuse in valleys without government oversight. According to miners, the practice has resulted in more usable flat land for commercial industrial development and for farm development. According to environmental groups, the practice has resulted in too much debris in streams that causes flooding. The changes, which would require the practice to be subject to government regulation, are proposed by the U. S. Department of Surface Mining. More than 200 people attended the hearing. One woman said, "It's time to start thinking of us and jobs instead of the environment." A man said, "I'm not against mining, but we should not destroy our planet." The wife of a coal miner said, "Mountaintop mining provides jobs." A member of Franklin County Environmentalists said, "These jobs have not helped the economy. Look at the town of Appalachia. The economy is in horrible shape in spite of the mountaintop mining." This was the third public hearing on the topic before the EPA decision, which is expected next month.

STORY 2:

The current maximum cost of a building permit in Sullivan County is $200. Commissioners may raise the top price to $550. The proposal was submitted to commissioners by the Zoning and Planning Board at last night's meeting, and the board is expected to vote on the proposal at next month's meeting. Zoning and planning fees have not been raised in ten years, and Zoning Director Maria Gomez says the increase will help her office recover costs. She told commissioners that the increase would bring in $17,800 more, raising income to $107,000 from the current $90,000 per year. Currently, the fee for a house valued at $150,000 or more is $200. Under the new rate structure, houses valued at more than $500,000 would require a $550 permit. The permit fee would be increased for each $50,000 of home value for those above a value of $200,000. All houses valued at $150,000 or less would cost $200 for the building permit.

Write a lead in each of the following tenses:

    a. Present tense (an accurate portrayal of what is happening now)

    b. Continuing present tense

    c. Present progressive tense

    d. Past tense

    e. Present perfect tense

    f. Future tense

    g. Distorted present tense (This exercise is to make sure you understand distorted present tense—not to encourage its use.)

2. In the stories given above, identify all passive-voice sentences and rewrite them in active voice.

3. Prepare the following for broadcast by giving the title before the name and writing as succinctly as possible.

    a. Kyle Shuman is the chief of the Wilson County Fire Department.

    b. Kyle Shuman is the chief of the Wilson County Fire Department and has been with the department for 27 years.

    c. Joann Simpson is treasurer of the city.

d. Lance Armstrong has won the Tour de France five times and is an American.

_____

_____

e. Anna Suzuki is 13 years old and has a pilot's license.

_____

_____

f. Tom Cruise has been an actor for many years.

_____

_____

g. Sam Jones was convicted of stealing more than $500, which is considered a felony.

_____

_____

WORK CITED

Potter, D. "I'd Like to Buy a Verb." *The Communicator,* July 2000, pp. 48, 49.

Shooting is music. It's a waltz; it's hip-hop, R&B. You put it all together

and it's a composition with rhythm.

ERIC SCOTT, WJZ-TV, BALTIMORE

SHOOTING VIDEO I

SHOOTING VIDEO, like making music, is an art. Anyone can pluck the strings of a guitar, but only a few become great guitarists. The same is true of using a video camera. Anyone can do it, but few achieve great quality. This chapter examines techniques and principles for well-composed and well-lit video that also captures sound effectively.

Video defines television, providing pictures that enhance a story and make it real. The pictures can be what some professionals refer to as merely "wallpaper"— pictures that get pasted on the screen merely to cover the story. Or the video can work with the story, define the story and make it clear and exciting to the viewer. You may have noticed that watching something on television can be better than watching the event in person. When you attend a concert, for example, you have one view of the stage from where you sit, in essence giving you the same picture the entire time. In contrast, a music video of the group will give you close-up shots of the lead singer from all sorts of angles, interspersed with a variety of views of the drummer, the guitarist and the keyboard player. The pictures provide angles and viewpoints that the music fan at the concert might never envision. In a music video, the imagination and creativity of the photographer help bring the music to life. Similarly, the work of the news photographer determines much of the success of television news. The gratification of completing a final product that is seen by thousands comes immediately.

As the quote at the top of the chapter indicates, shooting video can be musical. It also points out that the rhythm comes when the shots are put together or **edited.** The photographer determines the possibilities for the final editing of the story. Good television photographers understand good editing. A fabulously creative shot may be useless if it doesn't fit into the story. Other shots may be impossible to use if the photographer hasn't captured appropriate pictures that can tie them together. When photographers understand editing, they are more likely to get the appropriate amount of video and the appropriate kinds of shots. Good photographers understand the principles of editing, examined in Chapter 9, just as they understand the basics of good shooting.

DEFINING PHOTOJOURNALISM

News photographers have professional skill and expertise that go far beyond operating cameras and editing systems. The shooting and editing allow the news photographer to be creative and artistic, but the person with the camera must also master reporting skills. The appropriate title for those who do both the photography and the reporting in television news is **photojournalist.** And nothing insults a photojournalist more than to be referred to as a "cameraman" or "camerawoman."

The television photographer or videographer holds important responsibility for accuracy in reporting and also serves as a **gatekeeper.** A gatekeeper controls the entry of material into or out of media outlets. For example, a news photographer could make a protest by three people look like a major event by the way she photographs the marchers. The simple decision about where to point the camera carries with it the power to determine what to include or exclude from a newscast.

> The art stuff is good, but it shouldn't be a priority. The journalism is the most important. Everybody wants to be Steven Spielberg, but they forget about Edward R. Murrow. Some of the most important stories are the run-of-the-mill events like city council.
>
> *Mike Porras*
> **KCNC-TV, DENVER**

Photojournalists are responsible for both gathering information and getting pictures that advance the story. They must know how to talk to people and ask the right questions. They need to communicate the information clearly. Even when news photographers are working with reporters, they can make the story succeed or fail by the pictures they capture. One photojournalist gathered pictures for a business story assignment and was later frustrated when the story was rewritten to focus on an emotional aspect of the story. He commented that the story was OK, but "It's not the story I shot. I could have shot a story like that, but that wasn't what I was assigned to do." This reaction reveals a lot about a committed photojournalist. He took ownership of the assignment from the beginning, considered the specific purpose of the story and used his professional judgment in how to make the story work. His comment makes it clear that he would have done things differently if his understanding of the angle of the story had been different.

Much of the success of the news story lies with the photojournalist's understanding of news. Anyone who wants merely to shoot nice pictures without thinking about the context of what's happening will harm the news process. The photographer must first understand the story and why it is important. This understanding will require communication with the reporter and some background in the political, economic and legal forces at work in society. At the scene, the photographer will survey the area, attempt to understand the specific event and examine the possibilities of showing the context for the story: What's going on? What can you see? What do you hear? Where are the best shots? What caused the event and how can the causes be illustrated? All of these questions must be answered according to the purpose of the story: What are we trying to do? The photographer must always be alert: What is the interviewee talking about? What pictures will help illustrate the interviewee's comments? What will you have to do to get those pictures?

When covering breaking news, the photojournalist must anticipate. If police officers will be bringing a suspect out of the courthouse, which door will it be? Which way will they walk? If they change directions, how can you get the shot? How can you get pictures that will be different and better than anyone else's? What can you think of that no one else will consider?

Once photojournalists master a few basic principles of good video and understand the important role they play, they can choose from many shooting styles. Today, many photojournalists shoot so the camera moves constantly. Instead of a steady shot of a face, the camera will appear to shift slightly during the shot, perhaps upward or to the right or left. Instead of holding one picture on screen for a couple of seconds, the editing pace may be very fast, so that multiple images appear within a single second. This popular video style can be very effective, but steady shots, with lots of close-ups and slow fades from one shot to another, can also create a strong impact on the viewer. Moreover, good, clear video, edited smoothly and steadily, will always have its place. This chapter focuses on the classic shooting style of steady shots that are carefully composed according to fundamental artistic principles. As you gain experience in shooting, you may discover your own unique style, and you may decide to break the rules, but some basics remain constant for achieving quality video. Those who decide to shoot in other styles will need to master these basics first. Before looking at the how-to's of shooting, let's define the terms that apply to this part of television news reporting.

> The photographer has to believe in the reporter's idea because the photographer eventually takes charge of the piece. The reporter may say, "Here's my idea of the story," and they discuss it, but the two have to trust each other.
>
> *Dale Solly*

THE LANGUAGE OF VIDEO

Three terms are used almost interchangeably to describe those who shoot video for broadcast news. The word **videographer** came into use with the advent of video cameras in television news departments. The word merges video technology with the term *photographer,* which had previously applied to the person who took pictures with a still camera. Today, we often call those who shoot video "videographers," but we also continue to refer to them as *photographers* or *news photographers.* The term *photojournalist* is generally used to identify those who have responsibility for gathering both the pictures and the facts of the story. In casual newsroom talk, we may also refer to the news photographers as *shooters* or *photogs.* Remember that the professional responsibilities of those who carry the cameras go far beyond skill in shooting and editing video. Please keep these responsibilities in mind as we concentrate on the narrower instruction in shooting and editing video.

Today, the responsibilities of the photographer and reporter overlap more often as news departments use one person who both shoots video and reports—a practice still referred to as a **one-man band,** despite the fact that the one-man band is quite likely to be a woman. A more appropriate short reference is the *S-P-O,* or single-person operation. Today, the person with the ability both to shoot video and work as a reporter will find more career opportunities and won't have to forgo covering an important news event for lack of another person to help. We will use all of these terms—*videographer, photographer, shooter, photog* and *photojournalist*—interchangeably as we discuss the skills and responsibilities of those who use a video camera in television news departments.

> As a news photographer, you capture the most joyous moments of people's lives and the most tragic. People will love you and they'll scream hatred at you. If you don't recognize the emotions and feel them, you won't be a photojournalist.
>
> *Bob Burke*
> **KCNC-TV, DENVER**

When the photographer goes into the field to work on a story, he refers to the video he captures on a tape as the **shoot tape.** When the photographer takes the shoot tape back to the station, he copies selected images from the shoot tape to the **edit tape.** In the field, the photographer will concentrate on the basic types of shots: *wide, medium* and *tight,* referring to the distance the action appears to be from the camera. The wide shot that appears early in the story is often called an **establishing shot** because it gives the viewer a sense of where the action is taking place. The shot *establishes* the location.

The photographer captures action within the viewfinder, but she will sometimes provide motion in a *zoom* or a *pan.* In a **zoom,** the photographer moves the camera perspective in or out, toward or away from the subject, by depressing the automatic zoom control on the camera but without any actual camera movement. For real movement, the camera can be mounted on a tripod that sits on a **dolly.** The dolly is a set of wheels designed to hold a tripod to allow the camera to roll toward or away from the subject. In a **pan,** the photographer moves the camera to the right or left or from the top to bottom of the shot, by swiveling the camera on the tripod or by moving the camera on a dolly.

The photographer may shoot an interesting variety of **cutaway** shots, or pictures of things surrounding the primary action of the news story that make sense when juxtaposed or edited beside the primary action. In other words, when the editor needs to *cut away* from the action, the photographer will have provided plenty of video for that purpose. **B-roll** is a term for the pictures that cover the primary sound track in a video story. B-roll and cutaways can certainly contain action, but the terms suggest that these pictures are secondary to something else that is happening on the tape, such as the reporter narration or an interview.

The photographer often gathers appropriate video for **interview cutaways.** The interview cutaway may be a reporter reaction shot or B-roll related to the subject of the conversation. Most news stories include an interview with one or more persons who have some special credibility for commenting on the news event. The photographer thinks of the interview as a special type of shot because it is not a major action, not a cutaway and not B-roll.

The interview results in the *sound bite,* or the short part of the interview that is selected to be edited into the story. The interview may be set up as a **two-shot,** a picture composition that includes both the reporter and the interviewee, or a **one-shot** or **close-up,** where only one individual is included in the shot. Sometimes the photographer may zoom in to a close-up from a two-shot as the interview progresses. Similarly, the reporter's **stand-up** requires a different approach.

As discussed later in this chapter, a reporter uses a stand-up for a variety of purposes: to provide a visual when there is no appropriate video, to reveal something, to show participation or location, or to provide transition. To shoot a good stand-up, the photographer and reporter will work together so both have a clear understanding of the goals of the shot and where the focus will be. The reporter may stand still and speak directly into the camera, in which case the photographer will compose and hold a steady shot. If the reporter walks or demonstrates something, the photographer must ensure that the action gets the proper focus and that the shot composition remains in balance. For example, the reporter might open a dry ear of corn during a stand-up to demonstrate the devastation of a drought. If the report is from a carnival, the reporter might use the Ferris wheel in the background to emphasize the location. The reporter may walk a few steps from the opening of a pipe to the edge of a stream to show the source of pollution. In all these cases, the photographer will need a clear understanding of how the stand-up will be executed to maintain proper framing of the shot.

> When you arrive at a story, leave the gear in the car unless the house is burning. Shake hands with the subjects and find things in common . . . all the while trying to figure out a good interview location. If you take a few minutes to get to know people, they'll be more at ease and you'll get a better interview. Most importantly, they will know you as a person with a camera instead of a cameraperson . . . big difference!
>
> *Les Rose*
> **CBS NEWS, LOS ANGELES**

To summarize, the photographer goes into the field to capture video to bring a news story to life. Using a video camera, the photog captures images for use in the final news story. The news photographer is concerned with getting plenty of appropriate pictures and will think in terms of establishing shots and other wide, medium and tight shots. In consultation with the reporter, the photographer decides how to shoot interviews and stand-ups. To achieve these goals, the news photographer should learn the fundamentals of composing good shots. Some days your shooting will be "music" and the composition will be free and creative, but on the days when you don't "feel the music," you must rely on the basics.

FRAMING SKILLS

Once a videographer has learned the basic operation of the camera, the next goal is to learn to compose shots that look good. This chapter does not concern itself with basic camera operation, because each camera is different, and camera technology changes. However, the basics of composing a shot do not change.

When we talk about composing the shot, the skill begins with learning when to have the camera in record or pause mode and when to turn it off. The shot should be *composed* or *framed up* before the camera's record mode is turned on. Most often, the composing will be done in pause mode. When the shot is ready, the photographer will record and then return to pause mode. By judicious use of the record on–off button, the photographer actually does some *in-camera editing* by shooting only pictures that may be useful. Having the camera on while moving it into position for the shot leaves a lot of useless footage on the tape. Anyone who has ever left a camera running while carrying it back to the car and putting it into the case knows how irritating the shaky pictures of the ground can be. On the other hand, most cameras require a second or two to begin operating at peak performance, and we will offer advice later in this section on how long to hold a shot to ensure adequate footage. One of the first considerations in composing a good shot is to fill the screen.

Fill the Screen

Once the photographer understands the importance of steady video, the second goal is to *fill the screen*. What are you showing the audience? If you are interviewing someone, fill the screen with the person. You do not serve any purpose by having space above, below or to the right or left of the person.

Sometimes a neophyte photographer will frame a person at a desk with lots of space showing the wall behind. The beginner reasons that she should include the picture on the wall in the shot. Not so. First, the picture on the wall must be relevant to the story or it should not appear. Assume we are doing a story on an astronaut and the picture on the wall shows her with the crew of the space shuttle. In this case, the picture adds meaning to the story. Even so, including both the person and the picture in a shot means that the viewer will not see either one very well. Instead, fill the screen with the person, and then fill the screen with a shot of the picture to edit into the story. The audience sees a clear, close-up shot of the person, framed with mid-chest at the bottom of the screen and the top of the head close to the top of the screen. While the audience continues to hear the person's voice, a close-up shot of the picture appears. The picture will fill the screen, then the person will reappear.

At the site of tornado damage, you might want to capture a general shot of debris, but the viewer will recognize only rubble. If you want the viewer to see the teddy bear in the heap of devastation, fill the screen with the teddy bear. The full-screen teddy bear can follow the full-screen shot of rubble, and in both cases, the viewer sees what the photographer intended. An item that is large or small can fill the screen. The helicopter landing on the beach can be framed so that the aircraft fills the screen—top edge just above the helicopter blades and landing runners at the bottom of the screen. If the reporter is talking about a small paper carton of juice, fill the entire screen with the small juice container. You can argue that a wider shot of the grocery store aisle clearly shows the juice section and even the name of the product. Perhaps. But a shot of the juice section is just that—a section of the shelf. If the story is about a particular juice, let the viewer see the juice carton up close and clearly after the wider shot. If you want the viewer to look at an engagement ring, fill the screen with the ring, not hand and arm.

Think in Thirds

A sure way to fill the screen and feel confident that you have a well-composed shot is to employ the **rule of thirds.** In the rule of thirds, the photographer thinks of the video screen as a grid that guides the composition of the shot (see Exhibit 7.1). Imagine the screen divided into nine equal blocks by two evenly spaced vertical lines and two horizontal lines. In other words, draw an imaginary tic-tac-toe puzzle across the viewfinder or monitor. The primary focus—the part of the shot that is most important to see—should be at one of the intersections of the top horizontal line with the vertical lines. In other words, you want the focus of your shot to be slightly to the right or left of center instead of exactly in the middle and about one-third of the way down from the top. (See Exhibit 7.2.)

If you are shooting an interview, the person's eyes should fall along the top horizontal line. If you watch any news program or news magazine, you will discover that in virtually every shot of a person talking, the eyes will fall along the top horizontal line in the imaginary tic-tac-toe grid.

When a viewer looks at a video screen, her eyes naturally move in a Z pattern from the upper left corner of the center tic-tac-toe box to the top right corner

EXHIBIT 7.1   The imaginary rule of thirds grid guides the photographer in composing the shot.

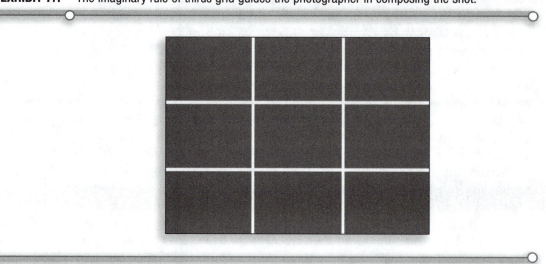

of the box, then to the bottom left and on to the bottom right. This expected pattern is known as the **Z-principle,** and it can guide photographers in composing effective shots (see Exhibit 7.3). (The "natural" movement in a Z pattern most likely comes from the habit in Western cultures of reading from left to right and top to bottom.)

The rule of thirds and the Z-principle apply to any shot. You should not frame a single object in the very center of the screen. Our normal vision patterns pull

EXHIBIT 7.2   The focus of the shot should be slightly to the right or to the left of center.

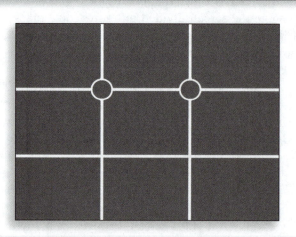

us to one of the top corners of the center square, even when there is lots of activity in the shot. (See Exhibit 7.4.) In a shot of a school bus surrounded by people, the person standing in the area at one of the two top corners of the center box will be the most noticed; accordingly, the photographer will want to choose exactly who or what is located in that area. In a shot of a ship on the ocean, the photographer will want to frame the ship along or slightly inside one of the right or left sides of the center box, preferably with the ship leading into or out of one or more of the corners of the center box. In a shot of a pharmacist scraping pills into a prescription bottle, the action should be framed in the focus areas alongside or slightly inside the corners of the center box. (See Exhibit 7.5 for examples of these shots.) Understanding the rule of thirds and the normal vision pattern of viewers enables the photographer to compose shots and decide exactly what will get the most focus.

To review, the most basic requirement for framing a good camera shot is to fill the screen with what you want the audience to see. Remember the rule of thirds so that the primary focal point falls at the intersection of the top horizontal line with one of the vertical lines, or at one of the top corners of the inside box of the imaginary tic-tac-toe grid. When the shot is framed properly, your next consideration is to make sure the camera runs long enough for useful editing.

The 10-Second Rule

When you have framed a shot and turned the record mode on, hold the shot for a count of 10. You'll think 10 seconds seems like an eternity, but when it is time

The natural pattern for looking at a picture follows a Z pattern: **EXHIBIT 7.3** from left to right, diagonally downward, and left to right again.

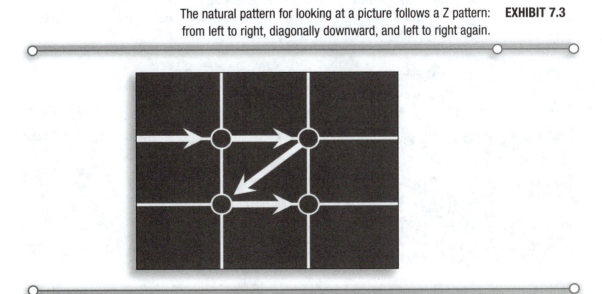

EXHIBIT 7.4 The rule of thirds and Z-principle apply to any well-composed shot.

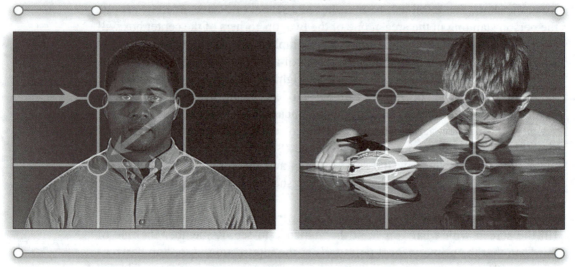

to edit, you'll appreciate having enough video to work with. In fact, some professionals insist on counting to 12 or 15 with the "one-thousand-one . . . one-thousand-two" method. Often, it takes a second or two to adjust the composition of the shot, or if there's a lot of action, you may want to use several seconds of an interesting shot. The old adage "better safe than sorry" applies here. If you have a shot but it's too short to use, you may as well not have it. You cannot wish a shot into becoming longer when you're in the editing room. Get plenty of shots, and make sure you have enough of each shot to provide flexibility in editing. To ensure that you have adequate video, frame the shot and hold it while you count to 10.

EXHIBIT 7.5 In any well-composed shot, the focus falls along the right or left vertical line in the imaginary grid.

Hold the Camera Still

For a quick lesson in how *not* to shoot video, go to a tourist attraction and watch amateurs shooting video. You will see people moving a camera up and down and right and left and back to the right, all very quickly, thinking they're doing a good job of showing the impressive height of a building or the large size of a crowd. Just watching the motion of the camera will make your head spin. Imagine how unpleasant it will be to watch the video.

A video camera *captures* motion. The camera does not need to *provide* the motion. For the beginning photographer, the most basic and important rule is to *hold the camera still*. Frame the shot, turn on the record mode and capture motion within the viewfinder. Do not provide motion by moving the camera.

Use a Tripod

Holding the camera still basically means using a tripod. In professional jargon, the tripod is sometimes referred to as *the sticks*. A tripod provides an easy way to hold the camera still. Even though carrying the tripod can be a nuisance, good photographers know that shaky video, especially on tight shots, can distract the viewer from the story's message. Even in breaking news situations, many professional videographers use a tripod. If it is not possible to carry a tripod, professionals use a table, wall or post as a method of steadying the shot, so they can direct the viewer's attention to the subject and not to the camera work itself. Some experienced photographers can manage to hold a camera steady enough that motion is virtually undetectable in most situations, but it is a mistake to watch a long-time pro shoot from the shoulder and assume that you can achieve the same quality.

When a Tripod Can't Be Used

Using a tripod is always best, but occasionally it is not possible. For the times when shoulder shooting is a necessity, remember that shots with a lot of action are less likely to reveal shakiness. For example, a shoulder-held shot on a football play can easily work because there is lots of action in the shot. If you're following someone walking down a street, a tripod is obviously out of the question, but the motion of the person's walking probably overpowers the shakiness of the shoulder shot. Conversely, a shoulder shot of a judge issuing a verdict from the bench in a courtroom cannot be steady enough to avoid the distraction of shakiness. If a tripod is simply not an option, a wide shot is much less likely to appear shaky than a tight shot. When a photog-

If it's important enough to shoot, it's important to get a good shot. . . . The excuses for not using a tripod are few and far between. Ninety-nine percent of the time, you can get it from a tripod. . . . Here's another tip for photographers. Carry a little flashlight. You can do wonders with it.

Steve Youngerman
KCNC-TV, DENVER

rapher is close to the subject and has to shoot from the shoulder, she zooms out to frame the shot. The wider field of view will make any movement less noticeable. If the project is important and you need steady video, take the time and trouble to use a tripod.

SHOOTING VIDEO IN THE FIELD
Get Plenty of Shots

Getting plenty of shots means getting plenty of B-roll. The term refers to the idea that the narrator or subject speaking on camera provides the foundation of a story: the *A track*. The pictures that cover the narrator provide the second track, or the B-roll.

When reporters get the opportunity to write, shoot and edit their own stories, they begin to understand the importance of shooting plenty of video. In some newsrooms, the shooter does not edit the story, but the editor hopes the shooter understands the editing process. With quick-paced editing designed to hold the attention of the viewer, a story demands many different shots. One shot may be used for a mere one or two seconds, so that if you cover a one-minute story with two-second shots, the story would need 30 different usable shots. Despite your best effort, not every shot will be usable, even though every shot will take time and energy to set up—another way of saying it's hard work.

> The best way to become a good photographer is to edit. You'll quickly discover the shots you needed and didn't get.
>
> *Steve Youngerman*
> **KCNC-TV, DENVER**

At an accident, the photographer shoots the wrecked vehicles from different sides and different angles, but he also looks for other pictures that can enhance the story or provide transitions or cutaways: the rescue vehicles, the bystanders, the road signs, the skid marks, the emergency medical team, the police officers directing traffic and those writing reports, the license tag, the cracked windshield, the backed-up traffic. This list includes 10 possibilities. A wide, medium and tight shot of each subject would yield 30 shots.

Video projects often require an entire day of shooting that will show up as a few seconds on tape. Prepare to spend lots of time achieving the quality that the average viewer takes for granted. The effort sounds thankless, but broadcasting colleagues recognize the effort, the audience knows whether the story is good or bad and, more importantly, you know whether you did your best. Get plenty of shots.

Shoot Wide, Medium and Tight

One way to get plenty of shots is to shoot wide, medium and tight on everything. The wide shot or establishing shot gives the viewer a sense of where the action is taking place. At the scene of a fire, first shoot a wide shot, perhaps showing a street sign in the foreground or some other identifying landmark with the burning building in the distance, to give the viewer a sense of location. The next shot will show a medium-distance view that includes the burning building, but none of the surroundings. Then find close-up shots of rescue workers or other interesting pictures. Remember, you can shoot wide, medium and tight on everything. Shoot a full-screen shot of the rescuer administering CPR and then tighten in to show a waist-up shot, followed by a tight shot of the rescuer's sweating face and furrowed brow.

> You can always rely on the basics—like wide, medium and tight—to get you through the stressful times and the freaky situations.
>
> *Bob Burke*
> **KCNC-TV, DENVER**

Angled Shots

In striving to get plenty of interesting shots, the photographer should work at finding interesting angles. Unusual angles can give the audience a perspective it would not ordinarily have. The standard angle for shooting video is tripod height—around stomach or upper-chest level. We are accustomed to seeing the politician speaking from a podium or the view of the horizon from this perspective. Shooting from different angles can add variety and interest to video. Consider a shot of the basketball team during a time-out where the photographer shoots from his back on the floor looking up into the center of the huddle. Instead of the expected tripod-level or shoulder-level shot from outside the huddle, the audience sees a view they would not ordinarily have access to. (The coach might veto the idea, or the photographer could get trampled, but the shot would be an interesting one.)

Angles and creative shots should reflect the viewer's perspective on the scene—and should not confuse the audience. For example, in a story about the boredom in life behind bars, an extreme close-up of a drip shot from above a water faucet as it falls and hits the drain of the sink could be either interesting or confusing. Assume the story begins with a shot looking from a walkway through prison bars and into the cell. If the next shot looks down onto the drip from above the faucet, the audience may not understand the connection to a prison cell. A more careful setup, however, could make the shot more effective. The viewer sees a wide view of the cell. Next, there's a tighter shot from behind the prisoner, where he sits on the bed looking toward the sink and the dripping faucet. Then, the angle above the faucet looking down as the water hits the drain makes sense. The photographer leads the viewer through a logical series of pictures and places the unusual angle on the drip into a context the audience can understand.

If your job is to capture video in a classroom, the first shot will be a wide shot of students at desks—the establishing shot. If the next shot is an extreme close-up from an angle at floor level showing a shoe digging into a spot on the floor, viewers may have difficulty understanding why they're looking at the shoe. When the photographer precedes the close-up of the shoe with a medium shot of one student at a desk staring into space and wiggling a leg, the next shot makes more sense and gives the audience more understanding about the student who is not paying attention. The floor-level angle is placed in context.

Shooting from different angles may require some reference point to help the audience maintain its perspective. If a news story requires pictures of an open land area chosen for the location of a new shopping center, shooting from different angles could confuse the viewer. If the wide shot of the land includes a barn, however, the medium shot could include one side of the barn and some of the area behind it. Keeping the building in the shot helps the audience to understand what they are seeing. If the series of shots leads us toward the barn and beside the barn, a shot from the loft of the barn might provide an interesting angle on the property and make sense to the viewer. A shot toward the window of the barn before the shot from the loft might help the audience maintain its perspective.

If you're shooting a building, shoot from an angle rather than head-on. Finding an angle will give depth to your shot. Try shooting from the corner so that the texture of the building shows. Frame the shot so that a clump of grass or a bunch of flowers adds interest, depth and texture to the shot.

Angles sometimes have social meaning. For example, the judge's bench sits on a level higher than the rest of the court participants. The judge's height forces attorneys and jury members to look up. We "look up" to people we respect. Arrogant people may "look down" on others. These angles can reinforce a message in video, so the photographer must make sure to choose an angle that appropriately represents the story. If a little girl is dying because her state's health care system will not pay for a kidney transplant, you would use a different angle from what is appropriate when a judge issues a ruling. The photographer might choose to angle the camera downward slightly to show the child in the hospital bed—the way she is most commonly seen. When the doctor is examining the girl, the photographer might kneel on the floor beside the bed and shoot up toward the doctor, for an angle that reflects the little girl's perspective. Reversing the normal angle can also be interesting. Instead of looking down on the homeless man sitting on the street and begging for money, the camera operator could sit on the concrete beside the man to capture his image. The audience is no longer "looking down" on the homeless man and may gain insight by seeing the world from his perspective. In short, rather than automatically shooting head-on, think angles.

Pans and Zooms

Remember from the discussion of holding the camera still that the action should happen within the viewfinder, not come from the movement of the camera. This principle basically means to *avoid pans and zooms*. Few people will disagree that camera motion can be distracting, but beginning videographers insist on zooming and panning despite all advice to the contrary.

Avoiding Pans and Zooms

Let's assume you're shooting a story about jail conditions and you want to show the rusty, leaking pipes, the broken handles and the falling-down ceiling in a narrow shower stall. You don't have much room to move, and you really can't get a good wide (establishing) shot. One possibility would be to start at the top and move the camera down to show the pipes and the handles and continue the movement to show the stopped-up drain—a pan from top to bottom. We might reason that this shot will show the entire shower stall, in all its broken, nasty condition. However, the result is a moving shot that gives the viewer a quick impression without detail. A much better approach would be to begin with a shot as wide as possible of the broken handles and stall. This allows the viewers to know they are seeing a shower stall, and they will understand the shots that follow: a tight, clear close-up of the broken handles; a tight, clear shot of the rotting ceiling; a tight shot of the stopped-up, moldy drain. This approach gives the viewer more detail than can be provided in a pan.

Pans and zooms can also make editing difficult. In the field, you might shoot a nice steady 10-second zoom. When the narration is ready, however, you need only five seconds of video. To use five seconds of the zoom, the editor has three alternatives: (1) starting the shot in the middle of the zooming motion and ending at the end of the zoom, (2) starting at the beginning of the zoom and ending the shot in the middle of the zoom, or (3) using the beginning and end of the zooming motion. None of these choices is easy to execute effectively. Special editing effects make it possible to fade or dissolve into a zooming action and diminish the jolt of a sudden, unnecessary action. However, editors in newsrooms do not always have access to the equipment necessary for this technique as they put together daily news stories. Remember that it's usually best to avoid pans and zooms—unless there's a strong motivation.

> In news, we are reflecting the human condition and the human eye does not pan, zoom or tilt. That is why we use tripods and steadybags, and shoot wide when we have to shoot off the shoulder.
>
> *Dave Wertheimer*
> **KSTP/KSTC-TV,**
> **MINNEAPOLIS/ST. PAUL, MINN.**

Motivated Pans and Zooms

If we always followed the rule to avoid pans, the video of a football game would be pretty dull. The football play will demand camera action—a **motivated pan,** a pan that follows real movement. Pans and zooms that follow real movement—motivated pans and zooms—can and should be used. Imagine the photographer composing the shot on the quarterback as he prepares to throw the ball. The camera remains focused on the quarterback as the ball leaves the quarterback's hands, sails down the field and is caught by a wide receiver, who then dodges tackles and makes his way down the field—all unseen by the camera. Obviously, the photographer needs to follow the action of the ball. What's the difference between panning to follow the football and panning from one building to another or from one side of the Grand Canyon to the other? The difference is that the movement of the football provides a reason to pan. With two stationary buildings, you can show their relationship with one steady wide shot. When someone is walking, you will follow the action. The camera moves to follow real movement.

Rules always seem to have exceptions. In fact, the motivations for panning and zooming do not always require real movement. We sometimes need to move the camera to the right or left or move in or out of a scene to show a relationship between a person and another person or object. Suppose you are shooting video of a rescue worker at the scene of an accident, and the worker is administering CPR in close proximity to high-speed traffic. In this case, showing the worker and then showing a shot of the traffic would not reveal the risk involved in the rescue, so you may choose to show the rescuer working on a victim and then do a short pan to the right or left, where the viewer can see cars speeding by.

Pans and zooms can be used effectively in other situations, but again, they are seldom required. In an interview, the photographer may zoom in for an extreme close-up when the source begins to reveal sensitive information. When a public official begins a statement that the reporter and photographer know to be a lie, the zoom-in emphasizes the fact that the public official is lying. The photographer may zoom out to reveal something about the surroundings at a particular time.

The motivation may be to provide movement in an otherwise static shot, such as in a news story that requires using still photographs. If you use a snapshot of a family that includes a murder victim, a zoom from the full picture to a close-up of the face of the victim would be an effective way to convey information about the victim's life and to emphasize the person's individuality. In a story that relies on historical photographs, pans and zooms can add action and interest to the shots. As the narrator indicates that an inventor married at age 19, the camera pans right from a view of the inventor in an old photograph to reveal the bride at his side. A motivated pan or zoom can work. Otherwise, avoid them.

How to Pan and Zoom

When there is a motivation to pan or zoom, the rule is to begin with a still and steady shot, then pan or zoom slowly and end with a steady, still shot. The hold time allows flexibility in the editing process. Think of the shot as if you're counting out dance steps. Frame the shot and hold-two-three. Pan slowly until you stop and hold-two-three. The same with a zoom. Frame a shot and hold-two-three. Then zoom in or out slowly until you have another nicely composed shot and hold-two-three. We say hold-two-three when we're talking dance steps, but in reality the count-to-10 principle is much better.

Panning and zooming *slowly* is an important part of the rule. If the movement goes too fast, viewers will be dizzy rather than informed. Again, there are exceptions. Sometimes the intention is to put the viewer somewhat on edge. In the television show "NYPD Blue," the setting is New York City and the subject is the gritty work of police detectives. The introduction to the show has the sound of pounding drums and video with lots of short, quick pans and zooms. The result sets the mood for the show in style and pace: a gritty, edgy, pounding city, and crime that makes our heads spin. Even though the technique works for a television drama, it is primarily limited to the introduction, and even in this instance, the pans and zooms mostly start and stop with at least a beat of a steady shot. When we see the pans and zooms within the show, they are infrequent and are usually used to introduce a new scene. Once a conversation begins, the camera movement is greatly reduced. A full hour of the introductory pace would be impossible to bear. Television news photography can have a dramatic impact, but it primarily comes from helping the audience understand a real situation. In news coverage of an actual crime scene and police activity, the viewer needs to see and understand what's happening rather than be led into a mood-setting montage of fast-paced camera action. If you use pans and zooms, make them slow and steady.

SHOOTING INTERVIEWS

Composing good shots is a skill that can always be improved, but steady shots with a full screen of information guided by the rule of thirds are sure to be effective. Avoid pans and zooms, and use them only with a good reason. A pan should be motivated, and the person talking or walking should have both the proper amount of *head room* and *lead room.*

Leave Head Room

The amount of space between the top of the head and the top of the screen is referred to as **head room** or **scan room.** The amount of head room varies depending on the style of the shot, but it is always minimal if there is any at all.

The amount of head room can relate to the formality of the shot. A shot of an anchor on the news set is more formal than a shot of an interviewee in the field. The anchor shot resembles a formal portrait of a U. S. president. The president's eyes will fall along the top imaginary horizontal line in the rule of thirds, and there will be some space between the top of the head and the picture frame (see Exhibit 7.6). Although it's not a professional term, the space is never more than a sliver.

When a shot is less formal than an anchor presenting the news from an impressive studio set, it may be tighter. Imagine a shot of a man framed so that the cutoff point is just below the knot in his tie at upper chest level. In this shot, the man's hair may actually disappear off the top of the screen. The shot could be framed even tighter, so that the cutoff is close to the top of the collar and the top of the screen falls along the hairline at the very top of the forehead. In an extreme close-up, the cutoff could even be at the chin line with the top of the screen at the top of the forehead. The composition of the shot can vary greatly, but when the cutoff is at chin level or above, the photographer must leave some indication that the body continues below the chin. (See Exhibit 7.7 for examples of good and bad composition on tight shots of a face.) Without a bit of neck showing, the head can look like it's been chopped off and is sitting on the bottom of the screen. Whether the indication that there is a body attached to the head comes from a shoulder behind the face, from the back of the neck or from some other clue, the camera work should not perform a video decapitation.

The framing of the shot may depend on the subject matter. In most evening news stories, the framing often has the bottom of the screen close to the level of the top button on a man's suit jacket, and there is some space above the head. The subject matter is general and the style is formal. When the mayor is being interviewed in front of City Hall about the campaign for re-election, the framing may fall below the knot of the tie and along the hairline. But if the topic is

EXHIBIT 7.6   In formal shots and portraits, the eyes fall along the top horizontal line in the grid.

The first tight shot (A) is poorly framed. The second tight shot (B) indicates the lines of the **EXHIBIT 7.7** body that extend below the frame, providing a more appealing composition.

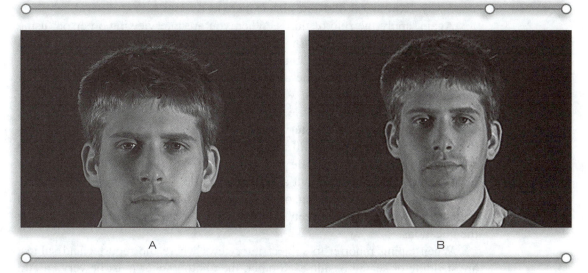

A   B

very intimate and sensitive, the shot may be framed more tightly. When a celebrity is somberly confessing to a drug addiction and the resulting pain to family members, the shot should be framed so the audience can concentrate on what the person is saying—the focus needs to be on the eyes and the mouth during the sensitive moments. This variation reflects the way we interact with others. For a job interview, we sit farther apart and take in a wider view of the person and surroundings. In a very personal conversation with a friend, we sit close together and look into the other person's eyes. Conversely, we would not tell a personal secret to someone from across the room, nor would we engage in a job interview sitting close and looking deep into someone's eyes. In a sense, the camera should reflect the level of intimacy we are accustomed to in our daily interactions.

Leave Lead Room

When you compose an interview shot or a shot that follows an action, you must give the subject forward space to talk into or move into—**lead room.** In the case of an interview, the lead room or space in front of the subject is also referred to as **talk space** or **look space.** In the stationary interview shot, the interviewee will be facing one side of the screen or the other, rather than facing the camera directly. This composition indicates that the subject is talking to the reporter, who is close but off-screen and out of the shot.

If a person is talking toward the edge of the screen with the nose close to the edge and extra space behind, viewers can feel uneasy even if they don't understand why. Exhibit 7.8 illustrates inadequate lead room.

Again, apply the rule of thirds. When you are interviewing a person, using either a chest shot or a tighter shot on the face, you want the person's eyes to fall along the top horizontal line. Frame the person in the screen along one of the vertical lines, and face him in the direction of the other vertical line. Exhibit 7.9 shows proper use of lead room.

It is best to avoid a profile shot; the camera should see both eyes. And because the person is being interviewed, we don't want him to look directly into the camera as a reporter would do. Instead, the interviewee should be angled somewhere between the profile and a direct look into the camera, with both eyes visible—probably at about a 45-degree angle, as shown in Exhibit 7.10B. The person should be talking or looking into space, which the viewer will understand is the space between the interviewee and the reporter who is asking the questions.

When taping reporter-to-subject interviews where the reporter and subject are standing or seated beside each other, the photographer must be very careful that the shot of the subject doesn't turn out to be a full profile shot (see Exhibit 7.11). If you frame up the shot before the conversation begins, you must account for the possibility that the subject may turn his head to look more intently at the reporter when he starts talking. Be sure you know exactly where the reporter and subject will stand or sit and in which direction they will look so that you get a clear view of the subject's face. Even though you may want a two-shot—a profile

EXHIBIT 7.8 In this shot, the photographer fails to provide lead room/talk space so the subject appears to be crowded against the edge of the screen.

With proper talk space, the subject will be aligned along one of the vertical lines   **EXHIBIT 7.9**
in the rule of thirds grid.

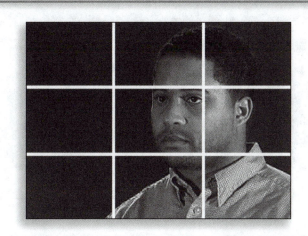

of the two people facing each other—to establish the setting, you should then move the camera closer to the reporter's shoulder to get a desirable framing of the interview subject.

Not all interviews take place with the reporter and subject sitting or standing motionless. Adding action to the interview can create interest.

A complete profile (A) cuts off half the subject's face. The subject should be angled (B)   **EXHIBIT 7.10**
so that both eyes are visible in the shot.

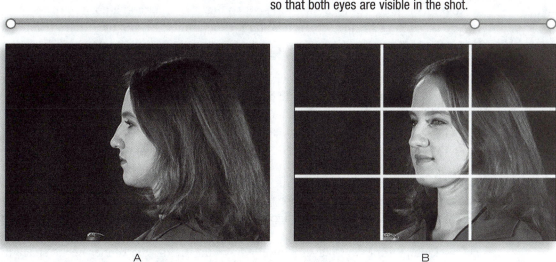

A

B

EXHIBIT 7.11   The photographer must plan ahead to guard against producing a profile of the subject (A and B). If the camera is set up for a shot of both reporter and subject, the camera will need to be moved closer to the reporter's shoulder for a suitable picture of the subject (C).

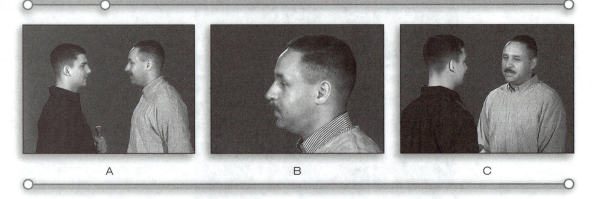

A   B   C

Include Action in the Interview

Consider shooting the subject talking to the reporter or camera while carrying out an action. Imagine interviewing an artist while she is painting a mural on a downtown building. Frame the artist with a chest shot and shoot the video while the artist is simultaneously painting and talking to the reporter.

After the interview, you will shoot the B-roll and capture a variety of shots that can cover narration or the interview. As always, shoot wide, medium and tight. The wide shot will show the building and the artist, including enough information to give an idea of the setting where the artist is working. The photographer might frame a medium shot so that the artist and a portion of the wall she is painting fill the screen. The tight shots might include the artist's palette, a close-up of the artist's face and perhaps some interesting angle shots from the ground toward the artist.

Talk to the police officer while she is putting up the crime-scene tape. Talk to the Civil War re-enactor while he is tapping gunpowder into his gun. Whenever possible, let the interviewee demonstrate something that gives extra information to the audience. Keep in mind that people will generally feel more at ease talking in the presence of a camera if they are engaged in some activity.

An action within the viewfinder requires the photographer simultaneously to apply the rule of thirds and to allow lead room for the person to move into. A person's profile should not be close to the edge of the screen: if a woman is walking with her profile close to the edge of the screen, it will seem as if she is pushing the edge of the screen out of the way in order to keep moving. See Exhibit 7.12.

Picture a football player running down the field—the runner needs space to run toward. Imagine the tic-tac-toe grid over the video screen. To follow the foot-

Without proper lead room, the subject seems to be pushing the edge of the screen (A). **EXHIBIT 7.12**
With proper lead room (B), the subject is aligned with a vertical line in the rule of thirds
grid and has space to walk into.

A   B

ball player, the best shot would have the player lined up on one of the vertical lines and facing the other vertical line so that he is constantly running into space. The player should not be in the center of the shot. The photographer will want the runner's face—or more accurately, the runner's helmet—to be at the intersection of the top horizontal line and one of the vertical lines, or at one of the top corners of the inside box.

During a football game, the videographer pans the camera to maintain the subject's position within the viewfinder. The same principle applies to someone walking. If the person is walking from left to right, begin your shot with the person aligned with the left imaginary vertical line and walking toward the right part of the screen. Move the camera as needed to maintain this composition. This technique gives the feeling that the person is walking into open space. In contrast, if the person is walking from left to right and is aligned with the imaginary right vertical line, it appears that the walker is having to push the edge of the screen out of the way to continue moving. If you're following a car in a race, you don't want the car in the middle of the screen—instead, provide space or lead room for the car to move into.

Maintaining lead room when there is an action within the viewfinder requires panning the camera. A movement of the camera for the purpose of following an action is called a *motivated pan,* which was discussed earlier in this chapter. However, pans and zooms generally are less desirable than other techniques for capturing images.

Protect Identity When Needed

Occasionally the photographer will need to shoot a subject in a way that protects the person's identity. She can photograph the subject in silhouette or in a way that does not show identifying characteristics. If the subject is trusting, the photographer can find lots of shots while the interview is going on that do not give away identity: the shadow on the ground . . . the back of the pants leg . . . a tight shot of hands. If there's no identifying goatee or beard, a very tight shot of the mouth can be both effective and protective. Shots from behind the reporter can give a sense of the conversation and show only the person's elbow and shoulder. If these shots are being taken during the interview, the camera will need to run continuously so the audio is not interrupted. As always, the photographer's imagination is the only limitation.

CONCEIVING AND SHOOTING THE STAND-UP

When the reporter appears on camera during a news package, this is a *stand-up*. The information included in the stand-up is a vital part of the story, and the photographer and reporter must work together to conceive and shoot the stand-up at the scene of the story.

The most familiar use of the stand-up is a closing statement by the reporter and an **outcue**—when the reporter identifies herself and the station at the end of the story: *This is Susan Smith reporting for WXXX News.* Newsrooms refer to their SOC, or the **standard outcue**—the order and specific wording for identifying the reporter and the station at the end of a package. For example, one newsroom may have all reporters end their packages by saying, *This is Susan Smith . . . Eyewitness News.* Another newsroom may require something different, such as, *Susan Smith reporting for Newscenter 5.* News departments want their reporters to become familiar to the audience and may require stand-ups to help achieve that goal.

The stand-up should always include valuable information about the story in addition to the outcue. The reporter should develop some idea in advance about how the story will be written so he can tape an appropriate informative stand-up before returning to the station.

Increasingly, reporter stand-ups come within the story. Well-known broadcaster Charles Kuralt is credited with advising reporters *never* to end a package with a stand-up. Because the last visual image of a package is most likely the one viewers will remember, the story should end with a picture that summarizes the story, *not* the reporter. However, news directors often want viewers to have a strong visual memory of the reporter because this helps to build the station's image among viewers.

Stand-ups being composed and taped.   **EXHIBIT 7.13**

Whether the stand-up is in the middle of the package or at the end, one requirement remains undisputed: anytime a reporter appears on camera, the appearance should be for a reason, and the shot should be composed accordingly. Exhibit 7.13 shows stand-ups being taped.

Some legitimate reasons for stand-ups include:

To show you were there. Stand-ups can emphasize the location of the story. If you send a reporter to Russia to do a series of stories on the Russian economy, you surely want to have a stand-up with the Kremlin in the background; likewise, the Eiffel Tower if you're in Paris, the Capitol in Washington, or Times Square or the Statue of Liberty in New York City.

In some cases, shots that show the reporter's presence can detract from the story. In a report on a schoolyard shooting, the video of the school building and the emergency personnel is more important than seeing the reporter standing with the scene in the background.

To reveal something. The reporter may do a stand-up to reveal important information. Two people are dead in a murder–suicide; the story begins with the who, what, when and where. Then, the reporter appears on camera holding a parking ticket and reports, *Police say the argument began over a parking ticket like this one.* In a story about drunk driving, the reporter says that Joe Smith and his two friends began their evening at the basketball game, followed by a stop at the local bar. In the stand-up, the reporter says, *The evening ended here when police say the car crashed into this telephone pole while traveling at 90 miles per hour.*

In a very dramatic stand-up, Baltimore reporter Mike Schuh of WJZ-TV began talking about a parolee who had reportedly killed someone. Viewers could see only some blue sky in the background. As the photographer pulled out to a wide shot, the audience realized that Schuh was standing on top of the jail. To illustrate the length of the rap sheet of the parolee, he held the top of the list of past crimes and let it fall—all the way to the ground.

To show participation. Reporters are not actors and should not attempt to become the focus of the story. However, reporter participation can help the viewer understand the story, if the action is realistic. If a story is about people who are afraid to drive through the Lincoln Tunnel, the reporter may give information about how many people request someone to drive them through the tunnel each week—while driving in the tunnel.

The reporter participation should be real and believable. It would not make sense for a reporter to be passing sandbags as a community attempts to hold back rising flood water, but it might be appropriate for the reporter to be standing in line to buy a lottery ticket in a story about the rush to buy chances on the state's biggest jackpot. A reporter would be more believable pulling cans from a grocery shelf while she talks about fat content in canned goods than pushing a grocery cart and adding cans from the shelf. It is not believable that a reporter would be grocery shopping while preparing a news story.

Reporter participation can add depth and can also remind the audience that the reporter is close to the subject and learning about the story that will be related to the viewers. In a story about a blight that is damaging a corn crop, the audience would not believe that the reporter needed to be helping the farmer water the crop. On the other hand, having the reporter shuck one ear of corn to see the underdeveloped growth could be quite appropriate.

To provide transition. The stand-up may be used as a **transition** or a way to move the story from one part to another. After introducing a farmer whose property taxes are going up, the reporter might do a stand-up in the cornfield, explaining that the tax rates are not determined on the farm—instead, they're decided at city hall. The next section of the story will focus on what lawmakers say about the new tax rate. The stand-up helps move the story easily from one part to another. If the story is about a drought and begins with the personal struggles of one farm family, the next part of the story may be about the state legislature's efforts to deal with the problem. The reporter may do a stand-up in the dry, dusty field and report that the legislature may be looking at a proposal to buy water from an adjoining state. Then the story would move to a legislator's office and proceed with that aspect of the story. A story about health care might begin at the headquarters of an HMO, followed by a reporter stand-up explaining that the new health care policy will change the way nursing homes bill their patients. The next part of the story takes place at a nursing home. Or a reporter might do a stand-up in front of the courthouse to make the transition between the prosecution's case and the defense. Reporter stand-ups can help the audience understand that the story is moving from one topic to another.

No appropriate video. The reporter may do a stand-up when there is no appropriate video. When covering a courtroom story where the camera is not allowed inside, the reporter may stand on the courtroom steps and describe the defendant's testimony. At the scene of an accident, the reporter may stand on the bank where the car became airborne and describe the way police say the accident happened. When someone is arrested for setting a fire that damages the school, you can show pictures of the person and of the fire damage. The stand-up might be the place to report that the suspect had previously been charged with arson.

Stand-ups offer an opportunity for creativity. If the story is about a controversial religious plaque in the courthouse, the reporter might walk into the shot of the plaque. But remember that the purpose of the stand-up is to advance the story.

LIGHTING

Despite the fact that camera technology is constantly improving and can help overcome many bad shooting situations, there is no way around the fact that good lighting is basic to good video. In fact, lighting makes the difference between good and excellent video and between excellent video and art. The best videographers always use a light—even outdoors. Under trees and in shade, a light can improve the shot. Lighting can soften harsh lines and shadows, provide depth and interest to a shot, enhance colors and draw attention to the desired parts of the picture. Light can also flatten a picture, increase undesirable shadows, ruin the colors or destroy the focus of the shot.

Camera Settings

The first step in ensuring good lighting is to make sure you're using your camera properly. Most news cameras require you to set a **white balance.** Generally, this process involves focusing the camera on something white so the camera can adjust its color balance to the color of the available light. For example, fluorescent lighting has a cool blue tint, whereas the sun has a warmer red tint. Without a white balance, the entire video can wind up looking blue or orange. White balances must be set anytime the light source changes. Moving from inside to outside, outside to inside, or from incandescent light to fluorescent light requires a new setting.

Second, videographers must evaluate the shooting environment and make sure the light is sufficient—sometimes a challenging objective, such as when they find themselves shooting outside in the dark. "Sufficient" may simply mean that the viewer can see it, or it may mean clarity with bright colors and defining shadows. Appropriate lighting for a formal interview with the governor and for an interview with firefighters working at dusk may be very different. The audience understands when breaking news occurs at dusk and results in dimly lit video. In these situations, dim light may actually enhance the feeling of being at the scene. On the other hand, if the scene is too dark, the viewers can become frustrated at not being able to see the picture clearly. The photographer may choose to allow dim lighting in the picture, but the amount of light should always be a conscious decision—not an accident.

When the videographer knows that the camera settings are correct and has determined whether the scene requires formal lighting or just the best light available for a breaking news scene, he must be confident that the lighting is providing the desired results on the video. This confidence involves understanding the difference between what the eye sees, what the viewfinder shows and what the final video will look like. The camera and the human eye see subjects differently. Sometimes, what appears to be dark to the eye will look just fine to the camera, and sometimes things may seem OK in the viewfinder but will be too dark when the tape is played back on a monitor. Only by experience with a specific camera can the photographer learn how the picture in the viewfinder will compare to the same picture on a monitor.

Lighting Scenarios

Flat Lighting

Lighting on a subject that may look OK to the eye can often result in video that looks flat in a monitor. We refer to light that is lined up with the camera lens, hits the subject directly and removes naturally existing shadows as **flat lighting.** In contrast, when the light hits a person at an angle, it causes shadows along the nose and other definitions of the face. Consequently, the worst two locations for a light source are on top of the camera and behind it—precisely where lights are located on news cameras. The attached lights are convenient for videographers who are shooting on the run—and bad lighting is better than a shot in the dark. However, the bright light will overpower the natural shadows on faces, give a washed-out look and flatten the picture. We've probably all seen an interview with a police officer or firefighter at a nighttime scene where the camera light is pointed directly at the person's face, is very bright and causes a washed-out hot spot where it hits the person's face. This type of shot offers no sense of depth or texture to the face because it lacks shadows. See Exhibit 7.14.

Another consequence of having the light directly in line with the camera lens occurs when the subject is standing or sitting in front of a wall or other background. The direct light will cause the background to appear to be very close to the person—almost like the person is positioned against the background. The more light cast on the subject without additional light on the background, the closer the

In this shot, the light hits the subject directly, making a bright spot on the forehead and   **EXHIBIT 7.14**
removing naturally existing shadows.

background appears—meaning that the shot has no depth. A light on top of the camera produces two results that harm your shot: a flat subject and no depth.

There are several ways to improve the shot. One remedy is simply to have the subject stand as far from the background as possible. This distance will allow a little natural light to fall on the background and provide some sense of depth. Second, you can soften the harshness by avoiding the brightest part of the light or by using reflected light. To use the softer part of the light, begin by pointing the light toward the ceiling above and slightly in front of the interview subject. While looking through the viewfinder, slowly move the light down until you see enough light on the subject to brighten the picture. By beginning to light the subject with the instrument pointed toward the ceiling, you will also bounce some light onto the background, which will help the subject stand out and give the appearance of more depth in the shot. Be sure to check the subject without looking through the viewfinder to see if the shadows and the amount of light appear proper. See Exhibit 7.15.

Good photographers find many ways to avoid washing out interview subjects. For example, you can take the light off the top of the camera and hold it at arm's length to the side so that it hits the subject's face at an angle instead of straight on. In a small room with a low ceiling and white walls, the photographer can sometimes aim the light directly at the wall in front of the interview subject to bounce the light off the wall and reflect it onto the subject. (When you do this, remember that a powerful light can burn the paint off a wall.) Instead of carrying electric lights, the photographer can attach the battery-operated portable light to a stand instead of to the camera. This allows more flexibility in positioning the light and eliminates the need for electricity at the scene.

EXHIBIT 7.15   Simply tilting the light upward can soften the lighting and help preserve naturally existing shadows around the nose and mouth.

Proper equipment can also help solve the problem of camera-mounted lighting. Light attachments are available for diffusing or softening the light. The light may come with removable filters that can improve lighting in different situations. You can even clip a piece of silk over the light to make it softer.

Three-Point Lighting

Formal interviews and other occasions that permit you to plan and set up lights allow the photographer to work with **three-point lighting,** the most desirable kind of light. "Three-point" refers to three light sources: the key light, the fill light and the back light. News departments usually have access to these **instruments** (the professional term for lights). The **key light** is the primary light on the subject. To set up the key light, remember not to aim the light straight onto the face, or the subject will look washed out and flattened out against the background. Think of a clock on the floor with the subject at the center where the two hands meet and with the camera at the 6. The key light should come from the bottom right, between the 4 and the 5, or from the bottom left, between 7 and 8, so it hits the subject at about a 45-degree angle. (See Exhibit 7.16.) This will make one side of the face brighter than the other side. The shadows that fall on the other side of the face give a sense of depth and texture and make the person look the way we normally see people—with a variety of shadows.

The height of the key light should allow the light to hit the subject's face from above at a 45-degree angle. (See Exhibit 7.17.) If the light is lower than the face, the shadows will be cast upward—exactly the opposite of the way we normally

If the subject is in the center of the clock and the camera is at the 6, the key light will **EXHIBIT 7.16**
come from between the 4 and 5 or between the 7 and 8.

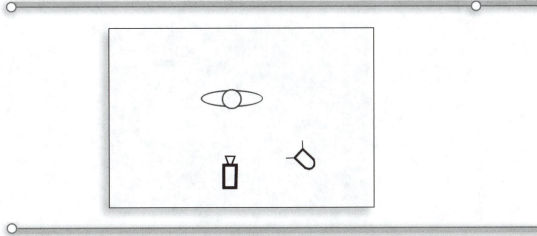

see people. Think of someone holding a flashlight under his chin, something you might see on Halloween or when someone is telling a ghost story. (See Exhibit 7.18.) This is probably not an effect you want for a newscast. A light hitting a person directly at the exact height of the face also casts shadows in an unusual way. The unique lighting could be very distracting, but it could also provide a desired effect. The height should always be above the subject and high enough to avoid

When the key light, the primary light on the subject, hits the subject at approximately a **EXHIBIT 7.17**
45-degree angle, shadows on the face provide pleasing depth and texture.

EXHIBIT 7.18   We are accustomed to light shining on faces from above. When the light comes from below, the shadows seem very unnatural.

brightness that will flatten out the picture. Again, with a powerful light, you might start by aiming the light at the ceiling and then tilt it down until the bottom edge of the light adequately illuminates the face.

To make the subject stand out from the background, a **back light** is very helpful. The back light is aimed toward the shoulders of the subject from the back, as shown in Exhibit 7.19. The back light comes from the opposite direction of the

EXHIBIT 7.19   The back light should be positioned approximately opposite the key light and will cause a slight glow around the shoulders and hair.

The fill light softens the shadows created by the key light. **EXHIBIT 7.20**

key light and should be a much softer, less intense light. The back light will cast a little bit of light onto the shoulders and back of the head so that there is a slight glow around the shoulders and hair. Only experienced photographers notice the defined edges of the shoulders and the illumination between the head and the background, but the viewer knows that the picture is natural and pleasing.

For a final touch, the photographer can use a very soft **fill light** or side light. The fill light softens the shadows cast by the key light. As described above, the key light casts shadows along the nose and other parts of the face. These shadows are desirable because without them, the face looks flat and unnatural. The shadows from a key light, however, are sharper than the shadows we are accustomed to seeing in natural lighting. The fill light comes from 7 o'clock and softens the edges of the shadows made by the key light at 5 o'clock. (See Exhibit 7.20.) The height of the fill light and the placement of the back light can be varied somewhat to suit the artistic judgment of the photographer.

Shooting Outdoors

When the photographer is shooting outdoors, the sun serves as the key light. If possible, avoid shooting when the sun is directly overhead, because the shadows under the eyes, nose and chin could be exaggerated and give the subject an unattractive appearance. Depending on how high the sun is in the sky, the shot may be set up so the sun is positioned like the key light from the 4 to 5 o'clock location on the clock face. If you are holding the camera and pointing it directly toward the subject, the sun would be behind your right shoulder. In a more creative and advanced approach, the photographer might avoid lighting the subject with bright sunlight that might make him squint and arrange the interview so that the sunlight bounces off a nearby light-colored building onto the subject. Once the photographer understands the basic purposes of key lights, fill lights and back lights, she can produce these light sources in many interesting ways.

In news situations, the photographer cannot always choose how to place the subjects. If the only available angle on a rescue operation at the side of the highway is shooting toward the sun, the lighting becomes more complicated. You cannot do anything about the position of the sun, but there are other options. The photographer can use a portable light, as long as it is bright enough, to offset the brightness of the sun. Or a *reflector* can bounce the sunlight back onto the subject.

Reflectors

Most simple light kits come with a **reflector.** One type of reflector is a specially designed disc that allows the photographer to bounce varying amounts of light onto a subject from the sun or from another light source. If you don't have a reflector, a large white card or a piece of aluminum foil stretched over a piece of cardboard can serve the same purpose and improve the look of your shot.

As discussed above, the most important light on a subject is the key light, which can be provided by a reflector. When shooting outside in the bright sun, you can use the reflector to bounce sunlight onto the subject. On an overcast day with no specific bright spot from the sun, the reflector can gather light and focus it on the subject. See Exhibit 7.21.

EXHIBIT 7.21   A reflector can bounce sunlight onto the subject or can gather light to focus on the subject when the sun is lightly obscured by clouds. The reflector can be used in either the key light or fill light position.

When the sun is used as a key light, a reflector can provide fill light.   **EXHIBIT 7.22**

On a bright day, when the sun is used as the key light, the reflector can bounce softer light and serve as the fill light, softening harsh shadows on the face. (See Exhibit 7.22.) If a key light and fill light are set up, you can use a reflector to provide back lighting for extra definition of the subject.

When key lights or fill lights are used indoors in small spaces, they may be too bright and too harsh. When either the key light or fill light is too bright, it can be moved farther away from the subject and the reflector can bounce a more appropriate amount of light on the subject.

Backlighting

Anytime the light is brighter behind the subject than on the subject, the picture will be dark, shadowy and unacceptable. We call this problem **backlighting.** The backlighting problem is different from the use of a soft backlight to help define the subject and make the picture look better. In fact, backlighting provides one way to totally conceal someone's identity. When a bright light is placed directly behind a subject, the person will be in a complete, unidentifiable silhouette. In the case of breaking news where the only available view of a scene faces directly into the sun, the photographer must overcome the problem of backlighting. Suppose you get a chance to interview an elusive, ill-tempered celebrity standing in front of a huge window. If the light is brighter behind the famous grump than in front, the video will show only a silhouette. A light brighter than the light coming from the window would solve the problem.

Another option is to open the iris on the camera. The **iris** works like the iris of the eye to control the amount of light that passes through. When the iris closes down to a smaller opening, the pupil is very small and less light comes in. That's why the pupils of the eyes are small in bright sun. When there is little light, the iris opens and the pupils dilate so that as much light as possible gets in. (Perhaps this is one reason why people look attractive in candlelight with wide, alert-looking eyes.) When a person is standing in front of a window, the photographer can manipulate the iris on the camera so that it opens wide to let more light in from the front of the person. Instead of seeing a silhouette, we will see a defined individual. The problem is that the depth between the person and the window flattens out and the picture isn't as attractive. (See Exhibit 7.23.) When a subject is backlit, the first step is to see if you can close drapes or blinds on the window or move the subject. If the photographer cannot control the backlight in these obvious ways, he will need to compensate with an artificial light or by opening the iris on the camera. A subject in front of a window always needs special attention for lighting.

Even though we have been talking about pointing the camera directly at a subject, remember that we ordinarily shoot the subject at a slight angle. Place the camera slightly to the side of the subject so there is depth in the shot and the subject will not be looking straight at the camera. Even in field shots of reporters doing stand-ups, a slight angle is better than a straight-on shot that flattens out the image. Studio-set shots are different because more sophisticated lighting is possible in the studio to prevent flatness in the picture. In the field, we also want to avoid shooting a person in profile, another setup that flattens out the image. Remember that shadows and angles can make your shot more pleasing.

EXHIBIT 7.23   Opening the iris can improve the lighting on a subject in front of a window, but as the iris opens wider, the picture flattens out.

Shooting at Night

The news business often requires covering events that happen at night in places without electricity at a pace that does not allow setting up special lights to make video look pleasing. In such situations, the photographer's priority may be just to capture video that can be seen clearly. The best option may be the use of the camera-mounted light. A flat, washed-out picture may be the only choice when an event occurs outside in total darkness. However, with the quality of today's cameras, too little light is often better than too much light. News cameras have a **gain control,** a camera setting that can be engaged to allow shooting in very low light. (See Exhibit 7.24.) Street lights, moonlight and police car or rescue vehicle lights might be enough for the camera in gain control mode. Creative photographers have used car headlights to illuminate a news scene at night.

The gain control mode, however, has disadvantages. When the camera is set up to bring in the most available light possible, the picture quality suffers. The video will look grainy, the colors may not be as vibrant as they really are, and the picture may look flat. When the video provides important information or context to a story, a grainy picture is better than no picture. For example, if photographers capture pictures of the mayor stopping on the side of the street and buying drugs, the picture need only be clear enough to validate that the person is, in fact, the mayor. Again, the imperfect grainy picture may be the only option in some situations. Photographers, reporters and editors will work together to make decisions about whether dark and somewhat grainy pictures are important enough to include in a story.

Gain control settings can be adjusted for shooting video in low light, but when gain control mode is in use, the video has a grainy quality. **EXHIBIT 7.24**

CAPTURING GOOD AUDIO

News videographers do more than shoot video. They shoot for sound as well. As the photographer is surveying the news scene and deciding where and how to shoot the best pictures, she is also noticing the sounds. What do I hear and what do the sounds tell me about the story? How can I best capture sound to make the viewers feel as if they were there? In addition to noticing **nat sound**—the natural sounds of the environment—the news photographer will have to get clear audio when the reporter talks directly to the camera or interviews people. Using headphones helps photographers ensure they are capturing good quality sound.

Requirements for good audio include using an appropriate microphone and having it in the proper location. Generally, the microphone needs to be close to the desired sound. The reporter may wear a wireless microphone to pick up a good audio level when he is talking. For an interview, the reporter may hold a microphone to capture his voice and move it to get audio when the interviewee is talking. In both cases, the shooter is responsible for the audio levels. For stand-ups and interviews, the videographer will need to notice whether there are distracting background sounds. If so, the reporter or subject may need to wait for a truck to pass or a siren to move out of hearing distance before speaking.

Photographers must pay attention to nat sound at a news scene. The microphone attached to the camera is usually sufficient for natural sound, and the photographer may let the tape run for 30 seconds to a minute solely to capture the natural sounds. At the scene of the fire, the natural sounds will include sirens, water hoses, people moving about and the fire crackling. At the park, the camera mic will pick up general sounds of people and animals, or leaves rustling in the wind. If the story is about inline skaters irritating business owners, the photographer might want to put the camera close to the ground to capture the sound as the wheels go by. At a banquet, the camera could be set up to get pictures and sound of glasses clinking or a knife being put down on a bread plate. These kinds of shots capture the natural sound and also make excellent cutaway and transition shots, as discussed in the next chapter. You can also edit the sounds under different pictures. For example, the photographer may have a distant shot of the president clinking glasses with a foreign dignitary to celebrate a new trade agreement. The editor can use the clink-of-glasses sound captured from another toast at a nearby table under the distant shot. If the crack-of-the-bat sound is better from a previous hit, the photographer may use that sound underneath the shot of the game-winning home-run hit.

Videographers can also accomplish a lot by using a **lavalier mic** or **lav,** which clips onto clothing so that the reporter doesn't have to hold a microphone. Subjects are usually more at ease and pay less attention to the microphone when it is clipped on rather than held in front of their faces. One problem with a lavalier mic is that the fabric moving across or near the mic can make a distracting sound, especially when the mic is clipped underneath clothing.

Wireless mics (see Exhibit 7.25) contain tiny transmitters that send the audio over the air for a short distance directly to the camera. Wireless mics are useful for interviews and can help you capture excellent natural sound. The dramatic-looking guy at the baseball game with the painted face and big hat could probably be persuaded to wear a wireless lavalier mic as he walks up into the stands to be seated. If he greets friends, orders a hot dog or makes casual comments, these sounds are good candidates for natural sound breaks, which will be explained in detail in the next chapter.

Wireless mics allow the reporter and photographer to do interesting stand-ups because the camera can capture clear sound from some distance away from the microphone. A photographer might be able to let the reporter conduct an interview while riding horses or walking down a street. Or the photographer could shoot through a window and receive clear audio even though the reporter is inside the house and the camera outside. The distance for good audio varies with the quality of the wireless mic.

A wireless mic. **EXHIBIT 7.25**

EXHIBIT 7.26 Omnidirectional mic.

Some microphones are **omnidirectional** (see Exhibit 7.26), picking up sounds from all directions. Other mics, with a heart-shaped pickup pattern, are more sensitive at the front of the microphone than at the back. **Shotgun mics** (see Exhibit 7.27) pick up only sounds within a narrow range and have a dead zone along the sides and bottom of the mic. Some shotgun mics can pick up sounds clearly from a great distance. The photographer must be aware of the sound and the type of microphone in use when framing shots. In a wide shot of a fire, the sounds will be more general if the microphone is an omnidirectional one. The mic would pick up a mix of the fire and peripheral noise. If you are shooting the fire scene from a distance with a shotgun mic, the mic would pick up the sound of the flames and mute the sounds of traffic, sirens and other peripheral noise.

Good videographers understand shot composition and proper lighting, and they also master the audio part of the camera. Knowing the type of microphone in use and its limitations can help you plan the audio portion of the story.

Shotgun mic.   **EXHIBIT 7.27**

CONCLUSION

Video defines television. Anyone can shoot video, but those who consistently shoot great video are rare. The videographer or news photographer has the opportunity to become an artist and to find great fulfillment in a creative profession. News photographers can develop their own unique style, and the work can be quite artistic, but it will always be at least acceptable if you follow a few basic rules. Good videographers begin with understanding the basics of steady, well-lit video and a screen filled with meaningful pictures, such as composing shots according to the rule of thirds. The rule of thirds provides two important focus areas and ensures that the viewer sees what the photographer intended.

Photographers must remember to allow lead room and the appropriate amount of head room for moving or talking subjects. Pans and zooms should be used sparingly and only when there is motivation. When they are used, they should begin and end with a long, count-to-10 steady shot. Photographers can go beyond the basics to improve their shot composition by following some fundamental artistic principles. This kind of creative work shows the audience a view of things that they might never have imagined.

Capturing good video also requires skill both in using natural and artificial lights and in capturing quality sound to accompany the video. Photographers must know how to assess and use the natural light at a news scene. Next, the photographer decides whether to use artificial lights and, if so, how to set up the key light and possibly a fill light and back light. Capturing clear pictures with appropriate lighting also requires knowing the capabilities of the camera and how to use white balance, gain control and iris settings. Video should always be accompanied by sound, and again photographers must understand the equipment they are using. They should learn to pay attention to the natural sounds and capture them clearly and effectively to enhance the audience's understanding of what it was like at the scene. They must choose the appropriate microphone, whether it's wireless, lavalier or handheld, omnidirectional or shotgun.

News photographers face an enormous challenge. They work as professional photojournalists with responsibility for gathering information and deciding which pictures to include in news coverage. In addition, they use artistic skill and creativity in composing and lighting shots and act as sound technicians as well. They also have the physical work of carrying and helping maintain highly technical equipment. In the midst of all these responsibilities, the photographer is an equal partner in the reporter/photographer team and must work well with many types of individuals to develop effective stand-ups and to produce the best possible video product. News photography is not for the faint of heart.

KEY CONCEPTS

edit	close-up	three-point lighting
photojournalist	stand-up	instrument
videographer	rule of thirds	key light
one-man band	Z-principle	back light
shoot tape	motivated pan	fill light
edit tape	head room	reflector
establishing shot	scan room	backlighting
zoom	lead room	iris
dolly	look space	gain control
pan	talk space	nat sound
cutaway	outcue	lavalier mic/lav
B-roll	standard outcue	wireless mic
interview cutaway	transition	omnidirectional mic
two-shot	white balance	shotgun mic
one-shot	flat lighting	

Activities

1. Watch a television program and pay attention to shot composition. Is the screen filled with video? Does the focus of the shot fall on one of the top two intersections of the lines in a tic-tac-toe grid?

2. Look for pans and zooms in a television newscast. Make a list of the pans and zooms you see, and explain the purpose of the camera movements.

3. The next time you go outside, listen for natural sounds. What do you hear? Imagine where you would put a microphone to best capture the sounds you hear.

SHOOTING ASSIGNMENTS

1. Ask two people to sit in two chairs beside each other and talk. Using a video camera, see how many interesting shots you can get. Think wide, medium and tight. Think angles. Think cutaways.

2. Shoot video of someone studying or eating. See how many interesting and creative shots you can get. Think wide–medium–tight–tight–tight.

3. Shoot video outdoors of someone talking into the camera. Use the sun as a key light. If you have someone to help, use a reflector as a fill light.

4. Shoot some video outside at night. With the camera in record mode, experiment with the gain control. Look at the video and notice the changing quality of the picture. Determine which settings you think would be acceptable for broadcast.

5. Shoot video of someone in front of a window or backlit in some other way. While the camera is recording, adjust the opening of the iris step by step until the person is clearly visible. Look at the video and notice the changes in brightness and in picture quality.

6. Set up a staged interview with one person asking questions of another. First, capture the audio using only the camera's built-in microphone. Next, have the "reporter" use a handheld microphone for the interview. Finally, attach a wireless mic to the interviewee. Watch and listen to the video. What differences do you hear? What are the advantages and disadvantages of each method?

We live by one credo: steady, sequenced video, meaningful and

compelling natural sound.

**DAVE WERTHEIMER, KSTP/KSTC-TV,
MINNEAPOLIS/ST. PAUL, MINN.**

SHOOTING VIDEO II

NOW THAT THE FUNDAMENTALS of good shot composition are under your belt, in this chapter, we discuss more complex decisions pertaining to shooting good video. After developing quick judgment in composing a good shot, the next step for the photographer in the field is to develop skill in using sequences, increasingly refined artistic judgment and more attention to sound.

CUTAWAYS AND JUMP CUTS

Good photographers will get plenty of cutaway shots. The term **cutaway** refers to shots of something other than the person you are interviewing. Cutaways are used to cover *jump cuts* or simply to cover the story narration. **Jump cut** refers to two shots edited back to back that are very similar but just different enough that the subject seems to "jump." A cutaway between the two shots solves the problem. The photographer must be aware of the editing problems related to jump cuts and provide the proper kind of cutaway pictures for covering the jump.

Interview Cutaways

Cutaways are necessary when an interview requires editing to shorten the person's comments. For example, assume you are interviewing the mayor, who begins the interview by saying, *I think the new parking garage will destroy the beauty and the quaint atmosphere of the downtown.* The mayor proceeds to talk about the design of the garage, its planned location and the process required to approve the plan. Then the mayor says, *Furthermore, the city can't afford to build anything without a tax increase.*

When it's time to write the story, you may choose to edit the comment about the beauty of downtown and the comment about the tax increase back to back. Anytime you cut material or put comments together out of sequence, there is the possibility of misleading the audience, and you must make an ethical decision about the edit. In this case, the two sentences edited together present a fair representation of the mayor's comments, and you can proceed. However, because the mayor said the sentences at different times, the edit will cause a jump cut. The mayor's face will appear to jump, even if the camera is stationary and the mayor is sitting in the same position throughout the interview. We move our heads slightly, blink our eyes and shift a little, even when we try to remain still. Even the guards at Buckingham Palace move. The mayor's face will jump at the edit point. The simple solution is to edit another shot over the jump—to cover the jump cut with a cutaway shot.

Sometimes editors leave the jump cut, and the audience recognizes that there has been an edit. Others use a dissolve between the two shots to convey the edit in a less jarring way. The most common practice, however, employs a cutaway shot to cover the jump. Let's look at two kinds of cutaways appropriate for editing interviews: reporter reaction shots and cutaway questions.

Reporter Reaction Shots

The edited pictures must always make sense to the viewer, even when we need a shot only to cover the jump at the edit point. If the subject is a major drought, the jump cut can be covered with pictures of the dry, cracked ground or dying plants to enhance the point of the story. In cases where appropriate video is not available, cutaway shots of the reporter can be used. A cutaway of the reporter, commonly called a **reaction shot,** should be used only when more appropriate video is not available. Reaction shots do have benefits: they can give credibility and remind the audience that the reporter was at the scene. The photographer will always want to get a cutaway shot of the reporter, in case the shot may be needed.

Reporter cutaways come in many varieties. If a reporter is interviewing a city administrator outside City Hall, the cutaway may be a wide or medium shot of the reporter and interviewee talking. Another choice is to show the reporter from over the shoulder of the interviewee to see the position of both people. The person's shoulder provides a bit of foreground, but the reporter is the focus of the shot.

The reporter may be holding the microphone, taking notes or simply looking toward the interviewee and listening. The photographer may frame the shot around the reporter, perhaps an upper-chest shot or a waist shot without the perspective of the interviewee's shoulder. The photographer can choose from many options in framing the cutaway, but for the editor's benefit should always get some kind of cutaway. Exhibit 8.1 illustrates several options for reporter cutaways.

Capture a variety of cutaway shots of the reporter for possible use in covering jump cuts.   **EXHIBIT 8.1**

Staging video means setting up shots in a way that did not actually happen. A reporter reaction provides the editor with an excellent way to cover a jump cut in an interview, but the editor must *stage* the shot. The picture sequence of the interviewee followed by a shot of the reporter makes sense to the audience because they understand the interview situation. However, the audience is also misled. Remember that the one camera remains focused on the interviewee throughout the interview. The cutaway makes it appear that there are two cameras: one focused on the reporter and the other focused on the administrator. The cut from one person to the other looks like a studio interview where a director is switching back and forth between two cameras, each focused on one of the two people. In fact, there is only one camera outside City Hall. In reality, the photographer gets a shot of the reporter listening to the interviewee either before or after the actual interview. During the interview, the camera remains focused on the administrator. The reaction shot can even be taken after the interviewee has left the scene, if the purpose is simply to show the reporter appearing to listen without showing emotion.

Ethical note: In the movie "Broadcast News," actor William Hurt plays an unethical reporter. In one of his news stories, he is seen with a tear running down his cheek, apparently crying in response to the interview he is conducting. Others in the newsroom, however, realize that the story was produced in the field using only one camera. The shot was staged after the interview was complete, and the reporter "acted" the tears, believing a show of emotion would endear him to the audience—a self-centered breach of ethics.

Cutaway Questions

Occasionally, there may be a reason to use a **cutaway question.** A cutaway question is field video that appears to show the reporter asking a question of a news source, but that was actually recorded after the interview ended. After an interview at the news site is complete, the photographer moves the camera and focuses on the reporter instead of the interviewee for a cutaway shot. The photographer can get a shot of the reporter repeating a question that was asked earlier. The shot can be used to cover a jump cut if the interview with the news source is edited.

Not only can a cutaway question be filmed after the interview is over, it can be shot after the interviewee is gone. For example, suppose a senator has steadfastly refused for months to reveal his plans about an upcoming election. During the interview for your newscast, the reporter asks about the upcoming campaign, and the senator, for the first time, reveals that she will retire at the end of the current term. The camera was focused on the senator when the question was asked. However, since the question revealed surprising information and thereby became important, the reporter might ask it again during a post-interview cutaway shot. When he puts the news package together, he could use the question after one of the senator's comments to make the transition to the new subject. Including a shot of the reporter asking the question emphasizes the importance of the question.

Ethical note: The ability to stage cutaway questions raises ethical issues. Why is it important to the story to see the reporter ask a question? Is it just to provide transition from one topic to another? Is it to provide a way to edit an interview and avoid the jump cut between two shots of the interviewee? Is it to focus on the reporter's ability to ask sensitive questions—to make the audience realize that the reporter has the ability to get the information the audience would like to know, but would never have the opportunity to ask? Sometimes the promotion department wants to use the reporter's question as a way of promoting the newscast without giving away the story in advance. In the above example, the senator reveals important information. Therefore, the question could be used to promote the evening newscast without giving away the answer. Unfortunately, reporters sometimes use the cutaway question as a way of promoting self and career, thinking that the question will impress a future employer. Reporters and photographers must consider the ethical aspects of the simplest decisions, such as when to show a reporter asking a question.

Sequence Jump Cuts

In addition to the jump cuts that result from editing an interview, we use the term **sequence jump cut** to refer to an edit that places two events back-to-back when, in reality, some time would have passed between the two shots. A jump cut creates a slight discontinuity in the movement on screen; a sequence jump cut creates a larger discontinuity.

If the president of the United States comes to town, we might see a shot of him descending the steps of the airplane at the airport. After he reaches the tarmac, he walks to a set of microphones and gives a speech. A shot of the president descending the steps from the airplane edited back-to-back with an excerpt of the president's speech would be a sequence jump cut. These two events cannot happen within a split second, and the video should give the clue that time has passed between the two shots. (See Exhibit 8.2.) Solving the problem of this jump cut may be as simple as showing a shot of the crowd. This cutaway indicates the passage of time and prevents the confusion of a jump cut. We know that while we're seeing the crowd, the president approached the podium and began the speech. The audience understands that the sound bite from the speech may have come at the beginning, middle or end of the talk. A shot of the crowd can also cover a jump cut in the sound bites from the speech.

If a police officer at the scene of an accident begins by putting out flares and directing traffic and later fills out an accident report form, the photographer should shoot all this action from a variety of distances and angles. However, the photographer should also know that editing a shot of the officer directing traffic back-to-back with a shot of her filling out the form would be a jump cut. The jump needs a cutaway shot. A shot of a suspect walking into a courthouse edited next to a shot of the suspect as the defendant sitting with his attorney in the courtroom would be a jump cut. (See Exhibit 8.3.) The two shots would need a cutaway to bridge the jump, such as a close-up of the gavel or a shot of the courtroom door. Photographers must understand the editing problem related to jump cuts and think about getting cutaway shots.

On a basic level, the audience does realize that it's seeing pictures that have been edited together and that pictures from different times can be placed back-to-back. We can use jump cuts and expect that if the audience is confused, the

These two shots show the same person in two locations. If the shots are edited together, **EXHIBIT 8.2**
they cause a sequence jump cut. The photographer will need to find cutaway shots that
can cover the jump.

EXHIBIT 8.3   The suspect and the officer cannot be outside in one instant and inside the next. These two shots edited back-to-back would cause a sequence jump cut. Good photographers will plan for editing by getting lots of cutaway shots.

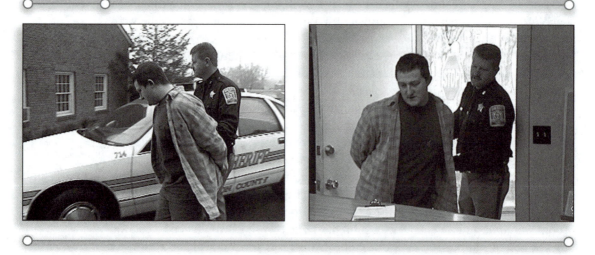

confusion will be very temporary. However, cutaway shots give viewers a clearer and more accurate representation of events. The photographer's efforts in getting workable cutaways make the final story better. These kinds of cutaways not only break up jumps, but they can also serve as *transition shots.*

Transition Shots

Changes in time or location within a story should be clear from the video alone. Shots that prepare the viewer for a new time or place are called **transition shots,** and the photographer must remember to shoot video that can serve as transition.

If we see the mayor at a school congratulating the coach when the team returns from winning the state championship and, in the next shot, we see the mayor talking from behind the desk in his office, a viewer could be jolted by the sudden change. The confusion would pass quickly, but inserting a transition shot can prepare the audience for the change and eliminate the possibility for confusion.

One way to execute a transition shot is to frame the shot in a way that the mayor and the coach walk out of the shot. They disappear from the shot and the audience sees a fraction of a second of the location without people. Without thinking consciously about the scene, the audience understands that the coach and the mayor have gone somewhere else. Next, when we see the mayor at his desk, it is clear that time has

To avoid jump cuts, shoot lots of tight shot transitions so you can edit in or out of anything.

Dave Wertheimer

**KSTP/KSTC-TV,
MINNEAPOLIS/ST. PAUL, MINN.**

passed, that the mayor has left the school and returned to the office. A common transition shot shows the reporter and the subject she will be interviewing coming down the street, passing the camera and walking out of the shot before we see the actual interview. Photographers who understand the need for transition will remember to let the subjects walk out of the shot at some point. (See Exhibit 8.4.)

At the scene of a four-car accident at a busy intersection, a close-up of the blue lights on the patrol car can remove us from the action of rescue workers and prepare us for an interview in a citizen's home where he explains his numerous unanswered requests for a traffic light at that particular intersection.

Allowing the subjects to walk out of a shot provides an easy transition before we see them in another location.   **EXHIBIT 8.4**

1

2

3

4

A sophisticated method for allowing people to walk out of shots involves using the two imaginary vertical lines in the rule of thirds. As you follow the movement of someone walking, keep the subject lined up with one of the vertical lines, and find a stationary object such as a mailbox or a sign on the street that she is approaching. As she reaches the stationary object, hold the shot still with the object matched up with the other vertical line. Then hold the shot so that the object stays in the same position while the person walks past it and out of the frame. You'll add creativity and depth to your shot. (See Exhibit 8.5.)

THE SHOOTING AXIS

Whenever you compose an establishing shot, imagine that there is an imaginary line on the ground extending from your left to your right, perpendicular to the direction you are shooting and just behind the focus of the shot. In other words, if we're looking at two people, imagine a line immediately behind them, as if they're leaning against it. Shooting various angles from one side of the line and

EXHIBIT 8.5 Following the rules of good shot composition, show a person walking in alignment with one of the vertical lines in the rule of thirds grid, with lead room in front. Then hold the camera still as a stationary object lines up with the opposite vertical line, and allow the person to walk out of the shot. This technique requires quick thinking and a thorough understanding of the rule of thirds.

editing them together would be acceptable, and the audience would understand the perspective. A view from the other side of the line would change the perspective and confuse the viewer. Although the photographer can move across this line in shooting, the editor cannot **cross the line,** or juxtapose shots from different sides of the line. Therefore, to provide usable shots, the photographer must also understand crossing the line. The crossing-the-line principle is also commonly referred to as the **180-degree rule** or the **shooting axis.** So that the line or shooting axis can be crossed in editing without violating the rule, the photographer must provide appropriate cutaway shots.

Without knowing the rule, your instincts will tell you that if you're shooting toward City Hall with the reporter and mayor standing face-to-face in front of the building, your next shot would not be a medium shot from the other side of the subjects, from between them and City Hall. Think of it this way: The reporter's profile is facing the right side of the screen. If the next shot is taken from the other side of the two people, the reporter's nose will suddenly be facing the left side of the screen. These two shots edited back-to-back would jolt and confuse the viewer. (See Exhibit 8.6.)

The requirement to stay on one side of the line will obviously need to be broken or you would be restricted to one viewpoint in any given scene. The photographer can cross the line without confusing the viewer by following yet another rule: *neutralize* the viewpoint before you cross the line.

Neutralizing Shots

To **neutralize** a shot is to take away the perspective the viewer has adopted in seeing an object or scene. We change the audience's perspective by interrupting the action with a different shot. Imagine two people sitting face-to-face across a table in a restaurant. We first see their profiles from a wide shot. The viewer now has

If the photographer crosses the shooting axis, the sudden change in perspective may jolt the viewer and distract from the story.   **EXHIBIT 8.6**

an understanding of the scene as a 180-degree span from an imaginary line crossing through the two people—like looking at a photograph or painting. The next logical shot would be to move closer and shift the angle to see a tighter view of one of the faces. We would naturally want to see a closer view of the other face. In the second and third shot, we remain on the same side of the line.

Now, we would like to shoot the couple from the other side of the table to show the other side of the restaurant. If we cut to the other side of the line, however, the noses will suddenly be facing in opposite directions. We neutralize the viewpoint by taking a close-up shot of the couple's entwined hands, a clock on the wall or the menu—something that changes the viewer's perspective. See Exhibit 8.7.

Now, if the following shot is from the other side of the line and the faces are looking in opposite directions, the audience understands that the camera has moved and the change is not jolting. The challenge for the photographer is to understand the editing possibilities and bring back shots that can neutralize the viewpoint so that the editor can change the perspective.

EXHIBIT 8.7   Viewers may benefit from seeing a wide range of shots in a particular setting. If the photographer captures appropriate cutaway shots, the editor will be able to cross the shooting axis and change the perspective without distracting viewers.

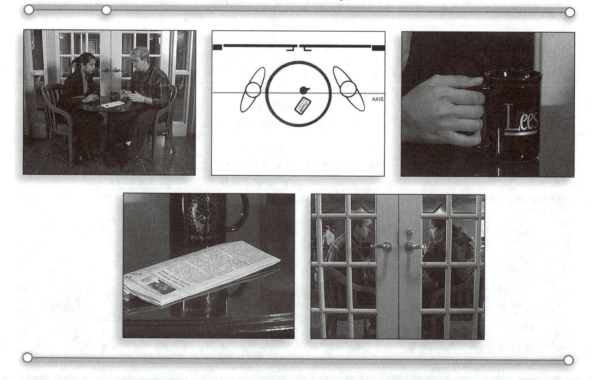

SHOOTING SEQUENCES

If the photographer provides workable shots and cutaways, the editor can enliven the story with video *sequences*. A **sequence** is a logical series of shots that fit together in a way that makes sense to the audience. Shooting sequences requires careful planning and diligent execution on the part of the photographer, who can prepare the appropriate video in several ways:

- by presenting a series of related shots
- by showing completion
- by juxtaposing an action with a reaction
- by shooting an action sequence

Wide, Medium and Tight Sequences

Skilled photographers shoot wide, medium and tight sequences. They understand that we shoot the same way that we look at things. We actually see in wide, medium and tight rather than panning or zooming with our eyes. Try it. Look around the room you are in, or even better, try this exercise when you enter a room you've never been in before. You will generally take in the entire scene at first: the wide shot. Then your eyes will scan to another location and focus on a section of the room: the medium shot. Even though your eyes are scanning from the wide view to the section where you stop, you're not really focusing as your attention moves to a smaller section of the room. Your eyes disengage for a second until you focus again. After you have looked at different sections of the room, you may find an item in the room that interests you. You may move in for a closer look, or even pick up an object to examine it carefully: the tight shot. When shots are edited together this way, they present the viewer with a logical series of pictures of something he has never seen before, the same way he would see it himself.

At the scene of a drug bust, the logical first shot would be wide, showing the street and the row of houses. The next shot would be a medium shot of the house in question, showing the sidewalk leading toward the door—maybe part of a mailbox or gate in the foreground. The following shot could be a close shot of the front door with attention drawn to the house numbers. The shooting sequence provides an order that helps the viewer understand the scene.

Shooting video of two people talking boils down to capturing wide, medium and tight shots that allow many possibilities when it is time to edit. Let's picture a reporter and the mayor standing face to face in front of City Hall. The first requirement is the wide shot or establishing shot, where we see both people from head to toe. We can recognize City Hall in the background. Next, we'll move closer for a medium shot from over the shoulder of the reporter so that the mayor is framed up according to our rule of thirds. We may include part of the reporter's shoulder for foreground. Then we will move to a tight shot of the mayor's face. (See Exhibit 8.8.)

The process of shooting wide, medium and tight can be used in every situation, and should be. It is a fundamental principle of getting good video. In fact, a better rule may be to shoot wide, medium and tight–tight–tight. A single establishing shot can give the audience the information it needs to understand the location and setting of the scene. A medium shot can give a bit more detail. However, the tight shots provide the most interesting views and the most opportunity for creativity.

> Avoid pans and zooms—unless they're motivated. Shoot close-ups and tight shots. Always remember wide–medium–tight. This adds a whole new dimension to your work.
>
> *Jay Webb*
> **WHSV-TV, HARRISONBURG, VA.**

Reversing the wide, medium, tight order can provide a rewarding surprise to the viewer and exciting possibilities in editing. This technique requires careful advance planning and close collaboration between the reporter and photographer. Imagine a story beginning with a tight shot of fingers on a keyboard. The next shot pulls back for a medium view of the side of a piano and the side of the pianist's head. The wide shot gives the surprise: the pianist has only one hand. Or, a story begins with a close-up of the lips of a singer at a microphone. You hear a powerful voice and see a cutaway shot of a volume meter. Then the wide shot reveals that the booming voice is coming from a small child. Or envision a paintbrush stroking a canvas. The next shot is a reversal of the first view: a shot back toward the artist from the ground, but this time we see the paint palette and only part of the artist's body. The wide shot reveals that the artist is painting by holding the brush in her mouth because she has no arms. A shoe commercial shows a runner beginning with tight and medium shots of the face, feet and body before the wide shot reveals that the runner has artificial legs. In all of these examples, the video conveys the essence of the story: an athlete or artist with an unusual

EXHIBIT 8.8   When shooting video of a news interview, shoot wide, medium and tight on the subject.

characteristic. The full package may give more detail in narration and sound bites, but the video has told the basics.

This powerful use of video can be accomplished only by a thinking, creative photographer. These examples also show the importance of teamwork among the reporter, shooter and editor. If the reporter wants to write the story with a surprise like the ones above, but hasn't communicated with the photographer, the shots may not be available. If the desired effect is not communicated to the editor, the idea may not be realized. Good communication between reporter and photographer always helps in the quest to develop excellent news stories.

Match the Action

To edit a sequence you will need the proper shots, especially when you wish to match an action. Anytime a photographer sees someone repeating an action that relates to the news story, the opportunity exists to shoot wide, medium and tight on the action. We'll use the example of a police officer directing traffic. The officer repeats the gestures of motioning traffic to move. The photographer captures the motion several times from a wide angle. Then the photographer shoots the motion several times from a medium angle. Finally, the photographer captures the same action several more times from a close-up view. Remember: wide, medium and tight–tight–tight.

Many other situations will allow a wide, medium and tight view of a repeated action: rescue workers administering CPR, a politician shaking hands with voters, a secretary answering a phone, a lawyer pacing the floor while awaiting a jury verdict. Photographers must remain alert for the opportunity to capture a repeated action from a variety of perspectives. We will discuss how to edit the sequence in Chapter 9.

A Series of Related Shots

Editing a series of related shots back-to-back forms the simplest kind of sequence. For example, three simple shots of a scene or an item—the wide, medium and tight—relate and fit together in a logical sequence. We see a wide view of a scene, go in a little closer and then focus on specifics, just as we process any view we have not seen before. As we drive down the highway, we see a wide view of an accident, take a medium look at the damaged car and then attempt to see a close view of the trapped driver.

In other cases, the related shots may not necessarily come in a series moving from wide to tight. If the city manager's sound bite relates to a recreation league for city employees, the photographer might find several shots of city employees engaged in different forms of recreation: a tight shot of someone's face coming up for air from the swimming pool, a wide shot of a softball game, a medium shot of the horseshoe competition. If a legislator is talking about new regulations for farmers, the photographer might find several interesting shots of farms and farmers. The sequence of related shots could be used as B-roll during the lawmaker's comments. In a story about rising college costs, a sequence of students working in part-time jobs relates to the story.

Completion

Human beings seem to have an innate need for completion, and showing the completion of an action can also form a sequence. We want to know how things end, and we don't feel right without finality. In music, hearing a melody that stops before the last note compels you to sing it yourself, even if only in your mind. (Try it: *The itsy bitsy spider went up the. . . .*) In a television show, if the cut to commercials comes just as the perpetrator raises a knife above a potential victim, you'll want to see how the action ends.

Shooting and editing video require that you consider this need for completion. When the quarterback releases the football in a spiraling pass, we need to see whether he completes the pass. When explosions are set off to bring down an old high-rise building, we need to see the scene after the dust has settled. If the story is about logging and we see the tree start to fall, we need to see the action completed. If a diver jumps off a cliff, we need to see how the jump ends. The list is endless, and the principle applies to the videographer in the field gathering news, just as it applies to the movie producer. Find the shot that completes the action. Only if the photographer gets the shots can the editor provide the sense of completion the viewer needs.

Action/Reaction

Another way to shoot so that the video works well in editing is to think in sequences of action and reaction. The **action/reaction sequence** can be as simple as two shots edited together that show an action and a reaction to it. (See Exhibit 8.9.)

At the scene of an accident, rescue efforts are the primary action, while pictures of the crowd that has gathered to watch reveal a reaction to the event. A famous author reading to children at a local school is an action; the reaction shot shows the faces of the children as they listen. When an angry citizen is protesting a city action at the council meeting, the photographer may show the citizen pleading to the council and the faces of the council members in reaction. In the action of a batter hitting a home run, the crowd reacts by jumping up, shouting and hugging each other. The photographer shoots the action on the field as the batter hits the ball—and also needs the reaction in the stands.

Getting action and reaction shots is not easy and not always possible. When the photographer goes to a baseball game with one camera, she cannot simulta-

If the photographer captures both an action and a reaction shot, the two shots make a   **EXHIBIT 8.9**
simple, effective sequence.

neously shoot the batter at the crack of the bat and the reaction of the crowd as the ball goes out of the park. However, the viewer is accustomed to seeing actions and simultaneous reactions. In the president's State of the Union address, we see the secretary of defense as the president comments on the funding for military projects. We see the reaction of the leader of the black caucus during the discussion of civil rights initiatives and the reaction of the secretary of education when the topic is school funding. During the State of the Union speech, however, there is one camera that remains focused on the president at all times while another camera finds the shots of key Congressional leaders. (In fact, the camera crew has a copy of the speech in advance so they know whom to find for upcoming shots.) A director is monitoring both cameras and switching live from one shot to another. News photographers don't work this way.

The lone photographer must compensate for the limitation of having only one perspective at a time. The task requires keeping the action/reaction requirement in mind and getting the shots at different times. If the camera focuses on the batter running around the bases, the photographer may need to shoot the crowd as it reacts to another big play. Or, if the photographer is in the stands shooting crowd shots when the home run is hit, he will need to think about capturing the cheers and perhaps getting a shot of the runner as he crosses home plate. If the run happens too fast to get both shots, the photographer thinks about getting pictures of the home run–hitting bat-

Think action and reaction. Shoot nat sound. You'll thank yourself when you get in the edit bay.

Dave Wertheimer
**KSTP/KSTC-TV,
MINNEAPOLIS/ST. PAUL, MINN.**

ter during another hit or during another run around the bases. During editing, it is possible to show the batter running the bases and the crowd reacting while the narration tells about the home run. Even though the shots are taken at different times and probably during different plays, the viewers will see a realistic presentation of the home run and the crowd reaction.

Ethical note: News photographers must be ever mindful of their power and must strive to make ethical choices. In sports coverage, showing the batter running bases with shots that have been taken from a different part of the game does, indeed, alter reality. Since the truth, however, is not distorted, the shooting practice seems acceptable.

Reversed Point of View

Another way to find short, interesting sequences is to reverse the camera perspective. A **reversed point of view** sequence shows a scene from one individual's perspective back-to-back with the perspective from another participant's viewpoint.

A reversal in a baseball game might show the perspective of the pitcher: first a shot from the pitcher's mound as the ball crosses the base and winds up in the catcher's glove. A reversed point of view would show the pitcher from the catcher's viewpoint (see Exhibit 8.10). In live coverage of a major league baseball game, viewers may see a shot that seems to be taken from immediately behind the pitcher but is actually accomplished by using a powerful studio-sized camera set up outside the field. With typical news cameras, this kind of shot is impossible during a game unless the photographer has a good life insurance policy and the station doesn't mind losing a camera in a line drive toward the viewfinder. But, during the pregame, the team manager or coach might agree to setting up shots that let the viewer see what the pitcher sees.

EXHIBIT 8.10   In this reversed point of view sequence, we see the perspective of one individual followed by another person's view looking at the individual.

The reversed point of view shot can be applied to most situations—generally with less complication and danger than in baseball. For example, after a shot of a programmer at a computer screen, shoot the screen as the programmer sees it. After a shot of the mayor presiding over City Council, show the mayor's perspective of the crowd. After the comments from the celebrity ducking into a car to avoid reporters, show the crowd of reporters pursuing the celebrity. After the shot of the rescue worker performing CPR, shoot from the level of the stretcher up toward the rescue worker. After the shot of the children in the new petting zoo, shoot from the perspective of one of the animals.

Efforts to capture reversal shots can be dramatic, but they always require good judgment on the part of the photographer. After showing the firefighter and fire truck, a shot from the top of the fire ladder could be stunning, but the fire department obviously doesn't have time to assist with such a shot while they are fighting the fire. In a reversal of the rescuer administering CPR, the videographer must be sure not to interfere with or distract from the rescue efforts. A shot from the perspective of the lion in his cage at the zoo might be dramatic, but also impossible. A reversed point of view can be interesting to the viewer, but the photographer's efforts to capture good quality video should not become the news story and should not be the cause of great inconvenience to others.

Action Sequences

Short bits of video from a series of movements that are put together in an **action sequence** can condense the actions and enliven the video. This sophisticated kind of sequence requires careful planning on the part of the photographer. Complicated action sequences are common on movie screens, but news photographers and editors can also set them up when time permits. For action sequences, the photographer decides how the action is broken into segments and gets corresponding shots. The photographer plans the transition between parts of the action during the shoot. The viewer understands that a transition shot can mean that time has gone by. If we want the audience to understand that someone has gotten out of a car, unloaded a box and carried it into a building, it is not necessary to show the entire action. Let's use this example to explain how the action sequence would need to be shot.

Getting a box from a parking lot into a building could take several minutes, but if we shoot a sequence properly, we can make the audience understand the full action in a matter of seconds. We must avoid jump cuts, so we don't want to show the person opening the car door and then cut to a shot of the person carrying the box because these two things can't be done in a split second. If we neutralize the action, the audience can understand that time has passed and the shots will make sense. The first shot might be of the person opening the car door and stepping out of the car and out of the shot. Once the person is out of the shot, the action is neutralized and the viewer can understand that time is passing. A tight shot of the door closing would make a nice second shot. The following shot could be taken from an open door into the backseat where we see the box. As the camera begins to roll, we see the person reach in from the other side of the car and pull the box out of the car. Again, the shot ends as the box and person disappear from the picture. Another shot shows the person walking toward a building. Then the camera could be set up inside the front door of the building. As the camera begins rolling, the person enters the building carrying the box. The person walks by the camera and out of the picture. In the next shot, the camera is set up behind the boss's desk, and we see the person approach the desk and set the box down. The entire sequence would take about 20 seconds and would give the viewer a clear understanding of an action that took much longer. For each shot, the viewpoint must be neutralized either by a cutaway or by having the individual walk out of the shot. See Exhibit 8.11.

Shooting action sequences makes interesting video, but it can also be very closely related to staging news and can raise serious ethical questions. When news events are happening, photographers and reporters do not want to become part of the news. Neither do news gatherers want to influence what happens in a news event. At the scene of looting and rioting, a photographer would obviously not ask a looter to put the TV back and grab it again to capture a different angle on the action. The ethical dilemma in asking a drug abuser in an exclusive interview to smoke crack for the sake of good video is also pretty clear. Less obvious is whether it is ethical to ask a protester to hold a sign in a certain way or to ask an investigator to hold a piece of evidence for the camera. The photographer has a great deal of power in deciding what pictures the audience sees and must work to present events accurately, just as the reporter does.

Designing action sequences at the scene of breaking news may be nearly impossible. Setting up action sequences in other news situations may result in serious breaches of ethics, such as those involving criminal activity. In cases where ethics are not an issue, the audience accepts and understands the standard procedures in video editing. In an interview where pictures of the mayor receiving a state award in an out-of-town location cover the mayor's comments about the banquet and ceremony, the audience accepts and understands that the ceremony is over, the mayor has returned from the trip, and she is in the office talking with a reporter. Viewers who see pictures of the mayor in the office juxtaposed with pictures at a banquet can understand the situation. The story does not mislead.

Many types of news stories or features present the opportunity for interesting action sequences that do not compromise accuracy in reporting. One common video scenario shows a reporter approaching a door and knocking. The next shot shows a person inside the house opening the door to reveal the reporter standing outside. The two shots are edited back to back and we see both actions within

Action sequences can be difficult to shoot but can allow viewers to understand a lengthy **EXHIBIT 8.11**
activity in a matter of seconds.

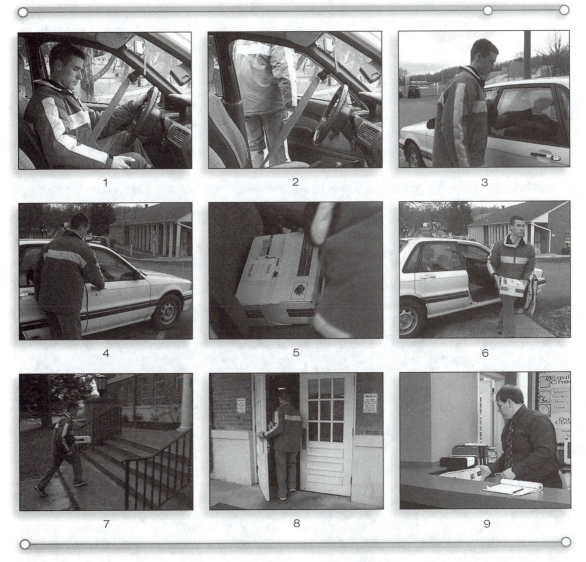

three or four seconds. The video sequence can allow time for introductory information in the story, and the audience accepts and understands these two shots on
several levels. Clearly, time has passed between the knocking and the opening of
the door, but because the actions follow in chronological sequence, they make
sense. On another level, the viewer understands that a camera is capturing the
action—from inside the house. Without thinking about it, or realizing how it is
done, the audience accepts the logic of the sequence.

To achieve an action sequence that will make sense to the viewer, the photographer will have to get the people involved to repeat the action. In the knocking sequence, the photographer will shoot a wide or medium shot as the reporter approaches the door and raises an arm. The photographer may ask the reporter to repeat the action so the camera can focus on a tight shot of his fist rapping against the wood. The photographer may then move to the inside and ask for the knock to be repeated to capture the sound from inside the house as the homeowner reaches for the doorknob. The reporter will be waiting as the door opens. See Exhibit 8.12.

The next shot could be from inside the living room toward an open doorway. This alerts the audience to the change of location but doesn't jump from a shot of

EXHIBIT 8.12   To capture this sequence, the reporter and the subject must repeat the action of knocking and opening the door.

two people at a doorway to the same people entering another room. After a brief moment in the new scene, the two people appear in the doorway and enter the living room, crossing in front of the camera and leaving the shot. After the shot of the people leaving the screen, the next shot might show the two as they settle onto the couch to talk. Again, the action will have to be repeated to allow the photographer to get a different shot of what will appear to the audience to be the same action. See Exhibit 8.13.

When appropriate and when ethical rules are not violated, the photographer can ask for actions to be repeated so that he can capture different angles and create sequences that make sense to the viewer and enhance the story. For example, in a news story about a new, non-invasive method of diagnosing colon cancer, the doctor might repeat the computer-imaging process. You wouldn't, however, ask a doctor to repeat a needle injection on a patient. News photographers are not movie producers and should not try to be, but careful planning in the field for action sequences can yield creative, interesting video.

This action sequence gives viewers more information about how and where the interview **EXHIBIT 8.13** took place. The reporter and subject will have to follow the photographer's directions about when to begin an action.

SHOOTING VIDEO USING ARTISTIC PRINCIPLES

Photographers apply artistic principles to shooting video; these include effective use of leading lines, movement, color, light and dark, balance and symmetry, foreground and background.

Leading Lines

The photographer has the power to determine which part of the picture viewers see first. This power comes from the knowledge that various components within the frame draw the eye to a certain point. The photographer can use **leading lines,** strong lines in the shot composition that pull the viewer's eye in a certain direction. For example, if the purpose of a shot is to show the front of a house, the photographer can frame the shot so the sidewalk leads the viewer's attention to the front door. In contrast, if a reporter doing a stand-up is standing beside a road and the center line of the road leads into the distance, the viewers' attention is drawn down the center line and away from the reporter. See Exhibit 8.14.

Leading lines are different from lead space for an action or an interview. Lead space refers to an open area for an action to move into. Leading lines refer to actual lines within the frame—the line along a fence row, the roof line on a building or the line of an arm as an action is performed in a shot. When the leading line extends past the edge of the viewfinder and is actually cut off by the edge of the frame, the line provides a **visual entrance** into the shot. The

EXHIBIT 8.14   Strong lines within a shot can pull the viewer's attention to the desired focus of the shot, as shown by the sidewalk's drawing focus to the building. In contrast, the strong lines can pull attention into the distance away from the desired focus on the reporter.

strong line pulls the viewer's attention into the shot at the point where the line meets the edge of the screen. A strong visual entrance overcomes the viewer's natural tendency to look at the shot in the Z pattern. For example, if a shot is framed so that we see an arm coming down from the top right side of the screen to feed a treat to a dog, the arm leads the viewer into the shot, and the line of the arm leads the viewer's attention in a pattern that is not the natural one. See Exhibit 8.15.

If the focus of a shot of a lunch counter is the tip under the coffee cup, the edge of the counter can lead the eye to the coins. Even though we naturally look in the upper left, the edge of the counter, beginning in the lower left, pulls the eye to the right. See Exhibit 8.16.

The leading lines can also pull the attention out of the shot. Imagine a shot looking down a railroad track as it disappears into the distance. The strong lines of the railroad track pull the eye to the point where the lines appear to meet. The picture gives the feeling of depth and distance. Consequently, if your shot of an accident is composed with the rescue squad working beside the railroad track, the viewer has to fight the pull of the rails in order to look to the right or left and concentrate on the action. See Exhibit 8.17.

Imagine a picture of a tree that has lost its leaves for winter. The trunk of the tree may pull attention within the shot and guide the eye up and down because it is the strongest line in the picture. (Depending on how you're imagining the tree, the trunk may also be the largest element in the picture.) After following the vertical line of the tree trunk, however, the eye follows the largest branches toward

The strong line of the arm pulls the viewer's attention into the shot from above, overcoming **EXHIBIT 8.15**
the natural Z pattern.

EXHIBIT 8.16 In this shot, the leading line pulls viewer attention into the shot from the lower part of the screen.

EXHIBIT 8.17 The strong lines of the rails pull the viewer's attention into the distance.

the edges of the picture. In fact, if a large branch on the right side of the tree pulls our attention to the right side of the screen, we may retrace the branch in reverse to the trunk before following the line of another large branch that leads off the screen on the left side of the screen. We are not likely to jump from the right edge of the screen to the left edge of the screen. The lines of the trunk and branches control our view of the picture, as Exhibit 8.18 shows.

The strong line of the tree trunk pulls the viewers' attention.   **EXHIBIT 8.18**

In contrast, imagine a shot of a large bell—the Liberty Bell, for example. Using the rule of thirds, we want the top of the bell to fall slightly above the top horizontal line, and we should frame the bell slightly off-center, so that the main focal point is at the intersection of the right vertical line and the top horizontal line. After focusing on the top of the bell, the eye naturally follows the curve of the bell down to the left bottom edge of the screen. (See Exhibit 8.19.) The natural tendency would be to return to the top of the bell and then follow the curve down the right side of the screen. The strong lines lead our vision.

Using this knowledge, the videographer can create interesting pictures and cause the viewer to see the effect she intended. On the other hand, ignoring leading lines can result in a picture where the viewer's eye is distracted from the part of the picture that is supposed to get the most attention. For example, if you interview someone beside a stairway with the railing behind the subject, the railing that leads up the stairs leads the viewer's attention away from the subject. Even if the videographer frames the face properly, the strong line of the staircase leading up and out of the picture pulls the eye away from the face of the subject. If the reporter is standing across the street from a building with its strong horizontal roof line behind her, the viewer's eye may be drawn away from the reporter. If you put a reporter between two buildings in a narrow alley, the vertical lines of the buildings will pull attention up and away from the reporter. Videographers must learn to notice the highway, street signs, trees, roof lines and other surroundings that provide strong lines to pull the viewer's attention. These leading lines can distract from the intended focus—or can be used by the observant photographer to enhance the shot. See Exhibit 8.20.

EXHIBIT 8.19   The lines of the bell pull attention down one side and lead back to the top of the bell and down the other side.

EXHIBIT 8.20   These shots demonstrate how powerful leading lines pull the viewer's attention away from the desired focus.

Movement

Movement is an even more powerful force than leading lines in pulling the viewer's attention. Photographers may use movement to direct attention as they like. Think of the railroad track with the rail lines leading the eye into the distance. Put a bunch of weeds flapping in the breeze at any location in the shot, and the movement demands attention. Based on the rule of thirds, the most unlikely place to look first is the middle of the bottom of the screen. But even in a shot of a line of refugees being driven from their homes, a piece of trash blowing across the ground at the bottom center of the shot will distract from the line of worried faces. Not all examples are so dramatic: traffic moving in front of or behind the reporter can distract from what is being said.

When the anchor is presenting a news update from the newsroom, we always follow the movement of the people walking in the background, even when they're out of focus. The flickering of flames in a fireplace draws attention, as does a flag flapping in the breeze or leaves blowing in the wind. The photographer must be aware of all that is going on in a shot to make sure that the pull of motion does not distract from the intended focus of the shot.

Color

Bright colors also attract attention, and the videographer must make sure that the effect is desirable. It's no accident that prisoners are issued bright orange jumpsuits and that hunters wear the same color to stand out in the woods. Imagine an escapee trying to blend into a crowd while wearing a bright orange jumpsuit. Even in a crowded football stadium, deputies can spot the orange—unless, perhaps, the criminal is wise enough to hide at a University of Tennessee football game, where everyone is wearing the color.

For a more pastoral example, look out the window onto a spring lawn and your eyes will be drawn to the yellow dandelions. Put a fire-engine red tie on a news anchor and viewers will see more of the tie than the anchor's face. Bright color attracts attention, and the photographer must be aware of the colors in the shot so that attention is drawn to the appropriate location and not away from the true focus of the shot.

Light and Dark

The amount of light and dark in a shot helps determine where the viewer's attention goes, just as movement and color do. Light and dark interact in a variety of ways, but in general, the eye is drawn to light. However, if the shot is composed mostly of light content, dark objects gain our attention. In a snowy landscape, the one dark bush will stand out, no matter where it is located within the frame. This principle is so basic, we automatically understand that the darker the letters, the more they show up on the side of the white airplane, and that the single clump of dark seaweed will catch our attention in the light sand. See Exhibit 8.21.

If most of the shot is dark, the light images attract attention. In a nighttime shot of a building, the one window with a light is the first place the viewer looks. If we want information to stand out, we choose light-colored letters on a black screen. Even if a shot is composed of gray or medium tones, anything white gets the most attention. The lightest part of a many-colored picture also gets the most attention. The milk mustaches on famous people's faces in the "Got Milk?" ads exemplify this principle. In a picture of faces that includes a variety of colors, a white mustache gets the first glance—even when the face is a well-known celebrity. The photographer

EXHIBIT 8.21 A dark object will attract attention in a light-colored background, but a lighter color will pull attention when the background is dark.

can use this principle to emphasize the focus of the shot. If an interviewee is wearing light clothing, a dark background will bring more attention to the subject.

Balance and Symmetry

Have you ever asked yourself what makes the world's most beautiful people so pleasing to look at? Pretty skin and pretty coloring are part of the reason, but balance is the most important. The most beautiful faces approach perfect symmetry: the right side and left side of the face are almost exactly the same. A good video shot does not require such detailed perfection, but good balance is a necessity.

Balance is a sense of equilibrium. In **perfect symmetry,** things are absolutely equal. Three bricks on one side of the screen are balanced by three bricks on the other side. A couch is framed by two identical end tables with two identical lamps. A see-saw is perfectly horizontal with a person of the same size on each end. See Exhibit 8.22.

If a reporter is looking directly into the camera and is situated in exactly half of the screen with a bare background, the shot will seem incomplete and unbalanced. For perfect symmetry, we could place the reporter on the left side of the screen, but we would need a person of the same size on the other side. In such perfect balance, the viewer's attention would normally be drawn back and forth from one person to the other. Because this type of formal balance is static and rarely desirable in news video, the videographer will use *asymmetrical balance* instead. **Asymmetrical balance** (also called *informal balance*) provides a sense of equilibrium even though the items in the shot are out of proportion or alignment. With the reporter on one side of the screen, something that appears much smaller in the dis-

These video shots show perfect symmetry and balance. **EXHIBIT 8.22**

tance on the other side can informally balance the shot. See Exhibit 8.23. Perhaps the reporter is doing a story on school funding and we see children on a jungle gym playing in the distance. Even though the shot does not have perfect symmetry, the focal point on the right provides a balance that makes the viewer more comfortable.

In many interview situations, you see the subject framed more on one side of the screen than the other, and a bouquet of flowers or a lamp is visible in the background on the other side, providing a sense of equilibrium. The subject can still be framed up according to the rule of thirds, filling the screen, with the eyes along the top line. In this case, the smaller item also helps provide depth to the shot. In asymmetrical balance, three bricks on one side of the screen could be balanced by one cinder block on the other. (See Exhibit 8.24.)

The balance principle applies to all visual media: The shot of a reporter in the camera lens must have balance, just as words on a magazine cover provide bal-

A shot with one person on one side would require another person on screen for perfect **EXHIBIT 8.23** balance. Perfect balance is not always desirable. Something small in the distance can provide effective asymmetrical balance.

EXHIBIT 8.24 The three bricks and one block form an informal balance.

ance to the picture. Designs on billboards, product containers and television screens all need balance. Photographers must master the concept of balance to produce good video work.

Foreground

The best photographers attempt to provide some kind of *foreground* in a shot. For this discussion, **foreground** is something that appears in the front of the screen that is not the primary focus of the shot. We actually want the viewer to concentrate on another part of the picture, but including something in the foreground gives the shot a feeling of depth and prevents the picture from looking flat. The sense of distance makes the picture more pleasing to the eye. In a picture of a landscape, for example, most of our attention focuses on the distance. However, including the edge of a building in the foreground helps give depth and richness to the shot. The leaves on a tree framing the top corner of the shot is a common way to provide foreground. (See Exhibit 8.25.) Now, prepare yourself for disillusionment. You have most likely seen a news story shot with leaves in the foreground, but . . . sometimes there's not even a tree where you see those leaves. Photographers have been known to hold a tree branch in front of the camera for the artistic purpose of establishing foreground and depth in the shot.

Every shot will not include foreground, but good photographers should be alert to the possibilities for giving depth to the shot. When you're interviewing a city administrator, the nameplate on the desk could be shot at an angle so that it is included in the foreground. For a wide, establishing shot of the administrator and the reporter, shoot from outside the office and use the door frame at the edge

The tree branch provides foreground that gives depth and richness to the shot.   **EXHIBIT 8.25**

of the shot to establish foreground. At the scene of a murder, use the yellow tape for foreground and show the white sheet over the body in the background.

Background

The use of **background**—something that appears in the back of the screen to provide depth but is not the primary focus of the shot—can also give depth to the shot. Although we want the viewer to concentrate on the front of the shot, including background makes the shot more interesting and pleasing to the eye. Often, the background shows part of what the person is talking about. When a witness is describing an accident, a blurred shot of wrecked cars in the background gives credibility to the interview by showing the person at the scene and adds depth to the picture. News photographers should think about setting up shots so that the foreground and background work together to give information and provide a well-composed picture.

Once the photographer understands the basics of good shot composition and learns the artistic principles that make a shot effective, she must take those skills into all kinds of situations, whether a stately banquet, the scene of a grisly murder, a quiet museum or a loud and dangerous drug bust.

SHOOTING TIPS FOR NATURAL SOUND PACKAGES

Sophisticated photographers and photojournalists can combine the techniques discussed in this chapter to prepare *natural sound packages,* commonly known in newsrooms as *nat sound packages.* A **nat sound package** is an edited package that tells a story using only the sounds of an event and sound bites from participants or observers—and does *not* use reporter narration.

Shooting for a nat sound package requires the photographer to get the basic information—the who, what, when, where, why and how—from interviews and sounds of the event, including bits of conversation picked up by the microphone. Nat sound packages allow enormous creativity and flexibility for shooters, who generally enjoy the opportunity to put one together.

Assume that the photojournalist is working alone and gets a call to cover a protest in front of the courthouse. In addition to capturing quality video, the shooter must make sure to get comments that explain who the group is, what they're protesting and why. The sound and video must also reveal, without reporter narration, where and when the event is occurring. Much of the story will be told with ambient sound. The ambient or nat sound is simply the surrounding sound—the sounds of the environment you're in, whether the chants of a protest or the sound of the breeze and chirping birds in a scene of nature.

At the protest, the photographer will make sure the mic picks up the chants of protest and will capture shots that clearly establish the location. The wide and medium shots might include street signs or landmark buildings. A shot of a clock or a calendar will clarify when the event took place—or perhaps a sound bite from an interview will explain, *"We chose today for the protest because the Council always meets on Wednesdays at two o'clock."* The creative photographer can find many ways to include the kind of information that is usually told in reporter narration.

> Listen to those around you. The best work I've ever done is always when the reporter and photographer are in complete partnership.
>
> *Richard Frohlich*
> **WFTV-TV, ORLANDO, FLA.**

As the photographer gains experience in planning for nat sound packages, she will learn to get several interview subjects to describe what they're doing, what they see and what they think. From the varied descriptions, the story can be told in an interesting way. The photographer will also want to set up in the interviews for variety and creativity. Rather than pulling the protester to the side for a standard interview shot, the photographer may walk beside him and get comments in the midst of the action. Talking to a protester who is taking a break and tying a shoe or repairing a sign can provide interesting video and valuable information at the same time. Shooting a nat sound package is a coveted opportunity for news photographers and photojournalists, and it demands both good video and good storytelling.

GENERAL TIPS

Practice Assertiveness

One of the most difficult challenges for the photographer is to find the proper balance between assertiveness and interference. It takes courage to walk in front of an auditorium full of people to get a close-up of the action on stage—or perhaps to walk onto the stage itself. At first, you will feel extremely self-conscious, as if all eyes are on you, and as if you are distracting from the occasion. However, remaining in the background will likely mean that you'll miss the best shots and the viewers will be cheated. Each situation has its own demands for propriety and requires careful judgment, but the public generally understands the role of photographers and is fairly forgiving. For example, no one should be disturbed when the videographer steps into the street to get a picture of an approaching parade. Stepping in front of the stage at an outdoor concert to get a close-up of the performer would not be disruptive. A political rally might be informal enough to allow the photographer to roam about the auditorium and walk freely in front of the stage. On the other hand, covering a famous speaker at a church service would require more restraint. Funerals of police officers or celebrities require sensitivity on the part of reporters and photographers. In the effort to do a good job in gathering news and video, it's easy to go too far. Videographers who are rude and disrupt or interfere cause harm to the reputation of media representatives and make it harder for those who follow in their footsteps. Doing a good job in gathering news video is imperative, but it also requires professionalism and good manners.

Understand the Story

Those who shoot quality video can be valuable to a news operation, but those who understand how shooting video fits into the overall news product are indispensable. For example, for a story about the destruction of a wetland area by a new road project, the reporter may ask an environmentalist how the loss of wetlands will affect people. The environmentalist may talk about two varieties of endangered birds that will lose more habitat with the project. The environmentalist may explain how the birds control the population of specific insects that damage garden produce. In this case, the photographer may need to ask some questions so that she can identify and get pictures of the birds and insects under discussion. By understanding exactly what the environmentalist is talking about, the photographer may be able to get shots in a household garden that show the insects' damage.

Finding the right pictures sometimes involves a special challenge. Mike Schuh, WJZ-TV, Baltimore, says, "I once saw a fascinating story about the Amish, shot by photographer Mark Anderson. Because of the religious beliefs of the Amish, you can't show their faces. He told a story of the people, but the pictures were of barns, horses, houses, cats, flags flapping in the breeze and other 'things.' It was great work and showed the potential of creativity with video."

The best photographers earn the title photojournalist because they, too, gather information and help the audience understand the story. Photojournalists listen carefully to the interview and use the information to formulate ideas about pictures. If the city recreation department manager mentions cracks in the tennis courts, the photojournalist remembers the comment and gets pictures of the cracks. The more the photographer understands about the story, the more valuable to the story the pictures can become.

Broaden Your Skills

The person who understands the possibilities for editing with a good variety of wide, medium and tight shots can get video that allows for more creative writing and editing. Shots have to work together in the edit room. Those who haven't experienced the frustrations of editing cannot possibly understand the need for video like those who have struggled to put a sequence together and realized the pictures just aren't there to do it. Likewise, when you've worked to write a script that makes the best use of video, you understand the possibilities for writing that good video allows.

More and more jobs in broadcast reporting require a variety of skills, but even when your job is restricted to shooting video, you'll do a better job and be more valuable if you also understand writing and editing. Extra effort is required to learn broader skills in news operations where tasks are compartmentalized. You may have to spend some of your spare time sitting with the editor if your sole responsibility is shooting. If you want to improve your writing, but you spend most of your time shooting and editing, you may want to write drafts of stories and ask another reporter or a news director to critique them. When you're learning and gaining understanding, your job offers more excitement and rewards.

Avoid Complacency

Any job can become routine. That's why it's called work. However, photographers should remember that the work is new to viewers with each and every story. You have the choice to make your job challenging. You can choose to become an artist and develop your own impressive style. Try to see everything. Ask how you can tell a story with pictures differently than someone else would. How can you make people *feel* what happened? Even though everyone in the city can look outside and see the snowstorm, how can you present it in a new way? How can you make an impression? How can you become the best at what you do? If you give yourself these challenges, you can avoid complacency and find satisfaction in your work.

Communicate

The most important requirement of a news operation is to communicate information to the general public. This process also requires communication between the photographer and reporter. When two people bring different approaches and ideas to one project, the decision-making process can become tense. Good photographers learn how to communicate their ideas clearly in a nonconfrontational way to reporters and producers. They also learn to listen and appreciate the ideas of others. Each newsroom will have an established decision-making procedure, and generally the reporter or producer's ideas take precedence over those of the photographer in the field. This does not mean that the photographer must simply follow instructions. Good reporters and producers appreciate creative input and enjoy working with other skilled professionals. They appreciate the thinking photographer who communicates good ideas.

CONCLUSION

After mastering the basics of shot composition, the news videographer will become more artistic, shooting sequences and lots of variety in content and angles. While working at the news site, the photographer may plan ahead for editing, making sure to get cutaways, transition shots, neutralizing shots and logical sequences. If there is an action that can be repeated without jeopardizing ethics, the photographer shoots an action more than once for editing and thinks about action/reaction and reversed point of view sequences. The news photographer or photojournalist should also listen carefully and understand the context of stories. Mastering the ability to tell a story without a reporter in nat sound packages will create opportunities for greater creativity. The job includes the physical aspect of carrying equipment and walking or running to get good video, but the job also requires clear, logical thinking plus a lively, creative mind. It's a wonderful combination of the physical and the mental, and a good photographer is indispensable for quality television news. Chapter 9 looks at the editing process and how to put the photographer's quality video to the best use.

KEY CONCEPTS

cutaway	180-degree rule	visual entrance
jump cut	shooting axis	balance
reaction shot	neutralizing	perfect symmetry
staging video	sequence	asymmetrical balance
cutaway question	action/reaction sequence	foreground
sequence jump cut	reversed point of view	background
transition shot	action sequence	nat sound package
crossing the line	leading line	

Activities

1. Watch a movie and make note of the use of sequences. What do you notice about reaction shots, reversals in point of view, and transition or neutralizing shots?

2. Watch a newscast and a syndicated celebrity magazine show. What do you notice about the different styles of the stories? The writing? The shooting? The editing? The content of the sound bites?

3. Watch a network newscast and a prime-time news magazine show such as "60 Minutes" or "Dateline." What similarities do you see in shooting and editing? What are the major differences?

4. Go to an art gallery to study the principle of *leading lines*. Where is the visual entrance for each picture or painting? Then watch a television documentary and look for similar implementation of the principle of leading lines.

5. Find a picture in a magazine that you like and study it in terms of color, balance and amount of light and dark.

Regarding Ethics . . .

6. You have gained access to a small group of people who are allowing you to shoot video of their illegal drug use. The young people are successful professionals, but also regular users of cocaine. You missed a good angle on a shot of one of the young women snorting the powder and you ask her to pretend to snort another line of the drug. She volunteers that she will be happy to actually snort another line as long as you're keeping your promise that the shot will not reveal her identity. What would you do? What *should* you do?

SHOOTING ASSIGNMENTS

1. Shoot a reporter interviewing someone. Shoot a reporter reaction shot, a cutaway question and other cutaway shots.

2. Set up an interview situation and get six cutaway shots from each side of the 180-degree line. Make sure that you get at least four shots that could be used as transitions to cross the axis.

3. Go to a sports event. Shoot several action/reaction sequences.

4. Find someone repeating an action, such as a telephone operator or someone putting mail in mailboxes. Shoot the scene from as many perspectives as you can think of. Be sure to get shots that could be used as transitions. Get shots from the reverse point of view.

5. Ask a friend to perform the action of getting out of a car, going into a building and speaking with someone. Plan the shots that you want and decide what transition shots you will need. Shoot the sequence.

6. Go to an event and shoot it so you can tell the story using only natural sounds and sound bites from people who are there. How is this process different from shooting a story where you can tell it with your own narration? Which is more difficult? Which is more effective?

Every action by the editor should reinforce the main story. Although the editor has the potential for endless creativity, you don't do something just because you can. The creativity comes in understanding and implementing the demands inherent in the story.

WALT REEDY, A. D.
PRODUCTIONS

EDITING

WHEN THE INFORMATION has been gathered, the story written, video shot and narration prepared, it's time for the editor to put the package together. Like every person involved in the process, the editor exerts a great deal of control over quality and holds responsibility for presenting the story truthfully and accurately. Even routine decisions will involve ethical concerns. The editor also has the opportunity to exercise creativity and artistic judgment—to develop a body of work that can be appreciated by viewers and colleagues and can become a source of professional pride.

THE EDITING PROCESS

The editor works with a script provided by the reporter, which indicates the recorded narration, sound bites and the location of stand-ups. Using an *edit controller* for a videotape machine or a computer, the editor selects and combines four basic components: the reporter's narration, sound bites, stand-ups and video with natural sound. Occasionally, news packages include music from CDs or tapes. (See Exhibit 9.1.)

In previous chapters we discussed terms that editors commonly use: *package, sound bite* and *stand-up, narration, nat sound* and *B-roll.* An **edit,** a change in the picture or sound, is also called a *cut.* **Cuts only editing** means that all the edits are instantaneous changes from one picture to another or from one sound to another, as opposed to dissolves or other ways of changing the images on

Everybody likes dissolves, but it slows the pace. It's better to use nat sound spikes in the track.

Pat Barry
KCNC-TV, DENVER

EXHIBIT 9.1   The basic components of a news package.

> **A NEWS PACKAGE INCLUDES:**
>
> ■ Reporter narration
>
> ■ Sound bites
>
> ■ Stand-ups
>
> ■ Video with natural sound
>
> ■ Music

screen. Most news broadcast editors use cuts-only edits for packages that are produced the day they air.

The editor works with a **video track**—the channel on the videotape or in the computer program designated for the pictures. For sound bites and stand-ups, the audio and video are recorded simultaneously. B-roll video may or may not include sound. The editor selects sounds and pictures from the shoot tape for the final package. There are two or more **audio tracks** for the sound, typically one for reporter narration and one for natural sound.

ELEMENTS OF EDITING

Pacing

The pace of the story is one of the major areas under the control of the editor. How fast does the story move from one section to another? Is the pace methodical and steady or is it varied? Even though you can determine pace to some extent by the writing, the timing on edits and the choice of pictures may make the story seem fast, or they can make the story seem faltering and slow.

The basic rule of pacing a story is to *edit tight*. In general, there should be no wasted time in the edited package, so that every second of the story—in fact, every fraction of a second—serves some purpose. There is no reason to delay moving from one section of the story to another. For example, there should not be a delay between the narrator's introduction and the beginning of the sound bite. After the reporter narrates, *"Investigator Jane Doe says her department is looking at several motives for the shooting,"* Doe should begin speaking immediately. At the conclusion of a reporter's stand-up in the middle of the package, the picture should change and the next part of the story should continue immediately. No purpose would be served by holding the shot on the reporter after she finishes speaking.

Tight editing can make a significant difference in the overall time of a package. Just leaving seven or eight extra frames (less than a third of a second at 30 frames per second) at every edit point can make a package five or six seconds longer than it needs to be. If a newscast has five packages and each one saved six seconds, another 30-second story could be included in the broadcast. An exception to cutting out additional time is the conclusion of the story. The editor will hold the final shot for several extra seconds. With the final shot or a concluding stand-up, the video runs for a second or two to give the director a chance to cut away from the story before the screen goes to black.

Tight edits do not always guarantee a suitably paced package. When there is too much video, even editing one shot tightly against another will not improve the pace of the story. For an extreme example of bad pacing, consider video of a boat sinking. A boat does not sink quickly, so if the video begins with the boat halfway submerged and maintains the perspective until the boat goes under, the pace will be painfully long and slow—impossible to include in a news package. Even if the second shot is edited tightly after the boat goes under, there's too much video. The audience does not need to see the whole process to understand what happened. A couple of seconds of the half-submerged boat, a reaction shot from the crowd watching from the beach, and the final few seconds of the bow being sucked under the water are enough. This might seem like an absurd example, but the principle of editing tight and controlling the pace applies in many other situations where the need is less obvious. Even though the shots may be great—a beautiful sunset, an endearing expression that transforms a face, a dramatic helicopter rescue effort—the editor must develop precise judgment about how much video is enough. A general rule is that once you've seen it, let it go. However, a singer's movement after the final beat of the song may be just the right touch.

> The pacing will be determined by the story that you're telling.
>
> *Dave Wertheimer*
> **KSTP/KSTC-TV,**
> **MINNEAPOLIS/ST. PAUL, MINN.**

In a story with little action, the editor can help keep the story from dragging by choosing shots that contain action. In a story about a community that has been without electricity for a week during the heat of the summer, the editor may want to create a story that is inherently slow. People can't do what they ordinarily do, and the heat makes everyone sluggish. The tape might include pictures of the main street with one person walking slowly across it. People sit on porches in swings. There is very little going on, which is the point of the story. The editor may want the story to reflect the pace in the hot little town, but he can still avoid having the story drag. Instead of using a series of motionless shots that would be very dull to look at, the editor may choose more interesting shots that include some motion. A shot of someone fanning a hand back and forth in front of his face or of the sole person on the street glancing over her shoulder provides movement and interest. Skill in choosing the right shots and knowing how long to hold them can give the audience the feeling of being there without boring them.

The editor could also fail to capture the mood of the small-town story if the pace is wrong. The action shots could move quickly from one shot to another: a door closes, a hand waves, the swing moves back and forth. By editing too much action back-to-back, the editor would destroy the reality of the story. She must pace the pictures and sound appropriately to match the mood and meaning of the story.

Even though sequences with many shots per second are common on television, they give only an impression, and news stories generally want to do more than that—they attempt to give information. It generally takes at least a couple of seconds for the audience to examine a shot and grasp the information it offers. Most shots may be held for a second or two. We want the audience to be interested in, maybe excited by and possibly mesmerized by the news story. The story needs to progress quickly enough to maintain interest, but not so quickly that the viewer gets lost.

Repetition

A basic rule of editing is not to repeat shots. Once the audience has seen a picture, that picture should not be used again. This rule always holds, except in rare situations. On the other hand, repetition is a powerful tool that can be used in many ways, including in the editing booth. Infomercials repeat a phone number over and over within a few seconds so the listener is more likely to remember it. Speech writers open with a story or example, refer to it again in the middle of the speech and use the same story for a dramatic ending. In editing, the use of repetition does not necessarily mean reusing the same shot. In a story about a children's carnival, we may see one child repeating, "Step right up!" throughout the package. Assuming the child spoke with dramatic flair and called out many times for people to "step right up," there may be several versions on the tape. You might use the expression a couple of times during the package from different angles, and a third repetition might provide a perfect ending to the package. If there is only one adorable "Step right up!" on the tape, it is possible to reuse it, but repetition in editing usually means using different shots of a repeated action.

A sudden, drastic change in the pace of your editing doesn't work well. You need to move gradually. From four-second shots, you'll need to put in a three-second, some two-second shots, and a one-second before you start the fast pace.

Everett McEwan
KCNC-TV, DENVER

In an April 15th story about the long line of people at the post office attempting to mail their tax forms before midnight, the action of the clerk's repeated stamping of the date on envelopes may provide a nat sound break to accent the interviews and narration. The editor could repeat the action, preferably from a variety of angles. In a story about a heat wave, shots of people getting water could accent the story: people at water fountains, people in water fountains, people spraying themselves with water hoses, drinking from upturned water bottles. Although the editor does not repeat the same shot, this video theme conveys the idea of people trying to cool off with water. In a similar theme, one editor used repeated shots of a swimming pool throughout a story about a record-setting hot day. The twist was that the swimming pool shots lasted less than a second and appeared to the viewer like flashes (*flash frames*). Then, at the end of the story, the pool shot appeared in full—a climax to the story and the solution to the heat problem. The audience had been teased effectively and was finally rewarded—all by the editor's use of repetition.

Timing and Punctuation

The nuances of timing that accent and punctuate a story provide the greatest source of pride for the editor. The editor's judgment in *timing* means choosing when to use a picture or nat sound, how long the shot or sound lasts and precisely when to end it. An editor *punctuates* a story by using the pictures and sound to emphasize, separate or dramatize the narration or other elements of the story. An old saying says that the devil is in the details, but precision and the art of editing are also in the details. For example, as the final shot in a story about a benefit concert by a famous jazz singer, the editor might use the singer's final bows with the sound of applause in the background. The bow and applause signify the end of the concert and provide a definitive ending to the package. Or the editor might choose a shot of the American flag waving in the breeze for the final shot of a story on a Memorial Day ceremony.

In a story showing a young man trying out the prototype for a wheelchair that actually rises up like a person standing, the first experience might be exhilarating and exciting for the man who had not been able to stand in years. The reporter's narration will set up the situation so the audience understands what is going on, and the editor will decide how to time the picture. Perhaps the wheelchair will rise to its full height just as the reporter ends the sentence that describes it. Perhaps the sentence will end, and in the next beat, the chair will reach its apex. If there is an exultant sound from the young man, the editor will decide the best timing for the sound: Will it accent and match the narration, or follow the narration? How long will it be held? How high will the volume be?

Surprise

As discussed in Chapter 8, shooting wide, medium and tight shots can provide the editor with the opportunity to create a surprise. Remember the story that begins with a tight shot of fingers on a keyboard followed by a medium view of the side of a piano and the side of the pianist's head? The wide shot gives the surprise: The pianist has only one hand. This technique allows the editor to tell a story within the story with a few pictures and without narration. A recent story about a pilot who volunteers each month to fly a child to another state for medical treatments because the family could not afford the time or money for the long trips provided a surprise to a news audience at a Virginia station. After most of the story had been told about the child, the video revealed the pilot being moved out of the plane and into a wheelchair. He was paraplegic, a video surprise presented to the audience after the package was well under way. After the revelation, the story gave more details about the pilot's paralysis and his special interest in helping sick children. By building a surprise, the editor can make a powerful impact on the viewer with a few pictures.

Characters

A news story is often personalized so that an issue is clarified through the story of one or two individuals. For example, a story on a new prescription plan for Medicare could tell about the Joneses—a couple who live on $1,200 a month and need $1,000 per month for medicines to treat their diabetes, blood pressure and other health problems. The story might explain how their lives will change if the new plan is implemented. These are the central characters of the written story and will also be the featured characters in the video.

The editor also has the opportunity to include video characters who are *not* described in the narration. In a story about opening day at a baseball park, the photographer might have captured pictures of a dramatic-looking young man with a painted face, wearing a gigantic hat. As discussed earlier, the editor must be careful about violating someone's privacy or showing the person in a way that would obviously embarrass or humiliate without a legally sound reason to do so. In this case, because the fan has appeared in public and on public property where he has no expectation of privacy, the editor knows that using the person's image is legally protected. If the editor has doubt about whether the person was on public property or whether he was the willing subject of the video, the editor should consult the photographer. Assuming the editor is confident about the legality of the video, the story may begin with the colorful character entering the ballpark with his friends. Later in the package, we see him eating his hot dog. Toward the end of the story, we see our new video acquaintance celebrating the team victory with high fives and shouts as he leaves the ballpark at the end of the afternoon, perhaps at the end of the package. The editor has told a story about one person at the game by the choice of three shots. Photographers learn to be alert for the little stories that occur as they are shooting footage, and editors learn to make the most of these serendipitous incidents.

LINEAR EDITING

Until recently, most newsroom editing was done on videotape with **analog** signals, in which a pattern is added to magnetic videotape that represents sound or picture. Analog editing is commonly known as **linear editing** or **tape-to-tape editing.** The image from the shooting tape is reproduced on another tape. The editor moves the shooting tape forward and backward as necessary and copies the desired shots in sequence onto the edit tape. Once the sequence is edited, making changes in the middle of the story may not be possible without redoing all of the subsequent edits. Tape-to-tape editing is still in practice, although less and less frequently. Digital tapes may also be used in linear editing; here, a digital signal, rather than an analog pattern, is recorded onto magnetic tape. The editing equipment operates much like the older analog tape-to-tape editing. That is, the editor shuttles the digital tape back and forth in a tape machine.

The Countdown

In linear editing, a 10-second countdown goes on the tape before the story begins. Newsrooms may use a shorter countdown, but the countdown always ends at the number two—two seconds before the story begins. In the control room during the newscast, the director ensures that the story appears the instant the anchor finishes introducing it. In other words, after the anchor says, *"Rosie Reporter reports,"* the video appears—no wait, no black screen. (See Exhibit 9.2.)

Laying Black

If the editor is working with analog tape machines, she must prepare the edit tape so that control room personnel can work with it under the pressures of a live newscast. The first step in editing onto videotape is to prepare a **control track,** which means *laying black.* Preparing a control track is like a painter preparing a canvas. The control track provides the working space—the area on the tape where pictures and sound can be added. The editor will use **assemble mode,** a setting on the edit controller that allows the establishment of a control track. The editor should create a control track to last longer than the length of the story. If a story

A news package usually begins with a countdown. Even though zero represents the beginning point, the editor will bring in natural sound and video approximately one second earlier. This technique prevents an on-air mistake if the package is brought up early. **EXHIBIT 9.2** is expected to last less than two minutes, laying four minutes of black guarantees plenty of editing space. Editors always lay more black than they need because running out of control track means they can't continue editing. Destroying the control track on the edit tape means starting over; therefore, beginning editors may want to lay enough black so there is, in fact, room to start over if necessary.

In linear editing, timing pictures and sound to accent and punctuate the story often requires *back timing*. **Back timing** means selecting the **end** or **out point** first—the spot where the editor wants the picture or sound to stop—then working backward to determine the **in point,** the point where the picture or sound should begin. For example, suppose a story about a dental program for the poor says that student dentists sometimes *"pick up where the tooth fairy leaves off,"* and this was written expressly for use with a shot of a child who puts his head back on the dental chair and opens his mouth very wide. The editor wants the mouth to open a quick beat after the final word, so that the mouth opening gets full focus and the action punctuates the sentence. The in point will be found by back timing. In this case the editor will set the out point just at the place on the video where the boy has completed the movement. Then, the editor backs up the video from the out point and determines how much of the shot to include and where the in point should be. Perhaps the in point will coincide with a specific word in the narration, or it might be selected to accent other interesting characteristics of the shot. The essence of back timing is that the end of the shot is the most important and the in point is determined by working backward.

NONLINEAR EDITING

In **nonlinear editing,** the audio and video signals are edited digitally on computers. With a digital camera, the signal is encoded digitally and can readily be interpreted by a nonlinear editing system—the computer that is set up for video editing. In nonlinear editing, both the shooting and editing are done in digital format, and the playback is digital as well. The major newsroom change in the next few years will be to use video footage that is shot on digital cameras and stored immediately on a DVD or other storage device for computer editing.

Nonlinear editing provides more opportunity to work with **effects**—dramatic techniques for changing from one picture to another. The simplest and most common effect is a **fade,** when a picture gradually disappears into black. A **wipe** is another basic effect, accomplished by one picture seemingly pushing the other picture off the screen, from top to bottom, bottom to top, left or right, right to left or one cor-

> The best editing goes unnoticed. This is especially true with natural sound. You can blend audio back and forth, back timing and post timing up and down so that every piece of sound flows.
>
> *Dave Wertheimer*
> **KSTP/KSTC-TV,**
> **MINNEAPOLIS/ST. PAUL, MINN.**

ner of the screen to the opposite corner. Another effect is a **dissolve,** when one picture disappears as the next picture forms. Computers can generate an infinite range of effects, such as bringing in a new picture as pieces of a puzzle that settle into the screen. Whatever the effect, it must enhance the story. A dramatic burst of light and sound effect might be appropriate for changing shots in a feature on Fourth-of-July fireworks, but it would not be appropriate in a touching story about a child in foster care. Editors must resist the temptation to use dramatic effects just because they can. The story should drive the editing style.

LAYING THE VIDEO TRACK

Reporters write the script and strive to tell an interesting story, but editors also create stories when they lay the video track. The editor may choose to illustrate the words of the narrator or may choose a different video story to enhance the reporter's words. Before the editor can make creative decisions in telling the story, the video must be available. The shooter must have captured the establishing shots and a variety of wide, medium and tight shots with pictures from many different and interesting angles. Moreover, as with other parts of the process, dramatic editing decisions almost always involve teamwork. When the reporter writes to the video and discusses audio and video possibilities with the editor, the package is strengthened.

If the reporter, photographer and editor work well together, the script will be well planned for the best use of audio and video. The script may indicate the location of the stand-ups and sound bites. Despite the many predetermined elements, many opportunities remain for the editor to use skill and creativity that express an individual style.

When the editor and videographer are the same person, the available video will be familiar and the editing decisions will be easier. When one person shoots and another person edits, the editor's first task is to become familiar with the available video. Sometimes, the editor prepares a **shot sheet,** a list of specific shots and their locations on the shooting tape. The process of preparing a shot sheet is also called **logging the tape.** The reporter may prepare the shot sheet for the editor, or the editor may do it, if time permits. For major reports that involve lots of shooting tapes, someone else in the news department may log the tapes. Interns are often tapped for such time-consuming, although important tasks. In logging tapes, the tape begins at 0 minutes and 0 seconds. Suppose that an excellent establishing shot is located 10 seconds into the tape, and an excellent tight shot of a firefighter's face is located at one minute and 30 seconds into the tape. The shot sheet might indicate:

00:10   wide shot of fire scene

01:30   tight shot of firefighter's face

A story is often reported, shot and edited with little time to spare before it airs. In this situation, the editor simply looks through the tape as many times as necessary to choose the best shots. The editor might be looking at the tape while the reporter is writing. More and more often, the same person does the reporting, shooting and editing. The amount of hard work required of one person to complete all these tasks could be a disadvantage; however, for editing, the one-person system serves as an advantage in the sense that there will be no conflicts in creative vision, and that one individual will be familiar with all aspects of the story.

To demonstrate the importance of video storytelling, let's discuss an example of bad editing, or "wallpapering" a story: pictures are thrown on the screen with no investment of time, thought or creative energy. The story tells of the health risks to long-distance runners and includes a doctor's comment about the warning signs of serious health problems. The sound bite is in the middle of the story, and the reporter stand-up is at the end. As the reporter begins talking, a runner appears in the distance and continues to run, getting closer and closer to the camera, for about 20 seconds, until the sound bite comes up. After the sound bite, we see the runner going away from the camera during narration, continuing to run into the distance until the reporter stand-up ends the story. *Boring.* But why?

The video of one runner approaching the camera from one perspective and then running away into the distance is monotonous because the audience quickly grasps and understands the scene. Within a second or two, viewers understand all they can from the picture: One person is running. They see what she is wearing and may get some understanding of the location, but there's nothing else to glean from the picture. Choosing a variety of shots from the same situation, however, can make the video much more interesting. First, a wide shot of the runner. Then, a medium shot. Then, a tight shot of the runner's face, eyes squinting and sweat following the furrows in the brow. Tight shots of the legs, shoes as they land in soft gravel, pictures of the shadow cast on the ground by the runner's frame. Pictures of the runner stopping, hands on thighs, bent over and breathing deeply. Shots of the end-of-the-run stretching: wide and medium shots followed by close-ups of the runner from a variety of angles. Throughout the mini-documentary of this person's run, we hear the natural sounds of feet in the gravel, breathing, birds chirping and the sounds of other people in the park. The editor selects the shots, the order, the timing.

At this point, the editor's possibilities are determined by the video the photographer has captured. If there are no shots of the feet or close-ups of the face, the editor's creativity is limited. If one long shot of the runner approaching the camera is the only available video, the editor may have few options for making the story effective. When there are lots of good shots, there are lots of decisions

> You don't have to edit in the expected places. You don't have to begin a new shot with the beginning of a sentence. You don't have to edit with the phrases of music. Sometimes it's too obvious and you don't want viewers to notice the editing.
>
> *Eric Scott*
> **WJZ-TV, BALTIMORE**

to make. How many seconds is appropriate for the opening shot? Will each shot be held a similar length of time, or will the duration of the shot be determined by narration or by other factors? Will the video illustrate all the narration or only part of the narration? Will the video tell a different story from the narration? Special effects such as slow motion and special wipes, transitions or dissolves may be available through the editing equipment. All of these possibilities for the story rest with the editor. First, however, the editor needs to establish the scene so the viewers understand what they're seeing and where it is.

Establishing Shots

Almost every story begins with a picture that establishes the location and situation of the story—the **establishing shot.** Because the audience needs to understand what is going on and where, the establishing shot is usually a wide shot and often begins with a bit of full natural sound to help clarify the scene for the audience. If a house is burning, an establishing shot makes it clear whether the house is on a city street, in a subdivision or in the country. A story about a city commission might begin with a shot of City Hall or a glimpse of the commissioners at work. A network story about the Super Bowl is likely to begin with an overhead shot of the stadium from a blimp, an establishing shot to be envied by news operations with smaller budgets.

The establishing shot does not always have to begin wide. The editor may reveal the situation after one or more tight shots. A story about a street peddler might begin with a close-up of a bag being zipped, followed by the back of two feet walking out a door, and then reveal the wider shot of the roving salesman carrying his bag of goods down the street. A story about the Kentucky Derby may begin with a tight shot of a hand taking a ticket to enter Churchill Downs and then show wider shots of the line of people buying their tickets and a shot of a sign that identifies the location.

Whether the editor begins with a wide or a tight shot, the decision must be made how to bring the audience into the scene most effectively. The story will require an establishing shot, whether it comes first in the package or later, and whether the story begins with a nat sound open or with narration and background sound. For example, the establishing shot of a carnival could be the first shot with a wide view of the midway, or the first shot could be a tight shot with nat sound of bowling pins falling as they are hit with a softball, followed by a medium shot of the person who just threw the ball for a chance on the big teddy bear. In this case, the establishing shot may be the third shot in the package: We see the fairway and understand exactly where the story is taking place. The editor may make these decisions alone or may confer with the reporter during the script-writing process. After the scene is established, the shots that follow will continue to bring the viewer closer to the action.

Illustrating the Narration

In one of the most common approaches to editing news packages, the video directly illustrates the narration. As the reporter narration describes the police investigation, police officers are seen working at the crime scene. As the story describes a lawsuit, legal documents and working attorneys appear on screen. As the reporter gives information about a shooting-spree killer and tells about his childhood, education and membership in a hate group, pictures will show the man, his childhood home, his elementary school and a photograph of him with his organization. These pictures show exactly what the reporter is talking about and illustrate the narration point by point. The advantage of this approach is that the story is simple and clear for the viewer. There is no guesswork.

> Don't cram. Let things breathe.
>
> *John Antonio*
> WABC-TV, NEW YORK

Because viewers are so accustomed to seeing video that illustrates the narration they are hearing, editors should be careful not to mislead viewers. When the video is not a direct illustration, some explanation may be needed. For example, if you have a local story about a local group currently in Washington to protest a federal law, the station may not have footage from Washington. If the editor uses footage of the group from a previous local meeting where they planned the protest and does not label it as **file footage** (video from the station's archives), the viewers could think they are seeing the group in Washington. Again, the editor should make sure that every picture is accurate, and working closely with reporters and photographers can help ensure that the editor does not mislead or confuse the viewer.

Editors quickly discover that it is not always possible to illustrate everything the reporter says, as he says it, and that even if it is possible this may not be the most effective approach. For example, consider the difficulties of simultaneously illustrating each part of the narration when the reporter says that the new county park *"provides activities for people of all ages, including picnic areas and playgrounds for children and workout stations and walking trails for seniors."* If the editor attempts to illustrate each part of the sentence, the pictures will have to change quickly and there will be little time to make any of the experiences clear and real. (See Exhibit 9.3.)

> Fast edits will keep attention. The audience will watch, but they don't hear and understand as well when the video is changing so fast. Use the important audio with slower edits.
>
> *Deborah Potter*
> RTNDF, WASHINGTON, D.C.

Instead of including the quick edits of different scenes, the editor may cover the entire sentence with shots that give an indirect illustration. Wide, medium and tight shots of a grandparent unpacking the car or a small child playing could cover the list of available activities. (See Exhibit 9.4.) Then, while the narration proceeds to give information about the number of park employees and expected attendance, shots of people picnicking and seniors at the workout stations can be included—illustrating the narration completed earlier. The audience has already heard the description and will understand the pictures that follow. Similarly, in a story about a tornado, the reporter

In this time line, the editor gives a direct illustration of the words the reporter says. **EXHIBIT 9.3**

The editor may elect to show related pictures rather than illustrating the narration directly. **EXHIBIT 9.4**

might say that cleanup crews are dealing with downed trees, piles of rubble and remaining flood water. Using pictures to illustrate each of the three problems would require editing the shots very fast to match them to the narration. Instead, the editor may choose a picture of a worker putting on wading boots during the description of the three major problems for the cleanup crew and use pictures of rubble and downed trees later. The audience will understand.

Stories Within the Story

Often, the editor lets the video tell its own story while the narrator tells another. In other words, the editor can tell a video story or stories within the larger story. (See Exhibit 9.5.) In a story about a major traffic accident, while reporter narration describes the cause of the accident, the video can tell the story of the frustrations of the traffic backup: a wide shot of the traffic backed up into the distance, a medium shot of people milling around their stopped cars and talking with each other, a tight shot of a driver leaning on the steering wheel in frustration. While the narration tells about a fire, the video tells the story of the firefighters' battle against the sub-zero temperatures with shots of ice forming on mustaches and people rubbing their hands together and struggling with cold equipment.

As a sports story tells about a horse race, the video might tell the story of people betting, winning and losing. In a story about a child trapped in a well, an additional story about onlookers can be told in the video, perhaps including a picture of someone climbing a fence for a better view. In this instance, when people are talking about the story around the water cooler the next day, they may discuss the rescue, but they are also likely to comment on the intrusiveness of the gawkers and the guy who climbed the fence. The editor can enrich the package by telling video stories.

Using Cutaways

As discussed in relation to shooting video, telling video stories requires the use of cutaway shots to change the picture from the established perspective. If an action is taking place, the cutaway leaves the action to provide another view and then returns to the action. If the video shows a marching band coming down the street during a parade, the cutaway may show people on the sidewalk watching the parade. If the primary action is an interview, the cutaway temporarily changes the view from the person talking to something or someone else, such as the reporter listening. We have examined cutaways as a shooting requirement, but the major purpose of getting cutaway shots is for more effective editing. We have discussed shooting reporter reaction shots and cutaway questions for interview cutaways, transitions and neutral shots for sequential jump cuts, and cutaway shots that allow the shooting axis to be crossed. Now let's look at these concepts from the editing perspective.

EXHIBIT 9.5 A short sequence of shots can tell a video story within a larger news story. These three shots could let the audience know that the subject plays a musical instrument while the narration describes something else.

Cutaways in Interviews

A cutaway in a sound bite cuts away from the person speaking to a picture of something else. The new shot appears to be for the purpose of adding variety to the video, but it is primarily to cover the point where two sections of the interview are joined together. (See Exhibit 9.6.)

Modern editing techniques allow new options for handling jump cuts in interviews without using cutaways. Some editors use a digital effect between the two parts of the sound bite to indicate to viewers that an edit has taken place. The effect may be a dissolve between the two shots or an edge or color that wipes across the screen between the segments. These effects can work very well, or they can distract from the interview if they appear too suddenly and contrast too dramatically with the previous style of editing. The advantage to using an effect as a transition is in letting the audience know that an edit has taken place. The advantage of the traditional cutaway is that the inserted video can provide additional information to the viewer.

The cutaways can illustrate what people are talking about and add variety and interest to the package. If a city council member is talking about a no-smoking policy for the city, the cutaway shots could show city workers smoking and talking. During an interview about school board action on school safety, cutaways of children at school would be more interesting than pictures of school board officials talking during a meeting. Because the audience understands very quickly a picture of a person talking, the editor may use the majority of the sound bite for additional interesting pictures. When appropriate video shots are not available and digital effects are not being used, the editor may need to use reporter reaction shots and cutaway questions to avoid jump cuts in interviews.

The two nonsequential shots of a person talking cause a jump cut. The editor covers the jump with a cutaway shot as indicated in this illustration. **EXHIBIT 9.6**

Before

After

Cutaways for Sequence Jump Cuts

Editors must avoid creating the jump cuts that result from placing shots of two nonsequential events back-to-back. These edits show two events occurring in the same time frame when the relationship would be impossible. A cut from a teenager riding a horse to the same teen on a diving board in the next instant is an impossible jump from one situation to another. So is a cut from an investigator taking fingerprints inside a house to a shot of the same investigator getting into a car. The editor needs some kind of cutaway to neutralize the perspective and cover the impossible jump. (See Exhibit 9.7.)

Editing Sequences

An editor becomes excellent by achieving mastery in editing video sequences. A **video sequence** is a series of related shots that progress in an order that makes sense to the audience. By editing wide, medium and tight, the editor creates a meaningful series of shots. At the scene of a bank robbery, the first shot will be wide to show the location of the bank, followed by a medium shot of the building,

EXHIBIT 9.7   To prevent a sequence jump cut such as the one that occurs in sequence (A), the editor adds a cutaway to neutralize the location. The viewer recognizes that during the time the individual is not shown, he moves from outside to inside.

and then a tight shot of the door with the sign indicating why the bank is closed. The sequences do not always have to be edited back-to-back. In a story about a baseball game, three shots of a face-painted fan could tell a story within the story: Early in the package we see the character, later in the package we see the same fan eating a hot dog, and finally the package closes with a shot of the fan celebrating the victory. However, the same three shots could be joined by cutaways and edited into a short sequence to tell the story more quickly. When editing sequences, the editor strives to achieve interest, continuity and completion.

Creative Sequences

In the example of the story about a new park, the narration explains that the park *"provides activities for people of all ages, including picnic areas, playgrounds for children and workout stations and walking trails for seniors."* Using one shot to illustrate each part of the park not only would be too fast, but also achieves no more than a mere wallpaper effect. If the editor presents sequences, however, the viewers can feel as if they've participated in the excitement of opening day. A general sequence of a family getting out of a car and gathering picnic items could cover the sentence given above; shots of the picnic area, playground and senior citizen activities could follow.

For the sake of variety, we usually avoid editing two similar shots together in a sequence. A wide shot will be followed by a medium shot—not another wide shot. The medium shot may be followed by a close-up, followed by an extreme close-up and back out to a medium shot or some other variation. In some cases an editor may choose to break this rule. To illustrate the site of a planned construction site or the location of a new landing strip for the airport, we might edit wide shots back-to-back. If two people are arrested for burglary, the two tight shots of the suspects would be edited together. But generally, it is best to edit sequences in the natural order in which we process what we see: First, we take in the overall scene, then we focus on increasingly narrow parts of the big picture. Imagine a sign flashing, "Please wait." We could see it in a wide, medium or tight shot and understand what's happening, but how much more interesting to see it first in a medium shot as it flashes and disappears, followed by a cut to the close-up of the words reappearing. A very simple, but very effective two-shot sequence.

The use of various angles can make a sequence more interesting. In a story about Marines training on the fast rope, a wide or medium shot of one Marine coming down the rope gives the audience a fairly clear understanding of what the training involves, but when the next shot is from above looking down the rope, the audience gets a most unusual perspective. The final shot might be from back on ground level for a tight shot of the Marine's feet as they hit the dirt. This sequence of wide, medium and tight, from below, above and below again, provides a creative and interesting sequence.

Continuity

Edits should present a series of shots in a logical order. Maintaining a logical order of shots during editing is called **continuity.** It would not *continue* logically to cut from a girl at the top of a water slide to a shot of the same girl walking beside the pool. This would be a jump cut, as discussed previously. Likewise, if someone goes out an outside door and we see the same person in the next shot coming into a room inside a house, the shots don't make sense. Editors need to keep continuity in mind. Do the actions *continue* in a way that makes sense to the viewer? The editor protects continuity by using appropriate cutaways and transition shots. The challenge is to see the story the way someone who has never seen the video and doesn't know the circumstances will see it. The reporter, photographer and editor know a lot about the story when they begin. The editor must keep the viewer's perspective in mind.

Completion

In the previous chapter, we discussed the audience's need for completion. This sense of completion can be achieved through editing. When a pitcher throws the ball, we need to see the ending, whether the ball goes into the catcher's glove or out of the ballpark. Even without the shot of the home run, the editor can provide a sense of completion by cutting away to the crowd reaction and finishing with the slugger crossing home plate. If the photographer didn't capture the actual home run hit, the editor can even use the sound from the crack of the bat from another hit to make the sequence more realistic. A sequence tells a story, and viewers want a beginning, middle and end.

At the water slide, a few shots can make the event complete: a wide shot of the slide and kids hitting the pool at the bottom, a close-up of a child's face at the top looking down, a cutaway to the water from the top of the slide showing how scary it looks, a shot of the child hitting the water at the bottom. The sequence could be extended with a cutaway looking down at the water from the top of the slide, a shot of the mother's face watching her child, and perhaps a close-up of the child's face as he comes up for air after the successful journey down the slide, sputtering water and wiping eyes and nose. Add some dramatic music and you have a 10- to 15-second action adventure.

Editors can create effective sequences by showing an action/reaction, a reversal of perspective or a series of actions.

Action/Reaction

Showing an action and a reaction to it makes a two-shot sequence. After the shot of a bass drum going by in a parade, the shot of a little boy holding his ears shows a reaction to the drum. In a story showing police officers training to use bicycles, a shot of an officer attempting a fast-speed dismount could take on added meaning when followed by the instructor's gesture of approval. At the tennis court, one person serves the ball and the video cuts to the other person returning the shot. After shots of abortion protesters outside a clinic, we see nurses watching from the window. Following an action with a reaction shot makes a meaningful two-shot sequence.

Reversals

If the photographer has captured the appropriate shots, the editor can make sequences more meaningful with a reversal of perspective. After a shot looking down on a baby in a stroller, cut to a shot looking up at the person who's looking down. In a story about the long lines for buying tickets to a new movie, show a person approaching the ticket booth where the salesperson says *"Eight dollars please,"* then cut to a shot from inside the ticket booth looking out at the customer. Amazingly enough, viewers accept these sequences without question and without realizing that the photographer had to ask the customer to assist in accomplishing the split second of reality. After a shot of a performer on stage, cut to a shot of the audience. After a shot of a sick bear at the zoo, cut to a shot of the zoologist approaching with medicine in hand. A perspective and a reversal of perspective provide an interesting two-shot sequence.

Editing on the Action

Editing a sequence that contains movement requires special attention. When a wide shot is cut to a medium shot, movement within the shot can cause unacceptable jumps unless the editor matches the action at the edit point. This editing technique is often referred to as **match frame editing** or **cutting on the action** because the editor will choose the exact frame of video from the wide shot that comes closest to the movement of another frame of video in the tighter shot. (Again, the editor must rely on the photographer to supply a variety of shots that allow logical edits of an action.) For example, imagine the common interview situation where two people face each other and talk. Any movement within the shot requires attention. If the editor uses a two-shot of the reporter and interviewee and then cuts to a close-up of the interviewee, that person's position needs to match reasonably well. If we see the interviewee in the wider two-shot with hands gesturing at chest level, but the following tighter shot shows the person rubbing the back of her neck, the jump in position will be too drastic and likely to distract the viewer. In one instant, the hand will seem to jump from the front of the chest to the back of the neck. If the person is moving her hands in front of her chest in the wide shot, the tight shot that follows should show her hands in a similar position. Some editors work so precisely that they edit on eye blinks, which surely goes beyond the need for continuity in broadcast news stories. If the editor does not remain alert to matching actions reasonably closely, however, some strange sights can develop.

The editor can develop an action sequence from a repeated action. Cutting on the action of the repeated movement keeps the video moving and helps retain interest, as shown in Exhibit 9.8. In this example, the photographer shot a wide shot of the officer moving his arm from right to left. The photographer also shot medium and tight shots as the action was repeated. With the wide, medium and tight shots of the repeated gesture, the editor can cut directly from the wide shot to the medium shot by cutting on the action. If the wide shot shows the officer's arm on the right, the medium shot will begin with the arm in the same position but will continue throughout the gesture. The two shots will look like one action: the officer moves his arm from right to left.

If the photographer captures an action along with plenty of cutaways, the editor can create a dramatic sequence by cutting on the action. Imagine that a lifeguard and his friend are good-naturedly playing with a pool regular, a charming cut-up kind of kid. They warn him that they're going to throw him in the pool if he doesn't quit teasing them. He taunts again, they pick him up by the arms and legs, swing him three times and then throw him in the pool. This action could take a couple of minutes to occur. To shorten the event, the editor can use general cutaways. For example, the editor could use a quick shot of the kid taunting the lifeguard, then cut to a general cutaway of the water, then back to a medium shot of the action as the lifeguard and friend pick up the kid.

The entire sequence benefits if the editor also cuts on the action or matches the movement as much as possible. The three swings take quite a bit of time, so the editor might use a short clip where the two pick up the boy and swing him

EXHIBIT 9.8   If the photographer captures a repeated action from wide and tighter perspectives, the editor can cut from one shot to another on frames where the actions match. This editing technique is called cutting on the action or match frame editing.

away from the water. Next comes a brief cutaway of the water or of someone watching. Next, the editor uses the final part of the action where the two swing the boy forward and release him into the water. The cutaway allows the editor to edit the first swing just before the final swing and release, without an awkward jump in the video. The cutaway let us skip the middle swing and pick up where the action matched. The edit point took place at a matching point in different actions. The goal of telling the story quickly was achieved by the use of cutaways and matching the action.

LAYING THE AUDIO TRACK

The importance of audio cannot be overstated. Television is not just about pictures; it's equally about sound. First-time editors are sometimes surprised that the audio track goes down first when editing a news package, but the editor's first responsibility is to serve as sound technician and make sure that the audio levels are appropriate. The **audio levels** refer to the balance between the reporter's voice, interviewee voices and any background sound or natural sound that may be included. As mentioned earlier, the natural sounds of an event are captured by the photographer and can be used as background to the reporter's narration to make the video feel more realistic. Besides its use for background or a nat sound opening, natural sound is also used in **nat sound breaks.**

In nonlinear editing, more audio tracks are available, so music or other sound effects can be added easily. When there are only two audio tracks and the editor needs narration, music and natural sound, the music is often combined, or **mixed,** with reporter narration onto one channel. The proper **audio mix** balances the different sounds, allowing the listener to hear the most important sounds clearly and the other sounds in appropriate levels. Background sound that is too loud will distract from the reporter's information, but if it's not loud enough, the video will seem dull. If the narrator's voice is louder than the sound bite, the audience may be frustrated and attempt to adjust the TV volume. Moreover, each newsroom has standard audio levels to aim for so that when packages go on the air, they will all have the same audio levels.

To maintain appropriate audio levels, the editor uses a **V-U meter,** a meter on the editing equipment that indicates the volume of audio. Both analog and digital systems provide V-U meters, all of which look very similar and are designed so that the desired narration level is indicated. (See Exhibit 9.9.) However, different pitches recorded at the same level on the V-U meter may actually sound like they've been recorded at different volumes. For this reason, editors may use headphones to help ensure that the audio levels sound balanced.

In the basic process of putting a package together, the editor usually starts by laying down the complete audio track. Following are the steps typically involved in laying the audio track:

EXHIBIT 9.9   The V-U meter indicates volume units or loudness of the sound and may be in either analog or digital form. V-U meters indicate the ideal audio level. In the example on the right, the desired level is zero.

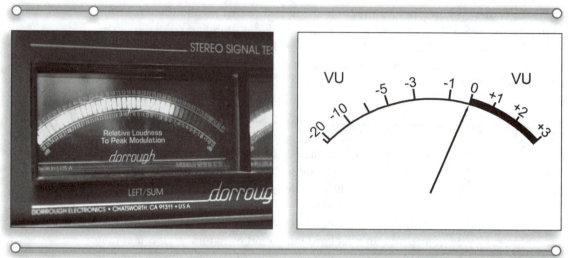

- The track usually starts with a **nat sound open,** which sets the stage and gives the audience a second to comprehend the location and subject of the story. When viewers hear full natural sound and see an event or location for one second or even less, they will be able to absorb the scene. For example, if a story begins with the sound of a bell ringing and students walking in hallways, this makes it clear that the setting is a school. Knowing the setting helps prepare the viewer to understand the story. The video is edited along with the sound. (Even though the audio track is the primary consideration at this point, it would be senseless to try to put only the sound on tape and try later to match the video.)

- The reporter provides a recording of his narration, made in an audio booth, or the reporter may record directly into the editing equipment. The editor transfers the first part of the narration to the edit tape or computer program—after the nat sound open. The narration will lead into a sound bite or a nat sound break. For now, this part of the edit tape has no video.

- After the first part of the narration is recorded and perhaps after a nat sound break, the editor adds the audio and video of the selected sound bite.

- The sound bite is followed by more reporter narration, additional nat sound breaks and usually a reporter's stand-up. Like the nat sound open and the

Video editors often complete the audio portion of the news package before adding B-roll. **EXHIBIT 9.10** This time line represents an audio track that starts with narration. The sound bite is added from audio from an interview; the sound bite's video is included in the edit. Reporter narration concludes the package.

If the editor begins the package with natural sound, the video will be included in the edit. This time line represents a completed audio track for a package.

In the final step, the editor will cover the reporter's audio with video and natural sound.

sound bite, the voice and picture of the reporter's stand-up and the audio and video for nat sound breaks are edited into the package simultaneously.

- Finally, the editor goes back to the beginning and adds the B-roll (video) and nat sound background over the reporter's narration to complete the package. We will discuss adding B-roll in more detail below.

A very simple package might be made up only of reporter narration and B-roll with nat sound. A more complex package may include more than one sound bite or nat sound break, more than one stand-up, and more than two sections of reporter narration. Even with simple packages, the editor always includes sounds (in addition to the narration) to bring the package to life.

Natural Sound

Imagine watching people dance without hearing the music, or seeing a home run without the sound of the cheering crowd. As an even more extreme example, imagine watching a singer holding a microphone and singing with great emotion—but you don't hear the voice. Editing video really means editing both pictures and sound. From the very beginning, editors should learn to include some level of natural sound when they cover a reporter's narration. The natural sound provides reality, emotion and interest and is fundamental to a good news package.

Good editing work always includes natural sound. In a story about an overcrowded highway system, we need to both see and hear the cars and trucks. When the video shows a keynote speaker concluding a dramatic comment, we need to hear the sound of the audience clapping rather than simply seeing people clap their hands together. Certainly when we see someone singing, we need to hear the voice. The video without the audio seems artificial and empty. Therefore, after the editor begins with a nat sound open and lays the reporter narration, nat sound breaks, sound bites and stand-ups, the final step is to cover the narration with video *and* nat sound.

> A lot of times, the sound will drive the package more than the pictures.
>
> *Pat Barry*
> **KCNC-TV, DENVER**

Including the nat sound should become an automatic part of laying B-roll. Whenever we see video, the audio track should be included—even when it seems that there's nothing to be heard. A long view of a mountain vista might not have a lot of natural sound. The wind may not be blowing and no birds are chirping. When the scene is edited into the story, however, the audio track should be included as nat sound. The audio from the shot of a mountain vista will at least have the slight hiss or static of reality. Even when we don't hear recognizable sounds, we do hear *something.* Editors should always include the natural sound to enliven stories.

Editors must be careful that the natural sound in the background does not distract from or overpower the reporter's narration. In a story about a street protest, the editor could easily let the audio level of protester chants remain too high. If the chants are recorded at a high level, the editor will have to compensate by keeping the editing volume level low. The editor can follow some basic guidelines for achieving proper audio balance, but skill in managing volume levels may come only with practice and experience. For example, analog V-U meters are designed so that the optimum level is at 0, meaning that the narration level should be as close to 0 as possible. (In fact, it will only hover around the 0, because our volume changes constantly while we talk.)

When working with interviews and reporter stand-ups, the editor is most concerned with the clarity of the person's voice. There may be natural sounds in the background, but there is generally no reason to want the audience to focus on the background sounds or natural sounds in interviews and stand-ups. At other times, the editor may want all the attention to go to the natural sounds.

Nat Sound Breaks

As previously mentioned, the editor sometimes uses natural sound brought up to full audio level at the beginning or within the story, a technique called nat sound opens or **nat sound breaks.** Especially in tape-to-tape editing, the editor's challenge in using nat sound breaks is to plan in advance. Even with digital editing, including the nat sound breaks as you go makes the process easier than adding them later. The reporter may write to the audio and indicate nat sound breaks in the script. For example, in a story about a new roller coaster at an area park, the reporter might write, *The gigantic double loop brings both delight and fear to passengers [ADD NATS].* The editor knows to include the sound of screams at that point. The reporter may remember a specific moment of dramatic audio or may have reviewed the tape and noticed a good segment of audio. Perhaps the reporter and photographer discussed the story after the shoot and shared the idea. The editor will decide whether the break lasts less than a second or perhaps a couple of seconds. During a nat sound break, the natural sound is not covered by reporter narration. The pure natural sound advances the story and conveys the emotion of the event much more effectively than the reporter describing the event—and more effectively than sound in the background of the reporter narration.

When the nat sound breaks are not written into the script, the editor decides where to interrupt the narration for a nat sound break. In a story about a new roller coaster, the script might say, *The riders waited in line for two hours to buy tickets.* At this point, the editor could insert a quick edit of the park attendant saying, *"Five dollars please."* Or perhaps the photographer has captured a shot of a child waiting in the long line and complaining, *"Mom, how much longer?"* The reporter may not be aware that such a shot exists, but the editor sees a place to use the question and convey more about what it was like to be at the scene, to enliven the story. In a story about large numbers of travelers on a holiday, the editor might use a quick nat sound break of an announcement over the PA system: *"This is a special train."* The nat sound break does not always include words. More often, the break is just sounds: a computer keyboard, a telephone, a door closing, a dog barking.

Nat sound breaks can provide transition from one part of the story to the next. After describing the new roller coaster ride, the long line and the thrills of the experience, the reporter says that the roller coaster is also providing excitement at City Hall. The mayor then describes how the new attraction is expected to increase tourism income by 25 percent. The editor needs to make a transition from the roller coaster scene to the mayor's office, so she might use a nat sound break of something other than the roller coaster to help the viewer make the shift in location: perhaps a quick edit of the sound of a cash register spitting out another ticket. The sound focuses the audience's attention on the financial transaction just before the mayor talks about the city coffers. Or natural sound from the mayor's office could help the viewer make the transition from the park to City Hall, perhaps the sound of the phone ringing or the mayor's secretary answering the phone. In a feature story about a child pianist, the story may shift away from music to the child's hobbies, so the piano music may fade and suddenly we see a blur and hear the full sound of children at play. We then realize that the blur is a soccer ball, and the audience sees the child playing soccer at the neighborhood park. The natural sound helps the viewer make the switch from piano practice to outdoor recreation. The possibilities for creativity in using sound are limited only by the imagination. The first step is to remember that natural sound is a fundamental requirement for good editing and nat sound breaks are essential for excellence in editing.

OVERLAPPING AUDIO AND VIDEO

The editor does not have to use the audio and video together exactly as they were recorded. In many instances the editor may overlap audio or video with pictures or sound from somewhere else. This is known as an **L-cut.**

One of the most common uses of overlapping video is in sound bites. The editor brings in the picture of the interviewee as the reporter is introducing him. This technique allows the audience to see the person before the sound is brought up to full audio level for the sound bite. (See Exhibit 9.11.) For example, in a story about a state bill to regulate the logging industry the reporter says, *"State Senator Bill Plam introduced the bill."* During the reporter's introduction, the viewer sees Bill Plam and hears him talking as background sound. When the narration ends, the audio level comes up full and Plam explains why he believes the bill should become law.

The L-cut requires more effort than just cutting to Senator Plam with full audio after the narration. In the normal cut, the editor sets the in point at the beginning of the sound bite with the appropriate audio level. However, in the L-cut, the in point for Senator Plam will occur a second or two before the sound bite begins, and the audio will change from background sound level to full sound within the edit.

The L-cut can also be used to continue the video of the interviewee with background sound level after the sound bite. In this situation, the picture and full sound of the interviewee appear for the sound bite; the in point is the beginning of the sound bite, but the out point will be set a second or two after the sound bite is complete. The sound is simply adjusted to background level after the sound bite. The difficulty of the process varies with the capabilities of different equipment. The editor will need to be comfortable with basic editing before attempting an L-cut.

Editors can use L-cuts to clarify and enhance news stories. Overlapping audio and video can create a strong impact when the editor includes sound that occurred at a different time than the video. For example, in a high-speed chess match, the players slap the timer when the move is over. The editor may include this sound while the viewer sees one of the players staring intensely at the board. In a story about a new Buddhist church, the story may end with a shot of the statue of

Buddha, but the background sound may be the chanting of monks or the sound of a bell. At the naturalization ceremony for new American citizens, the story may end with a shot of the American flag as the group recites the Pledge of Allegiance.

One familiar way of overlapping video is when the photographer has captured music as natural sound. For example, a musical group performs at the county fair. The editor shows the group performing with full sound, but adds video from various scenes at the fair. The editor may continue the music underneath the next section of reporter narration. (Remember, however, that copyright law requires permission for the extended use of someone's performance.) Like the L-cut, this technique builds on editing basics, which the editor should develop first.

Editors also use overlapping audio and video to make an edit acceptable that would otherwise be a jump cut. For example, when the president is walking down the steps from Air Force One, a cut to the president speaking at the podium would be a jump cut. The president cannot make that move in an instant, and a good editor would want to neutralize the shot by including a cutaway of the crowd or some other cutaway. However, overlapping the audio could explain the jump. For example, as we see the president de-planing, the reporter says the president's comments at this stop focused on poverty, and we begin to hear his comments about bringing business to the poor area. By overlapping the audio, the editor helps the audience make the transition from the president walking to the president's speech. In a story about a famous baseball player, the video may show footage from a recent home run, but we hear the sounds of a horse and the player talking about how he likes to get away from the world of baseball. As the video cuts to the baseball player riding alongside the reporter, the audience understands immediately that the interview is being done at a farm and that the baseball footage was to introduce the player and establish his identity.

In the L-cut, the soundbite audio is low until the narration is completed. then the **EXHIBIT 9.11**
interviewee's audio level is raised.

Some editors avoid overlapping audio and video, believing that when the sounds and pictures don't match, the audience will be confused. Confusion can certainly result if the technique is not executed carefully. Again, the editor's primary goal is to enhance the story and aid the audience in understanding. When used carefully, overlapping audio and video can become a powerful editing technique to enhance the audience's understanding and create interest.

USING GRAPHICS

Graphics are illustrations that are distinct from the video footage and are specially designed to be edited into a story. Graphics used to be limited mostly to computer-generated words on a colored background, but today's technology allows great variety and creativity in graphics. Words can be presented in many different styles and can be superimposed over still frames from the video or over other pictures. A **still frame,** shown in Exhibit 9.12, is one frame from video that is frozen and used for a dramatic effect or for a graphic background. The colors in still frames can be changed, the edges softened, the entire picture darkened or lightened. The words can fade in, float in, crawl or fly across the screen. For example, a story about gun control might include statistics on the number of crimes committed with handguns in the United States and in two other countries. To present the statistics in an attractive and memorable way, the numbers could be shown over a darkened still frame from video of someone holding a handgun. As the narrator gives the statistic for the United States, we might see the words "United States" fade in with the number of annual handgun crimes below, then fade out as the name of another

EXHIBIT 9.12 This video graphic was specially designed for a particular story and presents information that the audience might not be able to grasp quickly from narration only.

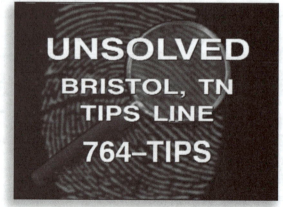

country appears with the number of handgun crimes below it. Or the names of all three countries and their statistics could appear together on screen.

In stories where numbers are important, the audience may remember more if they both see and hear the details. For example, in a story about hurricane damage, the narrator may give Red Cross damage estimates both in narration and in a still frame:

8,000 homes damaged

12,000 people injured

$20 million in damage

Like stand-ups, graphics can be especially helpful when video is unavailable. In a report about New York police officers charged with sodomizing a man, one network used a graphic of scales of justice fading in over video of police officers on the way into the courtroom, while the reporter described the allegations. In another network story, about economic policies under four presidents, editors used still-framed pictures of presidents Gerald Ford, Jimmy Carter, Ronald Reagan and George Herbert Walker Bush appearing one at a time until they were lined up across the screen.

For a description of three demands by a citizens' group at a city council meeting, the demands can be shown on the screen. In a story about tornado damage, while the reporter is telling the viewer that the tornado had winds up to 378 miles per hour and was reported to cover territory a mile wide, the audience might see a picture of the tornado with the label "378 mph" and then see another shot with the label "one mile wide." In a story about a merger of three major corporations, the company logos could be edited into the story. These graphics help the audience understand and remember.

Graphics can also emphasize points that cannot be easily illustrated with video. For example, if a corporation issues a written statement in response to charges of polluting the environment, there is no video of anyone talking. Graphics may be designed to highlight important parts of the statement. Several words from a sentence can appear to pull away from the paper and move forward on the screen. The technique of highlighting part of the quotation, also used in newspapers, is called a **pull quote.** In newspapers, the quote is often highlighted in a shaded box and stands alone. In television, the quote can appear to hover over a shot of the original document.

In all cases, graphics must be designed simply so the viewer can gain information or clarification quickly.

THE EDITOR'S RESPONSIBILITIES

The editor's task is to combine pictures and sound in a way that conveys the story with clarity and impact. As editor Walt Reedy indicates in his quotation at the top of the chapter, the story dictates the possibilities and limitations of editing. Like authors who listen to the demands of the characters they have created, editors are alert to what is appropriate or inappropriate in editing a story. Sometimes the job is easy and sometimes difficult depending on the available video. Because the editor's possibilities are tied to the available video, this chapter reinforces some of the advice in the previous chapter.

The trend in editing television news is toward fast-paced edits. Television news producers sometimes fear that if the audience is not constantly mesmerized by the pictures they see and the sounds they hear, they will change channels. This choice in editing style can quickly become a complex, philosophical question. Are we training people to require constant fast-paced audio and video stimulation and entertainment? Do we operate with the belief that the audience has *no* attention span? Are our citizens losing the ability simply to listen and understand the meaning of words? We cannot discuss this issue fully here, but thinking editors will want to consider the role they play in the presentation of news and recognize the responsibilities incumbent on the profession. Their simplest decisions have impact.

> You have to learn to work fast because invariably, you won't have the time you think you will.
>
> *Pat Barry*
> **KCNC-TV, DENVER**

Editors must be able to adapt to a variety of working situations. They must often work fast under extreme deadline pressures. The editing may be done in a truck in a remote location or in a hotel room in a foreign country. The editing may be done at a leisurely pace in a newsroom editing suite, or the story may be fast-breaking and the news team may give the script to the editor with 10 minutes until air time. In addition, editors in television newsrooms work with many different photographers and reporters, which requires adapting the editing style to the reporting and writing style of different individuals. Although the work is demanding, it can be fulfilling as well. When the story is finished, it will go on the air and be seen immediately by tens of thousands or even millions of people.

Television news editors use creativity and knowledge of state-of-the-art technology to tell stories with audio and video. Part of their job is to ensure the truth and accuracy of the story, and they generally provide the last checkpoint to make sure the story falls within legal boundaries. Following is a more detailed discussion of the editor's responsibilities.

Ensuring Truth and Accuracy

Despite the personal fulfillment editors may find in the creativity of their work, they must remember that the primary taskmaster is the truth and accuracy of the story. One of the first things photographers and editors learn is that they can control appearances and impressions. They can manipulate anything. What happened first can appear to have happened last or the other way around. Editors have the power of misrepresentation at their fingertips, and though giant violations of the truth would surely result in dismissal, smaller inaccuracies might not be caught. The entire process of broadcast news reporting must be driven by the desire to present the truth. As discussed in Chapter 1, news must be accurate and must be presented fairly and objectively. Video editors hold as much responsibility as anyone else in following these principles.

Adhering to Legalities

In addition to the ethical concerns facing the editor regarding truth and accuracy, decisions about putting pictures and sound together can be a legal minefield. Like the writer choosing words, the editor must be totally confident that each picture provides a truthful representation. Furthermore, the editor is the last person to work on the story before it is broadcast. Choosing the wrong picture can lead to a lawsuit for invasion of privacy, libel or copyright violation. When a story about a traffic accident says that police attribute the wreck to a drunk driver, the editor might choose the picture of a woman being pulled from the driver's side of a car. If, in fact, the drunk driver was in another vehicle, the woman could file an actionable lawsuit for damage to her reputation. In a story about eating disorders or theft, a general street scene may show an identifiable person who might be misjudged as a bulimic or a thief and who could sue for damages. In a story about a teacher's sexual assault on students, general shots during a class change could erroneously suggest that an identifiable student was one of the victims. In some cases, news directors or other legal specialists review the final version of a story, but more commonly, the videotape editor is the last person to see the package before it goes on the air. Editors are not required to be experts in media law and do not bear sole responsibility for the legality of the story. A careless editor, however, can find herself in a courtroom explaining how an editing decision was made. In contrast, knowledgeable editors can prevent errors if they know some basics of the law. Legal considerations will be examined in more depth in Chapter 11.

Exercising Creative Control

Like the reporter who chooses words and the photographer who frames up the shots, the editor exerts much creative control. Good editors enjoy their creativity and develop skill, judgment and finesse as they gain experience. Editors work in nuances, subtleties and timing that others may never notice but that define excellence. A poor editor may show too much of an action or too little, bring in a shot too early or too late, set the volume a little too high or too low. Without creativity and good judgment, the editor will achieve minimal impact. Television professionals often refer to ineffective video as **wallpaper**—it accomplishes

People respond to rhythms. Take them on a journey. Use clouds as transition. Ticks of the clock or rain falling in a bucket can make the audience feel the passage of time. Develop the rhythm of the story.

Eric Scott
WJZ-TV, BALTIMORE

nothing more than merely covering the narration. In contrast, an excellent editor can choose pictures and sound and develop sophisticated sequences for a dramatic, artistic effect that brings the audience to a story in a way that they could not have imagined. Like an athlete, an editor can "get into a zone" and feel the story flowing through her fingertips. Like a quarterback who sees the appropriate play clearly, puts the ball exactly where he envisions it and gets to the receiver with perfect timing, the editor can sometimes feel the pace and timing come from within. The editor tunes in to the purpose of the story and the editing choices come naturally.

Avoiding Sensationalism

To present information accurately, the editor must not only avoid misrepresenting the size of an event, but also avoid sensationalizing events. Because photographers often operate by the philosophy of shoot now and decide later, the shooting tape may be loaded with pictures that are inappropriate for use on the air. At the scene of a traffic accident, the photographer can gather pictures of a person trapped in the car with visible wounds, the crumpled vehicle and the efforts of rescue workers to extract the injured driver. There will be shots of ambulances, sounds of sirens, expressions of horror from bystanders. The door will make a cracking sound as rescuers use the jaws of life. The ambulance door will slam when the gurney rolls inside. In short, the editor could turn the story into an action thriller by choosing the most dramatic pictures and sounds, even if the story indicates that the rescue was routine and that all the injured are in satisfactory condition and expected to recover fully.

News stories certainly include emotion, and editors may legitimately choose to heighten emotion, but emotion should not take precedence over fact and information in news presentations. When the editor focuses on eliciting strong emotional reactions, the result can be a sensationalized story. Although the mother of a child who was killed with a family gun may grant an interview and break down into sobs, the editor must decide the amount of time appropriate for allowing the audience to understand the mother's grief without overemphasizing her expression of it. Sometimes, the implied can make a more powerful statement than the reality. Showing the hand of a corpse sticking out from the sheet that covers the body at the scene of a murder may hit the audience hard with the reality of the death, whereas a shot of the dead person's cell phone where it fell to the ground could be just as effective—or more so. At the scene of a car accident, the shot of a cracked windshield with a light blood stain will convey the message; it is not necessary to show the person's head wounds. The purpose is to help the audience understand, not to shock.

Providing Graphics

The editor's responsibility may include identifying people who are talking by **supering**—superimposing the name over the picture at the bottom of the screen. Often, however, the supers are added live during the newscast and are not the responsibility of the editor.

The lower third of the screen is used for superimposing names, titles and other identifying information about the shot. If pictures are used that come from the station's archives, the lower third usually indicates that the shot is from *file footage.*

Creating Animations

Graphic images may be designed to move for the purpose of making video more exciting and holding the viewer's attention. The animations can take place on the full screen or may be limited to a small portion of the screen. The titles—usually restricted to the lower third of the screen—may move on and off the screen or may crawl across the bottom of the screen. The station logo or channel number may spin or rotate in a corner of the lower third. The editor's primary goal and responsibility is to help the viewer understand the information. Graphics and animations that call attention to themselves may distract from the story and should be avoided.

CONCLUSION

Editors hold control over the creativity and accuracy of a news package. A poor editor can sensationalize a story and get the station into legal trouble by choosing the wrong picture or a wrong series of shots. An unskilled editor can simply wallpaper a story so that the video merely covers the narration, regardless of whether the pictures enhance the story or not. In contrast, the editor should strive to bring a story to life, add video stories within the overall news story and create a product that will have people talking about it the next day at the office. The editor must ensure that stories are technically ready for broadcast and that the audio levels of the voices and nat sounds are appropriate. With access to good video, the editor will include sequences such as series of wide, medium and tight shots, action/reactions, reversals and cuts on an action. Good editors are in control of a story's pacing and continuity, and they know how to punctuate a story with sophisticated techniques. Editing video can be challenging and exciting work for those who understand the complexities of the process.

KEY CONCEPTS

edit

cuts only editing

video track

audio track

analog

linear editing/
   tape-to-tape editing

control track

assemble mode

back timing

end point/out point

in point

nonlinear editing

effect

fade

wipe

dissolve

shot sheet

logging the tape

establishing shot

file footage

video sequence

continuity

match frame editing/
      cutting on the action

audio levels

nat sound break

mix

audio mix

net sound open

V-U meter

L-cut

graphic

still frame

pull quote

wallpaper

super

Activities

1. Listen for nat sound breaks and nat sound opens in a network newscast.

2. Look for video stories within the narrated story in network news packages.

3. Identify edit sequences in a network newscast. Do you see action/reactions? Reversed points of view? Full action sequences? Consider how the shots were captured by the photographer.

4. Watch the movie *Seabiscuit*. What do you know about the horse that provided companionship to Seabiscuit? How do you know it? How much time is devoted to this story within the larger story?

5. Assume that a news script describes a heat wave in the Southwest by saying, *Scorching temperatures have caused three deaths and are devastating livestock and fanning wildfires in three southwestern states.* You are editing the story and you have lots of good footage, including shots of medical personnel loading a gurney with a heat victim into an ambulance, cattle standing in front of a dried-up creek and lots of shots of wildfires and firefighters. Assume that you have any shots you can imagine. What are three options for illustrating the sentence with video?

6. If you decide to illustrate the narration directly in the example above with shots of a victim, livestock and wildfires when they are mentioned, where might you use a nat sound break and what would be a good clip of audio?

7. Consider the example in Exhibit 9.6, where a reporter cutaway covers a jump cut. List as many different cutaway shots as you can think of that could be used to cover the jump cut.

Regarding Ethics . . .

8. You are editing a script about a corporation that has made a policy of hiring workers with a variety of mental health problems. The script begins by saying, *The mentally challenged workers in this factory would challenge workers anywhere to beat their level of productivity.*

    The photographer has captured some wonderful pictures from the factory floor, and you want to begin with a close-up shot you see on the tape of a young man concentrating intently on his task. Is there an ethical question involved?

9. You are editing a package about the high costs to society of health treatment related to obesity. You remember some file footage of a weight control meeting and a picture of an enormous woman walking on a treadmill, and you would like to use the shot. Is there an ethical issue here?

10. A high-profile person in your community is on trial for rape, and the photographer has taken video of a group of people exiting the courtroom. The victim, who has not been named in any media, is included in the shot, but you would like to use the shot only as general footage. You know that a few people may know her and see her in the shot, but many will not. Is this an ethical issue? What would you do?

11. You are editing a story on the increased number of AIDS cases among heterosexual women, and you have pictures of women leaving the Health Department after an educational meeting on AIDS. The picture was taken on public property. Would you use the shot? Why or why not? What ethical considerations do you have?

12. You are editing a story on a child abuse case and you have footage from outside a courtroom of a small child sitting on a bench alone, crying. You want to use the shot, and it was clearly taken on public property. What considerations will you have in making your decision on whether to use the shot?

EDITING EXERCISES

1. Use the video you shot previously of two people sitting beside each other talking. Use the wide, medium and tight shots, the angles and the cutaways to edit a logical sequence.

2. Using a reporter reaction shot, cutaway question and other cutaways from an interview, edit the interview three times. Edit the interview either the same general way or three different ways. Eliminate each jump cut with

three different shots. Which one works the best? Why? Next, edit the interview using the reporter's cutaway question. Does it work well? Why or why not?

3. Using cutaway shots from each side of the 180-degree line in an interview setup, edit the interview so that the cutaways provide the transition for crossing the axis.

4. Go to a sports event. Shoot several action/reaction sequences. Edit the sequences together.

5. Using interview footage, create a narrated lead-in and edit the sound bite as an L-cut.

6. Using a variety of shots from a repeated action, edit a sequence that would appear to have been shot from different angles and perspectives.

7. Using video from a planned action sequence, such as a person getting out of a car and going into a building for an appointment, edit the sequence. Evaluate its effectiveness.

8. Shoot and edit a story that tells itself through video and accompanying nat sound (without a narration track).

Broadcasters don't need to have gifted tones and golden vocal chords. Anyone who can use grammatical language can develop the abilities needed by professional reporters. In some cases a little special training by a vocal coach may be in order, but in most cases, individual work is all that's necessary.

CARRIE CANNADAY,
WLFG-TV,
ABINGDON, VA.

PRESENTATION AND VOICE

VOICE QUALITY

Breathing and speaking come so naturally that we don't think about them in our daily routines. But for broadcasters, speaking is part of a product that is being sold to an audience and therefore needs attention and development. Singers train for hours each day to use their voices effectively, and they take special care of their vocal cords, which they often refer to as an "instrument." Actors also train their voices and, just like athletes, go through special warm-ups before a performance. The need to train the voice and prepare before a performance applies to broadcasters as well. Pleasant vocal quality is fundamental to a broadcaster's presentation. It requires work, but anyone can make improvements to voice quality.

Breathing

The most basic requirement for good voice quality is proper breathing. As odd as it sounds, many people don't breathe correctly. Good voice quality depends on full breath support, which is controlled by the large muscle partition between the chest and the abdomen, called the **diaphragm** (see Exhibit 10.1). Inhaling deeply should draw air down below the chest and into the abdomen so that the diaphragm expands and pushes the stomach out. As the air is exhaled, the abdominal muscles contract and control the air as it is released. If you watch a trained singer, you can actually see the stomach protrude when air is drawn in and watch it slowly contract as the

A voice with a problem is like a Chinese water torture for listeners. If you have a problem, get a vocal coach. You can overcome it.

Dave Cupp
WVIR-TV, CHARLOTTESVILLE, VA.

293

EXHIBIT 10.1 The diaphragm controls breath support for good vocal quality.

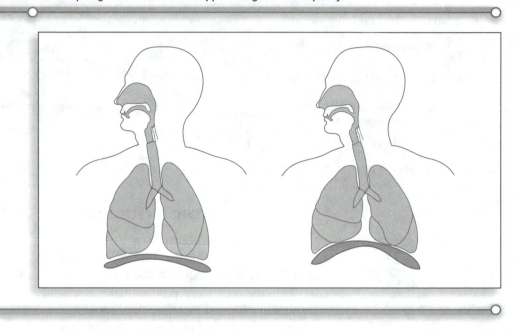

air is exhaled. Singers invest many, many hours in training these abdominal muscles, just as an athlete develops specific muscle groups. Broadcasters can also benefit from improving their breathing technique.

To find out whether you are breathing correctly, take in a deep breath. Where does the air go? If the air goes very deep into your abdomen and your stomach expands, you are breathing correctly. Put your thumbs around your sides pointing toward your back and let your fingers rest across the front of your stomach. When you breathe, your stomach should push your fingers outward. If you take a deep breath and the upper chest expands, the air is going to the wrong place and won't provide the necessary support for good vocal quality.

Try breathing into your chest and speaking, then breathing into your abdomen and speaking. You should be able to hear a noticeable difference in the vocal quality. If it is difficult to hear the difference in yourself, ask someone else to try it, and see if you can hear the difference when the person speaks.

Drawing breath into the chest, or shallow breathing, is the most common breathing problem. A foolproof way to feel where the breath should go is to lie on your back with a book on your abdomen and breathe in deeply. The book should move up and down. In a prone position, it is impossible to breathe shallowly and into the chest area. While in this position, breathe deeply and count slowly as you exhale. The farther you can count while slowly contracting the abdominal muscles, the better vocal control you will be able to exercise. Repeating this exercise while standing or sitting and counting to higher numbers is a way to improve breath control. Learning to draw in larger amounts of air and to control the exhaled breath for longer periods of time can improve the sound of the voice.

The purpose of good breath control is to cause the *vocal cords* to vibrate fully in a relaxed manner. **Vocal cords** are membranes at the top of the trachea, or windpipe, that vibrate to produce sound, as shown in Exhibit 10.2.

To visualize the way vocal cords work, think of a rubber band. If you hold the band taut between two fingers and pluck it, it vibrates and makes a sound. The stronger the pluck, the fuller the vibration. In our voices, the breath equates to the force of plucking the rubber band. The breath causes the vocal cords to vibrate— and the fuller the breath, the more complete the vibration. A weak pull on the rubber band does not allow much vibration. Thin breath support does not produce the fullest vibration or the best performance from the vocal cords. Broadcasters who want to get the best performance from their voices develop the ability to provide full, controlled breath support for their vocal cords.

After learning to provide the fullest possible breath support, the broadcaster must learn to direct the air properly. There are two ways for the breath to leave the body—through the nose or through the mouth. If the air is pushed primarily through the nose, the vibration will be mostly in the nose rather than in the vocal cords, producing an irritating nasal sound. Releasing the air fully and primarily across the vocal cords through the throat and mouth produces better sound quality. Some nasal resonation accompanies the vibration of the vocal cords and can enhance the sound, but try to limit the air that is pushed out through the nasal cavity. A simple exercise illustrates the difference: Breathe in deeply and count to 10, but try to push all the air out through the nose. In contrast, breathe in deeply, count to 10 and release all the air through the throat. The most comfortable and

Vocal cords in open and closed positions. **EXHIBIT 10.2**

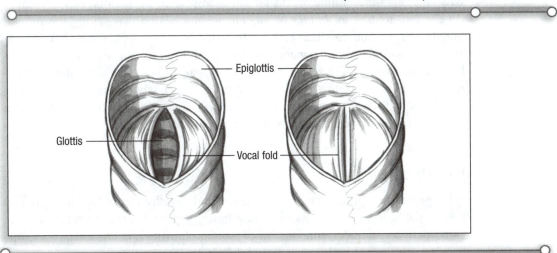

Epiglottis

Glottis

Vocal fold

natural sound results from releasing most of the air through the throat and mouth and allowing some slight resonation in the nasal cavities. (It is possible to force the air too much, resulting in a tight, harsh sound.)

Deep and fully supported breath with full vibration of the vocal cords goes a long way in producing a rich, pleasant sound, but the position of the mouth also plays a role in vocal quality. If the mouth or throat is tight, the air and sound may be restricted. The more open and rounded the throat and mouth, the fuller the sound will be. The position of the jaw, tongue and lips shapes the air and controls the formation of words. Again, think about singers. If you watch opera singers or even some popular singers, you will notice that they open their mouths very wide. An opera singer can produce an enormous amount of sound with the mouth wide open and lots of trained breath support. Popular singers don't attempt to produce as much sound, but they do relax and open their mouths and jaws to guide lots of air. Broadcasters should also produce a full, rounded sound, which is assisted by an open, relaxed mouth and jaw muscles. In summary, the muscles related to breathing combine with those in the throat and mouth to determine the quality of the voice. Broadcasters must prepare their voices before a presentation so that the throat and mouth are loose and flexible.

Warming Up

Like the athlete warming up muscles before a game, the broadcaster wants to make sure that the necessary muscles are warm and relaxed. The audience would surely not appreciate hearing a news anchor deliver the news sounding like he does when he first wakes up in the morning, before the vocal cords are warm and the air passages are clear. Anchors and reporters want to go far beyond getting rid of the clogged-up morning sound and may choose to do breathing and vocal exercises before a newscast. Those who want the fullest, most relaxed sound possible will employ some simple warm-up exercises, such as humming or breathing deeply and holding an *ahhhh* or *hmmmmmmmm* sound. Loosening the mouth, tongue and jaw muscles can be accomplished by repeating sounds that include vowels: *lalalalalalalala, memememememememe* and *sosososososososo*. The lips can be warmed up with the sound people often make when they are cold: *bbbbbbr-rrrrr*. All of these exercises should involve full, deep, abdominal breath support. Combined with the relaxation exercises we will discuss later in this chapter, these vocal exercises will ensure pre-newscast preparation.

DELIVERY

With proper breath support and a relaxed and healthy throat, vocal cords and mouth, the broadcaster can focus on developing a clear, interesting delivery style. Good delivery includes enunciation of words; phrasing and emphasis; and control of pitch, pacing and tone.

Enunciation

The broadcaster must form each word fully and carefully. She should **enunciate** each sound in each word—pronounce it clearly and distinctly—in order to accomplish *full word production*. **Full word production** means saying each consonant and each vowel sound. In casual speech, we typically jam some sounds together and skip over others. Because we are accustomed to the speech patterns of our friends and family, we don't have any trouble understanding them. For example, a friend may say something that sounds like *djeet'yet?* The combination of letters may look strange, but you would easily recognize the meaning: "Did you eat yet?" For broadcast news, the audience will hear content that includes new words and may introduce new concepts, so the reporter can't take a chance that the listener will miss the meaning if the sounds are run together.

> Practice your delivery. Read into a tape recorder. Anyone can develop the ability to sound professional.
>
> *Dale Solly*

The broadcaster must pronounce each consonant. *Found it* is *found It*, not *foun it* or *founi'*. *Going* is pronounced as *go-ing*, not *go'n*. Include each vowel, so that *go-ing* has both the *go* and the *ing*. The movie "My Fair Lady" gives a marvelous example of the struggle to produce sounds fully as Eliza Doolittle practices saying *The rain in Spain stays mainly in the plain*. Each word is a distinct presentation. Simply put, don't run the words together. Listening to Peter Jennings or Dan Rather during the evening news can be instructive when you notice how precisely and distinctly these broadcasters form individual words. On the other hand, effective broadcast speech involves more than just clear enunciation of individual words. The broadcaster must communicate the words in phrases with the proper emphasis.

Phrasing

While the broadcaster pronounces each word distinctly, he must also combine the words into groups and present them in phrases. Whereas the end of a sentence requires the reader to stop completely, **phrases** are segments of sentences indicated by slight pauses in the reading. Suppose that each word received the same amount of time and emphasis with a slight pause after each word. The presentation would sound choppy and irritating. Try reading Eliza Doolittle's exercise above, giving the same amount of time and emphasis to each word. *The . . . rain . . . in . . . Spain . . . stays . . . mainly . . . in . . . the . . . plain.* Reading in such a deliberate manner is quite difficult. Now try grouping each two words together and reading the sentence aloud. *The rain . . . in Spain . . . stays mainly . . . in the . . . plain.* The first two word groups make some sense when coupled together, but the remainder of the sentence clearly needs to be grouped differently. *In the* certainly doesn't work as one phrase. Neither would the sentence sound right to be read as one single unit. The most natural way to read the sentence would be in two phrases: *The rain in Spain . . . stays mainly in the plain.* The reader naturally pauses slightly after *Spain* before completing the sentence. We take natural phrasing for granted in common conversation, but speaking to a mass audience may require special attention to proper phrasing—beginning with the writing.

Presenting broadcast news in clear and effective phrases depends on good writing. Highly skilled broadcasters can make the most out of poorly written copy, but there's no substitute for good writing. Beginning reporters may quickly realize that their copy needs improvement when they try to read it out loud. When the writing is short, simple and conversational, the copy will easily fall into manageable phrases, but long sentences are very difficult to read clearly. Consider the following story by a reporter who investigated an illegal trash dump on a county road. He discovered that a church used to stand next to the site and found sunken spots in the ground, which indicated deteriorating wooden caskets in an unmarked cemetery. However, the county had no record of an owner for the property. Try reading his sentence aloud.

> Records at the Washington County Commission of Revenue Office reveal that no one has claimed the small tract of land where once a church and now a trash pile stand.

The sentence does not lend itself to manageable phrases, no matter how much breath control and skill in reading the individual brings to the words. Consider another way to give the information that makes it easier on the reader.

> County tax records show that no one claims this trash pile—or the land underneath where an old church once stood.

The second example is much clearer and easier to read. With the rewritten sentence, the reader has time to pause and, if necessary, breathe before continuing with the second part of the sentence. The audience will more easily understand the story because the writing makes it easier for the broadcaster to say it.

In a good broadcast presentation, the reporter or anchor says each word distinctly and groups words together in logical phrases. Very slight pauses mark the phrases, and there is a complete stop at the end of each sentence. The phrasing and sentence breaks allow time for the broadcaster to take an additional breath if necessary and help the listener understand the story. Skill in oral presentation is necessary—but remember that even the best broadcaster cannot overcome poor writing that does not lend itself to oral presentation.

When the story is written well so that the broadcaster can present it in clear phrases with full breath support, the final step in bringing the news story to life is to find the proper emphasis and pitch for individual words. These choices reflect the interpretation of the reader.

Emphasis

Broadcasters interpret a news story and bring it to life by choosing which words deserve more **emphasis,** or stress, than others. A speaker applies emphasis to a word by contracting the diaphragm and using additional force to push air over the vocal cords. Some words in a story are more important than others and need additional emphasis, whereas some words add little to the meaning. For example, the articles *a* and *the* don't generally add vital information to a sentence, whereas the subjects and verbs carry the most meaning. Therefore, the person reading the story would not likely emphasize or stress the articles in the following sentence:

The city's largest employer is now offering a generous scholarship at a nearby college.

Likewise, prepositions are crucial to the structure of a sentence but would not naturally be emphasized. Try reading the sentence with emphasis on the preposition *at.*

The city's largest employer is now offering a generous scholarship at a nearby college.

The words in the sentence that carry most of the meaning are *largest employer* and *scholarship,* so the emphasis would logically fall on those words.

The city's largest employer is now offering a generous scholarship at a nearby college.

The sentence lends itself to three phrases, but remember that the pauses between phrases are very short:

The city's largest employer / is now offering a generous scholarship / at a nearby college.

The broadcaster interprets the story for the audience by deciding how to phrase the sentence and which words to emphasize. The reader could make other choices. Perhaps the sentence could be read with different phrasing and different emphasis:

The city's largest employer is now offering / a generous scholarship at a nearby college.

Experimenting with emphasis reveals the possibilities for interpretation. Read the following sentence repeatedly, putting the emphasis on a different word each time:

I am going to town. I am going to town.

I am going to town. I am going to town.

I am going to town.

Changing the emphasis on the words can change the meaning of the sentence, making it important that it is *I* going to town rather than someone else, or that *where* you are going is the most important fact—*town* rather than somewhere else, and so forth. If the broadcaster understands the meaning and significance of the story, she can determine the appropriate places for emphasis.

As broadcasters develop the ability to interpret news by deciding when and where to emphasize words or phrases, they also learn to enhance the delivery with inflection: changes in *pitch.*

Pitch

Pitch, or tone, in speaking refers to the highness or lowness of the frequency of sound waves measured on a scale of musical notes. The most common example of pitch is when we hear someone sing all the notes in a scale: *do, re, mi, fa, so, la, ti, do.* In "The Sound of Music," Julie Andrews demonstrated pitch with the song "Do-Re-Mi." When we describe an individual as having a high or low voice, we mean high- or low-*pitched.*

Speakers need variety in pitch for a pleasant vocal presentation. Changes in pitch or tone within a sentence or within a word are called **inflection.** Without inflection, an individual speaks in a monotone, repeating the same or a similar pitch with almost every word. A monotone voice is, in short, boring and irritating. When reading a story to children, the experienced storyteller will often exaggerate changes in pitch to capture and maintain the attention of little people with short attention spans. Although adults don't want to be treated as children, we all appreciate some variety in pitch from a speaker or broadcaster. Consider how an expert storyteller might say the phrase *Once upon a time* to a group of small children. There may be changes of pitch from word to word and most likely within a single word. The pitch may be low in one part of the word and high in another part, such as *upon.* The *up* may have a low pitch, followed by a higher-pitched *on.* The word *time* may be extended so that the pitch slides from high to low. Words for broadcast news won't be as exaggerated in pitch as they are for telling stories to children, but nonetheless there should be lots of variety in pitch from word to word, and often within words. Consider the following sentence:

> The <u>standoff</u> between <u>hijackers</u> of a <u>jetliner</u> / and the <u>Indian</u> <u>government</u> / <u>con-
tinues</u> at this hour.

The changes in pitch might look something like this:

> (beginning pitch) *The* (up) **stand-** (lower than the beginning pitch) *off* (return to beginning pitch) *between* (slightly up) **hi-** (very slightly down) *jackers* of a (very slightly up) **jet-** (down) *liner* / (same pitch continues) *and the* (slightly up) **In-**

(back down) _dian_ (back up) **_govern-_** (back down) _ment_ / (same pitch) _con-_ (up slightly) **_tin-_** (back down) _ues_ (back up) **_at_** (down a little) _this_ (down a little more) _hour._

Attempting to mark pitch in this manner is awkward; pitch would be more appropriately distinguished by musical notes. Because everyone can't read music, however, the previous markings can help call attention to the fact that there is enormous variety in pitch as a broadcaster presents a news story.

Some examples from popular culture clarify the importance of variety in pitch. Think of the introduction to NBC's "Tonight Show": _He...eee...rrrrrre'ssss Jaa...aaa...ay Leee...eee...e...enoooooooooooooo._ Try to reproduce the variety in pitch. On Paul Harvey's radio news broadcast, you hear Mr. Harvey say, at the end of every presentation, "This is Paul Harvey . . . good day." The sign-off is a testimony to the power of pitch as Harvey seems to cover almost the entire scale of pitches in a few words. In contrast, the household expert Martha Stewart has a very limited range in pitch. Her broadcast presentations sound flat—and could be greatly improved with more variety in the range of her pitch.

In addition to making vocal presentations more varied and interesting, changes in pitch can clarify meaning. A single word can convey a variety of messages simply through changes in the pitch. A common exercise for acting students is to communicate different meanings by simply changing the pitch of a word. The word can be anything, or the students can simply address each other by name—_John_ and _Marsha,_ for example. The students use only the word or name to communicate anger, puzzlement, flirtation, irritation, chastisement, seduction, concern, excitement, sorrow, contentment or any other emotion. For the acting student, the exercise may help develop emotional reactions to someone else's expression of emotion, but broadcasters can use the same exercise to see the importance of pitch in communicating meaning. Try it. Does the pitch of the word go up or down when you express puzzlement? Excitement? Sorrow?

As you work with pitch and emphasis, you may think you are overly exaggerating changes even when you haven't yet achieved the amount of change you need. Beginning broadcasters frequently report that they think they sound ridiculous in changing pitch—when listeners say they have not yet achieved a desirable amount of variety. The previous descriptions of pitch and stress are somewhat technical and may not be helpful to everyone. Some individuals respond better to advice like, "Read it with more energy." "Read it like it's the most important sentence ever spoken." "Read it like you're telling it to children." These instructions may sound extreme, but again, beginning reporters are likely to be too flat in pitch with too little variety and may need to aim for a seemingly extreme standard to reach an acceptable one.

To improve your use of pitch as a tool in broadcasting, listen carefully to network broadcasters until you can identify changes in pitch as they speak. Then, use a tape recorder to record your own voice as you experiment with pitch and emphasis while reading news stories. Finally, you may want to ask broadcasting colleagues to listen to your voice as you experiment with pitch and emphasis and to offer suggestions for improvement.

Speech Patterns

When working to improve variety in pitch, individuals may fall into patterns of tone and emphasis that can become predictable and irritating. The most common predictable speech pattern is a *sing-song* presentation. The pitch in a **sing-song pattern** usually begins low, goes high in the middle of the sentence and ends on the low pitch. The next sentence repeats the same pattern of tone and pitch . . . as does the next . . . and the next. The pattern quickly becomes noticeable, predictable and irritating.

In another common pattern, speakers end each sentence with the pitch sliding upward on the last word. The pattern imitates the change in pitch for asking questions, even when the sentence is declarative. Say a question out loud, such as "Are you done?" Notice that the word *done* goes up in pitch. When this pattern is applied to declarative sentences, the resulting speech sounds tentative and lacking in confidence. Shy people often push the pitch upward on the final syllable of a sentence, betraying their lack of definitiveness. Try saying the following two sentences using the same pitch pattern in both.

Are you done?

I think so.

With an upward pitch at the end, the answer sounds like a question. In contrast, say the sentence again and emphasize the final word while pushing the pitch down.

I think so.

This time the sentence leaves no question about the intention of the speaker, who is definitely done. The repeated pattern of ending a sentence on an upward pitch creates two problems: tentative-sounding speech and a predictable pattern.

Broadcasters may tend to fall into the opposite pattern by pushing the pitch down and placing the emphasis on the last word the same way in every sentence. Although the downward pitch and final emphasis make the speaker sound confident and definitive, she should not repeat the pattern too often, because it may become noticeable and distracting. Listen to other broadcasters and try to follow the pitch of each sentence. Record your own stories on tape and listen for patterns in pitch. As you read copy and prepare for presenting it, pay attention to finding variety in pitch.

Pacing

Another skill in effective broadcast speech is in varying the *pace* of sentences and phrases. The **pace** of a sentence or phrase is simply the speed at which the words are delivered. Broadcasters not only break sentences into phrases with slight pauses and stop completely at the end of sentences, but they must also find the appropriate speed for each phrase. In the sentence about the hijackers, we indicated where the phrase breaks would be and which words to emphasize. We can also experiment with the pacing for each phrase. Read the following sentences aloud, applying the suggestions for pacing.

First, slow down the first two phrases and speed up the final phrase.

The standoff between hijackers of a jetliner / and the Indian government / continues at this hour.

Next, speed up the first and second phrases, then slow down the third phrase.

The standoff between hijackers of a jetliner / and the Indian government / continues at this hour.

Read the sentence again and speed up the first phrase, slow down the second phrase and speed up the third phrase.

The standoff between hijackers of a jetliner / and the Indian government / continues at this hour.

There are many possibilities for varying the pace of a sentence. Continue to experiment and determine how many variations in pacing you can find for the sentence.

Remember that both pitch and pace need variation. Try using a very simple sentence to experiment with varying both the pitch and the pace. For example, politicians often talk of the future and paint possibilities of grand achievement. They speak of economic prosperity and peace and say that the possibilities are real. About reaching these goals, they say, "We can, and we will." The promise may sound convincing, or it may not, depending on pitch, emphasis and pacing. Try it and analyze the effect of different combinations of pacing and pitch.

First, keep the pace fairly quick and constant with little variety in pitch.

We can and we will.

Next, break the sentence into two parts and slow the pace on the second phrase, ending with a downward pitch and emphasis on the word *will*.

We can . . . and we <u>will</u>.

Read it again with the same amount of emphasis on *can* and *will* and with the same pace applied to each part of the sentence.

We <u>can</u> . . . and we <u>will</u>.

Read it again with more emphasis on *we*. Read the first part slowly and speed up the second part.

<u>We</u> can . . . and <u>we</u> <u>will</u>.

The sentence may be read so that it sounds weak and questioning. Apply a constant pace and push the pitch up at the end.

We can and we will?

Send the pitch up after *can* <u>and</u> after *will*. The result suggests that we really don't have the ability to accomplish the vision, and we are not likely to.

We can? . . . and we will?

Or, the message can be that we have the ability, but we probably won't accomplish the desired goal. Slower on the first part—faster on the second.

We <u>can</u> . . . and we will?

Finding the appropriate variety in pitch, emphasis and pacing is an important skill for the successful broadcaster. These technical changes in the way the breath travels from the diaphragm over the vocal cords and through the mouth and nose carry important meanings to the listener. The reporter can develop effective delivery by concentrating on the technical process of producing the words or by thinking in more general terms, such as speaking with "energy." Regardless of how it is accomplished, the goal of interpreting information is fundamental to the successful broadcaster. To use radio newscaster Paul Harvey as an example again, remember his famous phrase, "And now you know the rest of the story." He slows the first four words and applies strong emphasis to each word, with a deep dip in pitch on *know*. Then he speeds up the final five words, again applying strong emphasis and drop in pitch to the final word. His presentation of this slogan shows a masterful command of pitch, pacing and emphasis. He has taken a common sentence and marked it with his own style. He has used the ability to speak—a skill that we all have—in a uniquely creative and memorable way.

Overall Tone

One final approach to vocal presentation is to consider the *tone* of the speech. Overall **tone** refers to the mood or attitude of the speaker. We've probably all had our parents refer to our tone of speech, as in, "Don't use that tone of voice with me!" The tone of someone's answers to questions may be friendly or hostile. The tone of an interview may be comfortable or tense.

Describing the technical aspects of producing a hostile tone or a warm tone amounts to an acting exercise, because the tone we are talking about represents emotion. We may speak in a hostile tone with shortened words, low pitch and a harshness in the force of the air in producing the words. We produce a warmer tone by a softer application of breath to word production and pitch variety in mid and upper ranges. Broadcast news anchors and reporters need a pleasant tone in their voices as they present their stories.

Different topics of discussion require different tones, and a live interview may require changing the tone in preparation for a new subject. For example, an interview with the mayor may begin with a light, friendly tone in a discussion of the mayor's vacation. The interviewer may even joke with the mayor about her still-apparent sunburn, but as the discussion continues, the interviewer will change the tone to prepare the mayor and the audience for a more serious topic. *"Now, Mayor, we need to move on to a more serious issue for the city."* The change in tone will be reflected in a slower pace, a lower pitch and an emphasis on the key words indicating the direction of the upcoming topic, like *serious issue.*

If the tone changes too quickly, the audience cannot prepare for a full understanding of the subject. Suppose the interviewer moves immediately from a joke about the sunburned mayor to the comment, *"Some people think you've burned the city's children by cutting the school budget, Mayor. What is your response to them?"* The tone would change too quickly and would make the question seem abrupt and rude—or the audience might not realize that the interview had become very serious. If the interviewer, however, took a moment to change the tone before the question, it would have more impact. A quick change in tone can be effective if you tell the audience about the upcoming shift. *"Excuse me, Mayor, for changing the subject, but there are some serious topics we need to discuss. Some people think you've been giving away the city's commitment to education by cutting the school budget. What is your response to them?"* In this case, with one sentence, the interviewer adapts the tone to the forthcoming serious question.

Attempting to reproduce an emotion is easier for most people than following technical descriptions for producing proper tones. In short, speak in pleasant tones with warmth and a smile in your voice when appropriate. When the information is more serious, let your tone reflect the importance. Speak with energy and interest in the story you are telling, speak to others with respect and interest, and you will likely have an appropriate tone in your voice.

Additional Considerations

Accents

Even though each individual has a unique way of speaking, certain groups of people have a shared, distinguishable way of choosing and pronouncing words—an **accent.** The words we choose and the way we pronounce them reflect the environments where we developed our speech, hence accents usually correspond to geographical areas. Broadcasters who may be speaking to a national audience, or who may move from market to market throughout their careers, will be more successful if they do not speak with a specific regional accent. A strong Southern accent might be acceptable in some Southern markets where the accent resembles the way most audience members speak. However, a more general audience in a large Southern city or another part of the country will be more comfortable with a more standard sound.

In the United States, Brooklyn, Southern and New England accents are readily identifiable with geographical regions. The stereotyped Brooklyn accent, "Brooklynese," is widely known; you can imitate it by saying the address 33rd Street, *Toity-toid Street.* In Brooklynese, an *r* is sometimes added to the end of a word so that *idea* becomes *idear.* At other times the *r* is replaced by an *a* sound, so that *your* becomes *yu-a* and *sure* becomes *schu-a.* The *th* sound is often replaced by a *d* sound or shortened to *t,* so that *the* becomes *duh* and *thirty* becomes *tirty* or *toity.*

Examples of Southern speech can be heard on television in re-runs of "The Andy Griffith Show." Flattened and extended vowel sounds are commonly associated with Southern speech: *right* becomes *rai-ut* and *thing* becomes *thang.* Other vowels are extended and turned into two syllables, so that *man* becomes *ma-un.* The *r* sound is dropped in some Southern regions, so that *father* becomes *fa-thu* and *bird* becomes *bud.* The city known as *Boston* may have the pronunciation *Bauw-stun* in the South.

President Kennedy's famous 1961 inaugural request lives in common reference today and exemplifies the New England accent: "Ask not what your country can do for you, but what you can do for your country." The *ah* sound in *ask* resembles the *o* sound in *hot* for most American speakers and illustrates a Boston accent. The common example of New England speech is *pahk the cah.* In the South, you might *pauw-rk* the *cauw-r.*

While actors and actresses may wish to study and imitate accents, broadcasters need to eliminate most accent in favor of **Standard American English.** Standard American English is not a formal way of speaking that one can find in a book and attempt to learn. Rather, Standard American speech is more generally the shared pronunciation of words by educated people across the country. Using Standard English also means using proper grammar; if you intend to succeed as a broadcaster, proper use of the language is expected. As they should, audience members will let you know quickly and unhappily by phone calls and letters when you mangle the structure of the language. This book does not attempt to instruct broadcasters in grammar. Review your grammar through a course or with a textbook as needed. Educated individuals using standard pronunciation do not have an identifiable accent, and neither should broadcasters.

Getting rid of an accent is not an easy task. We learned our speech patterns as children and have practiced them for a lifetime. Concentrating on saying each word completely may take care of some accent problems, such as dropping the *ing* from words. Southerners may have to work at producing the long *i* sound in *right* rather than using the more comfortable and flatter sound of *rai-ut*. New Englanders may have to work to put the *r* in *park* as Brooklynites are struggling to say the *th* in *thirty*.

The emotional aspect of attempting to change an accent is also important to consider. Those who have worked to change accents so that their childhood patterns of speech are abandoned know that family members and old community friends may resent the fact that their neighborhood pronunciations and manner of speech have been replaced. This feeling is perfectly understandable because our speech patterns contribute to our distinctiveness as individuals and help identify our background. For the broadcaster, however, Standard American speech is a job requirement. Reverting to older, comfortable speech patterns with family members and friends is perfectly acceptable. At work, however, more general pronunciations and speech patterns are tools of the trade.

By listening to standard English, some beginning broadcasters may be able to identify specific sounds that they need to change and make the changes on their own. In other cases, the work may be much more extensive, such as studying audio cassettes and practicing standard pronunciations. With very strong accents, a vocal coach may be necessary. Again, accents are deeply imbedded in our speech patterns and even in our individuality. They cannot be changed easily, but the broadcaster must do so, because a strong accent can interfere with effective communication.

Problem Sounds

As unique physical beings, we all have our own looks and individual fingerprints. We also have unique vocal sounds. In some cases, a person forms words in ways that are slightly different from the way others do, or a person may have trouble shaping the mouth and using the tongue to make certain sounds that others can easily accomplish. In some cases, a person's words and sounds may be noticeably unusual. When a broadcaster has these problems, they may be distracting and unpleasant to an audience. In other cases, the difficulty may be noticeable, but not problematic.

Many successful broadcasters have difficulties with specific sounds, including Barbara Walters and Tom Brokaw, whose efforts in making *l* sounds are noticeable. Obviously, their problematic *l*'s do not interfere with their ability to communicate even though, as enormously successful broadcasters, they might prefer not to be identified with difficulties in making particular sounds. Other broadcasters have overcome difficulties in producing certain sounds so that the audience never realizes the problem existed.

The most common speech problem is in producing the *s* sound. To make the sound correctly, the tongue is formed across the upper part of the mouth so that it maintains a depression in the center and pushes air up and forward. The flexibility of the tongue varies, and some individuals find it very difficult to maintain the position for producing this sound. The tongue may slide so that the *s* sound comes from the side of the mouth, or it may be rigid in a certain spot so that the *s* is shrill. Sometimes the tongue hits the teeth rather than the roof of the mouth and the *s* sound changes into a *th* sound, as in, "He'th going to thell the car."

When individuals have trouble producing specific sounds, they may be able to correct the problem on their own, or the work may require the help of a speech therapist. Speech therapists are trained in showing people exactly how to position the mouth, jaw and tongue to produce specific sounds. If appropriate, seek professional help in developing professional speaking ability.

> I've sought out a speech and diction coach on my own in every market. A lot of what you learn is the technique of relaxing to achieve your best vocal quality.
>
> *Kathy Soltero*
> **KCNC-TV, DENVER**

Local Pronunciations

Broadcasters often migrate around the country as they move up the professional ladder. When you find yourself in a new market area, learn to pronounce local names and locations. When new on-air reporters or anchors mispronounce the name of the mayor, the local high school or a small town, they instantly lose credibility with the audience. Viewers are unforgiving of these errors. Broadcasters show respect for people and their community with correct pronunciations.

Techniques for Improving Delivery

As broadcasters work to produce each word fully and to phrase and emphasize information so that it is clear to listeners, underlining copy and practicing out loud can ensure that each sentence gets the best possible interpretation.

Underlining Copy

When a reporter or anchor prepares to record a script or read a story live, he may find that underlining the script in advance will help improve the delivery. Underlining the most important word or words suggests the correct interpretation when the tape is rolling or the camera is on. (See Exhibit 10.3.) The reporter may

Each individual will choose to emphasize words and meanings in a personal style. This is one way a newscaster might underline words in a script in preparation for reading it.

EXHIBIT 10.3

2-08-05 HOME SCHOOL/PHYED/4662/NOONTHU/03:00

A:ann
HOME SCHOOLING IS BECOMING MORE AND MORE <u>POPULAR</u> . . . AND NOT JUST IN THE <u>LARGER</u> CITIES. IT'S AN <u>ALTERNATIVE</u> TO PUBLIC AND PRIVATE SCHOOLS . . . AND FOR SOME IT'S THE <u>MOST</u> <u>ATTRACTIVE</u> OPTION.
NEWSCENTER 5'S AMY LYNN SHOWS US A LOCAL PROGRAM THAT'S <u>MAKING</u> <u>SURE</u> SOME HOME-SCHOOL KIDS GET THE EXERCISE AND HEALTHY LIFESTYLE SKILLS THEY NEED.

TAKE PKG------------
****

T:2:41
!G 606
BRISTOL, TN
THIS IS WHAT WE ARE <u>USED</u> TO SEEING WHEN WE GO TO THE LOCAL GYM TO WORK OUT . . .

NAT OF ADULTS

BUT <u>THIS</u> IS WHAT YOU'LL SEE IF YOU VISIT THE WELLNESS CENTER IN BRISTOL FRIDAY AFTERNOONS . . .

NAT OF KIDS ON TRACK

!S MICHELLE WILCOX
!S EXERCISE TRAINER
"We just found that there's a need in the community for home-school kids to get out and participate in a phys ed class like you'd have in school so we put out notices that we wanted to start a program, and it's been going for a while now."

underline the most important words twice and less important words once. Some individuals prefer a red pen for underlining; others may find black or blue ink sufficient to draw attention to the important words. Sometimes, simply the act of underlining works as training and practice, which in itself helps the delivery.

Reading, thinking about interpretation and underlining prepare the broadcaster for the important task of clearly communicating information to the audience.

Although news anchors typically read from a teleprompter, they also have a printed version of the story in hand that they can usually review in advance. Reporters, of course, write their stories and use the script to prepare narration for a package.

> "Congress is trying to decide on <u>tax</u> <u>reform</u>." Tax reform are the important words. Underline your copy.
>
> *Steve Hawkins*
> **WCYB-TV, BRISTOL, VA.**

Practicing Out Loud

Although studying the script and underlining can be helpful, there is no substitute for reading copy out loud, even if you are the only person who hears it. Reading out loud to someone else is even better, but both ways of practicing can alert the broadcaster to sentences or phrases that may sound confusing—or that need shortening or improving in other ways. Sometimes, a sentence makes sense when you're looking at the words, but doesn't when you hear it. Practicing out loud will also show you how much breath you'll need and when you'll have the opportunity to get it.

THE QUALITIES OF A SUCCESSFUL COMMUNICATOR

Long before the printing press—much less the television camera—was invented, the Greek philosopher Aristotle recognized that a successful communicator embodies three basic characteristics: *logos, pathos* and *ethos.* We recognize *logos* as *logic.* A successful communicator exhibits intelligence and clear thinking and shows the audience the evidence that leads to specific conclusions. We like and respect the logical way the speaker thinks and talks. *Pathos* suggests the word *pathetic,* which means "to arouse pity or sympathy," but *empathy* is a closer definition for our modern understanding of *pathos.* If the speaker has pathos, the audience will identify emotionally with him or her. In simple language, you might say, "I understand how she feels," or "I feel for him." For reasons that viewers might not be able to explain, they find the speaker appealing and feel that they can relate to the person. Finally, the speaker has *ethos,* or character. We trust the communicator and believe him to be a good and honest person. The communicator is believable.

Aristotle's characteristics help explain the success of modern communicators. Think of today's most successful broadcasters: the anchors of the evening news, interviewers like Barbara Walters and Matt Lauer, or talk-show host Oprah Winfrey. No doubt, when you think of your favorite broadcaster, you would describe the individual as someone you like (*pathos*) and trust (*ethos*), and whose intelligence you respect (*logos*). These individuals give you the feeling that spending time with them would be enjoyable. Part of the reason you're attracted is that you think the broadcast interviewer would show an interest in you. You see that the communicator likes, respects and cares about people—whether the interview is with the president of the United States or a homeless person. Oprah and Matt Lauer would be polite in addressing a convicted murderer, just as they would in talking with the most popular movie star. Even if they were personally revolted by the interviewee, they would be cordial in the interaction.

> The best broadcasters are those who aren't that much different in person from the way they are on the air. They keep it natural.
>
> *Stephanie Riggs*
> **KCNC-TV, DENVER**

Any successful communicator, whether news broadcaster, politician, teacher or preacher, exhibits the Aristotelian characteristics of *pathos, ethos* and *logos*. Ideally, the characteristics are sincere and genuine, but in reality, the appearance of these characteristics can be imitated, developed and controlled for a positive response from an audience. With the understanding that reporters must be ethical, we also recognize that the broadcaster develops presentation skills so that the audience senses the desired characteristics of *pathos, ethos* and *logos*. A broadcaster who thinks clearly and is trustworthy and pleasant can fail in audience appeal if her presentation is weak. Our purpose in this section is to discuss how to develop a presentation style that does not undermine a reporter's good qualities and good work.

Appearance

A distracting appearance can prevent the audience from sensing the reporter's characteristics of ethos, pathos and logos and can result in the reporter's losing credibility, appeal and maybe the audience. By understanding some basic principles, most people can achieve a pleasing appearance, and contrary to common belief, outstanding good looks are not required for successful broadcasters.

One of the realities of television news is that the industry wants people with a conventional and professional appearance on the air. Tattoos, body piercings and unusual hair styles are out. The person appearing before a mass audience should simply strive to be neat, well-dressed and without distracting characteristics. Wrinkled, untucked or mismatched clothing suggests a lack of respect for the audience. A sloppy appearance suggests that it's not important to look your best for them and the job isn't important enough to require neatness. You've heard it often for a good reason: Neatness counts.

Other simple details can distract from the presentation of information. Hair that falls over the eyes, bright red fingernails or dramatic scarves and jewelry can pull the audience's attention away. Clothing with bold designs may be distracting, and some small patterns and stripes will shimmer or appear to move because the electronic scanner in the camera cannot discern them. Both black and white clothing can cause difficulty for the camera because the extremes require the iris to open very wide or to close tightly and may adversely affect other parts of the picture. Anchors and weather forecasters have to choose colors of clothing that do not interfere with the process that imposes their images over weather maps or other backgrounds. Makeup for women should be basic and fresh—no dramatic eye shadows or extreme colors in lipstick.

In larger markets, image consultants may assist reporters and anchors in making the most of dress and appearance, but striving for neatness and wearing basic colors in clothing are fundamental for broadcast appearance. Broadcasters often sign contracts in which they agree not to alter their physical appearance in any way that would detract from their ability to communicate with a mass audience. Sometimes the agreements are quite specific about facial hair for men and hairstyles for women.

A basic, pleasing look involves much more than just clothing and hair style. An appealing presentation also requires the broadcaster to look alert and energetic, to be erect and composed, and to maintain direct eye contact with either the person being interviewed or with the camera. Movement must be limited, controlled and careful. News anchors basically maintain one position, although slight movements of the head or hands and facial expression keep the static shot from being boring. Reporters doing stand-ups or field interviews often stand still, and when they do move in stand-ups, they have planned the move in advance and discussed it with the photographer. Sudden, unexpected movements can cause poor screen composition, so camera operators need to know what action to expect in a shot. Shifting from one foot to the other causes a distracting movement. We take the characteristics of on-screen presentation for granted, but they don't always come easily. In our daily routines, we all probably slouch in our chairs, mumble instead of speaking clearly and shift and move indiscriminately. These behaviors are unacceptable for a broadcast news presentation.

Courtesy

Just as courtesy and common good manners indicate professionalism, they also contribute to appearance and presentation. The broadcaster shows interest in others and is polite: *"Thank you for being here today." "Please explain more about your plan." "I understand that you're concerned about X, but what do you say to critics who believe Y?" "Thank you again for coming." "Have a nice day." "Please stay tuned."* If you watch a morning news program and focus on the niceties, you will be amazed at the number of times you hear *good morning, please* and *thank you.* In fact, if you're counting, it might almost seem ridiculous how many times the hosts, news anchors and guests express politeness. The audience, however, is not generally counting nice comments but rather gets the feeling that everyone likes each other and enjoys what they're doing. As a result, the audience member enjoys participating in the pleasant event.

One way of showing courtesy is by indicating interest in others. Focusing on the guest and not attempting to draw attention to oneself is a common courtesy. The audience quickly resents any hint of rudeness or selfishness on the part of the broadcaster. No matter how obnoxious someone may be to the reporter or broadcaster, the professional communicator is expected to maintain control. Even though a reporter's question may be indelicate or daring, it must be asked politely. Sarcasm is especially offensive coming from a professional journalist. Audiences appreciate courtesy.

Dressing neatly, sitting up straight, reading a script and asking questions with energy and good eye contact sounds simple enough. Courtesy is not difficult to practice. But what about working toward a relaxed demeanor?

Nervousness

Knowing that thousands of people will be watching you cranks up the pressure and prompts nervous responses. Nervous symptoms such as sweating and shortness of breath can certainly interfere with the appearance of professionalism, and the audience won't be focusing on the information and its credibility if it's distracted by the reporter's unease. In contrast, nervousness is expected and is, in fact, desirable for the individual facing a large audience. A heightened nervous response and the resulting increased adrenaline flow can actually help make an individual more alert and add desired energy to a presentation. The broadcaster should also realize that the audience basically wants the presenter to do well.

After accepting that nervousness is normal and helpful, the broadcaster can use several techniques to help diminish the feelings of fright and nervousness. Repeatedly breathing very deeply and slowly exhaling the air can be calming. For best results, breathe in as deeply as possible and release the air as slowly as possible, either by exhaling lightly through the mouth or by counting as high as possible while releasing the air. After a couple of deep, slow intakes of breath and long, slow exhales, the body will feel noticeably more relaxed. Repeat this procedure as often as necessary.

Relaxing the muscles can help reduce feelings of nervousness. Concentrating on one group of muscles at a time, make them tense and then release. For example, while sitting in a chair, tighten the leg muscles as much as possible, hold for a count of 10 and then release. Concentrate on releasing the tension as much as possible. Then choose another group of muscles, like arms, hands, feet or buttocks; tighten, hold and release. This technique can be used in a standing or sitting position and won't be noticed by others around you.

Rigorous exercise warms up muscles and helps relax the body. It might not be practical to run a mile before delivering a news report, but it may be possible to do a few jumping jacks or run in place for a few minutes. If vigorous movement doesn't seem appropriate, stretching muscle groups may be easier. Loose, warm muscles and relaxed breathing simply won't allow a noticeable nervous response.

Remember that most symptoms of nervousness do not show. Reporters and other public speakers often admit to being extremely nervous and feeling very uncomfortable on the inside when there are no noticeable outward signs of it at all. The viewers are naturally going to be on your side and want you to do well; they will not notice most of the nervousness that you may feel.

Finally, the best way to fight the nervous response and improve your performance is proper preparation. Practice reading the copy several times, and review your writing to make sure it sounds conversational with short, declarative sentences. Think about the message of the story you're trying to communicate, and concentrate on the audience's response to the information rather than on your own feelings. Breathing deeply, making sure you relax your muscles, and preparing properly cover most of the problems of nervousness in the beginning. Experience will take care of the rest. The more you appear on camera, the easier it becomes, and you may eventually find yourself missing the extra excitement of nervousness in your presentation.

PRESENTING STAND-UPS

In the chapter on storytelling and writing, we discussed writing stand-ups and fitting the stand-up into the structure of the story. The television news professional must also develop skill in presenting the stand-up effectively. A good stand-up presentation includes all the delivery skills described in this chapter: proper voice quality, enunciation, phrasing, emphasis, pitch, pacing, tone and pronunciation. Moreover, the reporter must convey the words while interacting appropriately with the camera lens.

Before we give more detail on doing a good stand-up, let us remind reporters that they should not do a stand-up unless it contains important information for the story. Otherwise, the audience will think that the reporter is getting unnecessary attention. When the reporter is confident that the content is important and the primary goal is to provide information, the reporter can then proceed in preparing a stand-up.

Use of Clear, Simple Language

The first requirement for a good stand-up is the use of clear, simple language. Convey one idea per sentence. Save the big words for the doctoral dissertation. Why *utilize* when you can *use?* Simple language sounds conversational and is easy for the audience to understand quickly and remember. If you are clear and focused about the message you need to communicate, you are likely to be successful. When using clear, simple language, you are also more likely to avoid flubbing words and forcing the photographer to shoot lots of failed stand-up attempts.

When there are several points that must be covered in a stand-up, reporters can develop anxiety about remembering them all. This concern leads to a debatable question: *to memorize or not to memorize?*

To Memorize or Not to Memorize?

Some reporters insist that memorizing what they will say on camera is the only workable method for them. Perhaps so, and the advice *If it ain't broke, don't fix it* certainly applies to those individuals. If you forget what you're supposed to be saying in a memorized sequence, however, you are more likely to become totally lost than if you are speaking extemporaneously. Thinking and speaking on your feet are abilities that contribute to successful reporting, and they allow the reporter to maintain direct eye contact with the camera throughout the stand-up. Looking down for prompting on facts can be acceptable in a stand-up and is quite common in the live shots we will discuss shortly. Therefore, reporters often hold a clipboard or notebook with a large, visible list of points that need to be covered when standing still and speaking directly into the camera.

If the jury has just issued its verdict in a major murder case, it could be difficult to remember all the details. Suppose you want to say, *The jury has returned a verdict in the Sam Halston murder trial. Halston has been found guilty of the stabbing murder of his wife. This trial has been underway for three weeks here in the Washington County Circuit Court.* There's a lot of detail in this information, and all of it is important. If you memorize, it would be easy to forget a sentence or to stumble and have difficulty remembering what's left to say. Instead, a list can indicate the most important information, which can be said in different ways. It's advisable to write the letters large so that you can see them easily.

Jury verdict—Sam Halston

Guilty in stabbing murder—wife

3-week trial

Washington County Circuit Court

As long as you convey the message accurately, the joining words and phrases are not important. It is a good idea to practice the presentation over and over the way you want to say it, but don't try to recite it from memory. When you have a bullet list available, you may not need it at all, but it's there in case you do. The list can also give you a chance to make sure you've included everything you intended to in a quick glance. Whether you choose to memorize your presentation or use a list, always take a moment before going on camera to think about the message you want to convey.

Stationary Stand-Ups

When the stand-up is intended to cover a part in the story where there is no appropriate video or to serve as a transition, the reporter may stand perfectly still and speak directly into the camera. Similarly, if the stand-up is meant to establish a location, such as that you are reporting from Moscow, you may stand still with the Kremlin framed in the shot. These circumstances require specific behaviors.

For any stand-up, the reporter will always look directly into the camera for a second or two before talking. If the reporter speaks and the camera rolls simultaneously, there won't be enough lead time on the video to allow the editor to find a good in-point. So, after the camera is rolling, the reporter stands still, looks directly into the camera for a beat or two, and then begins speaking.

Delivery of a stationary stand-up is very simple: the reporter simply talks and looks directly into the camera lens. The eyes must remain focused on the camera.

If a reporter looks to the side or rolls the eyes up or looks down while trying to think of something, it will look very odd to the viewer. Stand-ups require reporters to talk to the camera lens as if they are talking and maintaining eye contact with one individual. In fact, when we talk to our friends, we don't maintain constant eye contact. We generally talk for a few seconds, look away and look back. The camera in the field, however, requires constant, direct eye contact.

At the end of the stand-up, the reporter must continue the direct eye contact and remain stationary for a few seconds after the presentation. If the standup ends with a standard outcue, such as *Jane Doe—News 4,* Jane will need to conclude the outcue, look at the camera and wait. If Jane completes the words *News 4* and immediately looks down, looks away or, worse, begins moving away, the editor won't be able to include the end of the outcue without the distracting action or movement. The shifting eyes or movement out of the shot will make it appear to the audience that the reporter has no more interest in the story and is rushing away. So, at the end of the stand-up, remember to remain still, look directly into the camera and wait. Except in rare cases, the beginning and end of stand-ups require standing still and looking directly into the camera for a beat or two both before and after speaking.

Action Stand-Ups

During a stand-up—that is, *after* providing stationary lead time for the editor—the reporter may choose a variety of actions for the purpose of revealing something or showing participation. Actions can strengthen a stand-up. Some professionals advise always using something to point at, show or touch in stand-ups, but the reporter should remember that the action should support the story and add information. In a story about a drought, the reporter may take a step or two, bend down and pick up rocks from a dry riverbed and explain that the rocks were under water a few short weeks ago. The action will be sandwiched in between the steady, still beginning and a steady, still ending.

To show participation, a reporter traveling with troops and covering a war might open an MRE (meal ready to eat) and take a bite. For a story on police training, the reporter might do the stand-up while sitting behind the wheel of a police car or while demonstrating functions on a radar gun. In one of those rare instances where the stand-up doesn't begin or end with the reporter standing still, the reporter may talk to the camera while moving alongside a person who is walking across the country to protest federal environmental policies. In more typical examples, the reporter may want to show the difficulty in opening a tamper-proof package, or point out shattered glass from a broken bottle used in an assault, or turn over a leaf of a tree to show a particular kind of plant disease.

In all these examples, the reporter and photographer must plan the exact action and decide where the shot will be focused throughout the duration of the stand-up to maximize the creativity and effectiveness of the stand-up. The photographer needs to know how and where the reporter will move in order to maintain good shot composition.

When the reporter completes any kind of action in a stand-up, the movement must be limited. On stage, actors make large movements so they can be seen in the last row of the theatre. For the camera, movements are small: a slight nod of the head rather than a movement of the entire face and neck; two steps instead of ten; a gesture from the wrist to fingertips rather than from shoulder and elbow to fingertips. Notice the action that occurs in any situation comedy or dramatic program. The actors seldom cover much distance; they keep their arms and hands close to their bodies; their gestures typically move smoothly and slowly. Likewise, a reporter walking toward something will take only a few steps.

Reporters and photographers execute a good stand-up with the rhythm of music. Look at the camera and hold . . . speak and hold. When there's an action, look at the camera and hold, then begin speaking, and perform the action . . . look at the camera and hold. Conducting a stand-up requires all of the presentation skills previously discussed—plus a slow dance with the camera.

LIVE SHOTS

Broadcasters are increasingly called upon to use their professional voice and presentation skills in live telecasts. The general skills of using the voice properly with proper enunciation and varied, interesting delivery remain the same for live broadcasting, but there are other considerations as well.

First, reporters need to understand the value of live shots. One of the primary reasons for the live shot is to take the audience to the scene for the latest information. If a fire is burning or a bridge has collapsed, broadcast news can keep the viewer apprised of the most recent changes in a situation: *Two hundred more fire-fighters are arriving tonight to try to control this fire. Twenty people have been taken to the hospital and we understand that one man is in critical condition.* The live coverage also gives the audience the feeling of experiencing the event firsthand.

Live shots also add variety to a newscast. If the anchor presents a series of reporter packages, the audience hears a series of similar introductions. *Joe Smith has the story. Brook Holly reports. As John Seymore tells us, the trial should be winding up tomorrow.* A live shot changes the pace. And finally, live shots allow the audience to become familiar with reporters in the same way they become acquainted with anchors.

In general, reporters doing live shots in the field need to have a clear understanding with producers and with the camera operator about what is expected. Will there be both an intro and a close to a pre-produced package, or just an intro? How much cross talk will there be with the anchor? Will the anchor ask a follow-up question and what will it be? How much time is allotted? When everyone involved is clear on expectations, there is less likelihood of serious mistakes.

The reporter and camera operator must have an understanding of the composition of the shot. The reporter needs to know what the camera operator sees in the viewfinder and what the viewers at home will see. Clearly, the reporter would not want to tell viewers, *As you can see . . .* if they can't see what the reporter is talking about. When the reporter knows what is or is not visible, he can make decisions about pointing or gesturing. Similarly, the photographer needs to know about any movements the reporter is planning in order to follow smoothly with the camera.

You should not use gestures or reporter movement within the live shot without a clear purpose. If a fire is blazing behind the reporter, there is no need to gesture and say, *As you can see, the fire is still blazing.* If the fire is burning on the third floor, however, but started on the opposite side of the building on the ground floor, the reporter might point while explaining, *The fire started on the ground floor over there and moved quickly through the second floor. Blazes broke through the third floor about 30 minutes ago.* If the camera angle does not show what the viewers need to see, the reporter might take a few steps as she gives the account and let the camera operator follow the movement to reveal more of the building. In these examples, there is a reason for movement. Reporters who have a fondness for some particular action that is not motivated will be calling undue attention to themselves. One reporter became noticed in her market as the woman who always takes two steps and gestures at the end of her packages. Viewers would not have focused on the repeated action if there had been a reason for it.

Three kinds of situations make up most of the live presentations by broadcast reporters. Knowing what they are will help you prepare for live broadcasts.

The Wraparound

A broadcast reporter's first experience in live broadcasting will most likely be a *wraparound* from the site of a news story. A **wraparound** is the reporter's live introduction and outcue to her own story. The presentation style is like that of a stand-up.

Wraparounds can be straightforward and simple, with the reporter standing still and speaking directly to the camera throughout. For example, if you cover a major city festival, the news director or producer may ask for a live shot from the scene. You should have been at the festival much earlier and should have already prepared a news package about the event, either in a field truck or back at the station. During the newscast, you will be back at the scene. The anchor will announce that the festival is underway and tell the audience that you will be giving more information. The anchor then talks to you from the set and you appear. You greet the anchor by speaking directly into the camera and proceed to introduce your package. The intro might be something like this:

> Good evening, Diane. I'm here at Funfest in Kingsport and organizers say the crowd is larger than ever this year—by ten thousand! They're not sure where everyone came from, but the city had a hard time handling the traffic. . . .

At this point the package rolls, showing traffic snarls and fender-benders from the hot afternoon. The story may go on to say that despite traffic problems, the skydiving show was a huge success, and a sellout crowd is expected for the concert tomorrow.

In a wraparound, the package will not end with the reporter's standard outcue (*Joe Smith reporting for Eyewitness News*). Instead, the story ends and the live shot returns to you in the field, where you add more information:

> The good news, Diane, is that city police say they will have the traffic problems solved for tomorrow.

At this point the anchor might ask a follow-up question, to which you respond. As we mentioned, you should plan follow-up questions in advance. Suppose that the anchor asks the reporter how much longer the festival lasts and the reporter doesn't know. Both the reporter and anchor are embarrassed. When the reporter is surprised with a question and doesn't know the answer, it's hard to pretend otherwise. Not knowing the dates of the festival would be a serious reporting error, but it is understandable that a reporter might not know the answer to a legal or technical question that the anchor might ask unexpectedly. In these situations, it's probably better to say something like, *That's a good question and I'll work on it and let you know.* As discussed earlier, if you don't know, you can't fake it, and trying to do so in a live shot is a formula for disaster.

Finally, the anchor thanks you, and you may respond, but you will stand still and continue to look directly at the camera until you are sure the shot is no longer on you.

EXHIBIT 10.4 Wraparound script. The live intro is indicated in the shaded box. "Ad lib" at the end refers to closing live shots that will be ad-libbed.

ERWIN HIGH WATER-LIVE   500 PM [11/19/05 17:00]   Duration: 1:12

[Anchor: Gomez]
[Read Rate: 15]
{***GOMEZ***}
RESIDENTS IN UNICOI COUNTY, CALIFORNIA HAVE BEEN DEALING WITH FLASH FLOODING SINCE DAY BREAK THIS MORNING . . .
    THAT'S WHERE WE BEGIN THE TOP STORIES . . .
    AN ABUNDANCE OF RAIN IS CAUSING NUMEROUS PROBLEMS FOR RESIDENTS . . .
[TAKE: BOX SHOT]
{***BOX SHOT***}
    NEWSCENTER FIVE'S TARAH SCOTT JOINS US LIVE IN UNICOI COUNTY WITH MORE . . .
TARAH?
[TAKE: LIVE SHOT FULL]
{***LIVE SHOT FULL***}
[CG :TARAH SCOTT\ ]
[CG :1 Line CG\UNICOI CO., CA]

    IT'S BEEN A DAY OF FEAR AND FRUSTRATION HERE IN UNICOI COUNTY
    A 12 HOUR STORM CAUSED NEARLY EVERY CREEK IN THE COUNTY TO BREAK OUT OF ITS BANKS . . . FLOODING HOMES AND STREETS

[TAKE VO]
{***VO***}
FROM TEMPLE HILL TO LIMESTONE COVE AND UNICOI, RESCUERS HAVE SPENT THE DAY CHECKING ON RESIDENTS AND EVEN EVACUATING SOME. AT LEAST 20 FAMILIES HAD TO BE REMOVED FROM THEIR HOMES. MOST FOUND A SAFE HAVEN WITH A RELATIVE WHILE OTHERS TOOK COVER IN A RED CROSS SHELTER. RESCUERS SAY THEIR JOB WON'T BE FINISHED TONIGHT UNTIL THE WATER'S GONE.
[TAKE SOT
OUTCUE: "GET THEM OUT."
DURATION: 0:16]
{***SOT FULL***}
[CG :2 Line CG\CLYDE BRYANT\CAPTAIN, UNAKA MTN. SEARCH & RESCUE]
{NO VERBATIM AVAILABLE}
[TAKE: CONT VO]
{***CONT VO***}
    THE WATER IS CONTINUING TO RECEDE AT THIS HOUR AND OFFICIALS ARE HOPEFUL EVERYONE WILL BE ABLE TO RETURN TO THEIR HOMES TONIGHT. COUNTY ROAD CREWS ARE CURRENTLY ASSESSING DAMAGE—ALREADY ESTIMATED TO BE AROUND 100-THOUSAND DOLLARS.
[TAKE: LIVE SHOT FULL]
{***LIVE SHOT FULL***}
AD LIB

<mos>
ERWIN HIGH WATER
</mos>

In preparing a package for a live wraparound, the reporter essentially writes two beginnings and two endings to the story. The package itself needs to be able to stand alone, perhaps to be used in a later newscast. (In this case, the reporter's standard outcue will be added, most likely from a recording that editors have on hand for this purpose.)

Those who can communicate lots of information without giving up eye contact with the camera are fortunate, skilled or both. However, sometimes there is much information with important detail that you don't want to risk forgetting in the live shot. In this case, it is totally acceptable to hold a visible clipboard or notebook and to let the audience see you looking down for information. After all, the information is important.

The Live Shot Interview

The live shot will often include a short interview with someone. Once again, simplicity and clarity are fundamental. Questions should be simple—one at a time. The tone of the interview is important. The broadcaster always has the responsibility for making the conversation pleasant, or at least cordial, no matter how difficult the topic. Even if the person being interviewed is abrupt and sounds rude, the broadcaster must remain polite.

The major challenge of the interview in a live shot is working within the time limitations. You may have a maximum of two minutes to ask questions, and one or two may be all that time allows. Reporters quickly develop an acute sense of time with live-shot experience. On the other hand, people you are interviewing in the live shot may not be as experienced and may either talk too long or give very short, undeveloped answers. The reporter should prepare the interviewee before the interview by explaining exactly what will happen and how much time there will be. The interviewee will appreciate an explanation of where to stand, where to look and how much to say. If the reporter is holding a microphone, the interviewee should be advised not to try to hold the mic. For such short interviews, it may be acceptable to tell subjects what the questions will be, unless there is a reason to think they may avoid an issue if they have time to plan ahead. You may warn them that time will go by more quickly than they expect, and determine a signal to let them know to quit talking. For example, you may be able to touch them on the arm, since you will be standing much closer than people normally stand for the shot to look properly composed on camera. If the interviewee continues to talk when time is up, the reporter may need to interrupt the conversation—always politely. In more difficult cases, the polite, firm *thank you* may require a little extra volume.

As always, action during the live shot requires special attention. The reporter must plan each movement in advance, and the subject and camera operator must be clear about the plan. The reporter may begin by talking directly into the camera and then turn toward the interviewee, being very careful that the camera doesn't capture a total profile of the subject. After asking the questions, the reporter may turn back around to talk into the camera. If the interviewee expects these movements, the interview will go more smoothly. An unexpected action by the reporter could surprise the subject and interfere with the flow of the interview. In live-shot interviews, careful planning puts everyone at ease so that the reporter can concentrate on the message and ask clear, simple questions and the interviewee can think about what he is saying rather than being distracted by unexpected activity.

Extended Live Coverage

In important breaking news, reporters may remain at the scene and present extended live coverage. In major stories, reporters may go live for several minutes without a break, perhaps giving new information and conducting interviews in the same segment. When the cameras are off, the reporter may have to rush to talk to people and gather new facts for the next live shot. In these pressure situations, the basics are especially important. Make sure that everyone involved knows the plan: how long before going live again, how much time there will be to fill and what action or movement is planned within the shot. The reporter must also find time to concentrate on the message to be communicated: What is the latest information? What can I show and what can I tell that will help the audience understand the story? Normally, reporters have significant experience in live-shot wraparounds and live interviews before they are assigned to extended live coverage in a major breaking news story. At times, however, beginning reporters may find themselves at the place where a major event happens and may have to handle the live coverage. The basics of all live coverage are essentially the same as for all news broadcasting: tell a story, simply, clearly and accurately.

Additional Presentation Factors

The Food Factor. Broadcasters should avoid foods that can interfere with vocal quality before a broadcast. Greasy foods and milk can coat the throat and interfere with the vibration of the vocal cords. Too much caffeine can cause the vocal cords and jaw to be tight. Too much carbonation can cause gas in the stomach that makes it difficult to push air out in a steady, controlled manner. Acidic foods may stimulate the salivary glands. Individuals should know or learn how particular foods and beverages affect them and learn what to avoid before a broadcast.

Drugs and Alcohol. Alcohol is a depressant and can have an adverse effect on broadcast presentation. Even though it might seem like a good idea to have a drink to depress feelings of nervousness, the alcohol slows brain functions at the same time it reduces palm sweating. Moreover, reliance on alcohol or drugs is simply not a workable solution for the long term. Nervousness diminishes with experience, but dependence on alcohol or drugs for an enhanced performance will increase and create more serious problems than butterflies in the stomach or sweaty palms. Even if the alcohol is used for recreation rather than as an antidote to nervousness, social activity and job responsibilities may interfere with each other. Drinking while there is work to do is simply not wise. Drugs and alcohol can become addictive, and no career is worth the devastation of lives that comes with addiction. Do your job in broadcasting without drugs or alcohol.

Tobacco. Most of us have heard the rattling lungs and raspy voices of long-term smokers. Young smokers may not see a connection between themselves and the 40-year-old with the rattling lungs. However, 40-year-olds know that they're in their prime career years. They are ready to reap the benefits of experience with higher pay, better hours and a better quality of life. Struggling with damaged lung capacity, shortness of breath and dried-out vocal cords from smoking should not be part of the midcareer scenario. Smoking is not healthy and should be avoided, especially by broadcasters who rely for their professional success directly on the parts of the body most harmed.

CONCLUSION

Voice quality and presentation skills are important elements of news broadcasting. Broadcasters can and must develop skill in reading and reporting news to a mass audience. They can develop and improve voice quality by practicing and using good breath control. They can enhance delivery by enunciation, careful phrasing and emphasis, and variety in pitch and pace. They should practice the pronunciations of Standard American English and minimize regional accents that may not be appealing to a general, perhaps national, audience. They can correct even basic problems in producing specific sounds, although they may need professional assistance from a speech therapist. They can learn to look neat and attractive, be alert and make a courteous presentation while controlling the appearance of nervousness. Whether broadcast presentation is pre-recorded or live, the goal is to speak well and tell an accurate story clearly. In summary, the skill an individual uses in speaking to an audience is part of the broadcaster's professional package that earns the paycheck. Like any skill, vocal delivery and presentation usually improve with study and practice.

KEY CONCEPTS

diaphragm	emphasis	tone
vocal cords	pitch	accent
enunciation	inflection	Standard American English
full word production	sing-song pattern	wraparound
phrase	pace	

Activities

1. List the three Aristotelian characteristics of a good communicator and explain what they mean.

2. Gather your thoughts to give a description of the weather and your plans for the day. Present your comments to the class in a pleasant, energetic manner.

3. Study the examples on pacing in the chapter. Practice reading them out loud and then read them to the class according to the directions.

4. Practice saying *Once upon a time* in an extremely exaggerated manner. Prepare to perform your most extreme version for your class.

5. Find a partner. Either using the names *John* and *Marsha* or using your own names, say the names to each other over and over. Each time, indicate a different emotion, such as excitement, sadness, love, irritation, etc. Notice how the tone of your voice and your emphasis change.

6. Choose a nursery rhyme or a line of poetry from memory and say it three times. On the first time, try to push all the air through your nose. On the second time, try to push all the air through your throat. On the third time, find a comfortable balance in pushing the air out through both the nose and mouth. Compare to your normal speaking pattern and evaluate your sound quality.

7. Practice several of the techniques for controlling nervousness described in the chapter. Evaluate the potential and effectiveness of each.

PRESENTATION AND VOICE EXERCISES

1. Use a tape recorder to listen to your voice. Analyze your speech patterns. Do you produce all the sounds in words? Is your pitch comfortable to listen to? Do you speak slowly? Is there variety in your pitch and pace?

2. Read several sentences into a tape recorder. Try getting deeper and fuller breath support as you read them again. Can you hear the difference?

3. Tape your voice and then do a series of warm-ups and breathing exercises. Tape your voice again. What differences do you hear?

4. Tape your voice and a network news anchor back to back. Play them back and compare.

5. Record a news story on tape and have classmates or colleagues critique your vocal presentation.

Knowledge is power. If you know about the legal system and the legal

limits, you're free to achieve more powerful reporting.

ERIC SCOTT,
WJZ-TV, BALTIMORE

LEGAL CONSIDERATIONS

EVERY NEWS STORY hurts someone—or so it is often said. This claim may not be totally true, but certainly most news stories have the potential to cause difficulty for individuals, even if the story is as simple as reporting a traffic violation. In our society, we have accepted the idea that some individuals will face embarrassment to protect the free press and the open flow of information. The law does, however, provide remedies for people who suffer unjustly at the hands of news reporters.

THE CONSEQUENCES OF CARELESSNESS

You can be sued and your station can be sued if you cause undeserved problems for people through what you say or show in your newscast. If you lose, the person suing is likely to be awarded large sums of money.

The consequences of a news story are easy to understand. Suppose you hear on the evening newscast that your neighbor is accused of rape, or perhaps stealing from an employer. You are likely to reconsider your relationship and alter the way you interact with the neighbor. A typical television newscast is seen and heard by a minimum of tens of thousands of people, if not by millions, so your neighbor's other acquaintances may be doing the same thing. These actions represent serious damage to your neighbor's quality of life. Although these consequences may not seem inappropriate for a rapist or thief, *what if the story is not true?* The individual facing the charges may have been another person with the same first and last names, but a different middle name and different address who worked at an entirely different company from your neighbor. You can see why the neighbor might want to recover a financial judgment to help compensate for lost business, a damaged reputation and the emotional pain and suffering of the experience—not to mention the possible desire for revenge. For the individual who is erroneously identified in connection with a crime, the mistake can harm the person's reputation as much as if the charges were true. The follow-up story that clears the subject's name, however, never seems to carry the weight of the initial story.

In another scenario, the reporter may accurately name the person who was charged, but the individual may turn out to be innocent. The charges may be dropped when officials realize the mistake—or the case may proceed through trial where the person is acquitted. Because arrests, indictments, charges and court proceedings are public record, the courts will protect reporters from legal liability when they report truthful information from legally obtained public records. Our judicial system refrains from punishing the media for accurately reporting information from public documents.

Reporters need to understand the legalities surrounding their jobs to stay out of court, but they must also hold to moral standards. Morality and legality are not the same and there can be a lot of difference between what is legal and what is right.

LEGAL VS. ETHICAL

Celebrities and public officials have a very difficult time winning lawsuits, and publishers and their attorneys know it, so public people often just accept exaggerated, embarrassing or even false stories as part of the territory of being well-known. Stories about celebrities and elected officials that falsely accuse them of drug abuse, sex crimes and even murder are not uncommon. In the sensational tabloid television programs and magazines that we discussed in Chapter 1, there is often no evidence—just a claim. These stories of unsupported accusations appear, are discussed for a short while, and then the story dies. We seldom hear about related lawsuits because the publisher or broadcaster most likely has legal protection in presenting these stories. These tabloid papers and television programs masquerade as news and push the limits of the law, ignoring ethical considerations. If there are legal loopholes, the story runs, even if the writer has serious doubts about its accuracy. Sadly, the story sometimes runs even if the writer knows it is false.

If there's a source who says a presidential candidate used cocaine or who accuses the president of murder, the tabloid media may run the story based on the one source. The writer may know for certain that the source is not trustworthy or may at least be skeptical. Legally, however, the story may be safe because the writer can claim to have believed the source. We'll talk more about the difference in legalities in reporting on public people and private people later, but the point here is that reporting some things may be legally sound, but may not be the right thing to do.

This country's tradition of protecting speech and press often protects reporters who make big mistakes, and sometimes protects them even when the reporting is totally irresponsible. This chapter is not intended to show you how to use loopholes in the law for protection against making mistakes, but, instead, to show you ways to be more careful in your work.

One way to ensure that a story is both legally and ethically sound is to be fair and balanced. **Fairness** means giving both sides of a story, or maybe more than two sides. If someone accuses a candidate of doing something wrong, make sure the candidate gets to give the other side of the story. If the city manager is being interviewed and accuses a contractor of doing a bad job, get the contractor's comments. Some stories that may not seem to have another viewpoint do, in fact, need balance. For example, if a congressional representative introduced a bill that would require prayer each morning in public schools, many people might rejoice to hear of the proposal, and the reporter might be prepared to interview the representative for further details on the bill. A deeper look at the issue, however, would reveal a long legal history overturning such bills, and most attorneys could explain the opposing viewpoint. Good reporters attempt to present a variety of viewpoints so that the members of the public can make their own decisions about which arguments to believe.

Television news people hold great responsibility. They hold the power to ruin lives with a word or a picture. Therefore, each word and each picture must be carefully chosen. It only takes one mistake. The one day you are slightly careless could be the day your work lands in court.

Even though the First Amendment guarantees free speech and a free press, it does not protect you if you make mistakes in certain areas. In the area of *libel,* judgments are awarded to plaintiffs when information that is both false and damaging to a reputation is published or broadcast. In addition, the media must (meaning, it's a legal requirement or legal standard) exhibit some level of fault in getting and presenting the information—ranging from simple negligence to publishing information while knowing that it is false. *Invasion of privacy* suits can be won even when truthful information is published or broadcast. Privacy suits often relate to information gathered on private property, the use of someone's identity for commercial purposes, a misleading use of information or information that is considered both embarrassing and very private. *Copyright law violations* involve using the creations of others, in words, pictures or music, without proper permission. Other areas that commonly involve reporters in legal issues relate to access to public information or efforts at gathering news that may bring the reporter into conflict with the court system.

LIBEL

Libel law provides protection against defamation of a person's reputation. If the old rhyme claiming that sticks and stones can break bones but words can never hurt were true, there would be no libel laws. Words do hurt people. Defamation law is designed to redress the problems caused when a reputation is ruined or when people are shunned or ridiculed because of false information that is presented about them. When the defamatory statements are spoken to another individual or individuals, the defamation is called **slander.** When the defamatory statements are printed, the defamation is called **libel.** However, broadcast speech is considered to be libel because the communication often comes from a written script, and even if not, it is delivered to a large audience simultaneously.

> Lots of times people don't like your story and will threaten legal action, but when you have documentation that proves you're right, the threat won't go anywhere.
>
> *Dale Solly*

The first important concept to remember about libel law is that libel laws are state laws and vary from state to state. Therefore, the discussion of libel here is general, and reporters should familiarize themselves with the particular statutes of the state in which they work. Another fundamental of libel is that the law is designed to protect people from *false* information that defames them. For this reason, the general guideline is that *truth is an absolute defense* against libel charges. Avoiding libel suits is really quite simple. Every single word in a story must be true, and the reporter should know before the story goes on the air that every word could be proven if necessary.

The plan to present only the truth in a news story sounds simple, but the practice is not so easy. Good reporters work carefully to present the facts, but like all human beings, they make mistakes. The reporter may misread something or write something down incorrectly, or quote a trustworthy source who made a mistake. Time constraints may prevent checking information as thoroughly as desired, or the reporter may ignore a small doubt that turns out to be a serious oversight. Beginning reporters may simply lack the experience to recognize problems.

Because it is so easy to make mistakes and because the justice system recognizes the problems of working under tight deadlines, the reporter and station do not, in fact, have to prove that every single word in a story is true when they are taken to court. On the contrary, the person bringing the libel suit has to prove that the information is false. But despite the fact that the law is generally on the side of the media, it is still a good practice to make certain that every word of the story is correct and that every picture is an accurate representation.

In a general sense, the person who claims defamation and brings suit—the plaintiff—will have four things to prove: *defamation, publication, identification* and *fault*. First, was there **defamation** that caused injury? Was there damage to the reputation because of publicized false information? Did the story cause the person to suffer, to be shunned or ridiculed, to lose friends or business? In many cases, there's no question. If a story refers to someone as a thief, murderer, pimp or rapist, these words are clearly defamatory. Without some factual basis for the claim, the media would surely be held **liable,** or legally responsible, for the libel. (Notice the difference in these two words: *liable* refers to responsibility and *libel* refers to defamation.) Other references may or may not be libelous depending on the context in which they are made. In any case, the person suing will have to show that defamation resulted from the story.

Second, the plaintiff will have to prove that the story was **published**—printed or broadcast. As mentioned previously, slander is considered to have occurred if a false, defamatory statement is made by one individual to another individual about a third person. In broadcast libel charges, it's not hard to prove whether or not something was published. A script may be on file containing the defamatory words, or people will be able to verify that they heard it.

The plaintiff must prove that she was **identified** in the story. When someone is identified in a story, it means that viewers understand who the information is about. If Mayor Juliana Wilson claims to have been defamed in a story that falsely accused her of using city money to pave her driveway, there won't be much question about the identification. The story may not even have included her name. If it said *the mayor,* there's only one in a particular city and she has been identified. In contrast, if John Smith was arrested last night and charged with rape, any town would have several John Smiths who could possibly claim to have been libeled. Is there other information included in the story that would specify which John Smith was arrested?

Finally, the plaintiff will have to prove **fault,** a level of error on the part of the broadcaster. (Please notice that the lawsuit will be filed against the station, but the reporter will probably also be named in the suit, and the reporter's actions will be under examination on the witness stand.) The court will consider whether the reporter was working under deadline and whether the mistake was a reasonable one. Was a minor mistake included in a story that was substantially true? And how true is true? If an observer says a customer was "angry" and "yelling obscenities" before breaking something and running out, how can we judge the truth of the observation? When does frustration or irritation become anger and which words are obscene? Was there reason for the reporter to believe the information was accurate? Did the reporter attempt to verify the story? Was the source a reputable source of information, and why did the reporter think so? Did the reporter question the accuracy of the information or even doubt the accuracy? Is it possible that the reporter even knew the information was false? Maybe the falsity was a simple mistake, like writing John C. Smith instead of John D. Smith.

The level of fault that public people must show in libel cases is much harder to prove than the simpler requirements for private people. Let's look at the differences in legal protection for reporters covering public and private people.

> You can't be effective if you're afraid of litigation. Get your facts right and don't worry. People love to scream and threaten, but most of the time, they don't sue.
>
> *Richard Frohlich*
> **WFTV-TV, ORLANDO, FLA.**

Libel and Public Figures

The world changed for American journalists in 1964 when the Supreme Court handed down a decision in the case of *New York Times Co. v. Sullivan* (376 U.S. 254). The Sullivan case changed the standard of fault in libel cases related to **public officials,** those who are paid with public money and hold responsibility in doing the work of the government. The Supreme Court held that an Alabama police commissioner was a public official who could not win a judgment against The New York Times even though false information was printed that related to him. The *Sullivan* standard offers so much protection that the media can win libel suits even when the information about the public official is both false and defamatory. Today, a public official has to prove more than defamation, publication, identification and fault to win money in a libel suit. The public official has to prove that the information was published with a level of fault known as **actual malice:** a standard indicating that the reporter or others involved actually knew information was false or gave little or no attention to whether it was true or false. In legal terms, actual malice means that the people who created the story showed *reckless disregard for the truth* or presented the information with *knowing falsehood.* Think about the difficulty of proving that the reporter knew the information was false or that the reporter didn't care whether it was true or false. The **burden of proof**—responsibility for proving something—rests on the plaintiff, who must prove that the libel was broadcast with actual malice. Proving actual malice is very difficult.

Several years after the *Times v. Sullivan* decision, the Supreme Court expanded this burden of proof to public figures as well as public officials. No longer did a person have to be an elected representative or someone who worked on behalf of the public to hold the burden of proving that the report was presented with actual malice. **Public figures**—celebrities and others who are well known to the public—have the same burden of proof in libel cases as public officials. Therefore, if a tabloid television show broadcasts false claims that a movie star used cocaine at a party after the Academy Awards, the celebrity would have to prove that the writers knew the story was false or were reckless in evaluating the truth of the story, in order to win a libel judgment. A tabloid program could pay two sources for interviews in which each claims to have seen the movie star using the drug. Sadly, the sources may be willing to say anything for the money, but the people who prepared the story can testify that they had two separate sources for the information and did not know the sources were lying.

The law makes it difficult for public people to prove libel because these people willingly put themselves into the limelight and know that their actions will be conversation for the public. They seek public office or pursue careers that require constant publicity, and it's also easy for them to get access to the media to disseminate their own comments and opinions if they get unfavorable news coverage. Public officials also have easy access to the media because they are doing the public's business—our business. They're spending our tax money and making decisions that affect all of us. They are expected to be publicly evaluated and criticized.

These legal protections are important to our social system. If an opposing candidate claims that the mayor is misusing public funds, the media must have the freedom to broadcast the charge. Of course, responsible journalists would strive to verify the accusation with some evidence before it is broadcast, but as long as reporters do not know the charge is a lie and are not totally reckless about the truth of the charge, they are not likely to lose a libel suit. Public officials should expect to be the subject of public debate. Citizens must be able to talk freely about their representatives—and both citizens and reporters alike will inevitably make mistakes. The law will protect the media even when they're irresponsible or wrong in reporting about public officials, as long as the mistakes were not knowing or reckless. This does not mean that journalists have a license to be careless. It means that great freedom requires great responsibility and that journalists hold our democracy in their hands. The journalist will do everything he can to be sure the story is true, accurate and balanced.

All too often the freedoms given to the press for these noble reasons are used to smear public people. Open debate about elected officials has little to do with whether a mega-celebrity is sleeping with her manager, but if a couple of people say it and the media report it, the same arguments apply: Was the information broadcast with knowing falsehood or reckless disregard for the truth? Celebrities generally appreciate publicity because the better known they are, the more attention they get for their movies, concerts or lectures. And like public officials, public figures have ready access to media sources when they want to dispute a news item.

This area of libel law offers so much protection for the media that tabloid programmers can get away with totally irresponsible reporting. Even so, legal scholars believe the good outweighs the bad. Such protection for the media is unheard of anywhere else in the world. These laws protect free-flowing debate among citizens so that voters can freely express their ideas and opinions about government. The fact that some publishers and broadcasters abuse this privilege does not mean we must restrict the freedom, but it does require citizens to be able to tell the difference between important information and trash.

Libel and Private People

Although the law seems to protect egregious reporting about public people, it is much less forgiving when reporters make false defamatory statements about private individuals. Private people do not seek the limelight and do not have ready access to the media to correct mistakes or gain publicity for their opinions. Private people are likely to be more seriously hurt by defamatory reporting than are public officials. Therefore, the law makes it easier for private people to prove libel. The legal standard for determining whether the media is guilty of libel against a private person is **negligence.** In gathering and presenting the information in question, did the reporter do what a reasonable person would do to guarantee that the information was accurate?

The question of what a reasonable person would do to guarantee accuracy for a story can be quite difficult to answer. For example, what should a reporter do if the secretary in the prosecutor's office says in a phone call that drug charges are being filed against William Smith of Johnson Road, Salem?

- Use that information?
- Go to the courthouse to see the official written charges before reporting them?
- Call someone at the courthouse to verify the information?
- Make some effort to find out whether there might be another William Smith living on Johnson Road?

What if the secretary has long been a source of accurate information? What if the secretary is new? What if there are two William Smiths who live on Johnson Road? Is it negligent not to look in the phone book under the name William Smith? What if the secretary gave the information over the phone and misread the report—maybe it was really William Johnson of Smith Road. Has the reporter been negligent? Would a reasonable person find a way to verify the secretary's information? If you are the innocent William Smith, how will you define negligence?

Good reporters, of course, will be equally careful in all their work, whether the subject is a private individual or a public official, and must guard against letting the daily routine lull them into carelessness. News affects individual lives in serious ways, and the reporter must get the facts right.

Defenses Against Libel Lawsuits

Even reporting perfectly accurate information can result in a libel suit if a full context is missing. When reporters find themselves facing libel action, there are several ways to defend against the charges, including *truth, fair comment* and *privilege.*

Truth

Generally, truth is an absolute defense against libel charges. If your story claims that John Smith has been charged with murder and public records show the charge has been filed, John Smith will not go far with a libel suit even if he is acquitted of the murder charges. You have reported the truth and you have documents to back up your claim. On the other hand, reporters must remember that the truth that provides an absolute defense is *factual* truth. A factual truth can be proven, but all news is not factual. Sometimes, news is comprised of people's opinions. Mainstream media news does not include the opinion of the reporter, but opinions of those involved in a story can be important information. The opinions of others can also be libelous, and the media can be sued for including libelous opinions from news sources in their stories. At other times, even libelous opinions from news sources may find legal protection.

Pure opinion finds great First Amendment protection, as discussed later, but sometimes people masquerade their opinions as claims of fact. Whether an opinion is "true" can be difficult to determine. As discussed previously, if a private citizen named John Smith has a cousin who holds the opinion that Smith is a murderer and a liar, the broadcast of the claim can be libelous—even though the reporter gave a truthful report of the "opinion." It is true that the cousin made the claim, but the claim may not have supporting evidence and may be wrong. Whether someone has murdered someone or lied is more than a question of opinion—murder and lying either happen or they don't. Reporting libelous comments from others is the same as saying them yourself and can mean losing a libel suit and paying damages, even when the comments are labeled as opinion and are accurately reported.

> If you say, "Police have arrested two robbers," you've just convicted two people without a trial.
>
> *John Antonio*
> **WABC-TV, NEW YORK**

In determining the truth of a story, reporters must be especially careful to distinguish between *suspects* and *convicted criminals*. Until a suspect is found guilty, the media must not pronounce guilt or ascribe unproven actions to the suspect. A reporter should not say that the suspect walked through the door and shot three people. The man may face charges or police may even say he did it, but unless the reporter saw it and personally knows it for a fact, the story should not say that the suspect committed the crime. The story cannot say that "police have their man" in connection with yesterday's shooting spree. This statement clearly implies that the man is guilty. Someone who is merely charged with a crime has a legal right to object if anyone says or implies that he is guilty.

Remember that in libel cases, the plaintiff bears the burden of proof and must show that the information was published with some level of fault. If a libelous comment relates to a public figure, the public person must prove that the reporter knew that the information was false or recklessly disregarded the truth of the story. If a private person brings the charge, she must prove that the reporter was negligent in evaluating the truth of the story. If the reporter can prove the information is true, the lawsuit is not likely to happen in the first place.

Fair Comment and Opinion

Some opinion is considered **fair comment** and finds some legal protection when the opinion relates to matters of public interest. The opinions of citizens about political candidates would carry more protection than the opinions of neighbors about a man who was just arrested. Suppose that a neighbor of an accused murderer tells a reporter that the accused used to steal bicycles and no one in the neighborhood trusted him from the time he was 9 years old. This statement is obviously opinionated and quite damaging to someone who has been arrested and charged but has not been proven guilty of a crime. Broadcasting unsubstantiated, damaging opinions about a private individual can result in legal judgments against the media. However, if a restaurant critic says that the vichyssoise at Chez Robert was "inedible," the chef may feel that his reputation has been ruined and want to sue for damages. In this case, the chef may find that the courts protect such comments as fair opinion about the restaurant. Likewise, if a movie critic says that Julia Roberts cannot act and doesn't deserve a penny for her performance in her most recent movie, Roberts' claim that her reputation has been ruined is not likely to go far. The courts will say that a movie is a legitimate topic of discussion and opinion, even if the opinions are damaging ones. If the opinion goes far beyond the legitimate public discussion of Roberts' professional life, a libel case may be more likely.

Exaggerated opinions that cannot possibly be proven true or false are also generally protected. If a commentator calls a city council member a "stooge" or a "clown," the public official could claim that the charge was false and defamatory. But how do you prove whether or not someone is a "stooge"? And if the city council member is wearing a suit and tie instead of a big wig, floppy shoes and white face-paint, it's pretty clear that the public official is not really a clown. The claim is clearly an exaggerated opinion and is likely to find protection under the law because the behavior of a public person is open to public comment and opinion. If the food critic says that you couldn't have cut the medallions of beef with a chain saw at Chez Roberts', the chef could say that the claim was false. Reasonable readers have no doubt that the claim is false and they recognize the comment as an exaggerated opinion about a matter of public interest. The food critic will be safe in defending a libel suit.

The opinions that are "fair" relate to matters of public interest and are either based on clear evidence or are exaggerated opinion. If a sports commentator claims that an athlete is a criminal, the defense that the charge is simply opinion will not work. If there are no convictions, the athlete is not a criminal and the commentator may be found liable for libel.

If a political commentator claims that the mayor has shown a pattern of "stealing" from the taxpayers for the benefit of her own pocketbook, the mayor may sue, claiming that her reputation has been ruined and the claim that she "steals" is false. What if the reporter asserts that the comment was merely opin-

> The most important thing for photographers to remember is to roll tape, roll tape, roll tape. Tape is evidence. When in doubt, roll tape. And I recommend the National Press Photographers' Media Guide for Emergency and Disaster Incidents. Memorize it.
>
> *Dave Wertheimer*
> KSTP/KSTC-TV,
> MINNEAPOLIS/ST. PAUL, MINN.

ion? The mayor's behavior certainly qualifies as a matter of public interest, but whether someone steals or not can be proven true or false. In this situation, however, the columnist may be protected in accusing the mayor of stealing, if the charge is clearly presented as opinion based on evidence. For example, the commentator may point out that the mayor hired her spouse as a cultural director for the city, had road crews put in a new sidewalk in front of her house and hired a contractor to build a new school who then gave the mayor a trip to the Bahamas. As always, the reporter must be sure that the incidents are true and should verify them. After naming these incidents, the commentator asserts that the mayor is "stealing" from the taxpayers. In this case, the commentator has clearly reached an opinion based on specific documented facts that are presented along with the opinion. In any situation, opinions are better when they based on fact, but in court, they are also safer.

Absolute Privilege

In official government proceedings such as city council meetings, the floor of the state legislature and courtroom hearings, people often say false and damaging things about others. If individuals could be sued for these comments, citizens would be unlikely to speak in public forums and elected officials would be subject to huge financial penalties when they portray their opponents in false, damaging ways. Instead, the law provides an **absolute privilege,** or protection against legal action, for comments made in official government proceedings. A senator may accuse a large business owner of stealing taxpayer money during comments in Congress, and the charge may be totally false. When the charge takes place on the senate floor, there is no chance of a lawsuit. This absolute privilege applies to those participating in the proceedings in legislatures, Congress, local government meetings and courtrooms.

Qualified Privilege

Absolute privilege does not apply to reporters—only to those participating in public meetings. Even though reporters are not participants in the public forums, our legal system has decided that the media should not be punished for a truthful, accurate report of comments made in government proceedings. Reporters have a **qualified privilege,** or limited protection against legal action, when they present a truthful and accurate portrayal of a public meeting that includes false and defamatory comments. The reporting privilege is not absolute—it is restricted, or qualified. If the reporter does not present a balanced and accurate report about defamatory public comments, the privilege is lost and a successful lawsuit may result.

For example, if the camera is rolling during a city council meeting when the mayor calls a citizen a thief, the reporter who precisely and accurately presents the story will be protected against libel charges from the citizen, even if the claim has absolutely no factual basis. The protection applies to the accurate presentation of what happened in the official proceeding, even if the reporting defames someone. Coverage of courtrooms provides the same protection.

If cameras are not allowed in the courtroom and the reporter stands on the courthouse steps and describes the witness testimony, accurate reporting is unlikely to cause a problem. However, if the reporter interviews the witness outside the courtroom, and the witness changes the accusations slightly or expands the scope of the falsehood, these comments do not qualify for privileged reporting. Reporting these comments is not protected by the privilege that allows reporters to present official government proceedings accurately.

Consent

Consent may be a defense against libel charges. Individuals may **consent,** or agree, to have libelous statements broadcast, but why would they? If a reporter tells the mayor that a city council member is accusing him of stealing, the mayor is not likely to say, "Oh, fine. Go ahead and run the story. I don't mind." However, the mayor may agree to an interview and deny the charges and accuse the council member of mounting a political attack without any evidence. If the mayor agrees to the interview and comments on the accusation, he has *implied* his consent to having the story broadcast. Even though he did not directly state his agreement to having the accusation broadcast or sign a consent document, the fact that the mayor responded on camera is a clear indication that he knows the accusations will be included in the story. The mayor realizes that his response will be meaningless unless the reporter gives the details of the council member's charge. He has consented to the broadcast of the libelous claim. We will discuss the issue of consent related to using someone's picture in the following section about public and private property. This discussion is intended to remind reporters that an individual's reply to libelous statements implies consent to broadcast both the accusations and the reply.

Retraction

Even though a retraction is not an actual defense, retracting a story may be helpful in reducing or mitigating libel damage. If a false, defamatory story is broadcast about an individual, the person will surely call to complain or have a lawyer issue a complaint. Often, if reporters have made a mistake, a retraction or apology will help avert a lawsuit. Sometimes, the apology isn't enough and the case winds up in court. At a trial or before a judge, an on-air apology or retraction may help reduce the amount of damages the media will pay. Obviously, when reporters publicly admit making mistakes, the credibility of the entire news operation suffers. The only way to protect the credibility of the news medium and to stay out of legal trouble is to get the facts right. When the information is correct, a retraction won't be necessary.

Unfortunately, even accurate reporting can present legal trouble if the information constitutes an invasion of privacy, as explained in the following discussion.

PRIVACY

Libel suits are brought against the media for reporting false information that defames someone. Privacy suits are an entirely different matter. The media can lose invasion-of-privacy lawsuits by reporting information that is true but private. Privacy laws vary a great deal from state to state, so, as we have often advised, reporters need to know the laws in their own states. In general, privacy suits fall into four areas: *intrusion, false light, private facts* and *appropriation*. (See Exhibit 11.1.)

Intrusion

When people think of privacy, they are often considering our right to be left alone. For example, we expect privacy in our own homes. We do not accept that reporters can listen to our conversations or videotape our interactions in our own living rooms and kitchens. The law offers strong protection against media **intrusion**—invasion into private areas where we can reasonably expect to be left alone. But what about the front porch or the front yard? What if the kitchen window is close to the street and news photographers can easily see in? Can we expect privacy from media observation in a restaurant, at the ballpark or in a mall?

Public Property vs. Private Property

When reporters attempt to determine how far they can go in gathering information, the first and most important rule is to recognize the difference between public property and private property. The law generally protects news gathering on public property, where people can expect to be seen by anyone who happens

Four types of invasion-of-privacy suits. **EXHIBIT 11.1**

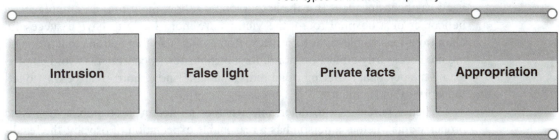

Intrusion · False light · Private facts · Appropriation

to be there. Public streets, parks and stadiums are paid for by taxpayers and are open to everyone. An individual cannot reasonably expect to have privacy in an open, public area. So, news photographers often take pictures of people walking down the sidewalk, picnicking or swimming at the public pool, or cheering the team at a football game. If a woman is with someone other than her spouse in these areas, hoping not to be seen, but shows up on the nightly newscast, the claim that her privacy was invaded will not succeed. On the other hand, a public restroom is also open to anyone, but an individual can reasonably expect privacy there. The governor's office is also public property, but that does not mean that the governor could expect someone with a camera to walk in at any time. So, after asking whether a location is public property or not, the photographer or reporter will also need to ask what the expectations of privacy would reasonably be in a particular situation.

> I've been in situations where home-owners have told me that I couldn't shoot video on their property even though I was on public property. When you know your rights, you shoot the video and do your job. Crossing onto their property is another situation. And remember that if a police officer gives you consent to enter someone's property, that's *not* consent.
>
> *Jay Webb*
> **WHSV-TV, HARRISONBURG, VA.**

One of the first experiences a news photographer may have related to legality is likely to come with the first assignment to cover a fire or an arrest. The homeowner watching the house go up in flames often tells the person with the camera to go away and not to take pictures of the fire. The homeowner's feelings are understandable, and offering legal reasoning to a person watching a lifetime of work go up in flames will probably not be successful. However, the photographer does have a legal right to be on public property and to shoot pictures of a scene that could be observed by anyone using the taxpayer-funded streets or land. If the publicly funded fire department is working in a location that is visible from public property, the homeowner cannot legally prevent the photographer from completing the assigned task. If the photographer walks onto private property, the matter changes completely. The owner can file trespassing charges if the photographer refuses a request to leave.

When rescue workers are trying to pull a victim from a crushed vehicle at the scene of a head-on collision, the action is usually on a highway—on public property. Even though people don't like to be seen by others while they are in pain, injured and helpless, they are not likely to be successful in claiming that their privacy has been invaded. But if photographers follow them into an ambulance, a helicopter or a hospital room, the victims are more likely to have a successful claim to a reasonable right to privacy. Remember also that actions that are legal are not necessarily ethical or moral. Responsible news departments avoid emphasizing the personal suffering of an individual and find a more creative way to tell the story of an accident.

When reporters try to determine whether an action is on public or private property and whether a person has a reasonable expectation of privacy, the legalities can become quite intricate. Do people inside a privately owned mall have a reasonable expectation of privacy when the mall functions like a downtown? Surely people know they will be seen by others in a mall, so why can't photographers take pictures there? Can people inside a restaurant, which is a privately owned business, have a reasonable right to expect privacy when the doors are open to anyone who walks in? The legal answers to these questions are not clear, so reporters and photographers should be alert to the dangers of taking people's pictures without their permission when they are on private property. The safe thing to do is to get permission—and remember that just because the owner says you can take pictures inside a restaurant does not mean that the customer agrees. Just because the owner or manager of the mall says it's ok to take pictures of shoppers does not mean that the shoppers agree. Although it's hard to imagine why someone would object to having his image included in a news story about increasing retail prices, there are many ways the video can cause problems for an individual—and if there is a reasonable right to expect privacy where the story was shot, the media could wind up paying compensation for invading someone's privacy.

Hidden Recordings

If a reporter is using a hidden camera or hidden tape recorder, internal warning bells should be loudly suggesting the possibility of legal danger. The use of a hidden recording device is not always illegal, but secret recordings surely suggest that privacy law might apply. Secretly taping a private conversation between other people is usually illegal, but some states permit an individual to secretly record his own conversation with another person. In some states, it is also illegal to secretly record your own conversation with someone else. The famous Monica Lewinsky presidential scandal began when Lewinsky's friend Linda Tripp secretly recorded their private conversation, wherein Lewinsky described her affair with President Clinton. The recordings were done in Maryland, where such recordings are illegal, and resulted in an indictment against Linda Tripp. If the recording had been done in the District of Columbia, it would have been legal. When reporters plan to secretly record an interview, the first step is to be sure that there is no other way to get the important information. If using the hidden recorder passes your own ethical test of right and wrong, the next step is to check the law.

When ABC's "20/20" secretly videotaped the handling and sale of out-of-date meat at a Food Lion store, the reporters knew that secret tapings were not illegal in North Carolina. So, when Food Lion sued, the company did not try to claim that its privacy had been invaded. Instead of filing an invasion-of-privacy suit, the grocery store chain claimed that ABC had committed fraud by having reporters lie to get jobs in their meat departments and won. The fraud lawsuit was a different issue from the question of the company's right to privacy. (Neither did the company claim it had been libeled. There was no dispute about the truth of the story.)

False Light

Privacy law protects individuals from being portrayed inaccurately, or in a **false light,** especially if the information is offensive to reasonable people and if the media is reckless in deciding whether the information is true or false. These kinds of cases are common when a dramatic presentation such as a book or made-for-TV movie portrays a real person as wicked or evil, or when a fictional character is clearly based on a real person.

Cantrell v. Forest City Publishing Co., one of the most notable legal cases in the area of false light, resulted from a reporter's portrayal of a family as poor and struggling. The story originated when a man died while trying to save victims of an airplane that crashed into the Potomac River in Washington. In a follow-up story a year later about the family's struggles, a reporter attributed quotes to the man's wife. In fact, the woman was not even present when the reporter visited the home. The objectionable portrayal of poverty in combination with the reckless disregard for the truth by the reporter resulted in a judgment against the media. The false light portrayal was an invasion of privacy.

Private Information

As previously mentioned, some private information is off-limits to the media. The law provides privacy protection that punishes the media for publicizing information about an individual that is true, but very private—a truth that should never be told. Whether a person has AIDS or has had an abortion, has been raped or has been sexually abused are considered too private for media attention. Financial status and details of sexual relationships and practices are also very private matters. Even so, the law generally protects the broadcast or publication of this truthful, private information when it is found in legally obtained public records.

In many cases, the media often withhold truthful, private information as a matter of ethics even though they would be protected in revealing the private information. The most common example is media protection for rape victims. When rape charges are filed, the victim's identity becomes a matter of public record, but the media generally do not reveal the victim's name. Moreover, when an adult is charged with sexually abusing a son or daughter, the name of the adult is often withheld in the media as a way of protecting the identity of the child involved.

The names of juveniles involved in crimes are regularly withheld from stories even though reporters know exactly who they are. The media and the courts generally subscribe to the idea that young people make big mistakes that they would not likely make as they mature. So, courts close the records on juveniles and the media withhold their names to let them enter adulthood without having their reputations ruined by the mistakes of youth. In recent years, however, juvenile crimes have sometimes become so heinous that the media make exceptions. In schoolyard shootings, the names of accused juvenile murderers have been released, and when the courts decide to try a juvenile as an adult, the media then apply adult rules to the child defendant.

Reporters need to remember that some truths should never be told, and the media may be held financially liable for revealing extremely private information. Public people have a harder time winning invasion-of-privacy suits, and when information is true and legally obtained from public records, the media does not generally have to pay. What is legal is not always right, and reporters and newsroom editors must evaluate the importance of the news relative to the harm it might do to an individual.

Appropriation

Privacy law in the area of **appropriation** guarantees an individual control over his own image, likeness or other personal identifying characteristics when the image is used to make money. Many of the privacy issues in this area relate to advertising. For example, Tiger Woods' picture cannot be used to advertise a product without his permission. So, if he walks into an ice cream shop, and a photographer shoots video from the public street as Woods comes out with the ice cream cone in hand and the name of the store in the background, the video cannot be used in an advertisement for the store without the possibility of a successful lawsuit by Woods. If the footage is used in the evening newscast to talk about the fact that Tiger Woods was in town, the story and the video are protected because of the news value—and the purpose is not to advertise the ice cream store, even though business may increase just because people think if Tiger Woods likes it, it must be good. The same rule applies to private individuals: A person's likeness cannot be used for advertising without permission.

Even criminal suspects have the right to decide whether their images can be used for someone else's profit. Television programs like "Cops" are produced for profit even though they claim to be news programs as well. As mentioned previously, the court system has decided that even legitimate news photographers do not have the right to accompany police officers into private homes. The producers of "infotainment" shows negotiate with the suspects and get permission to use the footage that contains their likeness. The individuals, like everyone else, have the right to control their own image or likeness when it comes to making money.

Defenses Against Invasion-of-Privacy Lawsuits

Consent

The safest way to avoid an invasion-of-privacy suit is to get an individual's permission for her appearance in the media. Sometimes the permission will be written, but at other times the permission is implied. As previously mentioned, when television producers use someone's arrest inside his own home as part of their programming, they will need the owner's permission to enter the home and will want the insurance of a signed agreement before they broadcast the video. In other situations, the permission may be implied. If a television photographer walks onto private property after a flood with an identifying logo on the camera and asks the homeowner to talk about the tragedy, the person who talks to the reporter in front of the camera will have a hard time winning a lawsuit later by claiming that the grief was a private matter and should not be presented as part of a newscast.

Any time private information is used for commercial purposes, a written consent should be acquired. In some cases, an individual cannot give consent. Minors and mentally impaired individuals are not considered capable of recognizing the ramifications of releasing private information; permission from a parent or guardian is required. In summary, reporters should remember to respect an individual's right to control private information, especially if the information is used for profit. When in doubt, get consent.

Newsworthiness

When private information is revealed in important news stories, the law often protects the media against lawsuits for invasion of privacy. For example, if someone is stabbed inside a gay nightclub, the wounded individual cannot win a lawsuit claiming that being in a gay nightclub is private information. On the other hand, the media might lose an invasion-of-privacy suit if they revealed information about the injured individual that was not a legitimate part of the story. The specific romantic relationships an individual had in the past would not be relevant to his being stabbed in a gay nightclub.

When Oliver Sipple saved President Ford's life during an assassination attempt, reporters revealed that Sipple was homosexual. Sipple sued for invasion of privacy but lost the case, in part because his homosexuality was common knowledge where he lived. The story about Sipple became newsworthy when he came in contact with the president of the United States in such a dramatic way.

Newsworthiness is not always a defense in privacy cases. Some private details about an individual may be relevant but not integral to reporting the news, and some private information may be newsworthy but not usable because of the individual's reasonable expectation of privacy. If reporters gather information without intrusion, they may find some protection against privacy suits when they broadcast relevant private information in important news stories.

COPYRIGHT

Copyright law gives people the right to control and protect things they create. For a better understanding of this idea, imagine yourself in the role of the creator. You have produced a movie or written a song. Why should anyone be able to show parts of the movie or use the song without your permission or without paying you a fee? Likewise, if you write, shoot and edit a video about your hometown, you don't want others to use your video without permission or without compensating you for the effort you put into the creation. Similarly, you cannot use someone's song or parts of her movie or other copyrighted work in your video without permission.

Licensing Fees and Permission

Broadcast news departments often use music in the background of a news story, but they pay for the privilege. Typically, a station pays an annual fee to major music-licensing companies for the privilege of using music in the station's programming. The fee allows editors to use music in news stories, permits entertainers to sing songs as part of a program and covers other incidental use of music in the station's operation. When sportscasters edit game highlights to music, the station pays for the rights to use the song. If the station does not pay the annual fee to cover the general use of music, it must make a report to the licensing company each time a song is used in the station's programming and pay an appropriate fee. These general licensing fees do not allow an advertiser to use a song as a background to a commercial that will be played repeatedly. When music is synchronized to video for repeated use, a special license is required.

Just as video editors and television programmers must compensate the copyright holders for the use of music and video that others have created, others may not use the creations of the television station without appropriate permission. Although the law protects individuals in taping television broadcasts and using them for their own private viewing, the law does not allow someone to tape television programs and use the video for other purposes. To use the example of a photographer's video about her hometown, she could not legally tape town pictures from a series of newscasts, edit the pictures over an original script and then sell the videos. The television station owns the rights to the video created by its employees for its programs and can choose whether to permit or deny the use of the video by others. Similarly, the photographer who shoots video as an employee for the station does not have the right to use the video for individual profit without the station's permission.

Fair Use

In some instances, individuals and organizations may use copyrighted material without paying special fees. This opportunity is permitted under fair use provisions of copyright law. **Fair use** legal provisions allow the use of such a small amount of copyrighted material that it does not harm the market for the material. For example, if Aretha Franklin sings "Respect" at a local concert, her licensing agents would surely not allow the television station to tape the song and play it as a feature on a morning program. Likewise, the station would be violating copyright laws if it turned part of the song into a regular introduction to a specific program without getting permission and paying a special fee. On the other hand, if the news department prepares a story on the concert, a few bars of the song may be used as fair use without special permission because the story is considered newsworthy. Such use may also be permitted because seeing the small clip of the performance might cause a viewer to attend an Aretha Franklin performance or buy her records; thus it has served a promotional purpose for Franklin. The amount of the song that may be used under fair use would be very small, and it could not be shown repeatedly after the news value of Franklin's appearance had passed.

In other cases, using even a very small amount of a copyrighted work may *not* be considered fair. One line of a song might not be considered fair use because one line would be so clearly representative of the entire work. Using one line from a poem might not be fair use, whereas using an entire paragraph from a novel could be fair.

The legal decision about what is fair use is determined by several factors, including the effect on the market for the material, the nature of the work and the purpose of the use. If copyright holders perceive that the use of their material would prevent others from buying the original work, a court might agree. On the other hand, if an English teacher shows a five-minute clip from a movie to a class to illustrate a point about plot devices, the clip is a very small part of the complete work, is not intended to benefit the teacher and will not prevent the movie studio from making a profit on the film. In this case, the excerpt is surely a fair use of the copyrighted material.

News reporters, photographers and editors must remain alert to copyright regulations. As a general guideline, remember that anytime you are using work that someone else has created, copyright fees may be required. The chances of getting caught and going to court for copyright violation may be slight, and arrangements for compliance with copyright laws can be complex. Even though copyright compliance may take time and trouble, the Golden Rule applies: Comply with copyright requirements for others because you would want them to do the same for an original work of your creation. If the moral imperative does not persuade you, remember that there is always the chance of being sued.

Libel and privacy issues get lots of attention in media law because the cases are usually long and involved and the liability can be millions of dollars when the cases are lost. Copyright fees are routinely paid by broadcast stations, so lawsuits in this area are somewhat unusual. A number of other legal issues are more likely to arise in the daily routine of news personnel, however; these include denied access to information or conflict with an order from the court.

MEDIA ACCESS ISSUES

Courtrooms

Remember that part of the job of reporters is to make courtroom information available to the public. This basic right of access to courtrooms simply means the right to observe and report on the proceedings. Access to courtrooms does not include access to the individual court participants. Interviews with judges, attorneys, defendants and witnesses depend on each person's willingness to talk, although judges will almost never comment on a particular case. Remember that reporters are not allowed to talk to jurors during a trial and may find themselves before the judge on charges of obstructing justice if they try to do so. After a trial is over, reporters are permitted to talk to jurors if the jurors agree.

Although the broadcast reporter is allowed into an open court along with the public, each state has specific rules about whether news cameras are also allowed in the courtroom. When camera access is given, the permission is restricted to legitimate news cameras, and usually it is also granted for tape recorders for radio reporters and still cameras for newspapers. In some states, electronic media coverage is permitted in criminal court but not civil court, or in appeals courts but not other courts. Television reporters must know state requirements and follow the guidelines for getting permission to cover specific court action.

Public Meetings

As previously discussed, all government business is conducted in public, with a few exceptions, and the public, including reporters, has a right to observe. When the city council, state legislature or school board meets, the public, including media representatives, is allowed to be present. If the governing body attempts to meet in private, officials must indicate why they are going into a closed session. News cameras are typically allowed into public meetings, but even if cameras are barred, reporters are allowed into any open meeting along with the general public. If a reporter is asked to leave a public meeting, she should object and get legal support from her employer.

Prisons

Reporters have at least the same access to prisons and prisoners that the general public has, but they may also be granted additional access depending on individual prison policy. Some states or localities may grant permission for reporters to interview specific prisoners, and some may deny any and all such media requests. The first step in reporting on prisons or specific prisoners is to ask to see the individual prison policy for prison visits.

Schools

School officials are generally cooperative in allowing media coverage of educational issues and will assist reporters and news photographers. Children do not have the legal authority to agree to interviews without permission of a parent or guardian. Even though most parents enjoy seeing their children on the evening news talking about a special school project, a parent might object to a reporter asking a child for a reaction to watching a shooting on the school grounds. Asking the child about such an incident and showing it to a mass audience could increase the trauma of the event and result in a lawsuit to compensate for the emotional injury. Again, reporters must be alert to specific access policies as well as to the possibility of libel or privacy action. The reporter should find out the school board policy for allowing news coverage on school property, and even if the policy does not state the requirement, the reporter should get signed permission to broadcast pictures of or interviews with juveniles.

Crime Scenes

Law enforcement officials are generally accustomed to media coverage of crime scenes and will usually cooperate with reporters by giving information and allowing camera coverage. Occasionally, law enforcement officials try to restrict media access to crime scenes more than they restrict the general public. For example, police may be keeping the public behind a line of yellow tape but tell the news photographer she cannot shoot video from that location. In fact, the media has the same right of access as the general public in this situation. The news photographer in this situation should try to explain calmly why she is entitled to shoot video. If the police resist or the situation escalates, the photographer may need to contact station management for legal assistance. When police successfully prevent the photographer from capturing video from an area open to the public, station management and their attorneys should work with law enforcement to clarify the right of access for the future.

COURT ORDERS

Confidentiality and Contempt

Reporters often find themselves in conflict with the desires of law enforcement officials and courts. In the most extreme cases, these conflicts can result in contempt charges or even jail for the reporter. The basic requirements of gathering important information can bring about these conflicts. For example, consider the process of reporting on the use of illegal drugs in a community. Most people would agree that the community would benefit by knowing about the scope of illegal drug activity. If citizens know that drugs are rampant in the schools, they may be able to take steps to combat the drug use. If a reporter reveals that a common household product is being used by teenagers to get high and that it has caused brain damage to one student, then parents, teachers and those who sell the product can be more prepared to intervene when they see warning signs.

But how does the reporter gather the information? Those who are breaking the law seldom agree to be interviewed or featured in a television story. Those who talk to the reporter will insist that the reporter protect their identities. When a reporter agrees to keep the identity of a source secret, the reporter is promising **confidentiality.** If the law-breakers agree to participate in a television story, they may insist that their faces not be shown, their voices disguised and any other identifying pictures left out. The reporter and photographer may even be allowed to attend a party where the drug use is underway, if they promise not to show people in any identifiable way. The story runs. It may upset members of the community, and they may launch an investigation. If a grand jury convenes, the reporter, who clearly knows the precise individuals who were breaking the law, may be called to testify. The reporter has promised not to reveal the sources, but a judge may insist that the reporter talk to the grand jury. The demand to appear in court will come in a subpoena—a written court order. If the reporter refuses, the judge can cite the reporter with contempt. The court can fine the reporter or jail him for refusing to cooperate. Reporters have gone to jail on contempt charges and have been kept there until they were willing to reveal their sources. What does the reporter do now?

Refusing to comply with a court order is a serious act. To some, it would seem that the reporter would be doing a service to the community by revealing the identities of those involved in crime and should testify. If the reporter talks, the criminals can be arrested and the community would be safer. The reporter's perspective is very different. Reporters see their role as gathering information and presenting it to the public. The information is important for the public to know so the community can try to prevent the overall problem in an informed fashion. If news personnel gather information about crime and then reveal it for the purpose of apprehending criminals who served as sources, they are, in essence, becoming law enforcement officers. Many would argue that if the reporter can get the information, the police should be able to get it too. In fact, the reporter's public information as revealed to the general audience should be helpful to the police without any further assistance from the reporter. Reporters take their responsibilities for informing the public quite seriously and are often willing to face serious consequences to protect their sources, even going to jail.

The larger reason for protecting the confidentiality of sources is long-term. If this particular reporter promises people to protect their identities and then reveals them, the public may never trust the reporter again. We talked about the fact that sources will sometimes come to reporters with important information because they have seen the reporter's work and know that they can trust the reporter. The reverse is also true. If people know a particular reporter has broken a promise, they won't come to that reporter with news. Moreover, if people know that reporters generally break promises and give information to police, they will not trust reporters in general. This damages the function of the media. News sources dry up. Reporters can no longer serve the purpose of giving the public important information.

The First Amendment provides for a free press, and if reporters cannot freely gather and report information, the Constitution is compromised. To assist reporters in their special duties and responsibilities, some states have *shield laws.*

Shield Laws

Many people believe that reporters should have special protection from court orders that require revealing their sources. In addition, most states have specific laws that provide some such protection to reporters who refuse to reveal where they got information. These statutes are called **shield laws.** But reporters must know that the protection of shield laws is limited or *qualified.* Sometimes these laws do not apply when the reporter has witnessed a crime or do not protect a reporter from testifying in libel cases. If there is no way to get the information except from the reporter, the shield law may not hold up. Even though shield laws have limitations, they may help when a reporter is called before a judge and required to give up the identity of a confidential source.

In summary, reporters must be familiar with state shield laws, if they exist, and should give some thought to how far they will go in protecting the identity of a source. A reporter must never make casual promises to protect someone's identity in exchange for important information, because keeping the promise can mean serious legal trouble and even jail. The source should be made aware that protecting her identity could mean jail for the reporter and should be encouraged to provide the information publicly before confidentiality is promised. The reporter and source should discuss what would happen if the reporter does go to jail. Perhaps the source will agree to go on the record if the reporter faces charges of contempt and a jail sentence.

Subpoenas

Reporters can find themselves in conflict with the law for reasons unrelated to providing testimony in court and revealing confidential sources. Sometimes the court will attempt to gain information by issuing a subpoena to a reporter to provide news footage, the actual news story or even notes he took in the process of gathering information. The first step when faced with a subpoena is to contact an attorney. The subpoena does not require immediate action, and the reporter can challenge it. However, if a subpoena is upheld, the reporter must comply. Reporters should never attempt to destroy subpoenaed material. This is obstruction of justice and may lead to serious legal consequences.

Newsroom Searches

Newsroom searches are a frightening threat to freedom of the press. Congress emphasized the danger of law enforcement intrusion into newsrooms in the Privacy Protection Act after police searched student newspaper offices at a college in California decades ago. The Privacy Protection Act requires law enforcement agencies to meet several criteria before searching a newsroom. One restriction on law enforcement requires that information from the search could prevent death or serious injury. If the criteria are not met, the information will be sought through subpoenas, allowing reporters and station management a more methodical approach to evaluating the legal merits of police intentions and providing an opportunity to challenge the legality of the request.

CONCLUSION

Working in a news department requires some knowledge of the law, because the law provides the framework within which reporters and photographers carry out their responsibilities. Individuals can suffer serious consequences because of the words and pictures with which reporters choose to describe them. Reporters should always take care to ensure that what they say is true, accurate and fair. If the information is false and defamatory, a libel action may result, and a level of fault will be determined based on how the information was gathered.

In the case of public officials, news personnel have wide protection for making mistakes unless they presented the information with actual malice, meaning the reporter knew the information was false or showed reckless disregard for the truth. In contrast, reporters may find little legal protection for presenting false and damaging information about private individuals, who do not have as much opportunity to correct false information or to publicize their viewpoints as public figures do. Simple negligence in checking the facts may mean losing a libel suit to a private individual.

News personnel should also pay attention to an individual's right to privacy, especially on private property. Unlike libel cases that relate to false information, privacy law can punish the media for revealing the truth when it is private and embarrassing, when it is used for profit or when it presents people in a false light.

Copyright law also shapes the boundaries in presenting news. Using the creations of others, whether words, pictures or music, requires getting permission and most likely paying a copyright fee. News personnel deal with other legal issues as they gather news and present it to the public, such as gaining access to public information and public meetings and perhaps coming into conflict with the interests of law enforcement agencies and courts.

News personnel need to know some basic media law to be effective gatherers of information and must know and be able to defend their First Amendment rights. Members of the news media should know the law and be vigilant in protecting the rights that make their jobs possible.

KEY CONCEPTS

fairness	public official	intrusion
slander	actual malice	false light
libel	burden of proof	appropriation
defamation	public figure	copyright
liable	negligence	fair use
publish	fair comment	confidentiality
identify	absolute privilege	shield law
fault	qualified privilege	

Activities

1. Find your state libel laws.
2. Find your state laws regarding secret recordings.
3. Determine whether your state has a shield law and, if it does, find it and read it. Do you think it offers adequate protection for journalists?
4. Go to the courthouse and look at files related to criminal cases. Look for copies of search warrants, subpoenas and arrest records.
5. Watch a network news magazine program and determine whether the footage was shot on public or private property. If you see video from private property, what arrangements do you think the reporter made with the owners?
6. Compare and contrast the usage and meanings of the terms *defamation, libel* and *slander.*
7. What are the major differences between libel law and invasion of privacy law?
8. What are the most common areas of legal action that television news personnel face? Give an example of each.
9. Why does our society agree that it is acceptable to embarrass individuals by trying cases in open court and making private information public in news stories? Do you agree with the philosophy? Would you agree if you were on trial or a story about charges filed against you was published?

10. Evaluate the advantages and disadvantages of libel law that virtually protects the media in publishing irresponsible and even false information about public officials and public figures. Should the law be more restrictive on media?

11. Who has the burden of proof in a libel case and what does that mean?

12. What are the defenses against an allegation of libel? Describe scenarios where each defense would apply.

13. Compare and contrast absolute privilege and qualified privilege (how are they alike and how are they different?).

14. What are the four areas of privacy law?

Regarding Ethics . . .

15. You are doing a package about the high costs to society of health treatment related to obesity. You remember some file footage of a weight control meeting and a picture of an enormous woman walking on a treadmill and would like to use the shot. What potential legal issues are there?

16. A high profile person in your community is on trial for rape and you have video of a group of people exiting the courtroom that includes the victim. The victim has not been named in any media, but you would like to use the shot as general footage. You know who the victim is, and a few people may know her and see her in the shot, but many will not. What potential *legal* issues are there? Are the legal issues different from ethical issues in this case?

17. You are doing a story on the increased number of AIDS cases among heterosexual women and you have pictures of women leaving the Health Department after an education meeting on AIDS. The picture was taken from public property. What potential legal issues are involved? Are the legal issues different from ethical issues in this case?

18. You are covering a town council meeting. During the meeting a citizen tells the council that he's tired of the lousy way the city is run. He says the mayor is a poor manager, is running the town into the ground and is wasting taxpayer money. As luck would have it, the battery died during his comments and you don't have them on tape, so you ask the angry citizen to give you an interview outside after the meeting is over. The comments are even more colorful this time: *"The mayor is a scoundrel and a thief and is ruining our town—and on top of that, everyone knows he's a philanderer,"* says the citizen. What legal considerations would you have in running the comment? Are the legal issues different from the ethical issues in this case? If you run it and the mayor sues, what defenses could you offer?

19. Suppose you say the same thing the angry citizen in Activity 18 said, in a news segment clearly labeled *"Opinion."* How would you defend your use of the words *scoundrel, thief* and *philanderer?*

20. You are editing a new opening for a daily segment in the five o'clock news and you use five seconds of a new hit song while video shows various scenes in your city. Is this a fair use of the music? Why or why not?

21. You are covering an explosion at a local hotel. Police have put up yellow tape and you are shooting from behind the tape. There are lots of people around you who have gathered to see what is happening. A police officer comes and tells you to take the camera and leave. She does not tell anyone else to leave. What do you do?

22. You are writing the story of a famous basketball player who is accused of assaulting a young woman. The charges have been made public, but the name of the woman has not. You discover her name, and three people tell you on camera that she has a history of depression. Do you run the story? Do you use her name? How do the legal and ethical issues compare and contrast?

WORKS CITED

New York Times v. Sullivan, 376 U. S. 254 (1964).

Cantrell v. Forest City Publishing Co., 419 U. S. 245 (1974).

After 22 years, I still truly look forward to work every day. It's as good as it gets . . . a daily education, and, even on awful days, it still beats whatever is in second place. It's not something you do. . . . It's something you are.

LES ROSE, CBS NEWS BUREAU, LOS ANGELES

CAREERS IN BROADCASTING: GETTING IN AND MOVING UP

WE'LL ASSUME that most would-be broadcasters have a four-year degree and can display the basic skills discussed in this book: understanding the meaning of news, gathering information within legal parameters, writing a story in broadcast style and presenting it clearly in front of a camera. Let's also assume that you have basic video shooting and editing skills. If you have those qualifications, finding a job in broadcasting simply requires preparation and confidence—the same confidence you bring to the job itself. This chapter explains the job-search process, provides tips that will help you get the job, and describes what happens after you accept the job.

Every employer is looking for candidates who are skilled and dependable. But be patient—the broadcast industry can be a difficult one to break into. It may take up to six months to find your first job. If you and your family are not prepared for the possible wait, you'll grow discouraged and consider settling for something else.

DEVELOPING YOUR RESUME AND COVER LETTER

Successfully applying for a job requires understanding the application process, including how to prepare and use cover letters, resumes, resume tapes and letters of reference and how and when to make phone calls to prospective employers.

The Cover Letter

Often, the cover letter provides the employer's first impression of the potential employee. It must be flawless, with no grammatical errors. Use a straightforward business style. In the first paragraph, introduce yourself and explain your goal, including the specific position you seek. In the second paragraph, list the skills and experience you possess that make you a viable candidate. Ask for consideration for the position, letting the prospective employer know that you are enthusiastic about the job. Let the person to whom you have written know that you are qualified by offering additional information and materials. Go easy on the adjectives in describing yourself; it's better to let your work speak for itself. The cover letter's purpose is to introduce yourself as a viable candidate who deserves further consideration. See Exhibits 12.1 and 12.2 for sample cover letters.

The Resume

You may wish to consult one of the many books available about writing an effective resume. These resources offer valuable advice for getting it right.

Word processing programs offer many templates to help you assemble an effective, professional resume. Begin with personal information about yourself—name, address, phone number and e-mail address. Include a section that contains job experience and internships—where the experience was gained, what the job or internship entailed and perhaps a line that explains what you learned that is applicable for the job for which you are applying. Be specific about dates—it is best to list month and date ranges next to job experience so it is obvious that there are no "holes," periods during which you were not working. If there were such times, offer an explanation. Most employers want to hire persons whom other employers want, so being out of work for an extended period can be a negative. However, it is one that can be overcome with a brief explanation. If your work experience was brief and sporadic because you were working during the summer while in college, that would be considered a positive by most employers as it shows something of your work ethic. (Don't be like the reporter who quit her job to look full-time for another and had a difficult time because news directors could not understand why she quit. It was a year before she was able to find another position, a lesser job in a much smaller market, all because the hole in her resume looked suspicious to prospective employers.)

Education should be next on the resume so the employer knows where you attended college or graduate school and how that experience is pertinent. Include any special courses you have taken or relevant seminars you have attended

> Speaking of all those resumes . . . know that the news director's secretary is the real power base. Get to know her or him BY NAME . . . go for short chats . . . anything to get her to remember you . . . and with a little luck, your resume will keep on ending up on THE TOP of the stack.
>
> *Les Rose*
> **CBS NEWS BUREAU, LOS ANGELES**

NATALIE KLEIN

3170 Solar Blvd. #15
Billings, MT 59102

(406) 555-0702
natklein@earthlink.net

October 24, 2005

Judy Baker
Administration Assistant
WCYB
101 Lee St.
Bristol, VA 24201

Dear Ms. Baker:

I am writing in response to your MediaLine advertisement for a 5 pm anchor. I am currently working as the morning anchor at the NBC affiliate in Billings, Montana.

During my time here I've worked as a beat reporter, a producer, an editor, a writer and an anchor. I've covered stories from the Freemen hearings to the bison controversy in Yellowstone National Park. Overall, the experience I gained as a reporter gave me a solid foundation to become a strong and responsible news anchor. I tell a story compassionately and honestly. I connect with my viewers, and I believe my honesty and commitment shine through in my work.

I am a highly motivated and dedicated journalist and I'm eager for a new challenge. Enclosed please find my tape and resume. Please feel free to contact me either at work (406-555-2652) or at home (406-555-0702). Thank you for considering my application. I look forward to hearing from you.

Sincerely,

Natalie Klein

Natalie Klein

EXHIBIT 12.2 Sample cover letter.

JENNIFER VARGO

313 Clay St. Apt. B
Clarksburg, WV 26301

October 24, 2005

Judy Baker
News Director
WCYB-TV
101 Lee Street
Bristol, VA 24201

Dear Ms. Baker:

I would like to apply for the opening for a reporter at your station and am
enclosing my tape and resume. I would like to take advantage of the opportunity
to offer my experience and continue to develop in the communications field.

Currently, I am a reporter, producer and anchor at WDTV, the CBS affiliate
in Clarksburg, West Virginia. I generate creative, well-rounded stories on my own,
make quick decisions, and, most important, juggle a number of tasks. I am
responsible for complete and thorough coverage of the main county bureau. In
addition, I'm very proud of a special "Five on Your Side" community interest segment that I create every Wednesday. Previously, I worked at FOX 19 WXIX in
Cincinnati, where I gained invaluable experience as a news writer and field producer. I am ready to advance my career with my motivation, ambition and skills.

Thank you for your time and consideration. I hope we can speak with each
other soon. You may reach me at 480-555-1234 or by e-mail at jvargo43@aol.com.

Sincerely,

Jennifer Vargo

Jennifer Vargo

Enclosure

that demonstrate you have the skills necessary to succeed in the position for which you are applying.

Applicants sometimes include the line "references available on request" at the bottom of the resume, to save space and to encourage an employer to contact them. But that line can be seen as arrogant—forcing the employer to contact you personally before you'll provide further information that is important in considering you for a position. You want to make it as easy as possible for a station to hire you, so provide all the information that they may require in your package. The reference list should give the names of at least three people who can vouch for your qualifications, along with their phone numbers and e-mail and business addresses. Ask persons who know you, both personally and professionally, if they would be willing to provide a prospective employer with information about you. Make certain those persons on your reference list know a potential employer might call, so they will be prepared. For most employers, references provide confirmation that they have made the correct choice. On the other hand, employers have changed their minds about a candidate when references commented negatively about a job candidate or were not aware that the candidate had listed them as a reference.

It is most important that all information in your cover letter and resume be accurate; providing false information is a mistake from which it is almost impossible to recover. A one-page resume plus a list of references on a separate sheet should be sufficient for the information the station needs. See Exhibits 12.3 and 12.4 for sample resumes.

The Resume Tape

The tape containing examples of your work is the basis of most hiring decisions. Consider the cover letter and resume as the setup, convincing the station that you should be considered. If the job calls for two years' experience and your resume indicates that you have no experience, your tape will probably not be viewed. But if your cover letter and resume confirm that you are a qualified candidate, the resume tape is your opportunity to demonstrate your skills. The box and the tape should be labeled with your name, address, phone number and e-mail address. This information should also appear on the slate at the beginning and end of the tape.

Include a countdown to confirm that the tape is properly cued to the video you want seen. Bars and tones are not necessary for a resume tape. A small-market news director tells the story of receiving a resume tape that was cued to the end of the actual stories on the tape. Not knowing this, she played the tape—and saw raw footage in which the job candidate talked and joked with employees of the station where he had been interning about newsroom management and others on the news staff. To some viewers it might have been funny, but this news director took it as a lack of respect for peers and managers, which she believed the applicant would likely transfer to his next workplace. Know what is on your tape. Also, check before mailing to be certain that it is the right tape—not a copy of your favorite TV program, or worse, a home video.

EXHIBIT 12.3 Sample resume.

Julian Lewis Webb

P.O. Box 1423, Narrows, VA 24124 ■ 540-555-7264 ■ jlewis@rev.net

EDUCATION:	Emory & Henry College, Emory, VA (May 2000)
	Mass Communications Major/Art Minor

MEDIA EXPERIENCE:

Station Manager (1999–present)
WEHC 90.7 FM Radio, Emory & Henry College
- Organize staff of 44 for daily broadcasts of music, sports and news
- Fill the broadcast schedule Monday through Saturday, 8 a.m. until midnight

Radio Disc Jockey (1998–present)
WEHC 90.7 FM Radio, Emory & Henry College
- Hosted two radio shows each semester since fall 1998

Staff Writer (1997–present)
The Whitetopper, Emory & Henry College
- Reporter for men's and women's tennis teams

Staff Writer (Summer 1999)
Virginian Leader Newspaper, Pearisburg, VA
- Covered town council meetings, wrote hard news, sports and feature stories and was assigned to do photography work

Assistant Manager (1998–1999)
WEHC 90.7 FM Radio, Emory & Henry College
- Assisted in the daily operations of the college radio station

Radio Disc Jockey (Summer 1997)
WRIQ Radio, Radford, VA
- Involved with the Kool Country morning show, production and remote broadcasts

Publicity Director (1996–1997)
WEHC 90.7 FM Radio, Emory & Henry College
- Designed promotional material for special broadcasts as well as general promotion of the college radio station

OTHER EXPERIENCE:

Front Desk Clerk/Public Relations Department (Summers 1993–1997)
Mountain Lake Hotel, Pembroke, VA

SKILLS: Microsoft Word, WordPerfect, Windows, PageMaker, Microsoft Works, Eudora, Netscape, basic HTML and MINITAB.

HONORS: Alf Goodykoontz Journalism Scholarship and Outstanding Senior, the top awards of the Mass Communications Department, Emory & Henry College. Dean's list fall 1998, Emory & Henry College.

Sample resume. **EXHIBIT 12.4**

NATALIE KLEIN

3170 Solar Blvd. #15
Billings, MT 59102

(406) 555-0702
natklein@earthlink.net

EXPERIENCE

Current Employer October, 2002	**KULR-TV (NBC News affiliate)**	Billings, MT

Morning Anchor
- Produce, write and anchor hour-long "Today in Montana" show
- Produce, write and anchor "Today" show cut-ins

Noon Anchor
- Produced, wrote and anchored the "Mid-day Report"

Reporter
- Beat reporter, covered police, fire and courts

March, 2002	**KEZI-TV (ABC News Affiliate)**	Eugene, OR

Reporter, Medill News Service
- Developed political and business stories
- Reported, wrote and edited stories
- Sent packages over ABC NewsOne satellite feed

September, 2001	**Chicago Sun-Times**	Chicago, IL

Researcher
- Produced daily content analysis reports comparing the Chicago Sun-Times with the Chicago Tribune

May, 2001	**The Munster Times (100,000 circulation paper)**	Hammond, IN

General Assignment Reporter
- Covered legal and feature stories on daily deadline
- Researched stories using Computer Assisted Reporting

EDUCATION

June, 2002	**Northwestern University**	Evanston, IL

MSJ from Medill School of Journalism
- Concentration in broadcast reporting, writing and producing for television and radio

June, 2000	**Indiana University**	Bloomington, IN

- BA in Political Science

The Jerusalem Institute	Jerusalem, Israel

- Hebrew University, Year Abroad Program

AWARDS

Society of Professional Journalists, Pacific Northwest Region
- 1999 Investigative Reporting award for "Bison, Brucellosis and Bullets"

University of Michigan
- 1999 Livingston Award Finalist for "Bison"

REFERENCES

Dan DuBray, Former KULR-8 News Director, (202) 555-4601
Jim Ylisela, Asst. Professor, Northwestern University, (312) 555-0777
Elizabeth Pearson, KULR-8 Weekend Anchor, (406) 555-0084

EXHIBIT 12.5 Sample contents of a resume tape. The resume tape should indicate the reporter's versatility and ability to do hard news, feature reporting and live shots.

00:00–00:30	Graphics page (includes applicant's name, address, phone number, e-mail)
0:30–01:15	Montage (4 or 5 short clips showing reporter stand-ups)
1:15–2:35	Hard news package
2:35–3:40	Live shot or live interview
3:40–5:10	Feature package
5:10–5:40	Graphics page again with contact information

Ten to fifteen minutes of material should be sufficient, although if you do not gain interest quickly, only the first minute may ever be seen. And, whether you are applying for a job as a reporter, anchor, producer or videographer, your best work should be up front. If many persons have applied for the job, there is a good chance that very little of your work will be seen. So, be certain that what is seen is your best. The packages should not be long. One minute and fifteen seconds to one minute and thirty seconds is a typical package length.

Job hopefuls often agonize over what to put on the resume tape. Most news directors say they want a video montage—a collection of stand-ups demonstrating various kinds of stories and numerous situations. Your montage, a quick sample of a half-dozen of your best stories, should be at the beginning, whether you are applying for a reporter, anchor, producer or videographer position. Follow the montage with three or four complete packages (but not necessarily the same stories from the montage). News directors want to see various kinds of stories—straightforward or hard news, live or breaking news, human interest or features (which are usually softer) and stories that demonstrate writing and producing ability. Some say they want to see how you "use" television—a term that includes the following qualities:

- How comfortable you appear to be on camera
- How your stand-ups are woven into the story
- How smoothly you make transitions from narrative to interviews (and back to narrative)
- How you organize facts
- How you incorporate natural sound into the story
- How the story continuously moves forward toward the conclusion
- How believable and likeable you are

Aspiring reporters should keep all work produced for school projects, internships and entry-level jobs on a master tape. The resume tape can be prepared from the master tape. Choosing material from an existing tape is much easier than trying to find stories from a variety of sources later.

How Your Resume Tape Is Reviewed

News directors want to determine how you look, how you sound and whether you are someone viewers can believe and trust. One news director says she puts the tape in the machine and pushes play, looks over the experience section of the resume, purposely looks away from the screen, and listens to the beginning of the resume tape. She wants to hear the candidate first to determine how that person strikes her. Often, a voice lacking polish and confidence—indicating a lack of experience—is enough to urge her to move to the next tape. However, if the candidate sounds polished and professional, she'll turn and begin watching, often returning to the beginning of the tape to watch a second time. That person has made it into the "keep" stack.

It is very easy for most news directors to cut a group of 300 resume tapes in half. And again. And again. The task becomes increasingly difficult as the number of tapes in the "reject" stack grows and the number in the "keep" stack dwindles. Eventually, the "keep" stack contains only about two dozen tapes. At this stage, a news director may become very selective and may begin stacking the candidates' tapes in order. The next step is for the news director to contact at least the top half-dozen, to get acquainted and to ask for their most recent work. Your best work will get you noticed, but it's your average work that lands a job for you. Let's face it—reporters don't come up with resume-ready story ideas every day, and they don't produce resume-quality packages every day. But they're on the street reporting every day, turning in average to above-average packages.

> The resume tape? Some say make it like a newscast. I say GREATEST HITS at the top. Chances are you will only get their attention for about 30–45 seconds. If they like it, they'll keep watching. Don't bury the good stuff!
>
> *Les Rose*
> **CBS NEWS BUREAU, LOS ANGELES**

The resume tape is the tape that gets you in the "keep" stack, but it may not be the tape that lands the job for you. Have a second tape ready for those occasions when the call comes for more material.

PREPARATION MAKES THE DIFFERENCE

Many successful broadcasters say that early preparation is the key to landing a job, and you can't begin preparing too early. Internships, part-time work and networking can all help. Before graduation, research the markets and stations in which you wish to be considered, begin applying for jobs a few weeks before graduation, and plan to visit several markets that hire entry-level candidates. There are ways to make your job search shorter and more successful.

Internships

The word *internship* means different things to different people. For some, interns are free labor—students or recent graduates who put in up to 40 hours a week for little or no pay. For others, interns simply look over the shoulder of professionals and receive no hands-on experience. And for still others, interns are students or recent grads who are continuing or enhancing their education with hands-on experience in the newsroom, as editors, videographers, writers or newsroom assistants. News directors are passionate about whether or not their interns should be compensated. Some believe payment is only fair for those who perform work for the station. Others believe internships should be an educational experience, a kind of boot camp during which interns receive no compensation. But almost all agree on the importance of the opportunity. Taking part in an internship can definitely help recent graduates land their first job.

One television station in the Southeast pays interns minimum wage for 18–20 hours per week; the station teaches shooting video and editing, and, following a month-long intense training period, uses interns nights and weekends as videographers and editors. If the intern progresses to the point where he can do some writing, that's better for the station and the intern. Same for reporting. That station probably has a full-time reporter on the staff who began as an intern; he was talented and worked harder than everyone else. (People like that seem to make their own luck.) Check with professors in the broadcast program at your school for information about internships in your area, or contact the Radio/Television News Directors Association (RTNDA) or your state's broadcast association for internship opportunities.

Networking

Many of us land jobs because of who we know or where we've been. Often, those we know can connect us with others who can aid us in our job search. The effort of contacting people you know professionally, academically and personally in order to explore possible job opportunities is known as *networking*. Networking is a crucial skill both for seeking employment and for succeeding as a reporter. After all, if you aren't able to network and connect with people, how will you make story contacts later?

Many books have been written just on the subject of networking, and we recommend that readers refer to one or more of those books to learn more about this important skill. Here are a few guidelines to get you started:

- *Brainstorm about possible helpful contacts.* Make a list of everyone in your life who may be able to offer advice or information, introduce you or recommend you. Include everyone you can think of on your initial list: friends of friends, instructors and professors, advisers, clergy, local business owners, parents and other relatives, and so on.

- *Begin contacting people.* Be professional. Know what you want to ask ahead of time. (Books on networking and job search include sample questions.) Keep scrupulous records and be sure to keep appointments.

- *Set up informational interviews.* These interviews are for information seeking only; you should not use them for soliciting a job.

- *Be sure to get permission* before using someone as a formal or informal reference—that means, get permission even if you are simply saying "Jane Doe recommended that I call you."

- *Make the initial contact with an employer yourself,* even if you plan to have someone recommend you to a station director or other potential employer. Prospective employers dislike hearing a recommendation of someone who hasn't even bothered to contact them.

- *Use a road trip* to network and job search.

The Road Trip

Many entry-level job seekers land a position after a road trip. University courses often teach the strategy of setting up a series of interviews and taking a couple of weeks to visit stations and meet news directors.

The road trip may be an excellent way for students or recent graduates—even working journalists—to make contacts, see what other newsrooms are like and begin the process of finding a job. Most small-market and some medium-market news directors will agree to see a job candidate who is making plans to come to the station, especially if a position is available. Be realistic in planning such a trip; only visit stations where you have a chance of being hired, which will eliminate most of the top 75 markets and many of the top 100. Ask for an appointment to present your resume, show your tape and get acquainted. Road trips can be a win/win situation—news directors can meet applicants in person and learn more about them than from a resume and tape; the applicants are able to compare stations, make valuable contacts and receive feedback that can help to prepare them better for future opportunities.

Look at a map to plan the route—choose cities or communities with stations that are within driving distance of one another. The idea is to visit several stations each day and move on to the next stop. (See Exhibit 12.6 for sample routes.) Call several weeks in advance of the trip to schedule appointments, and call back several days before the visit to confirm. You will make a positive impression with your ini-

You are not going to get a job without meeting the person that hires, so say to the potential boss (if he or she has expressed interest), "If I fly out there, can I see you for just five minutes?" or whatever you can think of that is NOT a lie. Never lie. Don't forget that finding a job is a full-time job . . . and it's expensive. Save all travel receipts for tax time, too.

Les Rose
CBS NEWS BUREAU, LOS ANGELES

EXHIBIT 12.6 Sample road trip routes for individuals completing degree work at specific schools.

For a person preparing to graduate from the master's program at Northwestern University in Chicago:

> First day: Rockford, Ill., Quad Cities market (Illinois/Iowa)
> Second day: Peoria and Springfield, Ill.
> Third day: Terre Haute and Lafayette, Ind.

For a person preparing to graduate from the undergraduate program at Ohio University in Athens, Ohio:

> First day: Parkersburg, Oak Hill and Bluefield, W.V.
> Second day: Harrisonburg and Charlottesville, Va.
> Possible third day trips would include Springfield, Va., and Salisbury, Md., or Johnstown/Altoona, Pa.

For a person preparing to graduate from the undergraduate program at the University of Georgia in Athens, Ga.:

> First day: Columbia, S.C., and Augusta, Ga.
> Second day: Macon and Columbus, Ga.
> Third day: Albany and Savannah, Ga.

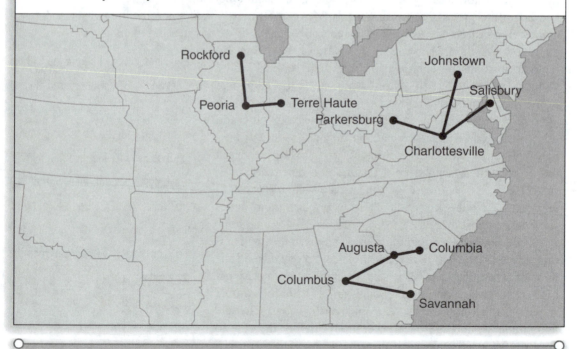

tiative, and you'll demonstrate your ability to plan and execute—two characteristics of a good employee. The personal visit also gives you the opportunity to call occasionally to check in. Your foot is firmly planted in the door.

Posting Your Resume Online

MediaLine offers an Internet-based job service called Talent Shop (www.media-line.com/resumes.htm; see Exhibit 12.7) that enables you to put your resume and a clip of your resume tape on its Web site. TV stations can gain access to the site by paying a fee for a week or month at a time to peruse the resumes and tapes. The employers can instruct the database to locate applicants who fit their specifications—level of experience, market size and qualifications. Stations can also place ads with their requirements on the MediaLine telephone service; job hunters gain access to the ads by paying a fee to hear available jobs.

Although MediaLine may be the best known, it is not the only source. Check with your university, look for ads in the back of trade publications, and ask your friends which sources they use. If you have the opportunity to talk with someone at a TV station, ask which sources he uses.

In addition to sources such as MediaLine, stations regularly place ads in national magazines such as Electronic Media or Broadcasting and Cable, with their state broadcasting associations, in their local newspapers, on their own Web sites and with colleges and other placement organizations. Online newsletters and employment services, such as Don Fitzpatrick's ShopTalk (www.tvspy.com/shoptalk.htm), provide daily news about the industry along with job information (see Exhibit 12.8).

Identifying the Position to Apply For

Don't apply for "anything"—your chances are best if you apply for a specific available job, so work the phone, send out postcards and scour trade publications and Web sites for specific positions that are available for someone with your skills. You should also be specific as to the person you are asking to consider your resume. Do not address your letter to *News Director* or begin your cover letter *Dear Sir or Madam* or *To Whom It May Concern*. Take the time to find out who the current news director is. (A news director told us she once received a resume package addressed to "News Director" with a cover letter that began "Dear Sir or Madam," and on the outside of the envelope the candidate had written "Personal and Confidential.") Remember, you are applying for a reporting job, so show that you can dig out a few facts. Employers know that people who overlook the little things often overlook the big things as well.

Understand that the broadcast news business is built on experience. Faced with two candidates from similar backgrounds and education, most news profes-

EXHIBIT 12.7   MediaLine's Talent Shop Web site (www.medialine.com/resumes.htm).

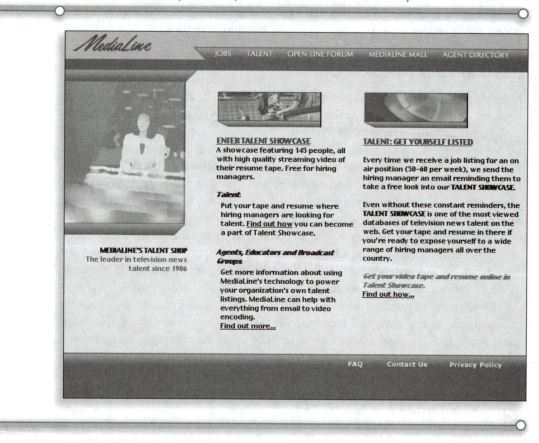

From Medialine.com. Reprinted with permission.

sionals will choose the one with experience. In medium-size markets, stations are generally hiring reporters for their second or third job. They fill the few entry-level jobs they have with interns who have been outstanding.

At most stations, the entry-level jobs may include reporter, videographer, editor or producer. The smaller the market, the more likely you'll be both videographer and reporter. Think of the first stop in a small market as boot camp. You give them a year of hard work and, in turn, they provide opportunity and training that will help you move up to the job you want. Most small-market stations are prepared to teach—much more so than in medium and large markets. So, even though an opportunity might come along in a medium or even large market, the small-market job may be best for you in the long run.

In the medium markets, stations begin to have full-time editors who are responsible for assisting with specific newscasts. These jobs can be opportunities

Don Fitzpatrick's ShopTalk Web site (www.tvspy.com/shoptalk.cfm).   **EXHIBIT 12.8**

From tvspy.com/shoptalk. Reprinted with permission.

to brush up on your editing and become both fast and proficient as you learn to judge the newsworthiness of story ideas, make video become a story and turn groups of stories into a newscast. In smaller shops, editing can be a springboard to a position as videographer, producer or reporter. The more skills you possess, the more valuable you are to yourself and the station you work for.

If you land an entry-level job, spend your downtime in other parts of the building learning about commercial and promotion production, and learn about the control room. There are many creative, talented people in television stations who can pass along tips that might be beneficial to you in the future. Furthermore, you'll begin building relationships that can be beneficial to your career. Broadcasting is a very small, closed business compared to most careers your friends might be considering; the people you meet in your first job will likely reappear in another station or another job somewhere down the road. The program director or sales manager you meet in your first job may someday be the general manager who hires you for your dream job.

If you can get market size out of your head (or at least admit that it has little to do with contentment), you'll be happier wherever you work. One news director tells a story about a reporter who put her first package at the station onto resume tapes and began calling news directors immediately after that package had aired. That's right: her first week on the job, she was actively looking for the next job. She was able to land it in about six months, and that one lasted for about a year. At that time, she landed another job in an even larger city. After that, just past age 25, she made it to a station in the top 20. She then realized she still had 40 years to work—in a situation that was highly competitive. There were hundreds of people who wanted her job, and the pressure to keep it was great. She later told a friend she had made at the first station that she wished she had moved slower and enjoyed some of the places in which she'd worked; they were all in beautiful parts of the country with a high quality of life. While concentrating solely on market size, she had missed out on quality of life, the real factor in determining personal happiness.

Another news director lost a reporter to a much larger market, simply because of the market size. The reporter left a dayside, weekday reporting job for a nightside job in a distant bureau—for less money than she had been making in the smaller market. All because she wanted to be able to say she worked in a top-60 market instead of a top-100. It was not a surprise to other staffers in the news department that within a matter of weeks she was unhappy and looking again. Contentment does not come from market size or from making numerous moves, but rather from enjoying your work.

It sometimes seems to managers that everyone who chooses broadcasting for a career wants to be an anchor. Although it is a good goal to aim for, don't expect to begin at the anchor desk, except in a very small market, unless you have some experience. Some smaller markets have opportunities fairly early on to anchor or to co-anchor a newscast. While you are investigating markets that interest you (and in which you might have the skills and experience to work), ask about such opportunities. Call one of the anchors on the staff and ask how much experience is necessary to fill in for one of the anchors who is vacationing. If anchoring is your ultimate goal, this might be the place to begin; however, beware of anchoring too soon at the expense of reporting experience. Although you may have the chance in a small market to become an anchor, any opportunity to move up will probably include some reporting as part of the job responsibilities. If you have spent most of your time on the anchor desk and have not been able to develop as a reporter, you run the risk of stalling your career—or at least slowing the opportunity to move up.

Entry-level employees can expect to work nights and weekends at first, while putting in long hours. The first couple of years in the business is the time when you will be paying dues. The other side of long hours and night work is the opportunity to produce many packages and to improve your skills. Regardless of size, in most markets, the more you know, the more valuable you are. Even if your goal is to report (and not shoot your own video), the experience of shooting and editing your stories may help you use both video and sound better. And remember that the television universe is a small one; your news director knows other news directors in other markets. If you make a good impression with your skills and work ethic, your first news director can help you find your second.

Producing may be the quickest way to move up while learning about the business. As stations schedule more and more newscasts, they need more producers to put those newscasts together. Producers are responsible for organizing and constructing the newscast, and, in some markets, for helping with story assignments and scheduling. Some stations look for persons who can help produce weekend newscasts and then report, or shoot and report, during the week. This can be a good entry-level opportunity because you have the chance to hone your writing skills, you get to learn how to determine which story possibilities are the most newsworthy, and you may be able to begin in a larger market than you would as a reporter. Because the demand for producers usually exceeds supply, producing jobs often pay better than videography or reporting positions. If you are organized, possess good writing skills and understand what is newsworthy, producing may open the door into the news business for you.

Finally, there is production assistant. Your responsibilities may be outside the newsroom but still connected with newscasts, as a studio camera operator, audio

To get started, do what you must. I worked overnight for fifteen months as a producer. I was fortunate to get the job even though the hours weren't normal and I knew that. If you like the business enough, you'll work the dirty schedules and climb the ladder. In five days, I went from producing the early morning news overnight to presenting live weather and news on television in another market. If you want a 9-to-5 job, look somewhere else.

Jay Webb
WHSV-TV, HARRISONBURG, VA.

board operator or character generator operator. In many markets, these are entry-level jobs: running the studio cameras or controlling the microphones during newscasts and production, putting story tapes in order and loading them in machines for playback during the newscasts, or creating on-camera visuals—supering names, creating full-screen graphics for story backgrounds or putting together sports scoreboards or weather forecast charts. Although, admittedly, it is not the first choice of most of those seeking jobs in news, working on the production crew may provide the opportunity to get your foot in the door. You'll learn about the technical side of television and make contacts who may be able to help you move to the newsroom or to another station. In many stations, the production crew has downtime between newscasts, which may allow you to help out in the newsroom by shooting and editing stories—learning skills to help you gain the next position in your career.

Defining Job Market Boundaries

Your first job will likely be in a small market, somewhere below market 100. There are some excellent television stations in small cities across the country. Each market, regardless of size, has best and worst stations. The person trying to get into the business would be better off seeking a job in the best stations in small markets instead of the worst stations in medium markets. How can you tell which is which? Remember, if you intend to be a reporter, your job will be seeking out facts. Investigate the markets you are interested in. This is the time to call in favors. Do you have friends already working in the business? Seek their advice on stations that are looking to hire or that regularly hire entry-level people. What do they know about specific stations and the reputation of their news departments? Are they considered good places to begin? Do entry-level workers receive instruction and critique to help them grow? Who do your friends know who might be able to help? Get a list of TV markets from TV Rates (www.tvrates.com/main-menu.htm) or another source and sit down with an atlas. Start at market 100 and work down the list, noting markets that are within driving distance of your location or of particular interest.

FINDING INFORMATION AND
GETTING YOUR FOOT IN THE DOOR

First, you have to get in the door. That means several things, including being noticed. A television news director in a medium market received a large envelope in the mail one day that was very light but thick in the center. When he opened the envelope, he found an aspirin bottle with a resume and cover letter crammed inside. He pulled the crumpled letter apart enough to read, "Dear News Director, you have just opened the solution to your headache—hire me!"

For him, it didn't work. The job candidate made the wrong impression—it was too gimmicky. For another news director, perhaps it would . . . or did. But, you have to make the decision—is it worth the risk of offending one person in order to interest another? At least one college instructor urges his students to use methods such as the aspirin bottle to get the attention of potential employers, but some employers are offended by what they consider to be backhanded tactics—they believe broadcast skill should be enough to land a job, and they consider gimmicks unnecessary.

Some reporter hopefuls have sent resumes designed as news releases announcing that person's entry into the job market; some employers might consider the package to be cute, while others would consider it unprofessional. Some candidates run ads in Broadcasting and Cable claiming to be exactly like a well-known ESPN anchor; most employers are not looking for a copy of another person, but an individual. And then there are the 8 × 10 glossies with the photo on one side and physical measurements (including clothing sizes) on the other—the candidate is available for work either as an anchor and reporter or actor and model. Most news professionals want to hire other professionals, not persons who just want to be on television—either as an actor or acting as a journalist. These methods may draw attention, but you must decide if it is the right kind of attention—the kind that results in your landing the job you desire. The goal is to help the prospective employer recognize your abilities, not your creativity and cuteness.

The medium-market news director who didn't care for the aspirin-bottle approach *did* respond well to the following: A candidate stuck a brightly colored piece of tape on the spine of the box containing her resume tape. She wrote her last name in bold print on the tape, and every time the news director looked at his shelf of resume tapes, he couldn't help but see hers. That almost constant reminder of her was probably a factor in his continuing to consider her for jobs. She landed a position elsewhere before he had an opening suitable for her, and she later confirmed that the brightly colored tape had played a role in landing the job she got. She drew the right kind of attention and made it easy to hire her. (News directors have actually had reporter candidates fail to put any kind of identification on their resume tape—not on the case, not on the tape, not in the video. One must wonder how good a reporter that person might have been. Most news directors wouldn't wonder that for long, because they would move on to the next candidate.)

That same news director notes that the reason he didn't consider the candidate who sent the aspirin bottle was the person's lack of experience. He was simply not qualified to perform the job, so his attention-getting device was not effective (or at least it could not overcome the lack of skill and experience). Even a good gimmick won't overcome a lack of experience when the job candidate is competing against others with experience. Although it is possible that if two equally qualified candidates apply, the one with the most creative presentation may land the job, most hiring decisions are made based upon skill and experience. There is no substitute for either.

Letters of Reference

Many employers are skeptical about glowing letters of reference from persons in positions of authority at stations. They wonder why, if this applicant is one of the best employees the manager has ever worked with (as many letters of reference will indicate), that manager is assisting the applicant in leaving. Some news directors who are not fond of letters of reference prefer that they be from colleagues rather than supervisors. Moreover, most employers are skeptical about writing them. Better to list a person as a personal reference than to include a letter of reference. You must decide if the information in the letter of reference is strong enough to overcome the possible skepticism about the practice. We suggest holding the letters of reference until they are requested.

Phone Calls

If the ad says "no phone calls," then respect the request. And don't try the "just checking to see if you got my tape" call—no calls means no calls. Wait as patiently as you can; if you don't hear, assume that your tape didn't make it into the "keep" stack. Take the opportunity to re-evaluate—why did you not get a call? Was it your cover letter? Your resume? Could there be a problem with your references? Did the tape not contain your best work? Were there weak stories on it? Ask friends or a trusted adviser to look over your package again, searching for weaknesses that can be repaired so you can resume your search.

Even if the ad doesn't indicate whether phone calls are acceptable, there is a fine line between calling to see how a job search is coming along and becoming a nuisance to the news director. If you call, ask if you are still under consideration for the job. If not, thank the person for looking over your materials and ask for suggestions—would you be considered for a future opening? Is the person aware of openings elsewhere? If you are still under consideration, ask what you can provide to help make a decision in your favor; certainly, offer to visit the station for a personal interview. If you call, be certain you listen closely; if you detect any hint of annoyance, don't call again. Just offer to be available as needed.

During the hiring process, stations are looking for reasons *not* to hire you. Their advertising efforts in national, regional and local publications will generally bring in a large number of tapes and resumes, so their task is to narrow the list. At a station in a 90s-size market, an advertisement in a national trade publication such as Electronic Media or Broadcasting and Cable or with a job service such as MediaLine may bring in up to 300 tapes. It's not physically possible to watch all of each tape. News directors narrow down the choices by looking for specific skills or experience levels. They will look at how effectively the candidates use the medium—how they use natural sound in their stories, how they weave sound and stand-ups into their work. The organization of facts, use of natural sound and interviews, effectiveness of transitions to the various parts of the story and reporter involvement in the piece will help the news director determine the skill level of the applicant, along with writing style, accuracy and the ability to collect and present the facts. Finally, of course, there is talent— the comfort level of the person appearing on camera and the professionalism that person exhibits in his work. Talent is often hard to explain, but for most of us, easy to recognize.

What if the call comes and you learn that you're being invited for an interview? After a (brief) celebration, begin preparing. You're a step closer.

THE INTERVIEW

An interview allows you and the prospective employer to get to know one another. It is an opportunity for you both to gain further information to decide if the job is a proper fit.

The interview may be your first experience with the art of selling yourself. The prospective employer has expressed interest and has invited you to come to the station for a visit. The pressure may be much greater than the pressure you felt while putting together your resume and tape—this one-on-one meeting may be the determining factor in your getting or losing the job.

Preparing for the Interview

You can expect the news director to ask you plenty of questions about your experience and skills, and you should be thoroughly prepared to answer them. But you should also come to the interview with questions of your own. What would you like to know about the job? About the station? About the staff and their responsibilities? About the station's policies and routines? The kind of stories they cover? The newsroom philosophy? Opportunities for advancement in the station or the company?

What do you want to be certain they know about you? How will you present your case in a professional and convincing manner that will result in your being offered the job? Assemble a list of questions and be prepared, as you would for an interview for a story.

Research the station and be prepared for any questions intended to determine if you have done your homework. If you failed to get directions to the station from the news director, call and get them from the receptionist. Plan your route so you'll be certain to arrive on time.

Visualize the Experience

As part of your preparation, conduct the interview in your mind. Visualize the situation and walk yourself through it. If the prospective employer asks about a rough situation that you made the best of, what will you say? What if she wants to know your strongest and weakest points? What situations have you handled well (or poorly)? What adversity have you faced, and how have you handled it? Don't apologize for your work and certainly don't do it in advance of your work being reviewed. You've made it this far; wait for the opportunity and sell yourself. If you are a hard worker, have some examples of situations that prove your work ethic. If you are determined, prepare to talk about several situations in which your determination resulted in success. We cannot accomplish anything that we cannot first imagine, so practice the interview in your mind and be prepared.

Second Impression Is Important

Your interview with the prospective employer will be her second opportunity to form an impression of you—the first was your resume and tape. When she meets you for the first time, she will form an instant impression of what you are like and even begin to decide whether she likes you. If the initial impression you make is negative, you may not have an opportunity to change it. Therefore, consider your interview, and the impression that you make, as your only opportunity to succeed.

A news director tells the story of a very recent college graduate who visited his office to talk with him about a job. The news director had invited the graduate to come to the station because he knew the person from the university, where he taught a newswriting course. The news director had seen some of the graduate's videography, which was very impressive, but the young man had a reputation for not working very hard. He arrived the Monday after graduation wearing a loose-knit sweater (without a shirt underneath), very old jeans, worn-out tennis shoes and no socks. He stretched out in the chair in front of the news director's desk and explained that he had done a lot of "work" during college, but he'd been so busy that he hadn't had the chance to put any of it on a resume tape. It should be obvious that the young man was not hired by that station (or any of the other television stations in the market). He was one of those hopefuls done in by not knowing what *not* to do.

Another job hopeful spent some time with the videographers on the staff and took the opportunity to give them tips on ways to do their jobs better. They beat a path to the news director's office after the person left the building to implore that he not be hired. Remember, you are seeking a job to learn and improve your skills. This person may have had worthwhile knowledge to contribute, but it was the wrong time and wrong situation in which to offer it. The other staff members felt the manager was considering a know-it-all who would be difficult to get along with. Most of us don't want to work, or associate, with persons who believe they already know everything and are prepared to share all their knowledge with us at any opportunity. If you have the opportunity to meet other staffers at the station where you are interviewing, consider the impression you might be making.

What to Wear

Proper attire for an interview is clothing appropriate for the job you want, or slightly better. It is difficult to overdress, but it is very easy to under-dress by wearing clothing that would not be worn by other persons applying for or performing the job. A suit for men or women, or a dress for women, will be appropriate for most interviews, even if you would not usually dress up that much for the job itself. Businesslike clothing is key.

A promotion director at a station believed in judging people by the "shoe theory." She believed that if the shoes were inappropriate, so was the person. Other managers at her station have admitted that they too look at feet now and, most of the time, they think there just might be something to the shoe theory. Most of us choose shoes that not only are comfortable, but also make a statement about our personality. Try it with recent acquaintances: What do shoes give away about the person? A good pair of shoes may not be absolutely necessary to get the job, but in choosing proper attire one should not overlook the shoes. The point is that you should take care in choosing the clothing and shoes you will wear for your interview. Experts on the subject say we should dress for the job we want, not for the job we have.

Attitude Is a Factor

You are visiting the station to convince management that you will be a good fit and will be a successful, contributing member of the staff. Arrive with a positive attitude, a smiling face and a strong handshake. Consider confidence as a part of your attire; you are a very good product, so be prepared to convince the prospective employer that you are the best choice. None of us wants to miss out on a good thing, whether we are looking for a job or hiring a person for that job.

In television newsrooms, as in the world, there seem to be two kinds of people: those who are happy and those who are unhappy. The happy ones arrived at the station that way; they know that happiness and contentment come from inside and are not "caused" by surroundings. Every station is looking for good people who are willing to work, learn and offer positive suggestions to make life and work better for all the staff. Every station would like to avoid negative people who offer nothing but complaints and suggest changes that would benefit only themselves. This may sound too simple to be credible, but think about the persons you associate with every day: Those who are basically unhappy never seem to change. Whatever the circumstance, they see what's wrong with the situation and how it affects them negatively. Those who really contribute are the ones who maintain a positive attitude and look for ways to solve problems, not complain about them.

A small-market news director whom we'll call "Bob" told us about a newsroom manager he knew early in his career. When asked about fixing any problem, the man would say, "So, what can you do to make it work?" Regardless of the situation presented to the manager, this was his response: How can *you* fix it? This was the case even if the problem did not seem to be the fault or responsibility of the person asking to have it fixed. When Bob anchored the late news, the small production staff seemed to make many mistakes. For example, tapes would play out of order, so Bob would be reading one story and the viewers would be seeing another. He went to the news manager to ask for help in fixing the problem and got the usual question, "So, what could you do to keep this from happening?" Angrily, Bob replied, "Well, I sure can't run the tapes for them!" The manager fired back with, "So, there's nothing you can do to help yourself have a better newscast?"

Bob began to think it over and came up with several ways he *could* help fix the problem. He could type up a list of tapes in the order in which they were to run. He could number the tapes and stack them in order. He even began putting his own label on the tapes and cueing them personally. Thus, Bob went to the studio with the knowledge that he had done absolutely everything he could do to make the newscast run smoothly. The results? Bob felt more confident as an anchor, because he knew he had provided all possible assistance to the production crew. And the number of mistakes was reduced significantly. When the news manager was promoted to general manager, guess who followed him as news manager?

A positive, problem-solving attitude will go a long way on the job and in an interview. Another important aspect of interviewing is knowing what not to do and what not to say.

Don't Oversell Yourself

Don't pretend to have experience you don't have. This applies to both out-and-out lying and *inflating*—making it seem you've done more than you have. A production manager had an intern in his department who called several months after leaving to ask if she could return after hours to work on her resume tape. He asked what she would like to do and she informed him that she'd like to put together a tape of some of the work she'd done while at the station. This person had interned in production and had run studio cameras, assisted with lighting and been involved in commercial and promotion production—not news production. But she wanted to put together a resume tape of news packages she said she had helped with, and she was applying for a news job in a smaller market. The production manager politely declined, not wanting to be a part of the former intern's attempt to deceive another station.

Sell *Yourself*

Many prospective broadcasters see themselves as being "like" someone else. Finding the next Matt Lauer would be a pleasure for most news directors, but they don't initiate a search by looking for someone who is like Matt Lauer. Most want to hire an original, not an imitation. Sell yourself based on your qualifications and skills, and at some point news directors may be looking to hire another person just like you.

AFTER THE INTERVIEW

Following Up

Some news directors object to job candidates calling to talk about a job. If the news director where you have applied accepts calls, be up-front and say you are calling to talk about the job, to see if it's been filled and to see if you can offer something else to help your chances. If the news director is not available at the time you call, leave a message or voice mail detailing your wishes and asking her to return the call. And ask the person to whom you are speaking if the news director is offended by phone calls or if calls are welcomed, if you don't already know.

Saying you are checking to see that your tape was received is too obvious; the postal service is more efficient than that and news directors see through the ploy. Your dishonesty may start you off on the wrong foot, resulting in your not being considered for a job for which you are qualified. Be honest. If you get the potential employer on the phone, this is your opportunity to sell yourself. It's a chance to show how you'll perform in the field when faced with a difficult interview.

If you call the station and get through to the news director, don't ask for an over-the-phone critique. Most news directors don't have the time to offer the service, and after looking at dozens, even hundreds of tapes, shouldn't be expected to recall specific information about one of them. If your tape was memorable enough, you're probably in the "keep" stack—the tapes they continue to consider for jobs. You might ask if the news director has any suggestions—other stations or markets you might want to consider, or anything she remembers that was good or bad about your tape.

Accepting the Job

If an offer is extended to you, before taking the next step you need to have an understanding of contracts, benefits, perks and moving expenses. Don't accept the position until you have considered what the station expects from you and has to offer you. Any special conditions that are discussed with you, but that are not covered in the station's employee handbook, should be put down in writing to ensure that both you and the manager remember the exact details.

Benefits

When you visit the station to discuss a job offer, make a list as you did before the interview. This list should contain your questions about the station's policies and benefits. You'll want to know things like:

- How much vacation does the station offer, and how long do you have to work there to be eligible?
- What is the policy on holidays, and what if you are needed to work on holidays?
- Is personal or sick time available to employees? Can it be scheduled as holiday time if you are not ill during the year? Can it be carried over from year to year if unused?
- Does the station pay overtime, or are you going to be paid a salary regardless of the number of hours or days you work?

These are all questions you should have answers to before accepting a job. You'll also want to ask questions about benefits, such as the station's health insurance program and the length of time you must work to become eligible:

- What percentage of the cost of the insurance plan will you be responsible for? Does the program include a co-pay (a set amount that you pay for any doctor visit)? Are dental and optical coverage a part of the insurance program? If not, can they be added as an option if you pay the cost?
- Is life insurance provided?
- How about a retirement plan, such as a 401k? How long before you are fully vested in the program (meaning how long until the full amount is yours)? What, if any, is the company match for each dollar you put into the retirement plan? Do you have the option of determining where your money is invested, and, if so, how often can you make that designation?
- Are there other benefits, such as health club membership?

Generally, stations will offer at least two weeks' vacation, which you may take after completing the first year on the job; six or seven holidays; and up to a week in personal or sick time. Most stations ask employees to pay a small percentage of the cost of insurance, and the insurance coverage will often be a plan that features a flat rate employees pay when they visit the doctor and a drug card that provides discounts on prescriptions. Usually some kind of retirement program, such as a 401k, is offered, with a small contribution by the station for each contribution the employee makes.

Perks

Some stations offer incentives to make their newsrooms more attractive places to work. These perks may include free or reduced-cost health club membership, hair care, makeup, shopping and vacations. Some employers offer tuition assistance if you choose to take continuing-education courses while you are employed. As you move up in a station, a clothing allowance might be a part of your contract, to defray the cost of clothing that you purchase for use in your job. Some stations offer a balloon payment at the end of contracts—a set amount that is added to your salary as a reward for completing the contract or re-signing with the station.

Contracts

You may be asked to sign a contract or a noncompete agreement, which will prevent you from working for another station in the same market for a period of time, usually three to six months. Contracts vary from station to station and market to market—from very restrictive, legally binding you to work for an agreed-upon length of time, to much less restrictive, allowing specific opportunities to leave before the end of the term. Usually, the larger the market the more complicated the contract. It would be wise to have an attorney check the contract before you sign it so you know exactly what your rights, and the station's rights, are. For entry-level employees, a one- or two-year agreement should be the maximum term you consider. Stations are more likely to offer longer terms, with guaranteed pay increases, after you've proven yourself. Be certain that all the terms you discuss and agree to are spelled out in writing so there is no confusion (or disappointment) later. (See Exhibit 12.9 for a sample employment contract.)

> I sent out 186 resumes before I got a two-week temporary slot that turned into a year and a half. . . . I just kept showing up until some lady from personnel asked, "Who is this Les Rose guy?" I knew that if you just showed up, newsrooms would generally put you to work! My foot was in the door so I just made sure the rest of the body made it in, too.
>
> *Les Rose*
> **CBS NEWS BUREAU, LOS ANGELES**

Moving Expenses

If the station is far from your current location, what will it cost for you to move to the new job? Will the station pay all or part of the cost for your move? Some stations offer loans to new employees to help cover the cost of moving. After a set period of time, the loan is forgiven—a double incentive because it makes it more attractive to remain with the station and it provides the employee with money to make the move. Before accepting the job, get an estimate of the cost for moving to the new location, so you know what you will need and what you might be able to negotiate for.

Before you accept the job, consider all the aforementioned topics and discuss them with your family and those close to you to determine if working for the station will be in your best interest.

EXHIBIT 12.9   Sample employment agreement.

EMPLOYMENT AGREEMENT FOR 2005

_____ (EMPLOYEE) AND WXXX DO AGREE ON THIS DATE TO A WORKING RELATIONSHIP WITH THE FOLLOWING STIPULATIONS:

(1) AGREEMENT TO RUN FROM JANUARY 1, 2005, THROUGH DECEMBER 31, 2005.

(2) EMPLOYEE AGREES TO NOTIFY WXXX 90 DAYS IN ADVANCE OF THE DECEMBER 31, 2005 TERMINATION DATE OF THE AGREEMENT OF INTENTION NOT TO RENEW FOR THE FOLLOWING YEAR.

(3) AFTER THE EMPLOYEE LEAVES HIS/HER EMPLOYMENT WITH WXXX, FOR WHATEVER REASON AND WHENEVER IT OCCURS, EMPLOYEE AGREES NOT TO WORK FOR, OR APPEAR ON BEHALF OF, ANY OTHER TELEVISION OR BROADCAST MEDIA IN THE _____ (ADI/DMA) MARKET FOR A PERIOD OF 180 DAYS.

(4) NOTHING IN THIS AGREEMENT SHALL BE CONSTRUED AS PROHIBITING IMMEDIATE TERMINATION BY WXXX FOR ANY CONDUCT DETRIMENTAL TO THE BEST INTEREST OF WXXX-TV.

(5) NOTHING IN THIS AGREEMENT SHALL REPLACE OR SUPERCEDE ANY PROVISIONS, POLICIES OR PROCEDURES CONTAINED IN THE WXXX EMPLOYEE HANDBOOK.

(6) EMPLOYEE AGREES TO THE FOLLOWING SALARY SCALE:

_____ ANNUAL PAY DURING THE CONTRACT PERIOD

_____   _____

EMPLOYEE   DATE

_____

WXXX-TV GENERAL MGR.

SUCCESS AND ADVANCEMENT

Success on the job can lead to personal happiness and career advancement, with your current employer or elsewhere. Many elements will determine success. Below we discuss some ways you can enhance—and make the most of—your career success.

Keep a Successful Attitude

When you begin a job with a successful attitude, you are more likely to be successful, even if the job you land isn't exactly what you want to do. CBS Reporter Wayne Freedman says it is his job to be a part of the solution for his employer, not part of the problem. Persons with that kind of attitude are regularly called on in critical situations and become staffers who can be counted on. Their successful attitude helps them become successful in their careers.

Make the Most of the Opportunity

If you move to a new city to begin work, you can enrich your experience (both personal and professional) by becoming involved in the community. You may find a place of worship where you are comfortable, accept invitations to visit civic clubs or volunteer for a nonprofit organization. By getting to know people and making friends in your new home, your stay there will be more pleasant. And there is the added bonus of the professional contacts you'll make. News stories often come from relationships, so the more people you know in town, the more meaningful will be the contributions you'll make to news meetings.

You will be more content for a longer period of time if your friends and acquaintances are not limited to the television station. People move more often in broadcasting than in many other businesses, so you are more likely to lose a close friend who works with you in the newsroom than a friend in town who works in another profession. The more friends you have and the more varied their backgrounds, the longer you'll be content in your new home. Having friends who are from the community in which you are living and working also helps you become familiar with the area.

What else does this new location have to offer? Does a nearby university have a good reputation as a business school? Perhaps you should consider taking classes to continue your education in areas not covered during your college years. Are there other ways to supplement your life education with classes or seminars? What is the community known for? Learn about your new home and see if there is something you can gain from living there besides the work experience.

Set Goals for Improvement

Find out what the news director expects from you and what he believes you are capable of. Try to set up regular sessions during which your work is critiqued.

Ask others in the newsroom to critique your work. One way to track your improvement is to look at your work again several weeks after completing it; if you are not as proud of it now as you were then, you're getting there! By the way, to critique does not mean to tell only what is good, but to point out what needs work and how to go about making improvements.

Set Goals for Advancement

What do you want from your career? Do you want to report? Are you interested in trying the anchor desk as well? How about producing; do you enjoy putting newscasts together, writing stories and determining story order? The answers to these questions will help you set goals for career advancement. The station you work for may provide the opportunity for you to fill in when one of the anchors is off—a way to try something different, and an opportunity that you might not have had at another station. Consider how content you are with your job. Will you be happy in that job for the next year? For two years? For five years? Happiness at work affects happiness outside work, so use these questions occasionally to help set goals for your future.

Know what the station expects and give more. Arrive at work early, offer to help in areas that are not necessarily your responsibility, and make it clear that you are there to do your best for yourself and for the station. If an assignment you were given falls through, offer to do something else. Look for ways to help out. You'll increase your value to yourself and to your employer, and the day will go quicker. It is likely you'll be more content on the job and in your personal life.

> No matter how successful you may be, you may get the rug pulled out from under you. Stay in touch with reality. You're only a reporter and only an anchor. You're only as good as your last newscast and the world does not revolve around you. I'm still in the business because it's in my blood.
>
> *Kathy Soltero*
> **KCNC-TV, DENVER**

Consider When to Move

Some stations in small markets do an excellent job of teaching. They regularly hire recent college graduates and are prepared to assist in furthering their education by providing opportunities, hands-on experience and critique. After working in such a newsroom for a year to 18 months, you may have made the most of the opportunity and gained about as much as is possible, if your long-term goal is to move to a different area to live or to work in a larger newsroom or city. It is possible to become comfortable and successful in a small market with a high standard of living. Many small stations are well-equipped (partly because they require fewer cameras, editors and so on) and are efficiently staffed. The next opportunity could come in that same station, moving up the reporter ladder to dayside Monday through Friday, getting the opportunity to anchor the morning newscasts, or perhaps combining anchoring and reporting on a weekend shift.

Why Move?

One of the reasons to move is to be closer to home. The person who graduates from college in Ohio isn't likely to have the skills to begin working immediately in Cleveland, Cincinnati or Columbus. A move to a smaller market may be necessary to begin climbing the ladder, after which he moves back closer to home. For example, the first job opportunity may be in Billings, Montana. After a year or two, the opportunity provided by the station in Billings may have helped the recent college graduate hone his skills to the point of being ready for a larger market. The next job may be in a medium market such as Tri-Cities, Tennessee, or Lexington, Kentucky. Another year or two of experience will help him prepare, now with up to three years of experience, for the move back home to the larger markets in Ohio.

Another reason to move is for a job opportunity that doesn't exist in the smaller market. Stations in medium markets that are looking for weekend anchors or reporters will often look to smaller markets for candidates. Experience in the smaller market as an anchor or reporter helps prepare the candidate for the opportunity in a larger market, and, generally speaking, the larger the market, the larger the salary.

Finally, there may come a time when you have gathered all the knowledge and experience available to you in your current job. Working in a larger environment with more experienced people and better resources and enjoying the lifestyle of a larger city may make a move attractive.

CONCLUSION

The broadcast news business is very much experience-based. You can plan your success by preparing for the job market and the opportunity you seek. To land a job, you must demonstrate your skills, first with a resume and tape and later in a personal interview. Your first impression—made by your cover letter, resume, tape and references—can make or break your chances of landing the job. Your tape should demonstrate your abilities, and the total package you present to a potential employer should make interviewing and then hiring you as simple for the news director as possible.

After landing the first job and gaining some on-the-job experience, plan your career moves based upon places where you would like to live and work and situations in which you can strengthen your skills, rather than solely on market size. If your goal is moving, or moving up, you can ensure career advancement by learning as much about the business as possible and expanding your skill base outside your main area of expertise.

Activities

1. Compile a resume. Follow the format used in the resume in Exhibit 12.3. Research the Web site shown in Exhibit 12.7 and find out how to post a resume online.

2. Write a cover letter for an entry-level reporting job at a small-market TV station. Use Exhibit 12.1 as a model or ask classmates, friends or relatives for a letter they have successfully used.

GLOSSARY

A-Block the first section of news in a newscast.

absolute privilege protection against legal action for comments made in official government proceedings.

accent a distinguishable way of pronouncing certain words.

accurate precise, exact and free from mistakes.

acronym a word formed from the first letter of a group of words; for example, NASA. Some very common acronyms may be used in broadcast copy, but both the person reading the story and the audience must be familiar with the acronym.

action sequence short bits of video from a series of actions, cut together to condense action and enliven the video.

action/reaction sequence two shots edited together that show an action and a reaction to it.

active voice describes sentences constructed so that the subject performs the action: *The judge sentenced the defendant to life in prison.*

actual malice a standard indicating that the reporter or others involved actually knew information was false or gave little or no attention to whether it was true or false. In legal terms, the people who created the story showed reckless disregard for the truth or presented the information knowing it was false.

affidavit a sworn statement revealing information about the suspected crime that supports the need for a search warrant. An affidavit should be available to reporters after the execution of the search warrant.

ambient sound the natural sounds in an environment.

ambush interview the technique of surprising people who won't agree to talk to reporters in order to catch them off guard and force them to answer questions.

analog describes a method by which a pattern is added to magnetic videotape to represent sound or picture patterns.

anchors individuals who present news and introduce reports live from a news set.

angle the focus from which a reporter introduces and tells a story.

appropriation using, without permission and to make money, an individual's image, likeness or other personal identifying characteristics. Privacy law guarantees an individual control over his or her own image or likeness.

arraignment open court hearing where the accused appears before a judge to hear a formal reading of criminal charges and has the opportunity to either claim innocence or admit guilt.

arrest the capture by law enforcement officers of someone against whom they have evidence of violating a law. Officers detain the suspect and indicate the reason in a sworn statement that becomes part of the arrest report. If the crime is serious, the suspect is taken to jail.

assemble mode a setting on an edit controller that allows the establishment of a control track on videotape.

assignment editors staffers who handle the daily scheduling of the newsroom, deciding which reporters and photographers work together, where they go and when. They maintain contact with crews in the field by radio, cell phones and pagers, and work with the producers as schedules change in the reporter's day. The assignment desk also maintains a file of upcoming stories.

asymmetrical balance   in photography, a framing technique that provides a sense of equilibrium even though the items in the shot are out of proportion or alignment.

attribution   identifying the source of information in a story or giving the audience as much information as possible about who provided it.

audio channels   tracks on the edit tape for the sound, typically one for reporter narration and one for natural sound.

audio level   the relative strength of the reporter's voice, interviewee voices and any background sound or natural sound, music or any other sound that may be included in a recording.

audio mix   the balancing of various sounds, allowing the listener to hear the most important sounds clearly and yet remain aware of the other sounds in appropriate levels.

audio tracks   channels on the edit tape for the sound, typically one for reporter narration and one for natural sound.

B-Block   the section of news following the first commercial break in a newscast.

back light   a light on the opposite side of the subject from the key light. The back light is usually much softer than the key light and is often used to cast a little light onto the shoulders and back of the head so that there is a slight glow around the shoulders and hair.

back timing   selecting the end point of the edit, or the spot where the editor wants the picture to stop, and counting back to determine the in point or the point where the picture begins.

background   the scenery or objects behind the primary focus of the shot. In using background, we want the viewer to concentrate on the front of the shot, but include background that provides depth and makes the shot more interesting and pleasing to the eye.

background sound   audio that is heard in the background behind the reporter's narration.

backlighting   a situation in which too much light behind the subject makes the picture unacceptably dark. In such cases the photographer may adjust the iris setting on the camera so that the subject in front of the light appears clearly. *Backlighting* may also refer to the use of a back light.

bond   an amount of money a defendant gives to the court as a guarantee that he will show up for trial. If the defendant does not show up at the scheduled trial, the state keeps the money. If the suspect cannot afford to pay the bond, she must stay in jail.

b-roll   the pictures that cover the primary sound track in a video story.

burden of proof   the responsibility for establishing the case. For example, the government holds the burden of proof in a criminal case. In a libel case, the plaintiff holds the burden of proof.

chronological order   the order in which events actually happened.

civil court   a court that hears civil cases. Parties go to civil court to settle grievances. Civil courts issue judgments rather than imposing fines or jail terms, as criminal courts do.

close-up   a shot that includes only one individual or object from close range.

confidentiality   protecting the identity of the source of information.

conflict of interest   the existence of two mutually exclusive desires, for example, a journalist's conflict between the need to report the story and the desire to protect a friend.

contempt   a charge made by a court against a person for refusing to cooperate.

continuing present   a verb tense that describes actions that continue to happen or happen repeatedly; for example, *People die in car crashes.*

continuity   maintaining a logical order of shots during editing.

control track   the area on a video tape that is available for pictures and sound.

convened   called together, as in *The state and federal juries were convened.*

convergence   when varied media work together; for example, have a joint presentation of material on the Web.

copyright law   law that gives people the right to control and protect things they create.

cross ownership   when a company owns more than one form of media; for example, a newspaper and a television station.

crossing the line   moving from one side to the other of an imaginary line that crosses the primary focus of the shot. Although the photographer can cross this line in shooting, the editor cannot juxtapose shots from different sides of the line.

cutaway   a picture of something surrounding the primary action of a news story that makes sense when juxtaposed with the primary action.

cutaway question   field video that appears to show the reporter asking a question of a news source; usually recorded after the interview was completed; see *interview cutaway.*

cuts only editing   editing in which all the edits are instant changes from one picture to another or from one sound to another.

cutting on the action   editing technique of matching movements at the edit point between a wide and a tighter shot.

deep background   describes information that the source and the reporter have agreed is not to be used by the reporter in any way. Such an agreement is suspect because it asks the reporter to know something, but pretend not to know it.

defamation   damage to an individual's reputation as a result of publicized false information.

defendant   the person against whom a civil lawsuit is filed or the person facing a criminal charge brought by the government.

diamond effect   a reporting technique in which the reporter introduces the viewer to a single person or a small group of people and conveys how the story relates to them. Then she broadens the scope to tell a more general story. In the end, the story returns to the person(s) we met in the beginning.

diaphragm   the muscle partition between the chest and abdomen used for breath support and good voice quality.

disposition   the final ruling of a court case.

dissolve   an editing technique in which one picture begins to disappear as the next picture forms.

distorted present tense   present tense used to describe events that have clearly happened in the past; for example, *Three die in plane crash.*

docket   a schedule of cases to be presented in a courtroom.

dolly   a set of wheels designed to hold a tripod so the camera can roll toward or away from the subject.

echo lead-in the use in an introduction of the same words that the source uses in the sound bite.

edit a change from one continuous piece of audio or video to another, also called a cut.

editing effect a dramatic technique for changing from one picture to another.

emphasis stress applied to a word by contracting the diaphragm and using additional force to push air over the vocal cords.

enunciation pronouncing each sound in each word clearly and distinctly.

establishing shot a picture that establishes the location and situation of the story; usually refers to the wide shot that appears early in the story.

fade an effect in which a picture gradually disappears into black.

fair comment opinion that relates to matters of public interest and is therefore legally protected.

fairness presenting both sides—or many sides—of a story.

fair use the use of such a small amount of copyrighted material that it does not harm the market for the original material and is therefore not disallowed.

false light the inaccurate portrayal of an individual, especially if the information is offensive to reasonable people and if the media is reckless in deciding whether the information is true or false. Privacy laws protect against portrayal in a false light.

fault a level of error on the part of those who broadcast libelous or defamatory information.

file footage archived footage from former news stories.

fill light a light used to soften the shadows cast by the key light.

flat lighting the use of a light that is lined up with the camera lens, hits the subject directly and removes naturally existing shadows.

foreground something that appears in the front of the screen that is not the primary focus of the shot. An object in the foreground can give a shot a feeling of depth and prevent it from looking flat.

gain control a camera setting that can be engaged to allow shooting in very low light.

gatekeeper an individual who controls the entry of material into or out of media outlets.

grand jury a group of citizens called together to examine claims against a defendant for the purpose of determining whether charges should be brought.

grand jury indictment a formal notice issued by a grand jury that has determined that sufficient evidence exists for bringing charges.

hard lead a straightforward first sentence of a news story that begins giving information immediately.

head room the amount of space between the top of the head of a photograph subject and the top of the frame.

holding without bond a court's requiring that a defendant stay in jail until trial. This happens when the court suspects that a defendant might flee or harm someone and does not allow the individual to use money as a guarantee that she will appear in court as required.

human interest stories that focus on emotional elements and generally do not affect people's lives in practical ways.

indictment a formal, written charge against an individual.

inflection change in pitch or tone within a sentence or a word.

instruments professional term for lights.

interview cutaway when an interview is shortened or edited and leaves a jump cut, the editor will use an interview cutaway to cover the jump. Typical interview cutaways include a reporter reaction shot, a cutaway question, or shots related to the interview topic.

intrusion invasion into private areas where one would reasonably expect to be left alone.

iris the part of a camera that works like the iris of the eye to control the amount of light that passes through. As the iris closes down to a smaller opening, less light is allowed in.

jump cut two shots edited back to back that are very similar but just different enough that the subject seems to "jump."

key light the primary light on a subject.

lavalier a microphone that clips onto clothing.

lead room on-screen empty space in front of the subject of an interview or an action shot that gives the subject space to talk into or move into.

lead the first sentence of a story.

lead-in the narrator's introduction to a sound bite.

leading lines strong lines within a shot composition that pull the viewer's eye.

liable legally responsible.

libel a defamatory statement that is printed or broadcast.

linear editing analog signals are copied from one magnetic videotape to another—or digital signals from one magnetic videotape are reproduced on another.

localizing finding the local angle to a regional or national story.

logging a tape the process of preparing a *shot sheet* to indicate where specific shots and sound bites are located on a shoot tape.

look space in the case of an interview, the lead room or space in front of the subject.

lowest common denominator refers to programming that can be understood by the largest pos-

sible number of people. The intellectual level of the programming must be low enough that everyone can understand it.

magistrate an officer of the court who acts as a judge with the specific responsibility of consenting to an individual's incarceration before a formal placing of charges.

mainstream media long-standing, reputable news sources that strive to present information objectively. Network news and local TV news departments; major news magazines, such as Newsweek, Time and U.S. News and World Report; and daily newspapers are examples of mainstream media outlets that we expect to present objective information.

match frame editing see *cutting on the action.*

motivated pan movement of the camera to the right or left or up or down for the purpose of following an action.

nat sound the natural sounds at a news scene.

nat sound break natural sound used in full volume in between segments of reporter narration.

nat sound open a nat sound break that begins a story, used to set the stage and give the audience time to comprehend the location and subject of the story.

nat sound package an edited package that tells a story using only the sounds of an event and sound bites from participants or observers and does not use reporter narration.

negligence failing to do what a reasonable person would do. Negligence is the legal standard for determining whether the media is guilty of libel against a private person.

neutralize in photography, to take away the perspective the viewer has adopted in seeing an object or scene.

news block the news content between commercial breaks. The A-block is the first part of the newscast and includes the most important news of the day. The B-block follows the first commercial break. The newscast also includes blocks of sports and weather.

news director the staffer who governs the structure of the newsroom. Responsibilities include hiring and firing, managing the budget, dealing with personnel problems and working with the station manager, engineers and other department heads concerning equipment, purchases, promotion and station image.

news package a report produced and edited prior to broadcast time, typically consisting of a reporter's recorded voice telling the story, pictures with accompanying natural sound to cover the narration, *sound bites* and usually a *stand-up*.

news photographer an individual who shoots video that clarifies and enhances the news story.

nonlinear editing a process in which audio and video signals are transformed into digital form and edited on computers.

nonmainstream describes information presented with a specific point of view or sensationalism that differs from objective points of view.

not for attribution describes information that the source and reporter have agreed can be included in a story, but only without an identification of the source. The information will appear as general knowledge or as an understanding by the reporter.

objective examining facts or events without distortion by feelings, opinion or prejudgment.

off the record refers to information that a reporter and a source have agreed will be used only when some level of protection is provided for the source's identity. However, there is no standard agreement on the specific meaning of the expression "off the record."

omnidirectional from all directions; for example, a microphone may capture sounds on a tape omnidirectionally.

on background describes information regarding the use of which the reporter and source have agreed to some kind of restriction. The use of the term varies.

one-man band one person who both shoots video and reports.

one-shot a shot in which only one individual is included.

pace in speech, the speed at which the words are delivered.

pan a movement of the camera to the right or left or top to bottom. The pan can be implemented by swiveling or tilting the camera on a tripod.

passive voice describes sentences constructed so that the subject is the recipient of the action: *The defendant was sentenced to life in prison.*

past tense describes an event that has ended; for example, *George W. Bush was elected president.*

perfect balance a framing technique in which aspects of a shot are absolutely equal; for example, three bricks on one side of the screen are balanced by three identical bricks on the other side. This type of symmetry is static and rarely desirable in news video.

perfect symmetry see *perfect balance.*

photographer an individual who shoots video that clarifies and enhances the news story.

photojournalist one who gathers information in addition to shooting video. Photojournalists often work alone in covering an event, with responsibility for finding facts, conducting interviews, shooting video and writing the story.

pitch in speaking, refers to the highness or lowness of the sound on a musical scale.

plaintiff   the person filing a civil lawsuit.

plea   a formal claim of guilt or innocence.

preliminary hearing   a court hearing in which a judge determines whether the state has sufficient evidence that a crime has been committed by the accused to hold the person for trial.

present perfect tense   describes an action that has recently ended; for example, *Congress has adjourned* or *The jury has returned a verdict.*

present progressive tense   describes an action that is happening in the present but may or may not continue; for example, *City Council is reviewing the proposal.*

present tense   describes actions that are happening now. The present tense can be *continuing present,* such as *People die in car crashes,* or *present progressive,* such as *City Council is demanding the mayor's resignation.* Universal truths and historical events can also be described in present tense.

pre-trial hearing   a court hearing in which a judge listens to requests from attorneys and decides matters regarding how the trial will be conducted.

private facts   information about an individual that is true, but very private—truths that should never be told. Private facts are protected by privacy law.

private person   an individual who does not seek the limelight and does not have ready access to the media. Private people are likely to be more seriously hurt than public officials by defamatory reporting. Therefore, the law makes it easier for private persons to prove libel.

producers   individuals who supervise and coordinate the overall content and flow of a newscast. They help determine which stories should be covered and how much time each story will get, and they are usually involved in a morning meeting where these decisions are made. They work on the rundown schedule, put stories in a logical order and keep up with news from wire services and the progress of reporters in the field. Producers write headlines and promotions for stories, plan graphics and keep track of time during the newscast. Producers review scripts before the reporter records the narration, checking for accuracy and good writing.

prosecutor   a government attorney who argues cases against defendants.

public figures   celebrities and others who are well known to the public. Public figures have the same burden of proof in libel cases as do public officials.

public officials   those who are paid with public money and hold responsibility for doing the work of the government.

published   printed or broadcast.

qualified privilege   limited protection against legal action when reporters present a truthful and accurate portrayal of a public meeting that includes false and defamatory comments.

question lead   a lead that asks the audience a question at the beginning of the story. Some experts advise against ever using a question lead. These leads should certainly be used sparingly.

reaction shot   a cutaway showing the reporter listening during an interview or someone reacting to an action, such as a fan's cheering after a homerun.

recognizance   term used when a person charged with a crime is trusted to show up for court without posting a bond.

reflector   a specially designed flat object with a reflective covering that allows the photographer to bounce light onto a subject from the sun or another light source.

reporters individuals who gather information, write and present it for viewers of the newscast. They may record narration for editing into a packaged news story, or they may write the story to be read by the news anchor. Reporters sometimes do live broadcasts from the field and introduce stories live from the newsroom or from the set. Television news reporters must interact well with people to gather information, recognize important news and be able to use public records and the Internet efficiently.

reversed point of view showing two shots back-to-back that were taken from opposite viewpoints, such as looking in through a window, then out through the window to the street.

rule of thirds a guideline for composing shots. To use the rule of thirds, picture the screen divided into nine equal blocks by two vertical lines and two horizontal lines. The primary focus of the shot should be at one of the intersections of the top horizontal line with the vertical lines.

rundown a list of stories in logical order for inclusion in the newscast.

scan room in photography, the amount of space between the top of the subject's head and the top of the frame.

search warrant a legal document permitting law enforcement officers access to private property for the purpose of a search for evidence in a crime. The warrant must specify what police are looking for and why they believe the items reveal information about a crime.

sentencing hearing a court hearing that follows a trial at which a suspect is found guilty, in which the judge announces the sentence: how much time the defendant will spend in jail or on probation, or other punishments.

sequence a series of shots that fit together in a logical way. A sequence may be a group of related shots or be designed around an action.

sequence jump cut an edit that places two events back-to-back that could not have happened so close in time.

shield law specific law that provides some protection to reporters who refuse to reveal their source(s) of information.

shoot tape the video captured on a tape by a photographer in the field.

shot sheet a list of specific shots and their locations on the shoot tape.

shotgun mic a microphone that picks up sounds only within a narrow pickup range and has a dead zone along the sides and bottom of the mic. Some shotgun mics can pick up sounds clearly from a great distance.

sidebar story a story that gives related information about a more significant news story.

sing-song in speaking, a pitch pattern that begins low, goes high in the middle of the sentence and ends low. When repeated, the pattern quickly becomes noticeable, predictable and irritating.

slander a defamatory statement that is spoken rather than written.

soft lead a lead that gives listeners only a general idea of what the story is about. The writer introduces the subject and attempts to attract interest without giving basic facts in the opening sentence.

sound bite a short segment of an interview or from someone's comments that a reporter chooses to edit into a story.

staging video the act of setting up shots in a way that did not actually happen.

Standard American English use of proper grammar and pronunciation, with no distinguishable accent.

standard outcue the specific wording that the reporter uses to identify himself and the station at the end of a package.

stand-up a shot in which the reporter speaks directly into the camera. Stand-ups serve a variety of purposes, such as making a transition from one part of a story to another, and often are used at the end of a story so reporters can identify themselves and the station.

still frame a frame of video that is frozen and used for a dramatic effect or for a graphic background.

stress emphasis applied to a word by contracting the diaphragm and using additional force to push air over the vocal cords.

subpoena a written order to appear in court.

supering superimposing letters or other images over a picture.

suspense lead a lead that establishes anticipation and expectation for a resolution. With a suspense lead, the story becomes a mystery waiting to be solved.

tabloids media outlets that are willing to pay people to talk or appear in their stories.

talk space the lead room or on-screen space in front of the subject of an interview.

throwaway lead a lead in which the writer entices the viewer to listen further without giving any real information about the story itself.

tone the mood or attitude of the speaker or story.

transition a way to move from one part of a story to another.

transition shots shots that prepare the viewer for a change in time or place.

two-shot a picture composition that includes both the reporter and the interviewee.

umbrella lead a lead that introduces more than one subject, such as different parts of the same story.

unequal balance a framing technique that provides a sense of equilibrium even though the items in the shot are out of proportion or alignment.

verb tense a distinction of form in a verb that indicates when an action took, is taking or will take place.

video editors individuals whose role is to combine reporter narration, portions of interviews, video and natural sound as required for packaged news reports or pictures and sound that accompany the news anchor's presentation of a story.

video track the channel on a videotape or in a computer program designated for pictures.

videographer an individual who shoots video that clarifies or enhances the news story.

visual entrance in photography, a strong line that pulls the viewer's attention into the shot at the point where the line meets the edge of the frame. A strong visual entrance will overcome the viewer's natural tendency to look at the shot in the Z pattern.

vocal cords membranes at the top of the trachea, or windpipe, that vibrate to produce sound.

voice-over the sound of the news anchor reading a script as the audience watches video. Also referred to as V-O.

VO-SOT a technique in which the anchor reads a story under video, a sound bite follows, then the anchor resumes reading as video continues.

V-U meter the meter on editing equipment that indicates volume units of audio.

wallpaper a term for video that covers narration but does not enhance the story.

watchdog the media role of maintaining surveillance over government, business and society; like a watchdog, the media alert citizens to what is happening.

whistle-blower the name for a source inside an organization who reveals newsworthy information to the outside world.

white balance an adjustment that a camera makes to the color of the available light. The photographer must focus the camera on something white to allow the camera to make the adjustment.

wipe a basic editing effect, wherein one picture seemingly pushes the other picture off the screen.

wireless mic a microphone containing a transmitter that sends the audio over the air for a short distance directly to the camera.

wraparound the reporter's live introduction and outcue to her own story during a newscast.

zoom movement of the camera perspective toward or away from the subject by means of the automatic zoom control on the camera lens but without any physical movement of the camera.

Z-principle the fact that viewers naturally begin looking at a picture in the upper left portion, look to the right, down to the bottom left and then to the right, in a Z pattern. Knowing this principle helps photographers compose effective shots.

Abbreviations, in writing, 168
ABC, 35
A-block, 28
Absolute privilege, 337
Accents, 306–307
Access, by media to venues, 347–348
Accountability, of reporters, 22
Accuracy, 9–10
    editing and, 286–287
    guaranteeing during interview, 65–66
    sound bites and, 10
ACLU, 6
Acronyms, in writing, 168
Action:
    editing on, 275–277
    including in interview, 198–199
    matching the, 233
    sequences, 237–241 (see also Sequences)
    stand-ups, 316–317
Action/reaction:
    shots, 234–236
    editing and, 274–275
Active voice, 157–158
Actual malice, 332
Advancement:
    career, 383–385
    goals for, 384
Affect vs. effect, 170
Affidavit, 95
Age, in stories, 163
Alleged, use of term, 171
AltaVista, 105
Ambush interview, 69–70
Amount vs. number, 170
Analog signals, editing and, 262
Anchors, 30–31

delivery and, see Delivery
Angle, determining an, 115–116
Angled shots, 189–190
Animations, 289
Appearance, 311–312
    job interviews and, 377
Appellate courts, 89, 90
Appropriation, 343
Arraignment, 93
Artistic principles, shooting and, 242–251
Ask Jeeves, 105
Assemble mode, 263
Assertiveness, 252–253
Assignment editors, 28, 30, 32
Asymmetrical balance, 248–250
Attitude:
    job interviews and, 377–378
    success and, 383
Attribution, not for, 59
Attributions, in writing, 159–160
Audience:
    attracting through entertainment, 36–37
    lowest common denominator factor, 37–38
Audio:
    laying the track, 277–282
    levels, 277
    mics and, 214–216
    mix, 277
    nat sound package, 251–252
    overlapping with video, 282–284
    track, 258
Axis, shooting, 228–229

Background:
    deep, 59

for interviews, 55–56
    on, 59
    shooting and, 251
Back light, 208–209
Backlighting, 211–212
Back timing, 264
Balance:
    symmetry and, 248–250
    white, 203
B-block, 28
Benefits, 380–381
Bias, by mainstream media, 4–5
Bill of Rights, 2
Birth records, 84
Blair, Jayson, 19, 63
Blocks, of news, 28
Bond, 94
Breathing, 293–296
    writing for, 164–166
Broadcast:
    formats for news packages, 123–125, 126, 127
    shooting video, see Video
    writing for, see Writing
Broadcasting, careers in, 355–386 (see also Careers)
B-roll, 181
Building permits, 84–85
Burden of proof, 332
Business reports, 86
Byrd, Robert, 9

Camera:
    settings/lighting, 203–204 (see also Lighting)
    tripod use and, 187–188
    in courtrooms, 97–100
Campaign disclosure, 85
Cantrell v. Forest City Publishing Co., 342

Careers (in broadcasting):
  getting foot in door, 372–375
  identifying position you seek,
    367–368, 370–372
  innovative search techniques,
    372–373
  internships and, 364
  job interviews and, 375–379
  making most of opportunities,
    383
  moving jobs, 384–385
  networking and, 364–365
  preparation for, 363–372
  resumes and, 355–363
  road trip and, 365–367
  success and advancement,
    383–385
Celebrities (*see also* Public
  figures):
  news and, 14
  trials of, 100
Characters:
  editing and, 262
  identifying in story, 111–112
Chronological organization, 121
Circuit courts, 89, 90, 91
City directory, 86
Civil actions, 96
Civil court, 96
Clichés, avoiding, 172
Clinton, Bill, 341
Close-up, 181
Codes of ethics, 20, 21–22 (*see
  also* Ethics)
Color, shooting and, 247
Commentaries, vs. news items, 4
Communication:
  successful, 310–314
  through shooting, 254
Complacency, avoiding, 254
Completion, sequences and, 234,
  274
Computer:
  assisted reporting, 102–105
  search engines, 105
  skills needed, 33

sources, 78–80
Confidentiality, 348–350
Conflict:
  as characteristic of news,
    11–12
  of interest, 40
Congress, 90
Consent, as protection against
  lawsuits, 338, 343–344
Consonants, 164
Constitutional law, 90
Contacts, networking and,
  364–365
Contempt, 348–350
Continuing present tense, 154
Continuity, 274
Contracts, job, 381, 382
Control track, 263
Control, creative, 287–288
Convened, 96
Convergence, 36, 135–144
Cooke, Janet, 19
Copy, underlining, 308–310
Copyright, 344–346
Countdown, 263
Couric, Katie, 32
Court:
  contempt of, 348–350
  orders, 348–351
Courtesy, 312–313
Courtrooms:
  cameras in, 97–100
  media access to, 347
  open, 87–89
Courts, 86–102
  circuit, 89, 90, 91
  civil, 96
  criminal cases, 93–96
  federal, 89–91
  grand jury proceedings,
    88–89
  juvenile proceedings, 88
  of appeal, 89, 90
  open courtrooms and, 87–89
  records of, 100–102
  state, 91–92

Cover letters, 355–356, 357–358
Creative control, 287–288
Credibility, of sources, 61–62
Crime reporting, 12–13
Crime scenes, access by media,
  348
Criminal cases, 93–96
Criticism, willingness to accept,
  23–24
Cross ownership, 35
Cross the line, 229
C-SPAN, 37
Curiosity, of reporters, 20
Cutaway shots, 180–181,
  221–224
  in interview, 181
  reaction shots, 222–223
  using, 270–272
Cuts only editing, 257
Cutting on the action, 275
Cynicism:
  during interviews, 64
  of reporters, 20

Dates, in writing, 167
Deadlines, 48
Death records, 84
Deeds, 101–102
Deep background, 59
Defamation, 330
Defendant, 93, 96
Delivery, 296–310
  emphasis and, 299–300
  enunciation/phrasing,
    297–298
  live shots and, 317–322
  nervousness and, 313–314
  pacing and, 303–304
  pitch and, 300–302
  stand-ups and, 314–317
  successful communication
    and, 310–314
  techniques for improving,
    308–310
  tone and, 305
Diamond effect, 114–115

Diaphragm, 293–294

Dilemma, 170

Disclosure, for elected officials, 85

Discrimination, 41

Disposition, 95

Dissolve, 265

Distorted past tense, 151–153 (*see also* Verbs)

Diversity, 40–41

Divorce records, 101

Dockets, 100–101

Dolly, 180

Drugs/alcohol, presentation and, 323

Dumb, playing, 67–68

Echo lead-ins, 130–131

Economics, television news and, 34

Edit (*see also* Editing):
tape, 180
controller, 257
defined, 257

Editing, 177, 257–292
audio track, 277–282 (*see also* Audio)
characters and, 262
countdown and, 263
cuts only, 257
editor's responsibilities and, 285–289
effects, 264–265
elements of, 258–262
establishing shots and, 267
exercises, 291–292
fast-paced, 286
graphics and, 284–285
illustrating the narration, 268–269
laying black and, 263–264
laying video track, 265–277
linear, 262–264
natural sound and, 277, 280–282
nonlinear, 264–265

on the action, 275–277
overlapping audio and video, 282–284
pacing and, 258–260
pans and zooms and, 191
punctuation and, 261
repetition and, 260–261
sequences, 272–277 (*see also* Sequences)
stories within stories, 269–270
surprise and, 261–262
tight, 258–259
timing and, 261
using cutaway shots, 270–272

Editor:
assignment, 28, 30, 32
responsibilities of, 285–289
video, 30

Editorials, vs. news items, 4

Effect vs. affect, 170

Effects, 264–265

Emotional impact, of news, 17–18

Emphasis, 299–300

Employment contract, 381, 382

End point, 264

English, Standard American, 306–307

Entertainment, news as, 36–37

Entry-level jobs, 368–371 (*see also* Careers)

Enunciation, 297

Establishing shot, 180, 267

Ethics (*see also* Legal considerations):
activities, 43, 76, 256, 291, 353–354
audience attraction and, 36
cutaway questions and, 224
defined, 19–20
legalities and, 287
reaction shots and, 223
reporting and, 18–20, 21–22
shooting decisions and, 236
vs. legal considerations, 328–329

Expert, as contributor to story, 112

Eye witnesses, 46

Fade, 264

Fair comment, libel and, 335–336

Fairness, 7–9, 329
of reporters, 21

Fairness Doctrine, 6

Fair use, 345–346

False light, 342

Fault, libel and, 331

FBI, 105

FCC, 35

Fear, government by, 39

Federal Communications Commission, 35

Federal courts, 89–91 (*see also* Courts)

File footage, 268

Fill light, 209

Financial disclosure, 85

First Amendment, 2, 6, 87, 335

Five W's, 111

Flat lighting, 204–206

Flexibility, of reporters, 24

Follow up, after job interview, 379

Food, presentation and, 323

Foreground, 250–251

Format, of stories/news package, 123–125, 126, 127

Former vs. latter, 170

401k, 380

Framing, 182–188 (*see also* Shooting; Shots)

Freedom of Information Act (FoIA), 81–82, 83
exceptions to, 81, 83

Freedom of information laws, 81–83, 98

Friends, as news sources, 50–52

Friendships, conflict of interest and, 40

Full word production, 297

Gain control, 213
Gatekeeper, 178
Gestures, 318
Goals:
  for advancement, 384
  for improvement, 383–384
Good manners, 312–313
Google, 105
Government:
  by fear and name calling, 39
  open, 77–83
Government in the Sunshine
    Acts, 83, 86
Grand jury:
  indictments, 96
  proceedings, 88–89
Graphics, using, 284–285, 289
Grid, rule of thirds and, 183–185,
    186
Ground rules, setting for inter-
    view, 58–63

Hard lead, 118
Head room, leaving, 193–195
Headlines, 5
  Web story and, 137
Hearing:
  grand jury, 88–89
  preliminary, 93–94
  pretrial, 94
  sentencing, 95
Held without bond, 94
Helping others, as motivation,
    54–55
Hidden recordings, 341–342
Holidays, 380
Hopeful vs. hopefully, 169–170
Human interest, 17–18
Hyphenation, 172

Identity, protecting, 200
Impact, as characteristic of news,
    14–15
Improvement, goals for, 383–384
Independence, of reporters, 22
Indictment, 88–89

Inflection, 300
Information:
  career, 372–375 (see also
    Careers)
  getting on the record, 60–62
  private, 342–343
  sources of, see Sources
Informational interviews, 365
Infotainment, 15
Inquisitiveness, of reporters, 20
Instruments, lighting and, 206
Insurance, 380
Integrity, of reporters, 21–22
    (see also Ethics; Legal
    considerations)
Internships, 364
Interrupting, during interviews, 73
Interview cutaways, 181
Interviews:
  ambush, 69–70
  asking tough questions, 70–71
  avoiding judgment, 71–72
  beginning, 64–65
  concluding, 74
  cutaway shots and, 221–222,
    271
  doing background work for,
    55–56
  getting information on the
    record, 60–62
  getting most out of, 63–73
  guaranteeing accuracy, 65–66
  including action in, 198–199
  informational, 365
  job, 375–379 (see also Job
    interviews)
  leaving head room, 193–195
  listening carefully, 66–67
  live shot, 321–322
  off the record and, 59
  planning what to ask, 57–58
  preparing for, 55–63
  protecting identity and, 200
  requesting, 52
  setting ground rules for,
    58–63

shooting, 193–199
silence during, 73
skepticism during, 64
source agreements, 59–60
using strategies, 67–73
Intonation, 171
Intrusion, 339–341
Investigative Reporters and
    Editors (IRE), 79, 102
Iris, 211
"Isms" in the newsroom, 40–41
It's vs. its, 169
Its vs. it's, 169

Jail, going to protect a source,
    62–63
Job:
  accepting, 379
  benefits, 380–381
  contracts, 381, 382
  market, boundaries of, 372
  search, see Careers
Job interviews:
  attitude and, 377–378
  following up after, 379
  preparing for, 375–376
  what to wear, 377
Journalism, Web, 135–144 (see
    also News; Stories; Writing)
Judgment, avoiding, 71–72
Jump cuts, 221, 224–226
  cutaways for, 272
  sequence, 224–226
Jurors, information about, 100
Justice, as motivation, 53
Juvenile:
  murderers, 342–343
  proceedings, 88

Kennedy, Ted, 58
Key light, 206–209

L-cuts, 282–283
Language, use of clear, 314–315
Latter vs. former, 170
Lauer, Matt, 32

Lavalier mic, 214
Laying black, 263–264
Leading lines, 242–246
Lead-ins:
    echo, 130–131
    informing with, 131
    to sound bites, 130
Leads:
    hard, 118
    question, 120
    soft, 118–119
    suspense, 120–121
    throwaway, 119
    umbrella, 119
Legal considerations, 327–354
    (*see also* Ethics)
    carelessness and, 327–328
    confidentiality, 348–350
    copyright, 344–346
    court orders and, 348–351
    libel and, 329–339 (*see also*
        Libel)
    newsroom searches, 351
    privacy and, 339–344 (*see also*
        Privacy)
    slander, 330
    subpoenas and, 350
    vs. ethical considerations,
        328–329
Legalities, adhering to, 287 (*see
    also* Ethics)
Lewinsky, Monica, 341
Liability, libel and, 331
Libel, 329–339
    burden of proof and, 332
    consent and, 338
    defamation and, 330–331
    defenses against lawsuits,
        334–339
    private citizens and, 333–334
    privilege and, 337–338
    and public figures, 332–333
    retraction and, 338–339
Licenses, marriage, 102
Licensing fees, 345
Light and dark, 247–248

Lighting, 203–213
    back light, 208–209, 211–212
    camera settings and, 203–204
    fill light, 209
    flat, 204–206
    reflectors and, 210–211
    scenarios, 204–213
    shooting at night and, 213
    shooting outdoors and,
        209–210
    three-point, 206–209
Linear editing, 262–264
Links, 143
Listening:
    as news source, 47
    during interviews, 66–67
Live shots, 317–322
Localizing, 16–17
Locations, news and, 16–17
Logging the tape, 265
LookSmart, 105
Look space, 195
Lowest common denominator,
    37–38

Magistrates, 93
Main point, organizational pat-
    tern, 121–122
Mainstream media, 3–6 (*see also*
    Media)
Malice, actual, 332
Marriage licenses, 102
Match frame editing, 275
Media (*see also* News):
    access issues, 347–348
    as watchdog, 2
    bias of mainstream, 4–5
    convergence and, 36, 135–144
    ethics and, *see* Ethics; Legal
        considerations
    imitating mainstream, 6
    in courtrooms, 97–100
    legal considerations and, *see*
        Legal considerations
    mainstream, 3–6
    nonmainstream, 6–7

open courtrooms and, 87–89
    ownership, 34–36
    political campaigns and, 3
    sensational, 7
Medialine.com, 367, 368
Medium shot, 188–189
Memorization, stand-ups and,
    315–316
Meters, V-U, 277–278
Mics, 214–216
Mixed sound, 277
Motivated pan, 191–192
Motivation, offering to sources,
    53–55
Movement, video and, 246–247
Moving:
    considering when to, 384–385
    expenses, 381
MSNSearch, 105
Mudd, Roger, 58

Name calling, government by, 39
Names:
    avoiding unnecessary,
        160–161
    delaying, 162–163
    including necessary, 160
    using titles with, 161–162
Narration, illustrating the,
    268–269
National Institute for Computer-
    Assisted Reporting
    (NICAR), *see* NICAR
National Press Photographers
    Association, 20
National Public Radio, 3
Nat sound, 214–216
    breaks, 277, 281–282
    open, 278
    package, 251–252
Natural sound, 214–216,
    251–252, 277, 278,
    280–282
Negligence, 334
Nervousness, 313–314
Networking, 364–365

Neutralizing shots, 229–230
News:
    accuracy of, 9–10 (*see also* Accuracy)
    as entertainment, 36–37
    blocks, 28
    characteristics of, 11–18
    conflict and, 11–12
    crime reporting, 12–13
    defining, 1
    emotional impact of, 17–18
    fairness and, 7–9 (*see also* Fairness)
    files, as sources, 86
    importance of, 2–3
    legal considerations and, *see* Legal considerations
    objectivity and, 4–6, 7–9
    possible bias of, 4–5
    prominence and, 14–15
    relevance and, 15–16
    sources, 45–76 (*see also* Sources)
    uniqueness and, 12–13
    vs. editorials, 4
    Web sites and, 135–144
News director, 27, 32
News Hour, 3
News operations, 3–4
News package, 123–125
    basic components of, 258
    sound bites and, *see* Sound bites
News release, as news source, 49
Newsroom:
    computer skills in, 33
    contemporary issues, 34–41
    diversity in, 40–41
    key players in, 27–31
    personnel, 24 (*see also* Reporters)
    routine of, 31–34
    searches of, 351
    television, 27–43
Newsworthiness, as protection against lawsuits, 344

Newswriting for Radio Web site, 134
New York Times, 3, 4, 63
    unethical reporter for, 19
New York Times v. Sullivan, 332
NICAR, 79, 102–104
Night, shooting at, 213
Nonlinear editing, 264–265
Nonmainstream media, 6–7
Not for attribution, 59
Numbers, styles for, 166–167
Number vs. amount, 170

Objectivity, 7–9
    vs. opinion, 4–6
Observation, as news source, 46–47
Off the record, 59
Officials, libel and, 332
Omnidirectional mic, 216
On background, 59
180–degree rule, 229
One-man band, 180
One-shot, 181
Online reporting, 102–105
Open courtrooms, 87–89
Opinion:
    blurring with news, 4
    libel and, 335–336
Opportunity, making most of, 383
Ordinals, 167
Organization, of reporters, 23
Organizational:
    patterns, 121–123
    records, 86
Out point, 264
Outcue, 200
    standard, 134
Outdoors, shooting, 209–210
Overtime, 380
Ownership, media, 34–36

Pacing, 303–304
    editing and, 258–260
Pans, 188, 190–193
    motivated, 191–192

Participation, showing through stand-up, 202
Passive voice, 157–158
Past tense, 156
PBS, 3
People:
    as news sources, 49–55
    getting them to talk, 52–55 (*see also* Interviews)
    interacting well with, 23
    interviewing, *see* Interviews
    talking to the right, 56–57
Perfect symmetry, 248
Perks, job, 381
Permission to use, 345
Persistence, of reporters, 23
Personalizing the story, 112–115
Phone book, 86
Phone calls, job search and, 374–375
Photographers, 30 (*see also* Shooting; Video)
Photojournalist, 30
    defining, 178–179
    shooting video and, *see* Shooting; Video
Phrasing, 297–298
Pitch, 300–302
Plaintiff, 96
Planning documents, 84
Plea, 94
Point of view, reversed, 236–237
Police information, 95–96
Politics, sound bites in, 39–40
Position, identifying sought for, 367–368, 370–372
Potter, Deborah, 150
Poynter Institute, 82, 102, 105, 106
Practicing, out loud, 310
Preliminary hearing, 93–94
Present, past, future, organizational pattern, 122–123
Present perfect tense, 156–157
Present progressive tense, 154–155

Present tense, 153–156
Presentation, 293, 310–325
  delivery and, 296–310
  drugs/alcohol and, 323
  exercises, 325
  food factor, 323
  voice and, 293–296
  warming up, 296
Press conference, as news source, 48–49
Pretrial hearing, 94
Printed materials, as news source, 47–48
Prisons, media access to, 347
Privacy, 339–344
  appropriation, 343
  false light and, 342
  hidden recordings and, 341–342
  intrusion and, 339–341
  protection against lawsuits, 343–344
Privilege, absolute vs. qualified, 337–338
Producers, 27–28, 32
  as entry-level job, 371
Production assistant, 371–372
Professionalism, when dealing with sources, 52–53
Programming, 37
  sensationalism and, 38–39
Prominence, as characteristic of news, 14
Pronouns, 171
Pronunciation:
  guides, 163–164
  local, 308
Proof, asking for, 72
Proofreading, 173
Property, public vs. private, 339–340
Prosecutors, 93
Public figures, 56, 58
  libel and, 332–333
Public meetings, media access to, 347

Public property vs. private property, 339–340
Public records:
  benefits of open government, 77–83
  birth and death records, 84
  building permits, 84–85
  disclosure forms, 85
  NICAR and, *see* NICAR
  tax records, 85
  zoning and planning documents, 84
Public trust, of reporters, 21
Publications, as news sources, 47–48
Pull quote, 285
Punctuation, editing and, 261

Qualified privilege, 337–338
Question lead, 120
Questions:
  "how do you feel?", 128–129
  asking sarcastic, 120
  asking tough, 70–71
  cutaway, 223–224
  planning interview, 57–58
  repeating, 72–73
  used as lead, 120
  yes-or-no, 73
Quotes, intonation and, 171

Radio talk shows, 6
Radio, writing for, 134–135
Radio-Television News Directors Association (RTNDA), *see* RTNDA
Rape victims, 342
Reaction shots, 222–223
Reader, 123
Receptionists, 80
Recognizance, 94
Record:
  getting information on the, 60–62
  off the, 59
  setting straight, 54

Recordings, hidden, 341–342
Records:
  divorce, 101
  public, *see* Public records
Reference, letters of, 374
References, on resume, 359
Reflectors, 210–211
Relevance, as characteristic of news, 15–16
Repetition, 260–261
Reporters:
  appearance and, 311–312
  career search and, *see* Careers
  characteristics of good, 18–24
  court orders and, 348–351
  delivery and, *see* Delivery
  helpful Web sites for, 82, 102
  job description for, 31
  news sources and, *see* Sources
  reaction shots and, 222–223
  shield laws and, 350
  stand-ups and, 181, 200–203
  subpoenas and, 350
Reporters Committee for Freedom of the Press (RCFP), 62, 82, 102, 105
Reporting (*see also* News):
  computer-assisted, 102–105
  crime, 12–13
Resumes, 355–363
  posting online, 367
  taped, 359, 362–363
Retirement plan, 380
Retraction, libel and, 338–339
Revenge, as motivation, 54
Reversals, editing and, 275
Reversed point of view, 236–237
Road trip, 365–367
Roosevelt, Franklin, 39
Routine, newsroom, 31–34
RTNDA, 20, 21–22, 82, 102, 97–98
  code of ethics, 21–22
Rule of thirds, 183–185, 228
Rumors, 51
Rundown sheets, 28, 29

Scan room, leaving, 193–195
Schools, media access to, 348
Scores, in writing, 167
Screen, filling, 182–183
Script:
    broadcast, 141–143
    radio, 134–135
    underlining copy, 308–310
    wraparound, 320
Search engines, 105
Search warrant, 95
Secretaries, 80
Sensationalism, 38–39, 288–289
Sentencing hearing, 95
Sequences:
    action, 237–241
    action/reaction, 234–236
    completion and, 234
    continuity and, 274
    creative, 273
    cutaway and jump cuts and,
        221–226
    cutaways for jump cuts, 272
    editing, 272–277
    matching the action, 233
    reversed point of view and,
        236–237
    series of matching shots,
        233–234
    shooting, 231–241
    wide/medium/tight, 231–233
Shield laws, 62–63, 350
Shooting, 177–256 (see also
        Shots; Video)
    action in interviews, 198–199
    artistic principles and,
        242–251
    assertiveness and, 252–253
    assignments, 219, 256
    at night, 213
    audio and, 251–252 (see also
        Audio)
    axis, 228–229
    background and, 251
    balance and symmetry,
        248–249

color and, 247
cutaway shots, see Cutaway
        shots
editing and, see Editing
foreground and, 250–251
framing and, 182–188
from different angles,
        189–190
holding camera still, 187–188
in the field, 188–193
interviews, 193–199 (see also
        Interviews)
leading lines and, 242–246
leaving head room, 193–195
leaving lead room, 195–198
light and dark, 247–248
lighting and, see Lighting
movement and, 246–247
outdoors, 209–210
sequences, see Sequences
stand-ups, 200–203, 314–317
ten-second rule, 185–186
terminology, 179–182
thinking in thirds, 183–185
using tripod, 187–188
Z-principle, 184–185, 186
Shoot tape, 180
ShopTalk, 369
Shot sheet, 265
Shotgun mic, 216–217
Shots (see also Shooting; Video):
    action/reaction, 234–236
    angled, 189–190
    close-up, 181
    composing, 182–188
    cutaways, see Cutaway shots
    establishing, 180, 267
    getting plenty of, 188
    jump cuts, 221, 224–226
    live, 317–322
    matching, 233–234
    neutralizing, 229–230
    pans and zooms, 190–193
    repeating, 260–261
    stand-up, see Stand-ups
    transition, 226–228

wide/medium/tight, 188–189
wraparound, 319–321
Sick time, 380
Sidebar story, 119
Silence, during interviews, 73
Simple, keeping stories,
        116–117
Single person operator, 180
Sing-song pattern, 302
Sixth Amendment, 87
60 Minutes, 117
Skepticism:
    during interviews, 64
    of reporters, 20
Slander, 330
Slug, 123
SOC, 134, 200
Society of Professional
        Journalists, 82, 102, 105
Soft lead, 118–119
Sound bites, 125–131, 181
    accuracy in, 10
    credibility and, 125
    lead-ins to, 130
    politics in, 39–40
    writing to, 129–120
Sounds, problem, 307–308 (see
        also Audio)
Sources:
    attributing, 159–160
    computer, 78–80
    court records, 100–102 (see
        also Courts)
    courts as, see Courts
    credible, 61–62
    deeds, 101–102
    developing, 50
    dishonesty of, 68
    dockets, 100–101
    friends as, 50–52
    going to jail to protect, 62–63
    interviewing, see Interviews
    listening, 47
    motivating, 53–55
    news release, 49
    observation, 46–47

of public information, 84–86
    (*see also* Public records)
people as, 49–55 (*see also*
    Interviews)
police information, 95–96
press conference, 48–49
public records, 77–108 (*see
    also* Public records)
shield laws and, 62–63
Speech patterns, 302 (*see also*
    Delivery)
Spelling, common errors,
    169–171
S-P-O, 180
Staging video, 223
Standard American English,
    306–307
Standard outcue, 134, 200
Stand-ups, 181, 314–317
    action, 316–317
    conceiving and shooting,
        200–203
    memorization and, 315–316
    reasons for, 201–203
    stationary, 316
    transition and, 202–203
Status, as motivation, 54
Stereotypes, 41
Still frame, 284
Stories:
    assignments for, 32
    attributions and, 159–160
    breaking, 33
    conflict of interest and, 40
    ending, 131–133
    finding an angle, 115–116
    format of, 123–125
    human interest, 17–18
    keeping them simply, 116–117
    leads, 117–121 (*see also*
        Leads)
    localizing, 16–17
    organizing, 121–123
    personalizing, 112–115
    print version vs. broadcast
        version, 139–143

sidebar, 119
sound bites and, *see* Sound
    bites
summaries of, 132–133
understanding and shooting,
    253 (*see also* Shooting)
using active voice, 157–158
within stories, 269–270
writing, *see* Writing
Storytelling, *see* Writing
Style:
    checklist for broadcast, 172
    for numbers, 166–167
    requirements for writing,
        166–168
    scores/dates/time, 167–168
    symbols and, 167
Subpoenas, 93, 350
Success, career, 383–385
Summary:
    of story, 132–133
    Web stories and, 143
Sunlight, shooting and, 209–211
Supering, 289
Supreme Court, 89–90, 91
Surprise, editing and, 261–262
Suspense:
    lead, 120–121
    ending the, 133
Symbols, use of in writing, 167
Symmetry, balance and, 248–249

Tabloids, 7, 15
Talent Shop, 367, 368
Talk space, 195
Tape-to-tape editing, 262–264
Tax records, 85
Technology, storytelling and, 109
Television (*see also* Broadcast):
    format for reader, 127
    format for VO-SOT, 126
Ten-second rule, 185–186
Tenses, verb, 151–156 (*see also*
    Verbs)
Thirds, thinking in, 183–185
Three-point lighting, 206–209

Throwaway lead, 119
Tight shot, 188–189
Timing:
    back, 264
    editing and, 261
Times, in writing, 167
Titles, using with names,
    161–162
Tobacco, presentation and, 323
Tone, 305
Toughness, during interviews, 69
Transition shots, 226–228
Transition, showing through
    stand-up, 202–203
Tree huggers, 7
Tricities. Com, 135–143
Tripod, using, 187
Tripp, Linda, 341
Trust, public, 21
Truth:
    as defense against libel,
        334–35
    editing and, 286–287
    of reporters, 21
TVspy.com, 369
20/20, 341
Two-shot, 181

Umbrella lead, 119
Underlining copy, 308–310
Uniqueness, as characteristic of
    news, 12–13
USA Today, 3

Vacation, as job benefit, 380
Verbs:
    avoiding "verb-free zone,"
        150–151
    avoiding distortion of te[nse,]
        151–153
    choosing correct tense,
        153–157
    distorted past tense, 1[ ]
    dropping auxiliary, 1[ ]
    past tense, 156
    present tense, 153–[ ]

Video (*see also* Shooting):
audio and, *see* Audio
color and, 247
editing and, *see* Editing
editors, 30
framing and, 182–188
holding camera still, 187–188
lighting and, *see* Lighting
movement and, 246–247
overlapping with audio, 282–284
packages, Web and, 143–144
rule of thirds and, 183–185
sequence, 272–273 (*see also* Sequences)
shooting, 177–256 (*see also* Shooting)
shooting in the field, 188–193
shooting sequences and, *see* Sequences
staging, 223
ten-second rule, 185–186
terminology, 179–182
track, 258, 265–277 (*see also* Editing0
Videographer, 178, 179–180 (*see also* Video)
Vietnam War, 3
Visual entrance, 242–243
Visualization, job interviews and, 376
V-O, 123
VO-B, 123
Vocal cords, 295
Voice (*see also* Delivery):
accents and, 306–307
active vs. passive, 157–158
breathing and, 293–296
exercises, 325
pitch and, 300–302

Voice-overs, 123, 125, 126
VO-SOT, 123, 126
Voters, news and, 3
Vowel sounds, 164
VSV, 123
V-U meter, 277–278

Wall Street Journal, 4
Wallpaper, 287–288
Walt Disney Corp., 35
Warming up, 296
Washington Post, 3, 4, 19
Washington Times, 4
Watchdog, 2
Web sites, news, 5
Web, writing for, 134–144
Whistle-blower, 60–61
White balance, 203
Who, what, when, where, why, 111
Why, asking, 73
Wide shot, 188–189
Wills, 102
Wipe, 264
Wireless mic, 215
Words:
choosing accurately, 159
commonly misused, 169–171
enunciation and, 297
Wraparound, 319–321
Writing, 109–176
abbreviations and, 168
acronyms and, 168
assignments, 145–148, 174–176
attributions in, 159–160
checklist for broadcast style, 172
choosing the format, 123–125

choosing words accurately, 159
common mistakes, 169–171
determining an angle, 115–116
diamond effect and, 114–115
ending the story, 131–133
five W's and, 111
for breathing, 164–166
for radio, 134–135
for the Web, 134–144
identifying the characters, 111–112
in broadcast style, 149–176
leads, 117–121 (*see also* Leads)
organizing the story, 121–123
personalizing the story, 112–115
preparing for, 110–117
pronouns and, 171
proofreading, 173
sound bites and, *see* Sound bites
style requirements, 166–168
summaries, 132–133
use of age and, 163
use of names and, 160–163
use of titles with names, 161–162
using active voice, 157–158
using verbs correctly, 150–157 (*see also* Verbs)

Yahoo!, 105
Yes-or-no questions, 73

Zoning documents, 84
Zooms, 180, 190–193
Z-principle, 184–185, 186, 243